Lecture Notes in Computer Science   1707

Edited by G. Goos, J. Hartmanis and J. van L

T0216603

Springer

Berlin
Heidelberg
New York
Barcelona
Hong Kong
London
Milan
Paris
Singapore
Tokyo

Hans-W. Gellersen (Ed.)

Handheld and Ubiquitous Computing

First International Symposium, HUC'99
Karlsruhe, Germany, September 27-29, 1999
Proceedings

 Springer

Series Editors

Gerhard Goos, Karlsruhe University, Germany
Juris Hartmanis, Cornell University, NY, USA
Jan van Leeuwen, Utrecht University, The Netherlands

Volume Editor

Hans-W. Gellersen
University of Karlsruhe, TecO (Telecooperation Office)
Vincenz-Prießnitz-Str. 1, D-76131 Karlsruhe, Germany
E-mail: hwg@teco.uni-karlsruhe.de

Cataloging-in-Publication data applied for

Die Deutsche Bibliothek - CIP-Einheitsaufnahme

Handheld and ubiquitous computing : first international symposium ; proceedings
/ HUC'99, Karlsruhe, Germany, September 27 - 29, 1999. Hans-W. Gellersen (ed.).
- Berlin ; Heidelberg ; New York ; Barcelona ; Hong Kong ; London ; Milan ;
Paris ; Singapore ; Tokyo : Springer, 1999
 (Lecture notes in computer science ; Vol. 1707)
 ISBN 3-540-66550-1

CR Subject Classification (1998): C.2, C.5, C.3, D.2, H.5, H.4

ISSN 0302-9743
ISBN 3-540-66550-1 Springer-Verlag Berlin Heidelberg New York

© Springer-Verlag Berlin Heidelberg 1999
Printed in Germany

Typesetting: Camera-ready by author
SPIN: 10704965   06/3142 – 5 4 3 2 1 0   Printed on acid-free paper

Preface

Truly personal handheld and wearable technologies should be small and unobtrusive and allow access to information and computing most of the time and in most circumstance. Complimentary, environment-based technologies make artifacts of our surrounding world computationally accessible and facilitate use of everyday environments as a ubiquitous computing interface. The International Symposium on Handheld and Ubiquitous Computing, held for the first time in September 1999, was initiated to investigate links and synergies in these developments, and to relate advances in personal technologies to those in environment-based technologies.

The HUC'99 Symposium was organised by the University of Karlsruhe, in particular by the Telecooperation Office (TecO) of the Institute for Telematics, in close collaboration with ZKM Karlsruhe, which generously hosted the event in its truly inspiring Center for Arts and Media Technology. The symposium was supported by the Association of Computing Machinery (ACM) and the German Computer Society (Gesellschaft für Informatik, GI) and held in cooperation with a number of special interest groups of these scientific societies.

HUC'99 attracted a large number of paper submissions, from which the international programme committee selected 23 high-quality contributions for presentation at the symposium and for inclusion in these proceedings. In addition, posters were solicited to provide an outlet for novel ideas and late-breaking results; selected posters are also included with these proceedings. The technical programme was further complemented by four invited keynote addresses, and two panel sessions. In addition, a tutorial and workshop day was organised, with half-day tutorials on the most recent developments and workshops on topics of special interest.

Submitted papers and posters came from a large variety of fields ranging, for instance, from middleware to interaction techniques, and from collaborative work to wearable computing. Balanced reviewing was not always an easy task, and I would like to express my sincere thanks to the members of the programme committee and the many additional reviewers for their very careful reviews, and for constructive comments towards improvement of the papers.

I extend special thanks to Prof. Peter Weibel, director of the ZKM Karlsruhe and symposium co-chair, for turning HUC'99 into a co-production of the University and ZKM; to Prof. Gerhard Krüger, head of the Institute for Telematics, for backing the HUC'99 organisation; to Joachim Schaper, director of SAP's CEC Karlsruhe, for tutorial arrangements and other support; and to Michael Beigl, Albrecht Schmidt, Birgit Schmidt, and Christian Segor for their efforts in taking care of all those additional issues that are essential for a successful symposium.

August 1999   Hans-W. Gellersen

Symposium Organisation

Supporting Societies

Association for Computing Machinery (ACM) with the special interest groups:
  SIGAPP (Applied Computing)
  SIGCHI (Computer-Human Interaction)
  SIGGROUP (Group Work, CSCW)
  SIGMOBILE (Mobile Computing)

German Computer Society / Gesellschaft für Informatik (GI) with the special interest group APS+PC (*Arbeitsplatzrechensysteme und Personal Computing*)

Symposium Chairs

Hans-W. Gellersen	TecO, University of Karlsruhe, Germany
Peter Weibel	Center for Arts and Media (ZKM), Karlsruhe, Germany

Programme Committee

Hans-W. Gellersen (Chair)	TecO, University of Karlsruhe, Germany
Peter Thomas (Co-Chair)	University of the West of England, Bristol, U.K.
John Bates	University of Cambridge, U.K.
Niels Ole Bernsen	Odense University, Denmark
Peter Brown	University of Kent, U.K.
Mark Day	Lotus Research, Cambridge, U.S.A.
Mark Dunlop	University of Glasgow, U.K.
Saul Greenberg	University of Calgary, Canada
Lars Erik Holmquist	Viktoria Institute, Göteborg, Sweden
Pertti Huuskonen	Nokia Mobile Phones, Oulu, Finland
Kori Inkpen	Simon Fraser University, Canada
Dag Johansen	University of Tromsø, Norway
Ying K. Leung,	Swinburne University of Technology, Australia
Gerald Q. Maguire Jr.	Royal Institute of Technology (KTH), Sweden
Günter Müller	University of Freiburg, Germany
Tatsuo Nakajima	JAIST, Japan
Reinhard Oppermann	GMD-FIT, Germany
Joachim Schaper	SAP AG, CEC Karlsruhe, Germany
Mark Smith	HP Labs, Palo Alto, U.S.A.
Ralf Steinmetz	GMD-IPSI and Darmstadt University of Technology
Constantine Stephanidis	ICS-FORTH, Greece
Chai Keong Toh	Georgia Institute of Technology, U.S.A.
Fabio Vitali	University of Bologna, Italy
Nick Wainwright	HP Labs, Bristol, U.K.
Terry Winograd	Stanford University, U.S.A.

List of Reviewers

Gregory Abowd	Georgia Institute of Technology, U.S.A.
Ana Paula Afonso	University of Lisbon, Portugal
Chris Baber	University of Birmingham, U.K.
Michael Beigl	University of Karlsruhe, Germany
Mark Billinghurst	HIT Lab, University of Washington, U.S.A.
Cora Burger	University of Stuttgart, Germany
Datong Chen	University of Karlsruhe, Germany
Keith Cheverst	University of Lancaster, U.K.
Per Dahlberg	Viktoria Institute, Göteborg, Sweden
Oliver Frick	SAP AG, Germany
Adrian Friday	University of Lancaster, U.K.
Mario Hoffmann	University of Freiburg, Germany
Fritz Hohl	University of Stuttgart, Germany
Dorota Huizinga	California State University, Fullerton, U.S.A.
Anne-Marie Kermarrec	IRISA, Rennes, France
Gerd Kortuem	University of Oregon, U.S.A.
Uwe Kubach	University of Stuttgart, Germany
Markus Lauff	University of Karlsruhe, Germany
Alexander Leonhardi	University of Stuttgart, Germany
Olivier Liechti	Hiroshima University, Japan
Robert Macredie	University of Reading, U.K.
Steve Mann	University of Toronto, Canada
Friedemann Mattern	ETH Zürich, Switzerland
Keith Mitchell	University of Lancaster, U.K.
David Morse	Open University, U.K.
Huw Oliver	HP Labs, Bristol, U.K.
Jason Pascoe	University of Kent, U.K.
Alex Pentland	MIT Media Lab, U.S.A.
Johan Redström	Viktoria Institute, Göteborg, Sweden
Nick Ryan	University of Kent, U.K.
Günther Schäfer	Eurecom, Sophia Antipolis, France
Alexander Schill	Technical University of Dresden, Germany
Jochen Schiller	University of Karlsruhe, Germany
Albrecht Schmidt	University of Karlsruhe, Germany
Markus Schwehm	University of Stuttgart, Germany
Jochen Seitz	University of Karlsruhe, Germany
Pavel Slavik	Technical University of Prague, Czech Republic
Harold Thimbleby	Middlesex University, U.K.
Walter Van de Velde	Starlab, Belgium
Leon Watts	Université Joseph Fourier, France

Publication and Local Organisation

Michael Beigl	TecO, University of Karlsruhe, Germany
Hans-W. Gellersen	TecO, University of Karlsruhe, Germany
Joachim Schaper	SAP AG, CEC Karlsruhe, Germany
Albrecht Schmidt	TecO, University of Karlsruhe, Germany
Birgit Schmidt	Hochschule für Gestaltung (HfG), Karlsruhe
Christian Segor	TecO, University of Karlsruhe, Germany

Table of Contents

Interacting with Handhelds

Panels

Posters

Design Probes
for Handheld and Ubiquitous Computing

Harold Thimbleby

Middlesex University, LONDON
harold@mdx.ac.uk
http://www.cs.mdx.ac.uk/harold

Abstract. In developing electronic gadgets, meters and oscilloscopes are used to probe into their workings, so that engineers can understand how they are behaving and how they can be improved. Analogously, this paper suggests a variety of conceptual probes that can be used to explore the process of design. The probes focus designers' attention onto successfully managing complexity and in coping with socio-economic influences on design practice in the real world.

1 Introduction

We may take it as self-evident that design should be good, yet it is also clear that it is difficult to make it so because technology is complex and because of pervasive and persuasive socio-economic forces that obscure a straight forward notion of "good." Regardless of the abstract arguments, there is additionally a wealth of circumstantial evidence that design fails: many systems are awkward to use. There is a large literature discussing design failure [1–4], as well as business literature on the way inadequate designs become and remain dominant [5]. (We discuss the specific example of consumer devices in Section 6.)

Thus there is a tension between economically-driven complexity and an ideal of usability, elegance and simplicity. Designers and users are part of the same socio-economic system, and it is hard (if not paradoxical) for designers to stand back and be aware of the influence of subtle cultural factors. Thus various forms of explicit design inspection are advisable—asking what you have done, why you have done it, and whether the results achieve the intended goals. This paper provides a preliminary selection of *design probes*, questions that help initiate, motivate and assess design inspections.

Furthermore, if design is to be good this begs what we mean and intend by "good" itself: this question is, by definition, an ethical one. There are issues to do with awareness and control of social consequences. Design is complex, embedded in society, and there are tacit goals that may silently conflict with good intentions—users have complex preferences, partly conditioned by design conventions. They may not want "better" design. Some of our later probes, therefore, home into ethical issues, of the designers' reflection on and commitment to an ethical framework and values.

1.1 Social forces on design

Design is difficult. Economics drives design complexity upwards. Complexity suits business, for psychological reasons including the manipulation of consumer demand. In other words, unless designers have high ideals, there is no standard by which to manage complexity—it is more profitable to exploit it.

Users are at a disadvantage compared to the designers. The designers know some of the system's structure, so they are able to compress its representation more effectively than users, and hence understand it more deeply. Moreover, a user—say a purchaser of a television in a street shop—has only a few minutes to experiment and explore the system, whereas the designers have an arbitrary time in the lead up to production. Let us use the word *obfuscation* for the system design that the user does not understand but which is understood by the designers. (Obfuscation has intention in it [6].)

A manufacturer that has a large market share may be tempted to increase obfuscation. Users who have grappled with one style of device will tend to buy new devices that work similarly—because this will save learning the subtleties of different devices. So they chose devices made by one manufacturer to ensure similar design. In communities, the effect of this sort of reasoning is profound. In a school community a classroom of different obfuscated products is hard for a teacher to manage, so the teacher will recommend a specific product. Naturally, this is likely to be the market leader. Thus by this strategy, the market leader obtains an entire class room as consumers of the same product.

Alternatively, if the user despairs of understanding the product, their choices are easier to manage. The user is no longer driven by rational processes based on an assessment of the quality of the product, since by assumption this is too hard to do. Instead, the consumer is guided by appearance, pricing, brand name, and so forth. All these are easier factors for a manufacturer to control systematically—for instance, by advertising, discounts, or product placement. Some manufacturers may simply promote several brands, and thereby increase the probability that consumers choose one of their brands. (If there was no obfuscation, the consumer could distinguish the brands, and not be fooled that they offered choices.)

Given these issues: design is difficult, systems are exceedingly complex, and manufacturers have no incentives to simplify. We end up with a society not using technology but driven by it—a designer who wishes to design well needs some sharp insights.

For further discussion, see [7–9].

1.2 Technical forces on design

A single line of Java code can easily generate hundreds of bytes of object code; a Java application includes packages written by other people and may end up being thousands of times larger than the Java program that specified it. What the code does is essential to understand, since this is what the device runs, and it specifies what the device does, step-by-step. Although a device may run the code directly, it is of course much more convenient for a human to write and understand the Java, because it compresses the program represented by the code.

This is a brief argument why high level programming languages like Java are used: they compress object code (which tells machines what to do) and make it easier to get the designer' minds around. Java is a successful language because it compresses useful programs more efficiently than many other languages, such as C or Cobol (though we tend to think of programs being expanded *from* Java, rather than Java representing the object code). Thus, programmers can produce more sophisticated programs with the same effort, or reproduce existing programs with less effort than before.

Now the nature of competitive computing business (brought about by ubiquitous computing) is that the market will force programmers to operate at the limit of their capabilities: for if they did not, some other programmers could produce cheaper, more reliable or more sophisticated systems at lower prices. The improved compression of Java does not make programming easier, at least under commercial pressure, it raises the threshold—programs are always designed at the limit of the programmers' competencies.

Unfortunately, the compression of object code is not sufficient; there is more to design than program text. Programs have dynamic behaviour that unfolds as they interact, and this is harder to compress than their static description in code. Some programs, of course, have trivial behaviour that is easy to compress and represent concisely. Such programs' behaviour is easy to understand; unfortunately, any program text that is easy to understand is likely to represent a program that is not very interesting to use.

Consider a program that interacts with a user, giving the user a modest ten choices every minute (for instance, from a menu or a selection of push buttons). At the end of just a quarter of an hour, the user will have selected one out of 1,000,000,000,000,000 possible outcomes. With more choices, making them faster, or spending longer interacting, the number of possible outcomes increases astronomically. It is clear that the designer cannot anticipate, except in the broadest of terms, what a user will do.

We now provide a concrete example to show how daunting complexity gets even in the most mundane applications. A simple digital alarm clock can display 1440 times (00:00 to 23:59), and the alarm can be set or not set to any of those times. At any time of day or night, the user may set the alarm clock for any time in the next day, so there are 2,075,040 (including the case of not setting the alarm) possibilities that the designer has to be sure work correctly. To check each possibility, the clock has to be run for a whole day to check the alarm sounds once at the right time (or not at all if it hasn't been set).

Doing the checking non-stop but exhaustively would take 5,685 years. Nobody— in fact, few civilisations!—can wait so long, so various cunning tricks are used instead of an exhaustive check. In practice, statistical quality control techniques would be used, but there are more analytic approaches that even the statistical methods assume ...

If we checked 1,000 alarm clocks *at the same time*, we could get the total checking time down to six years. Better still the designers should arrange the clocks so that they were sure that the clocks had symmetries—for instance, **if** they work between 1 and 2 o'clock **then** they will work between 2 and 3 o'clock, and so on. In fact, checking 1,000 alarm clocks assumes a symmetry, namely that when we make two alarm clocks they work the same way—they accurately "reflect" each other's design. By using symmetries, the task of checking can be reduced to manageable proportions. Fortunately many symmetries for alarm clocks are easy to conceive.

2 Symmetry

In everyday language, symmetry refers to mirror and rotational symmetries. Thus when a geometric object can be reflected or rotated and appear unchanged it is said to be symmetric. For example, a circle has both symmetries: reflecting or rotating a circle leaves it coincident with its former self. But further, a straight line can be moved along its length (i.e., translated) and left coincident with its former self. Thus translation is a symmetry. Translation through time is an important symmetry: if a system behaves like this today, it will behave the same way tomorrow. The notorious Year 2000 problem is a break in time symmetry, and an example of the seriousness of breaking symmetries people rely on to understand and use systems.

If the alarm clock (mentioned at the end of the previous section) was a mechanical one, with gears, the symmetries would be familiar ones: gear wheels that have regularly spaced teeth have simple rotational symmetry. Once you are sure a few teeth work, you can be convinced by symmetry that the others will. Other geometrical symmetries are important for checking: for instance, symmetry under translation ensures that the gear wheels still work if the whole clock is moved. Symmetry is a more general concept, however, and can be applied to non-physical structures, such as programs, that are not round and not even geometrical.

Humans are familiar with physical objects, with physical symmetries. The symmetries applicable to more sophisticated but less physical systems, such as video recorders or avionics systems, are harder to conceptualise or work out in the first place; quite possibly the necessary symmetries will be found less effective in compressing the descriptions of the systems. It follows that complex systems do not have convenient symmetries. Users—as well as programmers—will find them hard to understand.

Since designers are not sure what symmetries to require, and because computers are such flexible systems with large memory capacities, it is easy to introduce features to designs without any regard for the effect on the complexity of the system. Put in other words, systems often have large numbers of unrelated features, because it is easy to design them this way. Coherent features require a lot of hard design work, and anyway users can easily be sold features rather than comprehensibility. If computer memory was a restricted resource, then the program would have to be more carefully designed—typically by using a small number of carefully-designed general functions that can be applied in many parts of the program [10]. If the structure of these shared functions is visible in the user interface, then the system will have symmetries. For example, all scroll bars in a graphical user interface have rules that should be symmetric: changing scroll bar should not change the properties. However in a badly designed system, some scroll bars (or other features) may have been programmed specially, and therefore have some arbitrary properties.

Graphical user interfaces have become popular because a set of powerful symmetries are readily defined and agreed. Indeed they are inspired by familiar geometrical symmetries: windows and scroll bars work the same way under translation and scaling. The problem with push button user interfaces is that there are no very obvious symmetries; one might say that in the course of evolutionary time scales, push button-controlled complex gadgets have not had much impact on natural selection, and therefore humans are not selected for understanding them. Rather than wait many generations to experience selection forces (i.e., disasters), rather than wait for the lessons of numerous accidents to be widely learnt and intuitively appreciated by society, we need some more powerful methods for design. Until then, cultural pressures—such as those we described on the one hand forcing programmers to exceed their competencies, and on the other hand forcing users into a culture of complacent idolisation of technology (Section 1.1)—will drive design to be worse.

> **Probe 1.** *What properties does the design have that work in more than one place? Are there symmetries across the system (i.e., does it have a coherent design); are there symmetries from one system to another (i.e., does it provide useful communications properties)?* ◁

> **Probe 2.** *Are there properties shared with other material, such as user manuals, design documents ... ? Are there symmetries that work across media—the device, the manual, the user's head?* ◁

For further discussion, see [11, 12].

• • •

This paper continues with this structure: discussion of design issues, including a brief listing of probes. A discussion of the nature of probes, of the answers to probes, and how probes differ from design heuristics, is postponed to Section 10.

3 Drama

You are watching a film, a play or a TV programme. The story is engrossing, and your mind is following the story as it unfolds. What will happen next? Who will do what? These are real questions to the audience, yet in reality the play is running from a script and there are no choices. If the medium is a film, the reel has no junctions in it: it will unwind the one story it was made for. In reality, there are no choices, and everything is trivial! But that is not how it seems. The story may be exciting, frightening, worrying, or romantic. Our minds automatically create a wider world, and our feelings operate as if the media was reality. Of course that is the point, and a good play or film works its magic carefully to achieve its emotional impact. The drama need not be Shakespeare to work so deeply; it might be a simple demonstration of an interactive product. A story unfolds about how the product is to be used, demonstrating this feature and then that feature. Because our minds work the same way as before, we envisage a grander plan that we emotionally suppose the demonstration is but an example of, or a story within. But often a demonstration is not only just a linear story like a film reel, it was only designed as such.

A demonstration, then, can create the impression of a more sophisticated system than may actually exist. We know that Macbeth is fiction and we know some questions are just not worth asking—but someone watching a system demonstration does not know what is real and what is merely demonstrated from a script. The demonstration may even be stage-managed by a human, who works through a script behaving exactly as if they were using a fully working system. But there is no way to tell, merely by watching the scripted demonstration, whether there is any more to the system than is shown. Nevertheless, we imagine that there is, and we imagine that it all works as smoothly as the fraction we saw demonstrated. Reeves and Nass [13] argue that this is how our brains work: media is too new an invention for our emotions to have taken it on board. Evolutionarily speaking, up until very recently all experiences we had were real; only in the last few decades (with the exception of theatre) have we had media where reality may or may not be faked. Hence Reeves and Nass define the *media equation*: media equals reality, so far as we are subliminally concerned.

The media industry exploits this effect and we enjoy it. But in systems design, there are serious issues:

- A designer may demonstrate a system and marketers will become too excited by the potential of the design that they insist the product is ready. In fact, the product may be no more than a linear simulation.
- A user in a showroom may be shown a carefully rehearsed demonstration that makes the device seem much more effective than it really is (for that user in particular).
- A scientific paper may describe how a system works—and may deliberately or accidentally not mention that the paper is "but a stage," with edges. Beyond the edge of the stage, the media breaks down; the reader of the paper may imagine the system is more powerful than actually described. But the paper (even if completely truthful) may not define the system's general behaviour. The reader naturally assumes the paper describes a system with symmetries; if those imagined symmetries are not true in reality, the reader has a more powerful image than the writer of the paper had.

The purpose of drama, if that is what it is, is to stimulate, not to exaggerate. When people present papers or describe systems (possibly demonstrating systems) ask,

Probe 3. *Is the design as presented real or drama?* ◁

The problem with drama is that it takes a tiny view of a large, complex design. The complex design that the viewer imagines may not be the actual design. Unfortunate unwarranted generalisations from drama can be avoided by making design principles explicit: then any drama becomes an illustration of a principle the design satisfies.

> **Probe 4.** *Is the drama backed-up by explicit principles that it illustrates? In other words, is it made out to be an illustrative instance of a larger class of possible demonstrations, or is it a unique experience that illustrates little of general value?* ◁

For further discussion, see [14, 15].

4 Explanation

The Canon EOS500 has been one of the most popular automatic SLR (single lens reflex) cameras. The EOS500 manual [16] warns users that leaving the camera switched on is a problem. Canon evidently *know* that the lack of an automatic switch-off is a problem: there is an explicit warning in the manual on page 10:

> "When the camera is not in use, please set the command dial to 'L.' When the camera is placed in a bag, this prevents the possibility of objects hitting the shutter button, continually activating the shutter and draining the battery."

So Canon knows about the problem, and they ask the user to set the camera off—rather than designing it so that it switches itself off. Thus Canon is aware of design problems, but somehow fails to improve. The user manual for the EOS500N [17], an improved version of the EOS500, puts the same problem thus:

> "If the film is removed from the camera in midroll without being rewound and then a new roll of film is loaded, the new roll (film leader) will only be rewound into the cartridge. To prevent this, close the camera back and press the shutter button completely before loading a new roll of film."

It seems the manual writers have now discovered that as well as pressing the shutter button, the camera back must be shut too (it would probably be open if you were changing a film). But it does not seem like the camera designers read the EOS500's manual themselves. User manuals are obvious forms of explanation, to explain the design of a product to its users. Evidently if designers read user manuals (and were able to act on what they learnt) designs might improve.

> **Probe 5.** *Has a complete and truthful user manual been written, and what warnings did it make? Could the design be improved so that the warnings become unnecessary?* ◁

Probe 6. *Are the training procedures complete and truthful, and what warnings do they make? Could the design be improved so that the warnings become unnecessary?* ◁

Since having many views of the design that are complete and sound is essential, then we have higher-level probe,

Probe 7. *Are automatic methods used to guarantee all views, explanations, training material, documentation, and the design itself are complete, sound and consistent with each other?* ◁

For further discussion, see [18, 19].

5   Lottery effect

One of the best ways of handling complexity is to ignore it. In computing, we can write programs and never bother to try to understand them: thus, features are added, and the overall coherence of a design is never addressed. Of all features a sufficiently complex system exhibits, some will, just by chance, be rather effective. If we concentrate on those features, the system as a whole looks effective. The point is that we can find the effective features after an *ad hoc* design process, and in hindsight we can make the design look better than it really is.

Numerous organisations (and some countries) run lotteries. The media bombards us with the success stories: each week somebody has won lots of money, and this is news reported everywhere. Thus we become familiar with winning. As the media equation argues, we are not used to this mediation and we assume that if we are familiar with something then it must be probable. It is but a short step to think that as lots of people win the lottery, we are likely to win too. Of course, if newspapers reported each week the millions of disappointed people who failed to win, thus putting the one winner's chances into perspective, then we would have a very different (more realistic!) view of the lottery.[1]

In product design, we create a complex system and then describe part of it—in a paper at a conference, in a demonstration in a store, in a presentation to the marketing department—and the people who watch the demonstration are in danger of suffering from the lottery effect. If we emphasise success, for there is surely some success somewhere in the design, then the demonstration exploits the media equation, and gives the viewer a biased view of the design.

The lottery effect has a further twist. Many systems involve communications; anything on the Internet or using radio communications necessarily interacts with other people. Suppose such a system fails—for example, a web-based business fails—then nobody gets to hear about it. In fact, in a communications medium, people only hear from successful designs, and do not hear from unsuccessful designs (unless they are sufficiently notorious to be reported in the

---

[1] You are more likely to win in the UK National Lottery by betting at the end of a week—if you bet earlier, you are more likely to die than win.

media). Unsuccessful designs do not communicate, and they disappear. Thus not only is there the lottery effect, but there are actually "no failures" to report!

> **Probe 8.** *From the successful examples, how successful can we say the whole system is? If the examples were selected randomly, then their success suggests the whole system is good; if however the examples are selected with a bias, then we do not know much about the overall design. What method was used to select the design scenarios?* ◁

6   Blame incompetence

A very effective way of coping with unmanageable design complexity is to suggest that it is someone else's fault, or to find other reasons why it cannot be our fault. Better still, define social culture so that the scapegoats willingly accept their role.

The video recorder makes a classic example of this effect. (*i*) People find that their children can use a video recorder better than they can, and they conclude that they are getting too old. (*ii*) People find the manuals incomprehensible, and the technical authors (usually people in a foreign country who evidently don't speak the relevant language fluently) become the scapegoat. (*iii*) There are new models recently introduced on the market that solve the problems; if there are easier products on the market, the user must have made a mistake buying their current gadget. In short, the user is failing in their duty as a consumer to buy the newer, easier-to-use products. (*iv*) We haven't yet got books called *VCRs for Dummies*—as there are for computer programs—but the attitude, from all directions, is that users *are* dummies, and it is their fault [20]. (*v*) After any major disaster, the explanation is often human error, user error, pilot error, or operator error. All are familiar terms. The law, at least in the United Kingdom, requires individuals to take the liability for accidents. It follows that users are responsible.

All of these attitudes can be challenged:

(*i*) Children do not know how a video recorder ought to work, so they press buttons almost at random. This behaviour is likely to generate examples of what they want to achieve, and they can then generalise their discoveries to do what they want. In contrast, adults—having learnt how the world works—expect video recorders to work in a particular way. Since they do not, adults are forever frustrated. Furthermore, children are not responsible—they have not just spent lots of money on the gadget, and they are not worried about "breaking" it by using it the "wrong" way. In short, children are more successful at using video recorders, but not because adults are old and "past it" but because video recorders are badly designed for mature people to use [21].

(*ii*) Manuals are incomprehensible because a bad design has no good explanation, in any language. (This point is elevated into a probe in the next section, below.)

(*iii*) There are always new models being introduced on the market. Marketing for last year's models, at the time, presented the objects as desirable and solving the previous year's models. That there is always a solution to bad design (i.e., buying another design whose besetting problems will not become apparent to the user until a much later than the point of purchase) is not an excuse for bad design.

(*iv*) In the 1960s Ralph Nader intercepted a memo between two companies, asking how drivers could be trained to park cars better [22]. On a hill, cars not parked properly tend to roll down the hill. If parked cars roll down hill, then the driver needs training to do a better job: thereby the issue is presented as one of driver training, driver psychology, and even of writing good driving manuals. In fact even for reasonable inclines, the cars were hard to park on hills because the parking brake was flimsily engineered. Thus an engineering fault was being passed off as a user fault. Clearly *some* errors are user errors, but many are design errors passed off as user (or driver) errors.

(*v*) When there are substantial investments in hardware, as in avionics, it is tempting to blame "pilot error" since the pilot is unique, and if the pilot has made an error then nothing need be done to the expensive hardware. In contrast, if the airframe is blamed, there is a danger that an entire fleet of aircraft have to be grounded to fix the problem. Since pilots often die in accidents, there is often no strong argument that they are not to blame. Because of the cost of rectifying design errors in contrast to the cost of retraining (which is zero if the pilot is dead), there is an overwhelming tendency, regardless of the facts, to blame the human most closely involved at the moment of error—rather than the designer.

Finally note how one's difficulty with using a video recorder is celebrated as a joke: it is now difficult to treat the subject seriously. A satire of *Star Trek* had one of the security officers fumbling. The captain asks why the officer is not ready to go, and the officer replies that they cannot get their phasor to stop flashing 12:00! ... Nobody can get their video recorders to stop flashing 12:00, and the joke is that the officer's phasor has become as complex as a video recorder and now defeats its very purpose—namely to be a ready-to-hand tool.

If an interactive system does not work, there is a mismatch between the user and the device. It is easier, sometimes, to focus on the user's problems, rather than on the design problems. Users are "more easily changed" than systems, and in a marketplace, the users fixing "their" problems will cause more product sales—whether selling how-to manuals, or upgraded products promising to solve the spurious problems of the obsolete products. That millions of tons of electronics are thrown away and used as landfill every year is a testament to the economic power of persuading users that it is their fault that designs do not work, and that therefore the users should invest in new solutions—hence discarding old solutions.

Probe 9. *Are design failures discussed, and if so who is blamed for them?* ◁

Probe 10. *Are people defending bad designs with spurious arguments?* ◁

7 Scientific method

Perhaps it is hard to recognise, but all of the issues described above are analogous to issues of scientific method. The purpose of science is to have reliable knowledge of the natural world, and the scientific method has developed so that humans, with their limited abilities and tendencies to make errors, can work collectively to understand and check each other's results, and reach consensus [23]. In design, which we have been discussing, the issue is to understand artificial worlds, and to increase the community of people who understand and can use the underlying ideas. A successful design is replicated, and many people end up using it, employing the same underlying theory of operation. The current boundaries of science are precisely the still difficult-to-understand areas; the current boundaries of design are precisely the still difficult-to-understand ideas. In science, curiosity drives the boundaries; in design, economics fights back. In both, anything easy to understand is less interesting.

Both science and design, then, push human limits. In science a very clear set of protocols has emerged to help people resist and detect the temptation to cheat. One of the core principles is *replication*. Is a scientific result described in enough detail for someone else to replicate it? Was selective bias (cf. the lottery effect of Section 5) avoided in reporting the idea? If some data is held back, then it might be an error that the scientist is trying to conceal—or it might, if revealed, help another scientist to find a better explanation of the result than that claimed.

In computing we have exactly the same problem, exacerbated because most design products are seen, most often, in a consumer world where competitiveness and industrial secrecy rather than openness is the norm. The consumerist comparison is powerful because many consumer gadgets—on sale in stores—are sophisticated and powerful in comparison with experimental work; designers easily envy the seduction of consumer products and therefore aspire to "worldly" rather than "scientific" standards.

One difference is that a good design has expressible symmetries. These are the ideas that other people can understand (because they are expressed) and use in their own work (because they are symmetries). A bad design has inexpressible properties that are merely attractive, it has boundaries that break symmetries—in short, it works only as drama. The idea it represents is no bigger than the stage it is seen on.

Student projects in computer science make a good illustration of the tension. So many students work hard to build a thing. The thing is interesting in itself, but what remains of the student's work in a year's time? The system probably no longer works, because it relies on obsolete computers. All the project was, was a dramatic performance—despite containing a program that in principle could be replicated and run anywhere anytime, it was a program that merely created a time- and space-limited experience.

Probe 11. *Have the design ideas been expressed clearly and fully-enough for anyone else to replicate the core ideas? If not, what exactly has the design contributed to the future?* ◁

8 Ethical commitment

William Perry claims that we learn and understand subjects on a nine-stage scale of increasing intellectual sophistication [24]. Designers work at various positions within Perry's scheme. The initial position is that the designer believes in a basic duality: there are right and wrong answers. As they become more experienced, they realise that some authorities disagree—but they still cling to the idea that there are right and wrong answers, so that some of these authorities must be wrong. At least they are learning that their subject is hard!

At higher positions of intellectual development, designers realise that what is right or wrong depends on their commitment; there are different styles and approaches—they need to make a choice of what they want to be. Next—and this is a significant leap—they *make* a commitment. Perhaps they want to design better for the under privileged, or for the rich? Next, the last position, there arrives a higher level of intellectual sophistication: that the commitment itself is dynamic, contextual, and indeed a life's work.

Probe 12. *Is the design presented as right (as opposed to other designs that are wrong), or is a more mature view presented? Is the designer's commitment to the design orientation explicit, or not yet worked out?* ◁

In this paper we claimed that symmetry underlies good design, and that social, cultural, cognitive, evolutionary and economic forces conspired to make it hard to see clearly. We discussed probes, analytical tools to help designers climb out of the fog of complexity, to avoid the Siren songs of image over integrity. Nevertheless, we kept one factor implicit: the definition of good itself. Until a designer knows and chooses what sort of good they are pursuing, they will run the risk of being misled—of making arbitrary decisions. In an informal sense, ethics is the highest symmetry; a designer's ethics is that property that infuses all their designs, and is invariant from their mind's conception right through to the deployment, use and impact of the artefact in the hands of its users. Moreover having an explicit ethic gives the designer an integrity that they are not easily swayed from: each day, as it were, the designer reviews their behaviour and performance against their ethic and aims to avoid pitfalls next time. Only by having an ethic of which they are not ignorant have they a firm place from which they can see, and perhaps even anticipate, pitfalls. In short, designers need symmetries: properties that remain invariant from design to design.

One might derive a heart-warming feeling from being engaged in design and knowing design is doing good—a reassuring but hardly insightful thought. To be more specific, a characteristic of design (rather than art) is that there is an enormous scale-up (e.g., by mass production or software copying) from designer to user community; since a designer "lets go" of a product, for most people the relevant ethics involve the balance between the designer's greater influence as against the greater number of users.

Interestingly, we could make an analogy between designers of complex products—who define rules for the product's operation—and actual rulers, in the classical sense, of tyrants—who define rules for a society's operation. Indeed one might set up a translation of classical ethics from society and map it into design. There are good rulers and bad rulers; there are good designers and bad designers. Aristotle defines *justice* as that virtue concerned with doing good for others [25]. If justice is the ethics of concern for designers, it is disappointing that even after almost 2,500 years the correspondence between justice and design is obscure. However, in the 1970s John Rawls introduced an operational conception of justice [26].

A just society, according to Rawls, is one which was or was in principle defined by legislatives working under a so-called *veil of ignorance*. If I know who I am to be in a future society I am designing, I may design it so that it is advantageous to me, or to people who share some of my properties (such as my level of computing skill). If, however, I am under a veil of ignorance and I do not know who I shall be in this society being designed, I shall try to design justly—because I might be anybody, with any properties. In fact, almost by definition, I would be unlikely to be a privileged member of the society, and therefore my rules would tend to give rights to large sectors of society, since statistically I am more likely to be in these sectors.

If a designer acts justly (i.e., under the veil of ignorance) they cannot design for themselves; they must "know the user"—a standard design slogan, at least since Wilfred Hansen's classic 1971 article on design [27]—for if they do not they are creating a system into which they could find themselves with the "wrong" properties. For example, acting ignorantly they might design a system that requires hand-eye co-ordination; acting knowingly under the veil of ignorance, they would check whether their users had such co-ordination. Clearly, if their users are an ageing population, or car drivers who have to concentrate on the road rather than the in-car entertainment system [28], then knowingly acting justly will result in a more effective system.

> **Probe 13**. *What ethics does the design represent? In particular, is the activity just; does it do good for others?* ◁

Just design implies providing benefits to users (often balancing difficult trade-offs); but, as argued in Section 1.1, users have *counteradaptive preferences* [29]; clearly, design for users *with* such preferences (especially when they are unreflective) is different from innovative design stimulating rational choice.

> **Probe 14**. *Does design make user benefits explicit (or does it substitute fashion or consumerism)?* ◁

> **Probe 15**. *Does a design persuade users to do something the designers would not want to be persuaded to do themselves?* ◁

For further discussion of justice applied to design, see [30] (from where the last probe was taken) and [31].

9 Probing towards a global ethic

Design has been described so far as an almost private affair between the design and a group of people, the users. In fact users are far from homogeneous, and with international communications, design has become a global, multi-cultural issue. The global world of users are unlikely to agree on a common ethical basis. It is best, then, to make the ethical probes behind the design as explicit as possible.

Hans Küng in his *Global Responsibility: In Search of a New World Ethic* [32] proposes six rules for priority and certainty (which he attributes to Dietmar Mieth). Here, we have converted them into probing questions for designers.

Probe 16. *What problems are solved by the design?* ◁

There must be no technological progress that creates more problems than solutions. This probe requires us to think through the consequences of a new idea. It is perhaps too easy to think only of the advantages to some people in some conditions when promoting a new technology—this probe requires us to think about the problems too. Technology often causes problems; we must try to find designs whose advantages out-weigh their problems (so far as we can foresee them).

An important point this probe raises is the assumption that technology works as intended. Almost always, technology will solve problems. But what if things don't work out the way that was intended? What if the technology is less reliable, or if criminals find ways of subverting it? What if we have another problem on the scale of the Year 2000 bug?

Probe 17. *How do you know the problems are solved by the design?* ◁

Anyone who introduces new design must prove that it does not cause ecological, social or other damage. People make all sorts of claims about technology. How should we believe them? Have they done experiments, and what were the results? Society should require certain standards of performance, and then designers should meet those standards.

The Year 2000 bug is a nice illustration. Who, exactly, proved things would work? Why is no-one who made the faulty goods responsible for fixing them? . . . The answer is partly because no consumers ever made designers or manufacturers prove their original claims: we all took the benefits of computers on trust. This probe was not used; and now we are paying the cost.

Probe 18. *Does the design benefit a large part of society?* ◁

Interest in the common good has priority over the benefit of particular individuals, provided human rights are preserved (a comment guarding against a totalitarian view of "common use comes before personal use"). This probe of Küng's is an expression of user centred design (UCD) [3].

Probe 19. *Are more urgent issues being solved?* ◁

The more urgent (such as the survival of an individual) has priority over higher goals (such as self-fulfilment for the designer or for a particular user). This probe suggests, other things being equal, that implants like pacemakers are more important to develop and have than implants like calculators!

Probe 20. *Is the environment respected?* ◁

The ecological system has priority over the social system. The reason for this is that we can change designs, but that many changes to the environment are irreversible. It is hard to "lose" a design concept, but it is easy to lose a species, or to pollute some land. Since our children inherit the planet, then this probe suggests we think about the future, and that we should ask whether our technologies do good for our descendants.

Probe 21. *Is the impact of the design reversible?* ◁

Reversible developments should have priority over irreversible developments. For example, if we are going to have brain implants, we ought to be able to change our minds later.

Some people will not agree with what they see as implied political bias in the probes. But note that this is a list of probes; they are not rules. It may be that you are thinking about a new feature for a system design. There may be no obvious way that the idea is "reversible" or that it promotes the environment over the social system ... well, the probes are not rules. The point is that the probes will have helped designers think about significant trade-offs, and—in particular—started to ask questions about the human worth of what is being undertaken.

As Küng himself points out, this is a rational list. But as the probes are used, the more specific the probe's wiggling becomes, the more questions are begged about motivation, the degree of compulsion, and the ultimate issues of right and wrong.

10   The purpose of probes. What are the right answers?

Used appropriately, probes are constructive in the overall design process. However an intimidating number of probes were presented in this paper, ranging from ones concerned with the process of design, through to ones concerned with the ethical stance of the designers. Too many to be incisive! Indeed, if the probes were written down as a check-list, the reflection they are intended to inspire would not come about. There would be a serious danger of designers running down the list, ticking boxes quickly. The probes in this paper were instead intended to offer a selection from which a pertinent focus can be constructed. For example, a design company may wish to develop probes that closely match its corporate mission statement—or, conversely, it may choose a mission so that designers can operationalise it directly in their work.

Probes focus on key, but often ignored, properties of design, and help communication between designers, between designers and users and beyond. Unlike heuristic evaluation [33], the issue is not the design itself so much as the design process. Like probes on a volt meter, design probes are to be pressed home on the relevant parts of a process—even pressed on the designer—and to help obtain a reading of the "voltage" or other property. There is no *a priori* sense in which a high voltage or a low voltage is better or worse; it depends on what the purpose is whether one extreme or the other, or indeed an intermediate value, is desirable. But once we have a conception of "voltage" we can talk about it, get clearer readings, understand each other better, and improve the design processes in the direction we wish to go.

How do probes differ from design heuristics? A heuristic tries to make suggestions that would improve *a* design; for example *equal opportunity* is a heuristic [34] that suggests that user interfaces should treat input and output equally (a symmetry) and that doing so will make interfaces simpler and more powerful. In contrast, probes do not improve design; they improve thinking. There is no right answer for a probe—the point is that not having a good answer, or not being able to recruit an answer is, the problem that a probe would highlight.

Heuristics try to be constructive; they may be analytical and provide quite specific guidance, or they may be intuitive and inspirational. In contrast, probes are critical, though (like heuristics) they may be specific or inspirational in style.

In the long run, converting probes to constructive heuristics will be a valid research exercise, but it is not obvious how to proceed along this path at the moment. (See [35, 36] for examples of placing heuristics into a design process. In particular [18] suggests that, by using computers appropriately, design can be made concurrent, and hence, by being more efficient, better things can be achieved within given resources.)

I believe probes are an improvement on approaches that do not encourage debate with the designer (such as [37, 38]). It seems to me that the idea of probes allows us to start asking penetrating questions about where the design of interactive computing systems is taking us, where we want to go, and to warn us off diversions.

11   Conclusions

Design is complex, and it occurs in a complex world whose standards are different from the ideal of pursuit of good design. Thus the practical problem of design is to have clear discernment, to perceive the forces that result in compromises or, worse, in designs that look right but are inappropriate. Designers are agents of social change, yet, being at the top of a certain sort of social pyramid (there is one designer for a thousand users), they are caught up in conventional social forces. We believe designers and hence designs must have integrity. How anyone achieves that is a hard problem; this paper contributed by espousing a range of probes. The purpose of the probes was to raise issues, to raise consciousness of alternative points of view, and ultimately to show design as a political activity of changing the world—hopefully for the better.

The properties probes reveal are a consequence of symmetries; in particular, of properties that are conserved as they are translated from one mind to another. If there are no such symmetries, design becomes art, valuable because it is unique, and diminished if it is multiplied ("forged"); design becomes repetitious drama, transiently satisfying, non-interactive, ultimately predictable, and of no lasting value.

Acknowledgements

Ann Blandford, Penny Duquenoy, Peter Ladkin, Michael Harrison and David Pullinger made very useful comments for which the author is grateful.

References

1. H. Petroski, *To Engineer is Human: The Role of Failure in Successful Design*, MacMillan, 1985.
2. D. A. Norman, *The Psychology of Everyday Things*, Basic Books, Inc., 1988.
3. T. Landauer, *The Trouble with Computers*, MIT Press, 1995.
4. H. W. Thimbleby, "You're Right About the Cure: Don't Do That," *Interacting with Computers*, **2**(1), pp8–25, 1990.
5. C. M. Christensen, *The Innovator's Dilemma*, Harvard Business School Press, 1997.
6. L. B. Slobodkin, *Simplicity & Complexity in Games of the Intellect*, Harvard University Press, 1992.
7. N. Postman, *Technopoly: The Surrender of Culture to Technology*, Vintage, 1993.
8. E. Tenner, *Why Things Bite Back: Predicting the Problems of Progress*, Fourth Estate, 1997.
9. M. Piattelli-Palmarini, *Inevitable Illusions: How Mistakes of Reason Rule Our Minds*, John Wiley & Sons, 1994.
10. R. Bornat & H. W. Thimbleby, "The Life and Times of Ded, Display Editor," in *Cognitive Ergonomics and Human Computer Interaction*, pp225–255, in J. B. Long & A. Whitefield, editors, Cambridge University Press, 1989.
11. J. Grudin, "The Case Against User Interface Consistency," *Communications of the ACM*, **32**(10), pp1164–1173, 1989.
12. E. Gamma, R. Helm, R. Johnson & J. Vlissides, *Design Patterns: Elements of Reusable Object-Oriented Software*, Addison-Wesley, 1995.
13. B. Reeves & C. Nass, 1996, *The Media Equation*, Cambridge University Press.
14. H. Thimbleby, "Internet, Discourse and Interaction Potential," in L. K. Yong, L. Herman, Y. K. Leung & J. Moyes, eds., First Asia Pacific Conference on Human Computer Interaction, pp3–18, 1996.
15. B. Laurel, *Computers As Theatre*, Addison-Wesley, 1991.
16. Canon Inc., *EOS500/500QD Instructions*, part no. CT1–1102–006, 1993.
17. Canon Inc., *EOS500N/500NQD Instructions*, part no. CT1–1111–000, 1996.
18. H. W. Thimbleby, "Specification-led Design for Interface Simulation, Collecting Use-data, Interactive Help, Writing Manuals, Analysis, Comparing Alternative Designs, etc," *Personal Technologies*, **4**(2), pp241–254, 1999.

19. H. W. Thimbleby & P. B. Ladkin, "A Proper Explanation When You Need One," in M. A. R. Kirby, A. J. Dix & J. E. Finlay, eds., BCS Conference HCI'95, *People and Computers*, **X**, pp107–118, Cambridge University Press, 1995.

20. H. W. Thimbleby, "Minotaur," *Ariadne* (ISSN 1361–3197), **18**, p11, 1998.

21. H. W. Thimbleby, "The Frustrations of a Pushbutton World," in *1993 Encyclopædia Britannica Yearbook of Science and the Future*, pp202–219, Encyclopædia Britannica Inc., 1992.

22. R. Nader, *Unsafe at Any Speed*, Pocket Books, 1965.

23. J. Ziman, *Reliable Knowledge: An Exploration of the Grounds for Belief in Science*, Cambridge University Press, 1978.

24. W. G. Perry, Jr., *Forms of Intellectual and Ethical Development in the College Years: A Scheme*,[2] Jossey-Bass Publishers, 1999.

25. Aristotle, *Nicomachean Ethics*, Book **V**, in *Great Books of the Western World*, **8**, Encycopedia Britannica, 2nd ed., 1990.

26. J. Rawls, *A Theory of Justice*, Oxford University Press, 1972.

27. W. J. Hansen, "User Engineering Principles for Interactive Systems," AFIPS Conference Proceedings, **39**, pp523–532, 1971.

28. H. Thimbleby, P. Duquenoy & G. Marsden, "Ethics and Consumer Electronics," Ethicomp'99, in press, 1999.

29. J. Elster, *Sour Grapes: Studies in the Subversion of Rationality*, Cambridge University Press, 1985.

30. D. Berdichevsky & E. Neunschwander, "Towards an Ethics of Persuasive Technology," *Communications of the ACM*, **42**(5), pp51–58, 1999.

31. H. Thimbleby & P. Duquenoy, "Justice and Design," Interact'99, in press, 1999.

32. H. Küng, *Global Responsibility: In Search of a New World Ethic*, translated by J. Bowden, SCM Press, 1997.

33. J. Nielsen, *Usability Engineering*, Academic Press, 1993.

34. H. W. Thimbleby, *User Interface Design*, Addison-Wesley, 1990.

35. H. W. Thimbleby, "The Design of a Terminal Independent Package," *Software— Practice and Experience*, **17**(15), pp351–367, 1987.

36. H. W. Thimbleby, "Designing Interfaces for Problem Solving, with Application to Hypertext and Creative Writing," *AI & Society*, **8**, pp29–44, 1994.

37. H. W. Thimbleby, "Failure in the Technical User Interface Design Process," *Computers and Graphics*, **9**(3), pp187–193, 1985.

38. H. W. Thimbleby, "User Interface Design," in *Software Engineer's Reference Handbook*, J. A. McDermid, ed., pp57/1–57/14, Butterworth-Heinemann, 1991.

---

[2] This is the Library of Congress title; the title of the book is *Forms of Ethical and Intellectual Development in the College Years: A Scheme*.

Harold Thimbleby is Professor of Computing Research at Middlesex University, London, and Research Director for the School of Computing Science. Harold gained his PhD in 1981 in Human-Computer Interaction, and much of his research since then has been concerned with making complex devices easier to use. In 1987 he was awarded the British Computer Society Wilkes Medal.

He wrote "User Interface Design" published by Addison-Wesley in 1990. He has over 300 publications.

He has held visiting posts in Australia, Canada, New Zealand and Switzerland, as well as in industry. He has lectured widely from Norway to New Zealand, and has been widely reported on TV and radio.

Maintaining Context and Control in a Digital World

S. P. Stenton

Hewlett-Packard Laboratories
Filton Road, Stoke Gifford, Bristol, UK
Phil_Stenton@hplb.hpl.hp.com

Over the next three to five years most major electronics companies and service providers will be competing for the portal in your pocket. Your disposable income is their ultimate goal. We spend $27bn a year on music content alone. The humble and somewhat fragmented PDA market will be swept aside as our need to consume overpowers our need to be organized. The ubiquitous Internet has taken the potential for these devices way beyond the niche of electronic organizers. As clients to a pervasive infrastructure the processor in your pocket becomes a valuable source of advertising revenue in an attempt to provide whatever you want whenever you want it at a price you can afford. The internet represents the secon wave of change in this category.

The first wave of change was ushered in by the Palm Pilot. To date this most successful appliance-like PDA, has sold around 4m units since its launch at Demo 96. As a brave experiment in cut down functionality and pen input it was launched into a market littered with failed attempts. Its success has prompted Microsoft and partners to launch the PalmPC in an attempt to build on the acceptance of this form factor. For these devices the keyboard has already been relegated to an optional accessory. Freed from the dominance of the keyboard interaction designers can contemplate more exotic forms of I/O in the hope of hitting the right balance of affordance and value, as Palm computing did in 1996.

Speech as an interaction mode has promised much but has been restricted to cameo roles on PCs. Where it has taken center stage has been on voice only devices such as the telephone or dictaphone hybrids. Eyeglasses are, like CMOS imaging, coming of age and ready to take their place. Position sensing along with other contextual information will usher in a third wave of appliance PDAs based on situated computing to provide context dependent services. The days when the only input to the processor in your pocket was the keystroke from a keyboard or the selection of a mouse will be left behind along with the days when PDAs were simply electronic organizers. This presentation describes work on portable appliances and the ecosystems within which they are emerging.

Phil Stenton is the manager of the Personal Computing Department in Hewlett-Packard Laboratories Bristol. His PhD research was in the field of Stereovision where he worked with John Mayhew and John Frisby at Sheffield University. After a year at British Telecom's Martlesham Heath Laboratories he joined HP to work on interfaces to expert systems. During his 14 years at Hewlett Packard Phil has worked on Natural Language systems, Discourse Analysis, Interface Agents and Mobile Appliances. The work of his department includes research on Speech, CMOS imaging, Ultra-portables and future PC and Appliance systems.

Everywhere Messaging

Chris Schmandt

Media Laboratory
Massachusetts Institute of Technology
Cambridge, MA 02139 USA
geek@media.mit.edu

Abstract. This paper briefly describes a series of messaging applications for wearable and ubiquitous computing. The goal of these applications is to support location-aware messaging across a variety of devices and access media, in a manner which is transparent to message originators and configurable by the recipient. Location awareness includes learning which messages should be sent to which device's address as a function of location, and delivery of location-specific information when coupled with position derived from the GPS system. We explore a number of issues in alerting and message access via speech user interfaces, as they are appropriate when the user is busy driving or paying attention to other activities in daily life.

1 Introduction

Messaging is a wonderful application for wearable and ubiquitous computing as it is a service which is both essential and asychronous. Everywhere communication is already the norm for many people through their wireless telephones. But the usage paradigms for synchronous voice communication are not necessarily effective for asynchronous and/or text messages, and wireless phone owners can quickly become overwhelmed by excessive incoming calls.

Work and social mobility is only on the increase, as is email account penetration, and of course as the Web becomes pervasive we increasingly depend on timely information most readily available in digital form. Asynchronous messages or information delivery are by definition an interruption into our lives; whether this interruption is valuable or harmful depends on both the quality of the information being delivered as well as what other tasks we are performing at the arrival time. Interruption with the *right* information is useful and helps us be more productive, either at work or socially. We help our co-workers by providing needed information or decisions in a timely manner, and we coordinate with our family and friends in making day-to-day decisions. Interruption is also an essential part of the social protocols we may employ to communicate with each other in a more synchronous manner, as it help potential conversants synchronize informally. For exmaple, when I receive a message from you, you may be able to easily receive my reply right away, whereas if I were to wait an hour, you may be away from your desk or the office.

The downside to interruption is the cost it places on the attention of the interrupted person. Theis can range from welcome diversion (while waiting to meet someone who is late) to mild distraction (a pager beeping in the middle of a conversation) to potentially fatal distractions while driving. Note that for the whole range of possible interactions, their impact will be a combination of the timing of the event, the attentional state of the recipient, and they style of alert (beep, ring, vibration, etc) produced by the interruption.

Our work attempts to maximize the positive aspects of interruptions and minimize their distraction in three ways. First, we *filter* messages based on automatic and dynamic rules, to minimize the number of interruptions. Secondly, we factor in user *context*, i.e. what the user is doing, her location, etc. Finally, we aim to make alerts minimally intrusive through scalable notification mechanisms which are more or less invasive depending on the importance of the incoming message and the user's state. Our alerting is primarily auditory and many of our systems employ speech user interfaces, so they can be used while the user's hands and eyes are busy.

The remainder of this paper briefly describes four related projects into these research themes. Each explores a portion of the whole problem as just described.

2 Knothole

Knothole [1] uses two way pagers and simple text messaging to provide a filtered stream of email to the pagers, a proxy to hide the identity of the paging device from outsiders, and access to personal and external Web-based information sources.

Knothole builds a service layer on top of two way text message paging, and works with any device which has an internet address. Filtering of incoming messages is via the CLUES dyanmic filtering system. Our desktop computers have a large quantity of information about us, and CLUES takes advantage of this to decide a message is "timely" and hence worth forwarding. Specifically, CLUES uses calendar entries, address book (to map email addresses to phone numbers), outgoing and incoming (via Caller-ID) telephone call logs, and copies of outgoing email messages. Incoming email is tested against this information, which is recompiled automatically into a new rule set hourly, and if a match is found, the message is fowarded.

If a Knothole user responds to a message, or chooses to originate a new outgoing email message to any internet address or through personal address book lookup, the message actually goes to his desktop workstation. There it is reformated by this proxy server so that it appears to come from his main email account, not the address of the portable device. This hides the identity of the device, which is often desireable!

By sending a structured message (one that begins with a keyword) a Knothole user can invoke looking up personal information systems, such as reading from

---

[1] The name Knothole is meant to invoke the limited view of non-paying spectators peeking through holes in the wooden fence surrounding a sports arena.

his address book or reading or writing his calendar. He may also consult news, weather, and traffic services off the internet, and execute an arbitrary command line (with program output redirected to the pager as a reply message).

3 Active Messenger

Knothole causes subscribers to send many more messages, since it is easy to generate a reply, devices addresses remain confidential, and a wealth of information is available via the pager. A problem arises, however, when users have multiple portable devices, which they may use because of different costs of services or battery life characteristics in various areas. Even if the user has only a single device, what is the point of sending a message to a pager if it has just been read on screen?

Active Messenger uses CLUES to prioritize messages, and users may set these messages in various catagories by augmenting the CLUES rules (messages from my family may always be "important", those from my boss may be "urgent", etc). Active Messenger then follows the progress of each message it decides to forward, choosing devices in turn based on whatever sketchy knowledge of user location is available. For example, the user may have been seen (via Unix "finger") in his office a few moments ago, so Active Messenger will wait a few minutes to see if a message is read on screen there. Or the user may have phoned in recently from a distant location (which is determined by Caller-ID). Or the user may be sending SMS (160 character two-way text messages) using his GSM phone, which suggests he is in the metropolitan area.

In addition to handheld devices, Active Messenger can also phone up over a voice line and read email via text-to-speech, or send it as a fax. A key aspect of Active Messenger is that different priority messages are suitable for different sets of devices. This lets the user cut down the number of messages arriving when he is at a distant location and probably doesn't want to be bothered as frequently.

An important consideration of Active Messenger is that it is a *process*, not a router. It takes time to deliver messages to various devices, which may or may not have a back channel indicating whether they have been received, and Active Messenger must monitor the progress of the message through a heirarchy of devices, trying the least intrusive or expensive before escalating to try to deliver the really urgent messages by whatever means is possible. Also, since some paging services queue messages until the recipient is in range, but we do not wish to re-send messages which have subsequently been read using a different means while out of range, the device-specific queue managment is done by Active Messenger to avoid that of the service provider.

4 comMotion

comMotion uses GPS (Global Positioning System) data to determine a subscriber's physical location, and then delivers messages and items from to-do lists to the user as she nears locations of a particular class. For example, comMotion will remind its user of her shopping list as she nears a known grocery store, or her calendar as she approaches her office.

Lists may be a mix of text or digitized audio, and may be viewed on screen of a laptop computer or heard while driving. In addition friends may send the comMotion user location-specific reminders not already on her list. Web-based information services may be based on location or time of day, so the comMotion user may receive a list of films playing at the local cinema when she leaves work, but only on Fridays. Notification is by auditory cues since the user is almost always doing something else while in motion. The majority of comMotion features can be activated by speech recognition for use on the go. It has been used while on foot, while driving, or while riding a bicycle.

comMotion does not ask the user to describe all the coordinates of interesting places in her life. Rather, it observes her travel over time, detects places she frequents, and then asks her if she wishes to identify them. This is currently done by observing the loss of GPS signal when entering a building, and comMotion raises a query when a location has been visited three times. comMotion can also obtain map and services information for the user's current location from the Web, such as showing nearby grocery stores, banks, etc.; this is presented only via the visual user interface.

5   Nomadic Radio

Nomadic Radio explores the use of scalable auditory cues to alert a user to incoming messages. The goal of Nomadic Radio is non-intrusive alerting scaled by the priority of the incoming message against the user's current activity level.

Nomadic Radio is built upon wearable devices presenting a personal spatialized sound environment, with speech recognition input. It is designed for hands-free use while performing other tasks. As messages come in, higher priority messages result in more insistent auditory cues, and for known senders a voice snippet can often be played in the senders own voice (from the voice mail system). These auditory cues are *scaled* in a range of intrusiveness. Least intrusive is simply a change in background ambient sound (water flowing) to some network traffic to Nomadic Radio. Higher levels are auditory cues representing the sender of the message, the senders voice as a greeting, or simply reading the message aloud using text-to-speech synthesis, without waiting for a user responde.

Nomadic Radio usually monitors the user's response time and adapts notification as a result. For example, if a message arrives and is ignored, the user is not notified of similar priority messages, but only of higher priority ones (actually, the lower priority messages get a more subtle auditory cue as a gentle reminder that that continue to arrive). Nomadic Radio also monitors speech via its microphone, and uses this to adapt. If its wearer is speaking, for example, the system waits until she has finished before interrupting with an alert.

6 Conclusions

The four projects described above are meant to be examples of focusing on specific issues in alerting for everywhere messaging. The goal is to deliver the right messages to the proper location, in the manner which is least intrusive. It is hoped that approaches such as these will allow those users so inclined to be electronically reachable everywhere, in a manner which does not raise havoc in their lives.

More information on these projects can be found at http://www.media.mit.edu/speech.

7 Acknowledgements

Stefan Marti built Knothole and Active Messenger. comMotion is Natalia Marmasse's project. Nitin Sawhney created Nomadic Radio. These projects were supported by the Media Lab's News in the Future and Digital Life sponsored research consortia.

Chris Schmandt received the BS and MS degrees from MIT, where he has been building speech systems since 1979. He is the director of the Speech Research Group at the Media Laboratory, a position he has held since the creation of the Lab. Before that he worked on speech applications research at the Architecture Machine Group, including the "Put That There" and "Phone Slave" projects, as well as projects indigital video typography and gestural input for stereoscopic video displays.

His current research focuses on user interfaces and applications of speech processing technology, voice as a data type on workstations and hand-held computers, and computer-mediated telephony. Key to this work is gaining a better understanding of how people use speech for communication in a conversational context, and how to apply this knowledge to more effective voice interaction with computers.

Mobile, Ubiquitous and the Sense of Space

Marco Susani

Domus Academy Research Center
via Savona, 97
20144 Milano Italy

Introduction

Handheld and ubiquitous computing has the potential of disconnecting any computing activity from a single, fixed place of access. Most of the handheld, mobile devices we know and use today risk to generate a kind of *neutralization* of the sense of space. Mobile means, when we deal with portable devices, that we can access information no matter where we are; our territory of life becomes indistinct.

But future mobile, handheld and networked devices are more promising in creating a new relation between physical space and digital information. Mobile and handheld devices, in conjunction with contextualized and personalized digital information, could generate a layer of digital space connected to the physical space of the body, the architectural space, and the territory of the city.

The personalized, social, digital layer around the body

Psychology and architecture define the space around the body in terms of "proxemics". Social behaviors are influenced by the space of relationships around our person, and different cultures could be defined by different dimensions, and different interactions, between these social auras that surround our bodies. When dealing with mobile and worn digital information, the notion of proxemics needs to be updated.

First, we should consider that digital information "worn" on our body could be personalized and contextualized: we are wearing OUR information, and we access different information and different services according to where we are. This means that we are surrounded by our personal "aura" of information. Second, we can also consider that this aura can interact socially; that, in other words, our digital information can be exchanged in proximity of other auras, with the presence of other persons.

All this generates an addition to the social extension of our physical bodies, as described by the rules of proxemics: the intangible space of relation around our persons includes the digital extension of our physical bodies.

This notion of interactive auras around bodies have the potential of dramatically transforming the social space of relation.

The intangible, digital architectural space

Space, in architecture, has always had an intangible dimension. Architects can influence our perception of space using light, or sound, or the dynamic sequence of rooms with different proportions. Also the presence of media has a similar effect: even a non interactive, conventional TV, or a traditional corded telephone, have the power of reorganizing the space of a room with an intangible power of attraction(or repulsion).

Interactive media and telecommunication systems, connected with mobile and wearable devices, increase this power of reorganizing space. Architectural space that can recognize us also becomes active, and reactive, generating new hierarchies in space, attraction poles, as well as a different notion of closure and privacy.

The interactive territory of the city

Public spaces in the city are flooded with information (physical information, such as signs) and also flooded with information infrastructures (the cells for digital telecommunication cover all the urbanized territory) but still the sophisticated use of digital information in the city is unexplored. Ancient cities "spoke" with their walls and their buildings, communicated their history, conveyed the experiences of their inhabitants. Industrial cities are more inhabited by machines than by humans, and populated by signs that have the only functional reason to overcome the lack of sense of space. Future cities could reflect though digital information a new, updated "genius loci", a sense of local space that could deny the homogeneous space in the industrial, modern city. The use of mobile in connection contextualized information could make the city "speak" again, and give back a sense of local quality opposite to the uniform, globalized space of the web. The new interactive territory has the enormous potential to become the interactive media of the future, a place where experiences and knowledge could be diffused and exchanged through collective, participatory media.

Fluid, personalized, interactive, mobile spaces

The three categories of spaces that we mentioned could all be made possible by the new mobile and wearable technologies. But the connection between digital information and the creation of a sense of belonging to space will only happen if the design of the devices, of the information services, and of the new interactive media will acknowledge the need a shared, social, digital space. The theme of handheld, mobile and wearable devices should always be considered in conjunction with the creation of new social, collective environments that could be accessed through these devices. And with the creation of a fluid space that connects and includes both the physical, material collective space and the digital information space: a "Third Space" that doesn't belong solely to the material sphere or to the virtual one, but is the combination of the two that has original characteristics.

Marco Susani, July 1999

Marco Susani, Domus Academy, Milan, is an architect and industrial designer. He is director of Domus Academy Research Center, conducting projects, research and teaching on design and innovation. He also is responsible of the research area of interaction design and of the Interaction Design Course at Domus Academy.

His recent research focuses on interaction design, telecommunication, media spaces, multimedia, interface devices, robotics. He participated in writing the selected schema "Connected Community" for the Icubed calls of the European Union in 1996, and is coordinator of the Domus Academy participation to the Icubed projects Campiello, Lime, Presence and Pogo.

His works were shown at exhibitions at Triennale di Milano, Memphis Gallery Milano, Centre Pompidou Paris, Axis Gallery Tokyo, Grand Palais Paris and he has been speaker at "Doors of Perception" in 1994, 1995 and 1996.

In the past he has been partner of Sottsass Associati and consultant at Olivetti Design Studio.

The Children's Machines:
Handheld and Wearable Computers Too

Bakhtiar Mikhak, Fred Martin, Mitchel Resnick, Robbie Berg, & Brian Silverman

MIT Media Laboratory, E15-001, 20 Ames Street, Cambridge MA 02139

(mikhak, fredm, mres, rberg, bss)@media.mit.edu

Abstract. In this paper we describe the material of a construction kit designed to allow children to build their own handheld and wearable devices to meet their interests and passions. Children don't work with these machines, they learn, play and grow with them. Informed by the types of projects that children have done with this material in the context of educational research in science and engineering, we present a few scenarios for why children would build their own handheld or wearable computational devices. We believe that these application scenarios and their appeal to children are strong evidence for why we should rethink the design of computational devices, particularly for children.

1 Introduction: Handheld/Wearable Computers and Children

"Across the world children have entered a passionate and enduring love affair with the computer. What they do with computers is as varied as their activities...The love affair involves more than the desire to do things with computers. It also has an element of possessiveness and, most importantly, of assertion of intellectual identity. Large numbers of children see the computers as "theirs"—as something that belongs to them, to their generation."[1]

These images of the relationship between children and computers are what inspire the present work. In the past few years, small computational toys such as Gameboy™, Tamagochi™, Friend.link™, and Groove Connection™ have taken our children's relationship with computers to a new level. They now play and act out nurturing games, keep in touch and interact with their friends, and more broadly learn about themselves and the world with and through their machines. The diversity in children's interests in and expectations of their handheld computers is what has produced a growing market for a large number of specialized devices.

However, another way to address this demand is to provide children with a set of tools to build and reconfigure their own handheld and wearable devices. We have taken this approach because it also provides a natural context for many new learning opportunities. In the process of building devices that they care about, children get a

---

[1] *The Children's Machine* by Seymour Papert (page ix)

chance to look beyond and into the "black boxes" that surround them, and become proficient designers and critics of the tools they live and think with.

In this paper, we describe a Handheld/Wearable Computer Construction Kit, and propose a number of scenarios for what it would look like and what activities it could support. We will present a mixture of projects in various states of development. Some of the technologies we describe have been used extensively by children in a variety of classroom settings. Others are more forward looking and have only been used in our research lab. We discuss all of these to give a sense of activities for children in the coming years.

In other published work, we have focused more on the educational aspects of this work than we do so here. Earlier versions of this work, known as programmable bricks, was used primarily in robotic design with grade school children (Martin, 1988) and with university students (Martin, 1994). The latest work is part of our Beyond Black Boxes initiative, which encourages children to design scientific instruments for their own investigations (Resnick, et. al., in press; Martin, et. al. in press). Here, we will emphasize a collection of technologies most relevant to the ubiquitous computing community. Over the next year, we plan to have an extensive analysis of children's experiences in the activities we propose here.

2 The Handheld/Wearable Computer Construction Kit

2.1 Programmable Bricks

In earlier work we developed the Programmable Brick, a hand-held computer brick that could control motors, receive information from sensors, and run a program written in a dialect of the Logo programming language. Our first Programmable Brick was used with fifth-grade children who constructed games and play environments for small mobile robots built from it. This work focused on children's relationships with the cybernetic playthings that they had constructed (Martin, 1988).

In later work, we formed a core set of activities for exploring engineering design (Martin, 1996) and mathematics at the elementary school level (Hayward, 1995). This work served as a foundation for the LEGO Group's recent launch of the LEGO Mindstorms product, a robot design kit marketed both at the retail level and for educational use.

Fig. 1. A LEGO "Mini Fig" and the MIT Cricket (right)

Recently, we have designed the Cricket (Fig. 1), a tiny version of the Programmable Brick concept. The Cricket has fewer features than our earlier Bricks—for instance, it can directly power only two motors and receive data from two sensors—but because Crickets are so small, they open up new possibilities. Also, Crickets are designed with built-in infrared communications capability, and our latest versions include a multi-purpose "Bus Port," to which literally dozens of Cricket peripherals may be simultaneously connected (Martin et. al., 1999, in press).

2.2 Cricket Peripherals

As part of the Beyond Black Boxes work, we are developing a collection of sensors and output devices that can be used as building blocks by children in their projects. The Cricket Bus Port has opened up a whole new range of possibilities, starting with the fact that it once and for all ends the argument about how many sensor and actuator ports a programmable brick should have. Previous versions of our bricks had typically four motor ports and variously four, six, or more sensor inputs. With the Bus Port, the Cricket itself can have just two sensor inputs and two motor drivers, and additional devices may be connected to the Bus Port.

Much recent work has been devoted to the conception and development of new Bus Devices. Our present list of such Cricket peripherals includes:

- Heart Rate Monitor—Based on the Polar® exercise sensor, this device automatically tabulates a pulse measurement, returning a beats-per-minute reading that is updated every six seconds.
- 3-Digit Numeric Display—A large-character LED display, capable of displaying numeric values sent from the Cricket.
- Galvanic Skin Response (GSR) Sensor—A device that measures the resistance of skin, and provides a simple measure of excitement or stress.
- IR Proximity Sensor—Based on sensors used in public restrooms to detect (e.g.) your hands underneath the faucet, this device provides an accurate measurement to the nearest object within a range of 15 cm to nearly a meter.

- Voice Recorder—Based on technology used in answering machines and personal audio memo recorders, this device lets children record a number of sound snippets which may be individually played back under program control.
- MIDI Boat—A high quality, compact MIDI synthesizer that will generate music from instructions supplied by the Cricket.
- Motorola® CreataLink™—An interface to a national Motorola 2-way paging system, this technology allows Crickets to transmit and receive short data messages when located outdoors or in other remote locations.

2.3 Software Environments

An important dimension of the Handheld/Wearable Computer Construction Kit is the environment that children use to design the behaviors of their projects. We have two primary software environments: a text-based Logo language implementation, and an iconic version of Logo.

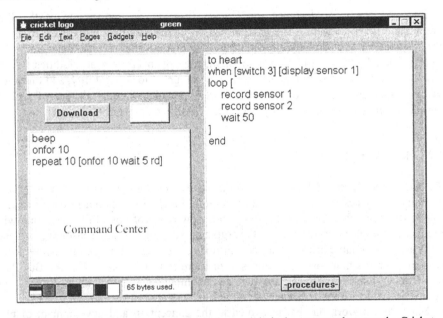

Fig. 2. Cricket Logo software interface. In the lower right is the command center; the Cricket immediately executes instructions typed in this window. On the right half of the screen is the procedures window; when the download button is clicked, all programs in the procedures window are transmitted to the Cricket.

Like traditional Logo software with screen turtles, our Cricket Logo (Fig. 2) includes a *command center*, an interaction window that acts as the main interface to the computational system. In a screen Logo, a child might type "fd 20" to make the turtle move forward 20 turtle-steps; in Cricket Logo, a child would type "onfor 10" to turn on a motor for one second. The facile, immediate feedback of the command center is critical to providing a powerful yet playful environment for learning how things work.

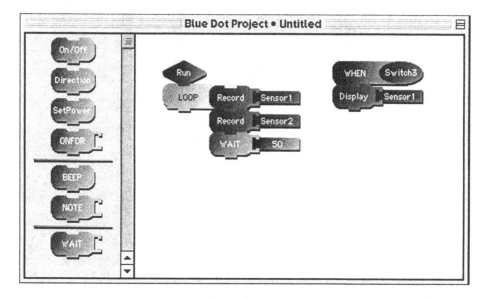

Fig. 3. Logo Blocks software interface. Program blocks are dragged off the palette on the left column and assembled into a program in the main screen window.

Our iconic environment, dubbed "Logo Blocks," is shown in Fig. 3. With Logo Blocks, children have visual color and shape cues that help them construct syntactically correct programs. All of the Logo commands are inside of blocks that may be dragged off of a palette and dropped into their program. We have found that many children who were frustrated or uninterested in traditional Logo programming have become quite engaged in programming using Logo Blocks.

Our plans are to bring these two distinct software systems into one. We are presently working on a version of Logo Blocks that will include "open code" blocks, into which one can type a traditional Logo program. Then after closing up the block, it will appear in the Logo Blocks palettes, ready to use as if it were any other "primitive" block.

3 Application Scenarios

This section presents applications inspired by projects that children have done with Crickets and Cricket peripherals in workshops and classrooms as part of the Beyond Black Boxes project. The top level goal of this project is to rethink science and engineering education fundamentally by developing a comprehensive set of tools, hardware and software, and sample projects that would allow children to build their own scientific instruments for investigation they care about. For further discussion of the learning value of these activities, please see Resnick et. al., 1999 (in press).

Fig. 4. Staying Cool

3.1 Staying Cool

Consider the wearable computer shown in Figure 4. It contains a heart rate sensor, a body temperature sensor, a 3-digit numeric display, and a touch switch. The computer records both sensors' values during the course of the day at a specified frequency. The program for the project, written in Logo Blocks, is shown earlier in Fig. 3. The set-up performs the following actions:

- The main program, on the left side, is triggered when the Cricket's RUN button is pressed.
- With the yellow LOOP block, three subsequent actions are looped indefinitely:
  - Sensor 1, the instantaneous heart-rate reading, is captured and stored in the Cricket's data memory.
  - Sensor 2, the temperature, is captured and stored.
  - A delay of 5 seconds is performed before the loop recycles.

The 3-digit numeric display is controlled by the piece of the program on the right side of the screen. The WHEN block sets up a background monitoring process that executes in parallel to the main data-collection procedure. Whenever Switch 3 (a button carried in the pocket) is pressed, the current value of Sensor 1 (the heart-rate monitor) is presented on the numeric display.

It is instructive to compare this program with that written in Cricket Logo (Fig. 2). We have found that younger children compose such a program on their own more often and more easily in Logo Blocks. However, as they gain more experience and write longer programs they would benefit from a programming environment that takes advantage of the strengths of text and graphics both.

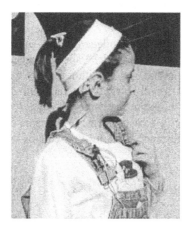

Fig. 5. Digital Mood Ring

3.2 Digital Mood Rings

The Digital Mood Ring consists of a Cricket, a galvanic skin response (GSR) sensor, and a display (Fig. 5). The sensor can be incorporated into one's clothing and the display can be playfully presented such that people can tell how stressed or embarrassed you are. Your stress or embarrassment levels can also be displayed through an auditory cue generated by one of the other Crickets bus devices such as the MiniMidi Boat or the Voice Recorder. Again we see that with a relatively small set of output/input devices, each of which is carefully integrated into a communicating system, children can build desired wearable or handheld devices easily with a little bit of programming.

3.3 Going Places

Equipped with pressure, bend sensor, and shock sensor, children can turn an exercise session into a study of their own body.

In one example, children can design their own pedometers by monitoring the readings from sensors that they embed in their shoes. In addition to recording the sensor values for determining the speed and the total distance traveled during the exercise session, the sensors' values can be used to generate music as they walk or can be studied to learn about the details of one's walking habits. Of course, any of these measured or calculated values can be displayed on the 3-digit display.

In another example, children can use the shoe sensors to measure how much time they are in the air when they jump—the famous "hang time" of pro basketball players. This is easily done with the combination of a touch sensor and near-millisecond precise timing of the Cricket.

3.4 Life in the Fast Lane

In a workshop held at Wellesley College in the summer of 1998, one of the participants designed her own Rollerblade™ speedometer. She used a magnetic Hall effect sensor affixed to her inline skates, with a magnet wedged in the hub of one of the wheels. Each time the wheel rotated past the Hall effect sensor, a signal was generated. She wrote a program to time the intervals between the signals, transforming it into a velocity measurement. In this sort of project, children gain an appreciation for time/rate/distance thinking that cannot be found in textbook-based school activities.

Fig. 6. Musical Friendship Rings

3.5 Musical Friendship Rings

A group of five friends get together and build the following functionality into their Cricket-based handheld devices. They all have MIDI boards attached to their Crickets and program their Crickets to send out a unique number to identify itself to the others. Together, they write or download a piece of music with five instruments in it. Each Cricket is programmed to play one of the instruments only. They can play their piece by pressing a button. When they come together, their Crickets handshake and synchronize and play the piece together. In this way they have developed a friendship "ring."

Other variations on this theme could be to also have a round or a fugue and designate one of the Crickets to be the conductor Cricket. If the conductor is present with all the others present then they will play a round. We are currently designing RF bus devices for the Crickets, which would allow for variations of these games. For example, we can expand and vary the interaction radius. This example is just an indication of the rich learning and play possibilities in which a group of children collaboratively design the behavior of their handheld/wearable computers.

3.6 Reach Out and Touch Something

With the Motorola® CreataLink™ interface, Crickets can send and receive short data messages over a wireless pager network. This means that a Cricket can originate a page or e-mail, or it can receive instructions sent by page or email. This opens up many possibilities for remote monitoring and control of on-going experiments or other activities. For instance, a child could set up apparatus in the woods behind their school for measuring and reporting on daily temperature, light levels, and other environmental data.

3.7 Talking to Things, Big and Small

The last application points to a much richer range of possibilities for the Crickets. With enhanced and multiple communication capabilities, Crickets will be able to talk to other handheld devices, big and small:

- games like Gameboy™ and Tamagochi™,
- communication tools like Friend.link™, Groove Connection™, and cellular phones
- programmable calculators
- personal musical devices like Walkman™, Discman™, or Watchman™
- home appliances and entertainment units
- and all other Cricket-based or tagged devices in the environment

We think of Cricket-like computational objects as an addition to the existing and growing collection of handheld and wearable devices that not only expand the range of possibilities, but also more importantly empower our children to open up the systems that surround them and take intellectual ownership of them. We see again and again that children relate to an open collection of devices that can be integrated into a functional unit of their choice in fundamentally different ways. Such construction kits allows them to move beyond being only consumers and become designers of the tools they use.

4 Evaluation and Future Directions

4.1 Evaluation

Over the last three years, the Cricket technology, Cricket Logo, Logo Blocks, and project ideas have been studied in a variety of settings:

- workshops for children in which they designed

  - robots that, for example, are attracted to walls, avoid edges, seek high temperature areas, or seek light sources
  - kinetic sculptures as artistic installations or interactive displays
  - visual or auditory displays for the data they accumulate with their own scientific instruments
  - activities for the body monitoring sensors
  - games similar to the ones that are popular in the kids' culture

- hands-on workshops for mentors and educators from

  - a number public schools in Massachusetts, Maine, Rhode Island, Colorado, Minnesota, and Montreal Canada
  - the five computer clubhouses[2], four in United States and one in Germany
  - a number of children's and science museums

In these workshops, participants built with the materials, discussed and reflected upon their constructions, and brainstormed about project ideas and application areas for their students.

- classrooms and playgrounds óf number of a schools in Cambridge and Boston

We learn valuable lessons from our interactions with children and educators that inform the next designs of the various elements in our construction kit. For example, by working closely with children, we have found that what often prevents many of the younger children from finishing their projects on their own is the syntactical complexity of Cricket Logo for beginners. The Logo Blocks programming environment was designed to provide a gentler entry point.

4.2 Ongoing Research and Future Directions

Our ongoing work includes both technology development and learning research. We are planning work with younger children, focusing on materials that will allow 5- through 8-year-old children to explore ideas of systems, functions, and mechanism (Resnick, et. al, 1999).

We are also focusing on the following technologies to expand and improve the handheld/wearable construction kit:

---

[2] The first Computer Clubhouse was established in Boston as a part of the Computer Museum a little over five years ago. Clubhouses are after-school centers in which children from under-served communities come together and develop proficiency with a number of computational design and production tools through creating projects that are meaningful to them.

- Communication Capabilities—RF transmitter and receiver bus devices
- More Sensors—to detect identification, position, orientation, and motion characteristics of people and things.
- New Input Devices—A vision system for detecting and tracking objects.
- New Output Devices—LCD displays and small printers similar to that Nintendo introduced for GameBoys™.
- New programming environments—Enabling children to program their devices with handheld WinCE machines and Nintendo GameBoys™.
- New programming paradigms—A graphical programming environment in which children will specify the components that they are using and make live connections between their iconic representations to specify the flow of control. The details of the design and implementation of this programming environment will be presented elsewhere.

5 Conclusion

One may argue that the approach presented in this paper exasperates the complexity that the proliferation of handheld devices has already introduced into our lives. One might wonder if we should not make special machines that integrate the functional units that we have found to be educationally and socially most appropriate for our children. The answer is not obvious and requires much more discussion.

> *"For the moment some of us old fogeys may somehow have acquired the special knowledge that makes one a master of the computer, but children know that it is a matter of time before they inherit the machines. They are the computer generation.*
> *What lies behind the love affair? Where is it going?*
> *Can it be guided by the older generation into forms constructive or destructive? Or is its evolution already out of our hands?"*

In *The Children's Machine*, Papert focuses on one aspect of these questions: How does the relationship between children and computers affect learning. We agree with him in that "understanding this relationship will be crucial to our ability to shape the future." We also add that as we move to an era where computers are being integrated into the daily lives our children, we should revisit these questions and broaden frameworks to take advantage of the inevitable enormous ubiquity of these machines. These are very hard problems indeed.

However, in regards to who should be designing the machines for our children and what should these machines be able to do, it is important to keep in mind that the current design of most handheld devices reflect the needs and abilities of (professional) adults. In designing handheld/wearable devices for children, we are not faced with the same constraints. In fact, a genuine recognition of the children's "love affair," styles of play, and their sense of ownership of computers compels us to give children as much control as possible over the configuration and the functionality of their machines.

Our responsibility is to provide our children with tools to not only probe and critique the existing machines, but also express their expectations and aspirations through their designs. Our sample designs and ideas can guide and influence these designs. Having concrete designs to share and discuss with others provides an excellent opportunity to share and reflect on the current and past design principles. A culture that actively engages in design and discussion of its artifacts is far more likely to not only make better choices about the their uses, but also recognize the true potential of the underlying technology. This is a culture in which we hope to live, play, grow, and learn with our children.

Acknowledgements

The authors would like to express our appreciation to all of the teachers who have participated in this work, including most especially Martha Greenawalt, Mike Petrich, Karen Wilkinson, Rami Alwan, and Phil Firsenbaum. We would like to recognize the contributions of other members of our research group, including Claudia Urrea, Vanessa Stevens Colella, and Genee Lyn Colobong.

Finally we would like to thank all of the children who have participated in this work. We hope that they got as much out of the experience as did we.

References

1. Hayward, M. "Lego My Penguin!" in *The Elementary Mathematician*, vol. 9, no. 4. (1995)
2. Martin, F. *Children, Cybernetics, and Programmable Turtles*, Master of Science dissertation, MIT Department of Mechanical Engineering. (1988)
3. Martin, F. "Kids Learning Engineering Science Using LEGO and the Programmable Brick," unpublished; presented at the American Educational Research Association. (1996)
4. Martin, F., Mikhak, B., Resnick, M., Silverman, B., Berg, R. "To Mindstorms and Beyond: Evolution of a Construction Kit for Magical Machines," in *Robots for Kids* edited by Alison Druin and James Hendler, Morgan Kaufmann Publishers, Inc. (In press, 1999)
5. Martin, F. *Circuits to Control: Learning Engineering by Designing LEGO Robots.* Unpublished PhD dissertation, Massachusetts Institute of Technology. (1994)
6. Papert, S., *The Children's Machine: Rethinking School in the Age of the Computer.* Basic Books. (1993)
7. Resnick, M., Berg, R., Eisenberg. "Beyond Black Boxes: Bringing Transparency and Aesthetics Back to Scientific Investigations," *International Journal of the Learning Sciences.* (In press, 1999)
8. Resnick, M., Berg, R., Eisenberg, M., and Martin, F. *Learning with Digital Manipulatives: A New Generation of Froebel Gifts for Exploring "Advanced" Mathematical and Scientific Concepts.* Proposal to the National Science Foundation. (1999)

Appendix: Supplementary References

In this section we provide references to material available on the web about the Cricket technology, the programming environments, and the workshops mentioned in this paper.

Crickets: http://www.media.mit.edu/~fredm/projects/crickets/
Cricket Logo: http://el.www.media.mit.edu/people/mikhak/sd98/CricketLogo.html
Logo Blocks: http://www.media.mit.edu/~fredm/projects/cricket/logo-blocks/
Beyond Black Boxes: http://el.www.media.mit.edu/projects/bbb/
Sensory Design 98: http://el.www.media.mit.edu/people/mikhak/sd98/

Pocket BargainFinder: A Handheld Device for Augmented Commerce

Adam B. Brody   Edward J. Gottsman

Center for Strategic Technology Research (CSTaR)
Andersen Consulting
3773 Willow Road
Northbrook, IL 60062 USA

{adam.b.brody,edward.j.gottsman}@ac.com

Abstract. The Internet has engendered a new type of commerce, commonly referred to as electronic commerce, or eCommerce. But despite the phenomenal growth of eCommerce, the vast majority of transactions still take place within the realm of traditional, physical commerce. Pocket BargainFinder is a handheld device that seeks to bridge the gap between electronic and traditional commerce. It represents one of the earliest examples of a new breed of commerce we call *augmented commerce*. With Pocket BargainFinder, a consumer can shop in a physical retail store, find an item of interest, scan in its barcode, and search for a lower price among a set of online retailers. The device allows customers to physically inspect products while simultaneously comparison shopping online (where prices are often lower.) As such, Pocket BargainFinder is an example of a disruptive technology that may well transform the nature of both electronic and physical commerce. With consumers able to find the best price regardless of where they shop, the physical retailer is left at a distinct disadvantage.

Keywords. Handheld computers, mobile computing, ubiquitous computing, electronic commerce, agents, augmented reality.

1. Introduction

Within the past decade, technology has contributed to an explosive growth both in the business and consumer sectors of the retail industry. The Internet, and especially the World Wide Web, has connected people across cities and continents. This new communication channel has dramatically changed the way people learn, entertain and shop. It has also give rise to a whole new class of programs, software agents, that help people find information on the web. One type of agent, the shopping agent, is designed to facilitate web commerce (commonly referred to as electronic commerce, or eCommerce). Shopping agents help people find the products or services they want at the best price. Examples of such agents include Excite's Jango [1], C|NET's Shopper.com [2], and Andersen Consulting's original shopping agent, BargainFinder [3]. Although these shopping agents have proven their usefulness, their versatility has been somewhat restricted. Until recently, agents could only be accessed via a desktop computer at home or at work. With the advent of personal digital assistants (PDAs) and wireless Internet connections, however, these agents are now accessible from virtually anywhere.

The rise of shopping agents in the virtual world is mirrored by the rise of discount retailers in the world of physical commerce. According to a survey conducted by LJR Redbook Research [4], discounters account for 63.6% of US retail sales in 1998, versus 43.4% in 1986. Consumers are willing to drive farther and shop harder to find those bargain-basement prices. According to a WSL Strategic Retail survey [5], consumers want some kind of tangible contact with goods as they shop, demanding to "touch it, drive it, listen to it, or wear it before they buy it." Thus, in a perfect world, a consumer would visit the store to touch, feel, and inspect the product, and then turn to cyberspace to find the best price. Pocket BargainFinder lets the consumer do just that: browse in the physical world, then buy in the virtual world.

Pocket BargainFinder combines the global scope of Internet shopping agents, the ease-of-input of a barcode scanner, and the portability of a PDA. The result is a convergence of electronic and physical commerce that we call *augmented commerce*. (The term derives from research into *augmented reality* [6], which explores the convergence of the electronic and physical worlds in general.)

Traditionally, shoppers have been forced to choose between the low-cost but intangible purchasing experience on the web and the tangible but often higher-cost experience of physical shopping: with Pocket BargainFinder, consumers can have the best of both worlds.

As its name suggests, Pocket BargainFinder is a small, pocket-sized device that finds the lowest price of an item in cyberspace. The current version is set up to find bargains for a book or similar item that can be identified by an International Standard Book Number (ISBN) number. Pocket BargainFinder scans the barcode on a book, translates that number into the appropriate ISBN number, establishes a wireless web connection, initiates a search at several electronic book retailers, displays the query results, and enables the consumer to place an online order for the book.

Pocket BargainFinder thus represents a potentially *disruptive technology* [7], providing perfect information in a hostile environment. In other words, physical retailers would not want customers logging on to compare prices—and make purchases—while standing in the aisles of their stores.

The following section presents a more detailed scenario of Pocket BargainFinder in action. We then go on to describe the hardware and software components used to create the device. We discuss Pocket BargainFinder's relationship to previous work in the areas of shopping agents and augmented reality. We then conclude with a discussion of some of the ramifications of this disruptive technology.

2. Application Scenario

The following scenario illustrates the power of the Pocket BargainFinder device. A shopper, armed with the Pocket BargainFinder (Figure 1) system, spends a leisurely afternoon at the local bookstore.

Figure 1. Pocket BargainFinder

After flipping through a few magazines (and enjoying an espresso at the coffee bar) our customer visits the Computer Programming aisle. After browsing for a few minutes, she runs across a book a colleague has recommended she read. Noting the price marked on the book, she takes out her Pocket BargainFinder unit and scans its barcode. Within seconds, she discovers that the exact same book can be purchased at an online retailer for less than the bookstore's price. (Figure 2) Taking note of the delivery time and shipping method, our user decides that the cost savings is significant and opts to order the book directly from the online retailer, which she does at that moment using her Pocket BargainFinder. As she leaves the store, she congratulates herself on a savvy bit of shopping. The bookstore has unwittingly lost a sale.

Figure 2. Pocket BargainFinder

Mastering Visual Basic 5
By Petroutsos, Evangelos
ISBN Number: 0782119840
Retail Price: $49.99 + Tax
Pocket BargainFinder found the
Following information.

Price	Merchant	Delivery
$36.40	USED – Powel	10-15 Days
$37.43	Kingbooks.co	14 Days
$37.44	alphaCraze.co	3-7 Days
$38.90	Fatbrain.com	3-7 Days
$38.93	Kingbooks.co	3-7 Days

This situation can take place in any bookstore, from a large super-chain to a small, family-owned operation. And Pocket BargainFinder is just as useful in contexts where books are not for sale (for example, in a library or a friend's house).

Currently, Pocket BargainFinder only works with books (and other items that have uniquely identifiable ISBN numbers). One can imagine a time when shoppers can purchase videos, audio CDs, and other common consumer products using a device similar to Pocket BargainFinder. Virtually no store would be immune from the effects of such a device.

3. System Design

The design of the Pocket BargainFinder system had to satisfy three important requirements. First, the device had to be portable and easily stored in a purse, briefcase, or pocket. Second, it had to be compact and comfortable to hold. Third, in order to be usable in the conditions of a retail store, the unit had to have a simple input scheme and an easily readable output.

3.1 Hardware

The Pocket BargainFinder unit requires three basic hardware components: a barcode scanner for easy input; a wireless communications device for accessing the Internet; and a small computing device for converting barcodes into a format that can be transmitted to web retailers. The original prototype (built in November 1998) used an AT&T PocketNet phone, a Hamp barcode wand, and a custom-designed CPU unit. (The latest version is more compact, making use of a Symbol Palm Pilot and a Minstrel Wireless IP modem—more on this below) A remote web server is also needed to support the Pocket BargainFinder in the field. The remainder of this section will describe the hardware components used in the latest implementation.

3.1.1 Barcode Scanner and Computing Device

Ease of data entry was considered crucial for usability in the conditions of a retail store. Manually typing in ISBN numbers is possible, but this is a tedious and error-prone process. Since each ISBN is uniquely represented by a barcode, and since barcodes are printed on nearly all book covers, we decided to use a barcode scanner as a simple means of entering the data.

The computing device serves as the link between the barcode scanner and the communications device. It also runs the software, including the operating environment and applications. For the computing device we decided on the SPT 1500, a PDA jointly developed by Symbol Technologies, Inc. and Palm Computing, Inc. The device is a combination of the standard Palm III handheld computer and the SE 900 scan engine. At 0.66" H, 3.16" W and 5.46" L, the SPT 1500 is light and compact.

3.1.2 Wireless Communications Device

Due to differing wireless service standards in the United States and Europe, two different communication devices were used. In the U.S., we chose the Minstrel, a 19.2 KBPS, CDPD wireless IP modem. The Minstrel fits snugly onto the SPT 1500, only adding a few inches to the overall dimensions of the device. In Europe, where the standard is GSM, we used an Options International Snap-On modem in conjunction with a GSM compatible cell phone. The transfer rate is 9.6 KBPS with data compression.

3.1.3 Web Server

The web server hosts all of the pages and scripts used in the application. In order for the process to run as smoothly and quickly as possible, the server was connected to the Internet with a T1 line connection. For this project, we used a Compaq Proliant 800 server.

3.2 Software

Pocket BargainFinder requires a number of software components: a micro-browser that can process HDML messages; a script that that can act as an intermediary between the HDML messages and the HTML-based shopping agents; and web server software that can host these other components. Each of these is covered in more detail below.

3.2.1 Micro-browser

We used a simple web browser (Created by AvantGo, Inc.) to load the pages from the appropriate server. The browser accepts simple HTML 3.2 web pages that include forms, button, and graphics. The AvantGo browser was the only one for the SPT 1500 that supports the use of the barcode scanner.

3.2.2 CGI Script

Most of the processing done by Pocket BargainFinder application is performed by a Common Gateway Interface (CGI) script stored on the web server. The script's first task is to read the data that is sent from the browser. The script then translates the data into the appropriate ISBN number. Next, it submits queries to roughly forty online book retailers, collecting such information as price, shipping time, and shipping cost from sites that respond within the 20 second time-out time period. After the query results are retrieved, they are sorted by price and formatted into a new HTML page. An alert message notifies the user that the information is ready. The user can then view the query results on the handheld device.

3.2.2 Web Server

We chose Netscape's Enterprise Web Server software to run the appropriate scripts and serve as the main connection to the Internet.

4. Related Work

We have seen how Pocket BargainFinder is an enabling and potentially disruptive application in the nascent field of augmented commerce. We now discuss its relationship to other research in this and related areas.

The idea of a comparison shopping agent was pioneered in 1995 by Andersen Consulting's BargainFinder [3], which was designed to find the best price for a given audio CD across all the music retailers on the web at that time. Since then, a number of other comparison-shopping agents have appeared, such as Jango [1] and Priceline [8]. However, these agents remain "disembodied," with no physical connection to the user's world. Pocket BargainFinder extends the capabilities of shopping agents by providing access at the point where the customer comes into physical contact with products.

A number of researchers are exploring the area of augmented reality, in which elements of the electronic world are used to augment the physical world. For example, the Touring Machine [9], developed at Columbia University, uses GPS to track a user's position, then displays information relevant to that location on the user's head-worn display. A Touring Machine user can look at objects in any direction, and the system will superimpose annotations for those objects on the scene as it appears in the display.

The Metronaut [10], a wearable computer developed by researchers at Carnegie Mellon University, serves as a schedule negotiating and guidance system. The device includes a barcode scanner, two-way pager, and computer processor. As the user moves around the campus, she scans barcodes at key locations. This information is sent to the hub of the system. The server then communicates with the user via pager, giving directions to the next scheduled meeting or alerting the user when she falls behind schedule.

Shopper's Eye [11] is a pioneering application of augmented commerce developed at Andersen Consulting. The system prompts the shopper to create a profile that includes items he wishes to purchase and other preferences. It then makes the profile available to merchants in a physically proximate area (e.g., a mall) via a PDA with a wireless modem. The merchants in turn use the shopping profiles to create specially packaged offers, which they transmit to the shopper as he passes near the store. The shopper can use this information to decide which stores to visit.

Pocket BargainFinder is most like Shopper's Eye in that both seek to provide information to a mobile shopper. The primary differences lie in how much information the shopper provides to the merchants and which merchants have access to the shopper. With Shopper's Eye, the shopper provides profile information, and the set of merchants is the physical retailers in proximity to the shopper; with Pocket Bargain-

Finder, the shopper provides a minimum of information (the ISBN number), and the set of merchants is electronic retailers in cyberspace.

Physical retailers are unlikely to welcome the scenario envisioned by Shopper's Eye, since the system provides a comparison shopping service that includes their physically proximate competitors. They will likely find Pocket BargainFinder even more disturbing, since it places physical retailers in direct competition with their web-based counterparts, who have very different operating constraints.

5. Conclusion and Future Work

The Pocket BargainFinder application has brought together some of the latest technology advances to produce a device that may turn the retail book industry on its head. Beginning with a simple prototype, the project is now a fully developed working device that could be used anywhere in the United States or Europe. There are, however, a few enhancements that could be made to make Pocket BargainFinder even better.

In an application such as this, speed is a defining characteristic. At present, it takes roughly 60 seconds to connect to the service once the modem is turned on. An instant connection, or at least one in the 10-15 second range, would make the device more attractive. Until this matter is resolved, the system's acceptance may be limited.

Second, adding other product categories would greatly expand Pocket Bargain-Finder's effectiveness. Support for consumer products such as videos and audio CDs would accelerate the acceptance of the product into mainstream culture.

Even with its limitations, Pocket BargainFinder has generated a tremendous amount of coverage in the media. Stories on the device have appeared in magazines, newspapers, television shows (ZD-TV) and network news reports (ABC World News Tonight with Peter Jennings). As a result, we have received numerous inquires about the availability of Pocket BargainFinder. At the current time, there are no plans to bring the device to market. However, it is inevitable that devices such as this will become commonplace.

Online book sales are expected to account for 10 percent of total book sales by 2002 [12]. The creation of an entirely new sales channel through devices such as Pocket BargainFinder may increase that number substantially. And expanding the application to work on multiple products in the retail industry could have a dramatic effect on eCommerce as a whole.

6. Acknowledgment

Thank you to Joseph F. McCarthy of Andersen Consulting for input and editorial review of this paper.

7. References

1. Excite Inc. Redwood City, CA. http://www.jango.com
2. CNET Inc. San Francisco, CA. http://www.shopper.com
3. Krulwich, B. The BargainFinder agent: Comparison price shopping on the internet. In Williams, J., ed., *Bots and Other Internet Beasties*. SAMS.NET, 1996.
4. Forest, Stephanie Anderson, Naughton, Keith, and Zellner, Wendy. I'll Take That and That and That.... In *Business Week*. (06/22/98) Page 38.
5. WSL Strategic Retail. How America Shops. New York, N.Y.
6. Suherland, Ian. A head-mounted three dimensional display. In *Proc. FJCC 1968*, pages 757-764, Washington, DC, 1968. Thompson Books.
7. Christensen, Clayton M. The Innovator's Dilemma : When New Technologies Cause Great Firms to Fail. Harvard Business School Press. June 1997.
8. Priceline.com Inc. Stamford, CT. http://www.priceline.com
9. Feiner, Steven, MacIntyrem Blair, Hollerer, Tobias, and Webster, Anthony: A Touring Machine: Prototyping 3D Mobile Augmented Reality Systems For Exploring the Urban Environment. In *Proceedings of the First International Symposium on Wearable Computers (ISWC '97)* IEEE Computer Society. 1997.
10. Smailagic, Asim and Martin, Richard. Metronaut: A Wearable Computer with Sensing and Global Communication Capabilities. In *Proceedings of the First International Symposium on Wearable Computers (ISWC '97)* IEEE Computer Society. 1997.
11. Fano, Andrew E. Shopper's Eye: Using Location-based Filtering for a Shopping Agent in the Physical World. In *Proceedings of the Second International Conference on Autonomous Agents (Agents '98)* ACM Press. Pages 416 – 421.
12. Italie, Hillel. Independents Fight Back. The Associated Press and ABCNews.com. April 29, 1999.

Scalable and Flexible Location-Based Services for Ubiquitous Information Access

Rui José[1] and Nigel Davies[2]

[1] Information Systems Department, University of Minho,
Azurém, 4800 Guimarães, Portugal
rui@dsi.uminho.pt
[2] Distributed Multimedia Research Group, Department of Computing,
Lancaster University, Bailrigg, Lancaster, LA1 4YR, UK
nigel@comp.lancs.ac.uk

Abstract. In mobile distributed environments applications often need to dynamically obtain information that is relevant to their current location. The current design of the Internet does not provide any conceptual models for addressing this issue. As a result, developing a system that requires this functionality becomes a challenging and costly task, leading to individual solutions that only address the requirements of specific application scenarios. In this paper we propose a more generic approach, based on a scalable and flexible concept of location-based services, and an architectural framework to support its application in the Internet environment. We describe a case study in which this architectural framework is used for developing a location-sensitive tourist guide. The realisation of this case study demonstrates the applicability of the framework, as well as the overall concept of location-based services, and highlights some of the issues involved.

1 Introduction

As computation and networking move from the desktop to ubiquitous features of our daily lives, location becomes an increasingly important component of many software systems. In particular, there has been considerable interest in supporting methods of information access in which applications dynamically select the information that is relevant to their current location. Typical examples of localised information are maps, traffic, tourist attractions or shopping places.

The current design of the Internet does not provide any conceptual models for supporting associations between information and location. Existing approaches are based on ad hoc solutions that are only valid for the narrow application domain for which they have been developed or for the specific underlying technology on which they are based [1–3]. The lack of abstractions on which to base the design of such systems makes their development a challenging and costly task, as developers must deal directly with every low-level detail of the system.

In this paper, we propose a scalable and flexible concept of location-based services as a generic approach for developing systems that need to associate information with location. In the context of our work, a location-based service is an, otherwise normal, Internet service with a scope that defines its usage in terms of a geographical area. For example, a service providing information on local parking availability may have a scope corresponding to an area of a town, while a service providing directions within a building would have a scope corresponding to that building. Our concept of location-based services is scalable because scopes may range from small locations to wide-area coverage without any significant effect on the systems performance. Furthermore, it is flexible because it is independent of any constraints imposed by specific location or networking technologies and is aimed at the heterogeneous environment of the Internet.

The location-based usage, which characterises the nature of these services, typically results from either some interaction with the physical environment, e.g. controlling the temperature of a room, or from the provision of information associated with a location context, e.g. a local map. In this paper, we focus on this second type of information-centric services and in supporting the association of information with location. Work on the former includes [3–5], and mainly addresses the issues associated with ubiquitous device interaction.

Location-based services represent a simple and yet powerful concept. They are simple because, as Internet services, they can fit in the normal framework of their usage, creation and in many aspects location. They are powerful because they provide a paradigm on which the development of a vast range of location-dependent systems may be based. They allow location dependency to be introduced into an application by adding appropriate service location mechanisms and by defining its behaviour as a function of the services available in its environment. The indirection introduced by the use of service location shields application developers from the complexity of the heterogeneous Internet environment.

This paper describes our model of location-based services, how we propose to support this model, and how it can be used as a generic approach for engineering systems that require localised information. In Section 2, we analyse existing systems, relating them to our work and discussing the reasons why, in our opinion, they are not generic approaches for supporting localised information. In Section 3, we describe the concepts, components and procedures of our architectural framework for location-based services. This is followed, in Section 4, by the description of a case study in which the framework is used for creating a location-sensitive tourist guide. The case study demonstrates the application of the framework and analyses some of the issues involved. Finally, in Section 5, we discuss our future work and present some concluding remarks.

2   Analysis of Existing Approaches

In recent years, a number of systems have addressed the issue of associating information with location contexts. What mainly distinguishes our approach is the focus on a generic concept, i.e. location-based services, supported by an architecture that is not bound to any specific application scenario or underlying technology.

In its overall objectives, our work has much in common with that of Schilit [6] and Brown [7] in the area of context-sensitive applications, namely we also aim to support systems that react to changes in their environment, and in particular location. Our approach is substantially different in that we build context-awareness from the range of services available in a given location context, whereas both Schilit's and Brown's approaches are based on the use of several types of environmental variables.

The Service Location Protocol (SLP) [8] is the standard proposed by the Internet Engineering Task Force (IETF) for service location within a single administrative domain. As an emerging standard protocol for service location, SLP is an important reference for our work, and we use some of its components. But there are several reasons why we do not consider SLP an adequate technology for the problem of location-based services. Firstly, SLP is not meant to scale to the wide area. It has been created as a dynamic configuration mechanism for applications in local area networks and under a single administrative domain. Secondly, the scope model used by SLP, as well as the corresponding protocol support, are very limited when used for modelling location scopes. In SLP, scopes are only a simple form of administrative service aggregation within a larger implicit scope, which is the administrative domain. They lack hierarchy or any other kind of relationship that could be used for modelling them as locations and they are only valid within the boundaries of their SLP domain.

Wide area service location [9] has been proposed to overcome the limitations of SLP in terms of wide area usage, thus enabling client software to find services in logically remote locations in the Internet. It differs from our work in that the objective is to select a server anywhere on the Internet regardless of location, whereas we use location as the basis for service selection.

Work on addressing and routing based on the Global Positioning System (GPS) [10], which aims to integrate the concept of physical location into the design of the Internet, can also be used to support geographical services. The possibility of geographically routing messages could be used by a server to advertise its services within a certain distance range. Clients could also use this mechanism for finding servers within a certain distance from their current location. This approach differs from our work in its assumption that every node can independently determine its own geographic position and also in its concept of proximity, which is based on the absolute physical proximity between the location of clients and servers.

The work by Imielinski on Wireless Information Systems [2] also explores the idea of location-dependent information services for the mobile wireless environment. This environment is seen as a collection of wireless cells, managed by Mobile Support Stations (MSS). Information pages are accessed from a set of mobile hosts that interact with MSSs to obtain the information they need. The different pages available on each MSS provide the basis for the introduction of location dependency. Our work may be seen as a generalisation of this approach. Our concept of location-based services may recreate the functionality of this system, while avoiding many of its assumptions such as the existence of a homogeneous wireless system.

The architecture proposed by Hodes in [3], while probably the work that is closest to our notion of location-based services, also presents some differences, both in goals and approach. Its Universal Interaction System is mainly oriented towards device interaction, focusing on the associated aspects of interface adaptation. This is in contrast with our information-centric approach and affects a number of system design decisions, most notably scale. Also, the scope model used in Hodes's system is closely tied to the network beacons and does not support any form of hierarchy. We propose a scope model that can model physical space and scale to the Internet level.

2.1 Analysis

Overall, existing systems present several types of limitations that restrict their applicability as generic approaches for supporting localised information in the Internet. Essentially, they provide pragmatic approaches to address specific requirements, rather than high level abstractions applicable to a broad range of scenarios. This lack of abstractions leads to systems which are excessively dependent on the specific characteristics of their underlying networking environments, and introduces assumptions that are unique to the specific problem domains being addressed. As a consequence, those approaches are only valid for the narrow and specific application scenarios for which they have been created.

We also consider that current systems do not address the issue of proximity in an adequate way, i.e. as a very abstract concept with significant variations in different contexts and for different activities. A common limitation is only supporting the notion of proximity that results directly from the connectivity range of the specific network technology on which the system is based. We consider it a key requirement that the system is able to support additional layers of proximity on top of the basic notion provided by the underlying technologies.

Another issue concerning proximity is the use of a proximity concept based on the absolute physical distance between servers and clients. This absolute distance does not provide a convenient model for many of our overlapping notions of physical context. For example, if searching for a petrol station while on a motorway a user is interested in the stations located in the service areas of the motorway and not necessarily in the stations in the physical neighbourhood of its current position. This is particularly important for larger scales of space, as the correlation between context and proximity tends to decrease as we enlarge our notion of proximity, i.e. more things that we do not care about will be in our proximity. Using the absolute position of servers has the added disadvantage of forcing servers to be located within the area for which they are providing location-based services. We believe this would be a limiting factor for many application scenarios.

3   Architectural Framework

3.1   Design Goals

Our system is designed to meet two fundamental goals. The first is to provide support for multiple views of space and notions of proximity over the same infrastructure. This is crucial for supporting multiple applications, as they may have very different requirements in how they relate to space and in the proximity range they use. This requirement is addressed by a flexible hierarchy of symbolic locations, which we use as the basis for scope definition.

The second goal is to support mechanisms for locating services that are effectively based on physical location. Such mechanisms should allow two collocated devices, attached to different networks, and under different administrative domains to have access to the same service information. To achieve this goal, we developed a service location architecture based on explicit location scopes and transparent to any network or administrative boundaries.

3.2   Location Scopes

A key component of this architectural framework is a model for representing service scopes in terms of physical space. A basic requirement for such a model is supporting explicit location scopes, i.e. scopes that are not based on any implicit forms of scoping, such as administrative boundaries or network topology. This is essential in guaranteeing that a scope can be shared by multiple applications in the same location, even if they are in different networks or domains.

The essence of our approach is to assume the existence of a shared set of symbolic locations that are used as contexts for service location. The way these locations are supported by the system will be described in the next sections. Servers, when registering their location-based services, use one or more of these location contexts to indicate the scope of their services. Clients, when searching for services, use one of these location contexts to indicate the area on which they wish to find services.

Location contexts are organised in a similar way to the location domain model described in [11]. They are partially ordered by the "contains" relationship, reflecting the spatial inclusion of the associated geographical areas, and they may overlap, forming a lattice instead of a tree, as exemplified in Fig. 1.

Our model for location scopes also includes the possibility of classifying location contexts according to the their type, e.g. building, room, or town, allowing applications to know the nature of the places in which they are located.

The names for location scopes are based on a composite schema, named "lbs:", that follows the generic syntax defined for Uniform Resource Identifiers (URI) [12]. The first component of the name, after the schema identifier "lbs:", indicates a Location-Based Services (LBS) server (described in Sect. 3.4), and the second a location context managed by that server, as in the following example: "lbs:lbs.lancs.ac.uk/engineering".

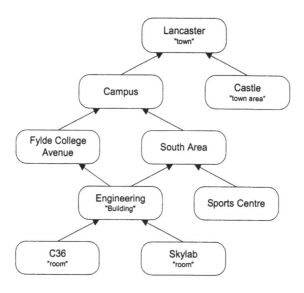

Fig. 1. An example of a location domain model

This naming approach for location contexts is based on two key decisions. The first has been to embed the name of the LBS server that manages the context. This speeds up the service location process by eliminating the extra level of indirection that would otherwise be required to obtain, given a location context name, the respective LBS server. The other key decision has been not to associate names with the hierarchy of location contexts, i.e. a location context is not necessarily a naming context for its contained locations. We expect the location hierarchy to be flexible and to support multiple views of the location space. Forcing the association between the organisation of locations and the organisation of naming would lead to a rigid and formal location hierarchy that would become a limiting factor for the dynamic of the context space. On the other hand, in some cases, simplicity may be more important than flexibility, as in the case of well structured places, such as a building. Whenever that is considered the best approach hierarchical names may also be used, e.g. "lbs:lbs.lancs.ac.uk/engineering/C36".

3.3 Mapping Between Networks and Location Contexts

Location contexts are not bound to any specific network, but each participating network must be mapped onto a location context. Such mapping allows a device, without any *a priori* information, to determine its corresponding location context as a function of its point of attachment to the network. A mapping of a network portion to a location context means that the area of physical coverage of that network is contained within the area corresponding to the location context. Multiple networks may be mapped to the same location context representing the physical overlapping of the respective coverage areas.

Even though we assume that this mapping will be available in any participating network, we do not define any specific mechanisms for supporting it. The most appropriate technique must be chosen for each specific case, considering factors such as the specific network environment or the desired granularity. Beaconing techniques provide an adequate solution for simple network infrastructures, especially cellular networks, but may be limited for more complex network infrastructures, in which it is difficult to set up a beacon per link and to define the boundaries of multicast traffic. More elaborate and flexible methods, possibly based on a combination of new techniques, such as Administratively Scoped IP Multicast [13] or GPS based routing [10], are essential before this mapping can be widely supported in multiple network environments.

Alternative forms of determining location, such as GPS, may also be used either as a substitute for the lack of information from the network or as a way of improving its granularity. However, the need to map the location information obtained from those sources into valid location contexts implies that the system must have some information about the location contexts available for its area of operation.

3.4   LBS Servers

The architecture of our system is based on LBS servers. The primary function of an LBS server is to maintain a dynamic repository of service registrations and satisfy requests upon that information. Service registrations and requests are done on a per location basis and each server is responsible for maintaining the registrations corresponding to a number of locations. Each service registration is identified by a "service:" Uniform Resource Locator (URL)[14], and may include attributes for describing the characteristics of the service and aiding service selection. Registrations are only maintained for a certain period of time, unless they are refreshed. This soft-state approach is similar to the one used in SLP, but more flexible refresh intervals are used.

The other function of LBS servers is to support the hierarchy of location contexts. This involves maintaining information about the location contexts and their relationships. Information about each location context typically includes service location policies and attributes describing the location context, e.g. its type and geographical coverage. Each location also maintains a set of links to other locations in which it is contained. The next section analyses the effect of these associations in terms of service location.

The existence of relationships between location contexts maintained by different servers provides the basis for the creation of LBS federations, such as the one represented in Fig. 2. A federation allows servers to share their respective service offer spaces, and thus form a larger location space, but the loose integration between location contexts allows servers to keep their autonomy and set their own policies. This cooperative and distributed process of creating relationships between location contexts is the basis for supporting larger location models.

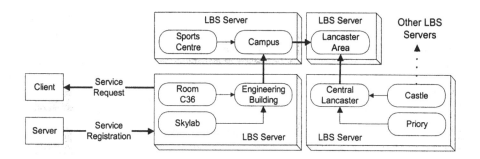

Fig. 2. A federation of LBS servers

3.5 Service Location

The overall process of service location can be described as follows. From its point of attachment to the network, and possibly with the collaboration of other locating technologies, a device determines its current location context. Since the name of the location context includes a reference to the respective LBS server, applications on the device (clients or servers) may start to interact with the appropriate server. This interaction is based on the exchange of protocol messages that are basically a subset and an adaptation of the messages used by SLP. Servers issue service registration messages, indicating the characteristics of their service and the location context at which it should be registered. Clients issue service request messages indicating the location context, the type of service required, and the attribute based criteria that the service must satisfy.

The Semantics of Containment. Location contexts are more than mere service aggregations, as the existence of relationships between locations has strong implications in the overall process of locating services. When a location context is contained within another, then the services registered in the containing location are also available in the contained location, subject only to systems policies. For example, a service registered in a "building" location should also be available to devices on the enclosed contexts, e.g. "room" locations. In contrast, a client searching for services in a "building" location should not receive information about services that are registered with "room" scopes. Supporting this cascaded service location means that an LBS server may have to forward a request to other LBS servers that maintain hierarchically superior location contexts before it can answer a service request.

Proximity. Another important aspect of service location is how multiple notions of proximity are supported by the system. Since there is no notion of service position, other than registration in a given location context, the basic level of proximity that a device may use to find services is the smallest location context in which it may assume to be.

Enlarging this proximity range, i.e. searching for services in a wider area, is achieved by changing the scope indicated in the service request to a higher location context. As a result, only the services that have been registered for that wider scope will be returned. The advantage of this approach is supporting a scalable notion of proximity, in which the range of proximate selection may be expanded without an exponential increase in the number of returned services. From an architectural point of view, this is substantially different from discovering the services that are located within a certain range, but it is consistent with our concept of service location in which the objective is to select services whose scope includes our current location context.

3.6 Implementation

We are in the process of implementing the various elements of this architecture. We have implemented an LBS server supporting multiple location contexts, contained relationships, and service requests. On the client side, we have a general functional model for the interaction of applications with the framework. The core of this interaction is an adapted version of the JAVA Application Program Interface (API) for SLP described in [15]. This API, modified to reflect the specificity of location-based services, provides an object oriented interface to the functionality of the framework and is designed to allow implementations to offer just the feature set they need. The use of this API greatly simplifies the development of applications and also allows common functionality, e.g. determining the current location context, to be shared by several applications. Also associated with this API, there is a file format for serialised service registrations, allowing legacy services to be registered and registration databases to be exchanged. All these implementation components have been used for building the case study described in the next section.

4 Case Study: A Location-Sensitive Tourist Guide

This section describes the application of our architectural framework to the development of a location-sensitive tourist guide. This case study is based on the requirements and infrastructure of the Guide system [1], currently under development at Lancaster University.

The Guide is a context-sensitive tourist guide for visitors to the city of Lancaster. As visitors, equipped with portable Guide units, move around the city, the system displays the information that is relevant for their current location. Examples of location-dependent information provided by the Guide are the local attractions, a map of the area, and a list of events. The system is based on a set of wireless cells, placed in key locations in town, that send beacons containing a reference to the information associated with that area.

4.1   Technical Description

The realisation of this case study involved four basic activities: the definition of
the location model; the realisation of the supporting architecture; the creation
of the location-based services; and the development of a location-dependent application that uses them to access information.

Location Model. The location model for the Guide case study is diagrammat-
ically represented in Fig. 3.

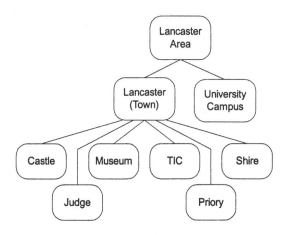

Fig. 3. The location model for the GUIDE case study

The model was designed to provide the maximum location granularity over
the wireless cells of the Guide networking infrastructure and to take advantage
of the respective beaconing system. This was achieved by a one to one mapping
between each cell and a location context, originating the set of location contexts represented in grey in Fig. 3. In order to better explore the possibilities of
location-based services, a simple hierarchy was created with the introduction of
some additional location contexts in which the basic locations were included.

System Architecture. The architecture used for this case study is represented
in Fig. 4, and is based on a single LBS server that manages all the location
contexts of the model. All available services are registered here at the appropriate
location contexts.

Since the association between services and locations is only dependent on the
location context indicated in the service registration, and not on the position of
servers, we used a single information server to support all the services created for
this case study. Services were modelled as Extensible Markup Language (XML)
documents available through the Hypertext Transfer Protocol (HTTP). Appropriate Document Type Definitions (DTD) were created for each type of service,

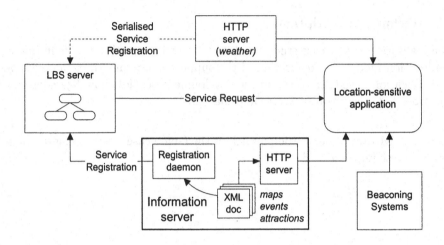

Fig. 4. The architecture of the location-sensitive tourist guide

but they all included data fields indicating the location context on which the service should be registered and its registration attributes. A registration daemon reads the XML documents and uses that information to register the respective services in the appropriate location contexts. The weather service was obtained from an existing server on the Internet, and its registration was based on a serialised service registration.

Location-Based Services. We have created a number of location-based services for satisfying the information needs of the tourist guide. More specifically, we have created services with information about local attractions, events in the area, maps, and weather forecast. The SLP service type definition [14] was used to distinguish between the several types of services, with an abstract service type being defined for each of the information services, i.e. map, weather, attractions and events. For example, the map service was identified as being of type *map:http*, being *map* the abstract type, which defines the nature of the information, and *http* the concrete type, which defines the network protocol by which it can be obtained.

Depending on the nature of services, different strategies were used in the distribution of services among location contexts. A service of type map was created for each location context. The map service registered at the Lancaster location provides a general town map, while the services in smaller locations provide more detailed maps of those areas. Several event services were also created for the various location contexts. The services in smaller locations offer more specific information about events that take place in the respective area, while the service for the town only lists the most important events, i.e. those whose scope surpasses the town area in which they occur. A similar approach was used with the attraction service, with the town wide service providing information about the major attractions in town. The weather service, given its granularity, was only available at the Lancaster area scope.

The use of a location hierarchy supports some interesting options in the association of information with location. For example, town-wide information may easily be associated with the town location context, thus avoiding the need to replicate it on each cell as it was the case with the original Guide model. Another interesting feature is the possibility of selecting the most appropriate proximity level for obtaining information. For example, tourists without much time to visit the town may only be interested in the main town attractions. They may prefer to use the town-wide attractions service instead of a service specific to a smaller area, even if it is their own current location. In these cases, the ability to specify the proximity range becomes a form of indicating the desired information detail, which may be an important feature for supporting such different contexts of information access as walking or driving.

The Application. The visible component of the system is the location-sensitive application, running on a portable unit, that visitors can use to access the relevant information to their current location. It determines its location context from the GUIDE beacons it receives and from a simple mapping function that translates that information into valid location contexts. This information is then used to find the services it needs, obtain the required information from those servers and, if requested, display the information to the user. We have used basically the same interface of the Guide system, but the functionality associated with some buttons was slightly changed to better reflect the new underlying architecture and its possibilities. The interaction with the LBS server is done through the API created for this purpose, thus keeping to a minimum the effort of implementing the application.

4.2 Analysis

The realisation of this case study has allowed us to evaluate several aspects about the applicability of our framework and the LBS concept in general. Despite being a fairly simple example, it has been extremely useful in highlighting a number of open issues and potential difficulties. One of those issues is how to define and support the information space of an application, i.c. the information it requires for its normal operation, based only on service location. If all that the application needs is any server of a given type, then the problem is trivial. However, in more elaborate cases, such as a tourist guide, creating the information space of an application may imply interacting with a large number of servers and may involve many more aspects, such as the characteristics of the services, user preferences in service selection or service content.

In general, our approach appears to provide a useful framework for the development of location-dependent systems. Furthermore, the abstractions introduced by the use of location-based services have provided the basis for transforming an essentially self-contained system into an open system with a much larger potential for evolution. New sources of information, even if not explicitly created for this purpose, may be added by simply registering new services. New types of information may be supported with the creation of new service types. Other networks, wireless or not, may be used for accessing the same services, depending only on the existence of a mapping to location contexts. The same information infrastructure may easily be used as the basis for new unpredicted applications. All these extensions are possible, and simple, because the abstractions on which the system design is based avoid hidden dependencies between its different components and provide a clear separation of concerns between its main functions such as information provision, location modelling, service location and application development.

5 Future Work and Conclusions

5.1 Future Work

Our work on location-based services is an ongoing project. We plan to extend our framework in order to address some of the existing issues, and we plan to develop further case studies. We are currently preparing a new, more ambitious, case study in the context of the AROUND project. This project, which has recently started at University of Minho, aims at providing transport related information, and will have a stronger focus on exploring the possibilities introduced by the use of location-based services. The prototype will have a larger number of services and service types, and will be based on multiple networks, including the Global System for Mobile communication (GSM). With the realisation of multiple case studies, with different characteristics in terms of applications and technological environments, we hope to evaluate the effect that several factors may have on the applicability of the LBS concept. The realisation of multiple case studies is also essential in demonstrating that the proposed framework can serve as a unified approach to several different scenarios, as this is one of its main advantages in comparison with existing approaches.

Security. We are aware that security is a crucial component of our framework. A comprehensive solution will require a careful analysis of the specific security requirements of location-based services and a clearer definition of the system administrative model. Our emphasis, so far, has been on the definition of such model, rather than on the introduction of ad hoc security mechanisms.

Hybrid Models. There are many cases in which plain service location may be inefficient for building the information space of an application. We will be looking for new solutions that, while still based on services and service location, may also combine some functionality commonly associated with other technologies, such as directory services and information retrieval. Depending on the nature of the services, prefetching and caching of service information may also be considered, not only as a way of optimising performance, but also as a way of supporting weakly connected operation.

Networking Environments. The emergence of new wireless network technologies based on short range connectivity, e.g. bluetooth [16], and the increasing number of devices equipped with network connections, possibly even more than one, represent a vast potential for applying the concept of location-based services to smaller location scales. Exploring the use of our framework in these highly networked environments is another objective of our future research.

5.2 Conclusions

There is a growing interest in systems that support associations between information and location, but there is a lack of generic approaches on which to base their development. As a consequence, developing such systems becomes a technically complex task, leading to partial solutions that are only valid for very specific applications and technological environments. In this paper, we have proposed a flexible concept of location-based services as a paradigm for supporting the use of localised information and described an architectural framework for enabling such service model in the Internet environment. The application of the framework has been demonstrated through the development of a location-sensitive tourist guide, which also served for evaluating the approach and for highlighting some of the issues involved in its use. The results of the case study have shown that the concept of location-based services can be used to develop location-dependent systems. Moreover, the characteristics of the resulting architecture, in terms of its openness and generality, suggest that location-based services can effectively be used as a more generic approach to support localised information.

Acknowledgements

To the GUIDE team, and especially to Keith Mitchell and Matthias Franz, for their collaboration in the preparation of this case study. To Adrian Friday for his comments on a draft version of this paper. To the anonymous reviewers for their attentive reading and valuable comments. This work was carried out as part of the PRAXIS funded AROUND project (PRAXIS/P/EEI/14267/1998) and supported by grant PRAXIS XXI/BD/13853/97.

References

1. Davies, N.,Cheverst, K.,Mitchell, K.,Friday, A.: Caches in the Air: Disseminating Tourist Information in the Guide System. Second IEEE Workshop on Mobile Computer Systems and Applications, New Orleans, Louisiana (1999)
2. Imielinski, T.,Viswanathan, S.: Adaptive Wireless Information Systems. SIG in Data Base Systems Conference, Tokyo, Japan (1994)
3. Hodes, T. D.,Katz, R.,Servan-Schreiber, E.,Rowe, L.: Composable Ad hoc Mobile Services for Universal Interaction. 3rd ACM/IEEE International Conference on Mobile Computing and Networking - MOBICOM97, Budapest, Hungary (1997)

4. Jini website, available as "http://www.sun.com/jini".
5. HAVi website, available as "http://www.havi.org".
6. Schilit, W.: A System for Context-Aware Mobile Computing. Columbia University, PhD Thesis (1995)
7. Brown, P.: Triggering Information by Context. Personal Technologies Vol. 2 1 (1998) 1–9
8. Guttman, E.,Perkins, C.,Veizades, J.,Day, M.: Service Location Protocol, Version 2. RFC 2608 (1999)
9. Rosenberg, J.,Schulzrinne, H.,Suter, B.: Wide Area Network Service Location. Work in progress from the Service Location Working Group of the IETF, Internet-Draft draft-ietf-svrloc-warsv-01.txt (1997)
10. Imielinski, T.,Navas, J.: GPS-Based Addressing and Routing, RFC 2009 (1996)
11. Leonhardt, U.: Supporting Location-Awareness in Open Distributed Systems. Imperial College of Science, Technology and Medicine, University of London, PhD Thesis (1998)
12. Berners-Lee, T.,Fielding, R.,Masinter, L.: Uniform Resource Identifiers (URI): Generic Syntax. RFC 2396 (1998)
13. Meyer, D.: Administratively Scoped IP Multicast. RFC 2365 (1998)
14. Guttman, E.,Perkins, C.,Kempf, J.: Service Templates and Service: Schemes. RFC 2609 (1999)
15. Kempf, J.,Guttman, E.: An API for Service Location. RFC 2614 (1999)
16. Bluetooth website, available as "http://www.bluetooth.com".

Enabling Context-Awareness
from Network-Level Location Tracking

P. Couderc[†] and A.-M. Kermarrec[‡]

† IRISA/INRIA
‡ IRISA/UNIVERSITY OF RENNES 1
Campus Universitaire de Beaulieu
35042 Rennes Cedex, France

e-mail : {pcouderc, akermarr}@irisa.fr

Abstract. The development of mobile computing combined with the exponential growth of the Internet makes it possible to access informations and services from everywhere. However, user's mobility also means that the context in which the information system is used change dramatically. To be useful in these new environments, applications will have to be adaptive, which requires context-awareness. We propose in this paper an efficient way to export context-dependent informations to applications by exploiting location knowledge available at the network level. This method is illustrated by a prototype using Mobile-IP and a context-aware Web browser.

Introduction

Mobile computing popularity and the development of the Internet are two important trends in current computer systems. They potentially enable people to access any information anywhere. However, these environments are characterized by important variations, since the user may access the information system from many different *contexts* (from his office, from his car, while shopping etc.), with many different devices (desktop workstations, notebooks, cellular phones etc.). These variations concern both resources (like network bandwidth) and relevant informations for the current context (like flight information in an airport and traffic information in a car). In this paper we focus on a way to provide some means to application to adapt their behavior to the user's context, which is known as *context awareness*.

Because context changes can usually be associated with a user's movement, detecting location changes is essential. To this end, we propose to exploit the information available at the network level to detect host movement. We assume the model of network mobility proposed for the Mobile-IP protocol. This model is described in Section 1. Context-dependent information are made available to applications through a server (*context-manager*) responsible for the local area, which is described in Section 2. To demonstrate the interest of this service, we developed a context-aware Web browser which was used to access location dependent information (Section 3). A comparison with similar works and some perspectives are given in conclusion.

1 Mobile system model

We consider a global system composed of the following elements: the information system, mobile stations, and access points (Figure 1). The information system provides resources and services that may be requested by the users. The mobile stations are portable computer or terminals equipped with one or more communication interfaces (wireless or not) from which the user may access the information system. Access points provide the mobile stations with a gateway to the information system in a limited area, called *cell* in cellular systems. In the rest of the paper, we also use the term cell for wireless LAN, and even for wired LAN like Ethernet (in this case the cell is simply the geographical zone spanned by the LAN).

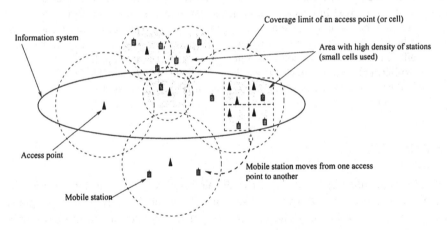

Fig. 1. Mobile system model

1.1 Access point organization

Access points geographical organization is determined by the size of the cells. Two parameters are have to be considered: geographical coverage and access point load. Using bigger cells reduces the number of access points to deploy for the coverage of a given area, but increases the number of mobile stations that the access points have to handle at a given time. Small cells handle less users but have to support more frequent cell switching (hand-off). Thus, different cell sizes are usually used depending on the areas: small cells for high user density area and bigger cells elsewhere.

As a consequence, the access point organization determines the granularity of the network level location system, because a mobile host movement is detected only when the mobile host switch from one access point to another.

Note that an access point may even mobile: for example, a train or plane may offer an access point to passengers mobile hosts through an embedded LAN. This access point would itself be considered as a mobile from stationary access points. Another example is network using low orbiting satellites like Iridium. In this case, even when the mobile host does not move (relatively to the earth) it's access point may change because the cells are moving.

1.2 Mobile-IP protocol

The information system we consider is the Internet: mobile stations and access points have to use the Internet protocols to communicate. In the Internet, IP addresses identify the network interface and the physical network to which the interface is connected. Mobile-IP solutions allow a host to keep its IP address wherever it is (independent on the physical network used), and hence do not require any modification to applications. Special routers (called foreign agents or FA) serve as temporary access points to the Internet for mobile hosts. When Mobile-IP is used in a wireless environment, the mobile support stations are usually configured as the FAs.

In the mobile-IP protocol [7], each time mobile hosts move, they are assigned a temporary IP address (in addition to their constant IP address). Mobile hosts register their temporary IP address to a special router (called a home agent or HA) connected to the mobile's home network, which manages the binding between permanent and temporary IP addresses. IP packets addressed to a mobile host are routed to its home network and delivered in the usual way if the mobile is connected at home. Otherwise, the HA forwards the packet to the FA via IP tunneling. Optimizations are used to allow mobile-aware hosts (i.e. running the Mobile-IP protocol) to communicate directly with mobile hosts once their current location is known, thus short-cutting the HA suboptimal route.

In our prototype, we exploit the temporary address registering scheme to update the current contextual server of a mobile station.

2 Prototype architecture

The prototype is composed of three elements: *context managers* which manage location-dependent informations, a mobile-IP implementation where changes of access point are detected, and an application (a context-aware Web browser).

2.1 Context managers

Context managers constitute the generic part of the prototype. A context manager is a server software associated with a geographical area or a mobile station, which manages a database of location dependent informations. In the current implementation, database items are simple pairs *(attribute, value)* and may represent any context parameter. A simple example could be:

Attributes	Values
location	city=rennes, latitude=48.10, longitude=-1.67
traffic_report	http://www.traffic.com/rennes.html
weather_report	http://www.weather.com/rennes/today.html
web_proxy	131.254.60.47:3128
network_type	name=ethernet, bandwidth=10mbs

Context managers accept GET and SET queries, which respectively return the value of a set of attributes (or all the bindings in the case of a GET *), and sets the values of specified attributes. Of course, some standardization would be required for attribute name and value format.

The mobile host also runs a local context manager, which constructs its context database by merging the local area's database with a description of the user and mobile station profile. This may include attributes like user's preferences (language, browser's colors and fonts etc.), or platform capabilities (monochrome or color display, cpu speed, etc.)

2.2 Detecting location change with Mobile-IP

The Mobile-IP temporary address registering represents a natural place to detect host zone changes. When a mobile host enters a new zone, it must discover a FA in order to be assigned a temporary IP address. Two schemes exist in mobile-IP: the FA may be configured to periodically multicast advertisement messages, or may be requested by the mobile host. In either case, when the mobile host registers itself to the FA, it just has to set the IP address of the new zone's context manager to the local context manager running on the mobile host (this IP address is usually the same as the FA one). This SET request for the attribute current_context_manager is treated as a special case by the local context manager. When it receives this address, it imports the context of current zone with a GET * query on the context server just discovered. Especially, this server should define the location attribute. These interactions between Mobile-IP and the context manager are shown in Figure 2.

We are aware that this scheme raises some security issues, as it may not be desirable to blindly import the attributes from the unknown context server discovered in the new zone. Our first prototype does not currently address these problems, but a more realistic one would have to provide some means to allow the user of a context server to attach access control information for sensitive attributes.

We used an implementation of Mobile-IP for Linux [2], compliant with the IETF specification [7]. This implementation allows a special operating mode which does not require a FA, but this mode is not supported in our prototype since the FA is used to discover the local context manager.

Note that what our design specifically requires from the access point is to provide the context manager service. We do not explicitly associate the current cell with the current location, but the access point of the current cell must be able to describe the current location, and this location may be obtained by any available means. For example, a mobile access point in a plane may obtain the current location from the embedded GPS receiver of the plane.

3 Application example: A context-aware Web browser

To demonstrate the interest of our context manager, we designed a simple context-aware Web client from an experimental HTTP-TCN compliant Web client [3]. HTTP-TCN [4] is a recent protocol which allows a Web client to negotiate transparently for the user a particular representation of a Web resource from a server when multiple variants exist. The selection of the most relevant variant for the context is based on quality factors affected to variants and attributes (readers interested in more details about transparent content negotiation should refer to [4]). The Web client consists of a Web proxy which interfaces with a standard HTTP 1.0 or 1.1 client (like Netscape Navigator) to provide a TCN-compliant user agent. We extended it in order to get TCN attributes values from the context manager, which change as the user move. The resulting architecture is depicted at Figure 2.

To test a location-dependent service, we have implemented a small transparent negotiating HTTP server implemented in Java, which provides location-dependent information for two places p1 and p2, represented by two Ethernet networks n1 and n2 (meaning that n1 was supposed to be p1's network and n2 to be p2's network). A mobile host which runs the client-side of the prototype was able to switch between the two networks and to transparently access to p1's variant on network n1 and p2's variant on network p2.

This architecture relies on the traditional pull-approach of the Web, which introduces a problem for mobile oriented-services: when a context attribute like 'location' changes while the browser is displaying a resource dependent on this attribute, it is not notified of the change. It is possible to solve this limitation by modifying the TCN proxy in order to use persistent connections with the browser for context-dependent resources. In this way, the TCN proxy would send the new value of a context dependent resource as soon as a context change is detected.

Conclusion and related work

In this paper, we have emphasized the importance of context-awareness in mobile computing. As context changes are usually induced by users movements, a location system provides a low-level way to detect them. We used the informations available at the Mobile-IP level to detect such changes and update the description of the current context. This description is managed by a server running in the local cell, which has the advantage of being a scalable approach. Similar

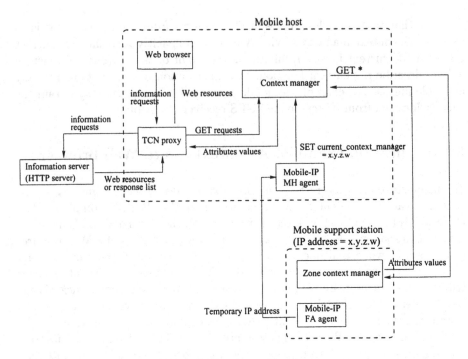

Fig. 2. Prototype architecture

works on context-awareness have been described. The importance of context-awareness was initially pointed out by works related to ubiquitous computing [9]. In this vision, computers system are closely integrated into the real world to implicitly assist people actions. The Parctab prototype [8] is an example of such environments. Like in our proposition, the location is determined from the cell used to access the network. However, the information system is a centralized database, whereas in our system the management of the context is localized on each cell and the information system is potentially the whole Internet. Cyberguide [1] is a location-dependent application for tourists using IR beacon for its location system; unlike our system the information system is fully hosted on the mobile station. This is an important restriction because informations can't be updated dynamically, and the size of the information system is limited by the storage capacity of the mobile station. Context-aware systems have also been developed with *wearable computer*: Shopnavi [6] is a context-aware shopping and city navigation assistant based on a wearable computer and a combination of GPS and IR beacons positioning system. Like our prototype application it uses the Web as its information system, but it relies on a central search server to index Web pages on their associated geographical position which may limit the scalability. Finally, JINI [5] is a recent proposition to allow dynamic integration and configuration of electronic devices like computers, printers, phones etc, into a network. Each JINI participant may discover services proposed by others and/or register new ones using a look up service. JINI is more specialized than our system, as it addresses services configuration problems while our system provide any context-dependent information, which may includes configuration information.

Among the possible improvements to our work, an important one is the design of a notification service for context-aware applications which would allow to register specific condition changes and to group common events for multiple applications. It would also be interesting to see if other applications could beneficiate of the context-manager as easily as the Web browser.

References

1. G. D. Abowd, C. G. Atkeson, J. Hong, S. Long, R. Kooper, and M. Pinkerton. Cyberguide: A mobile context-aware tour guide. *ACM Wireless Networks*, 3, 1997.
2. A. Dixit and V. Gupta. Mobile-IP for Linux. Available at http://anchor.cs.binghampton.edu/mobileip, May 1996.
3. K. Holtman. Conneg-uax v2.0. Available at http://gewis.win.tue.nl/~koen/conneg/, June 1998.
4. K. Holtman and A. Mutz. Transparent content negotiation in HTTP. RFC 2295, March 1998.
5. Sun Microsystems. JINI architectural overview. Technical White Paper, January 1999.
6. K. Nagao and J. Rekimoto. Agent augmented reality : A software agent meets the real world. In *Second International Conference on Multiagent Sytems*, December 1996.
7. C. Perkins. IP mobility support. RFC 2002, October 1996.
8. B. N. Schilit, N. Adams, R. Gold, M. M. Tso, and R. Want. The Parctab mobile computing system. In *Proc. of the 4th Workshop on Workstation Operating Systems*, pages pp 34–39, Napa, CA, October 1993.
9. M. Weiser. Some Computer Science Issues in Ubiquitous Computing. *Communication of the ACM*, 36(7):pp 75–83, July 1993.

Perceptual Intelligence

Alex Pentland

Academic Head, M.I.T. Media Laboratory
E15-387, 20 Ames St., Cambridge MA 02139
http://www.media.mit.edu/~pentland

Abstract. The objects that surround us —desks, cars, shoes and coats —are deaf and blind; this limits their ability to adapt to our needs and thus to be useful. We have therefore developed computer systems that can follow people's actions, recognizing their faces, gestures, and expressions. Using this technology we have begun to make "smart rooms" and "smart clothes" that can help people in day-to-day life without chaining them to keyboards, pointing devices or special goggles.

1 Introduction

Inanimate things are coming to life. However these stirrings are not Shelley's Frankenstein or the humanoid robots dreamed of in artificial intelligence laboratories. This new awakening is more like Walt Disney: the simple objects that surround us are gaining sensors, computational powers, and actuators. As a result desks and doors, TVs and telephones, cars and trains, eyeglasses and shoes, and even the shirts on our backs....all are changing from static, inanimate objects into adaptive, reactive systems that are more useful and efficient.

Imagine a house that always knows where your kids are, and tells you when they might be getting in trouble. Or an office that knows when you are in the middle of an important conversation, and shields you from interruptions. Or a car that knows when you are sleepy and should stop for coffee. Or glasses that can recognize the person you are talking to and whisper their name in your ear. All of these are examples of demonstrations we have built in my laboratory, and several have already become the basis of commercial products.

To change inanimate objects like offices, houses, cars, or glasses into smart, active helpmates they need to have what I call perceptual intelligence. They need to begin paying attention to people and the surrounding situation the way another person would. That way they can begin to adapt their behavior to us, rather than the other way around. If you imagine raising a child in a closed, dark, soundproof box with only a telegraph connection to the outside world, you can quickly realize how difficult it is for computers to become intelligent and helpful. They exist in a world that is almost completely disconnected from ours, so how can they understand our desires?

In the language of cognitive science, perceptual intelligence is the ability to solve the frame problem[1]: it is being able to classify the current situation, so that you know what variables are important, and thus can take appropriate action. Once a computer has the perceptual intelligence to know who, what, when, where, and why, then simple statistical learning methods are probably sufficient for the computer to determine what aspects of the situation are significant, and to answer a wide variety of useful questions.

2 Perceptual Intelligence, Not Ubiquitous Computing

My goal is to make machines that are aware of their environment, and in particular are sensitive to the people that interact with them. They should know who we are, see our expressions and gestures, and hear the tone and emphasis of our voice. People often equate perceptual intelligence with Ubiquitous Computing (or Artificial Intelligence), but I believe that my approach is very different.

For instance, I do not care that there are computers everywhere, or that they have Artificial Intelligence, because I believe that most tasks do not require complex reasoning. Instead, they require appropriate perceptual abilities and simple learned responses (e.g., 'perceptual intelligence'). Consequently, the fact that it is often convenient to have a general-purpose computer in the system is largely beside the point.

Moreover, I am against the idea of having everything tightly and continuously networked together. Such ubiquitous networking and its attendant capacity to concentrate information has too close a resemblance to George Orwell's dark vision of a government that controls your every move. Instead, I propose that *local* intelligences...and mainly perceptual intelligence...combined with relatively sparse, user-initiated networking can provide most of the benefits of ubiquitous networking, while at the same time making it more difficult for outsiders to track and analyze user's behavior.

3 Adaptive Interfaces

A key idea of perceptual interfaces is that they must be adaptive both to overall situation and to the individual user. As a consequence much of our research focus is on learning user behaviors, and how they vary as a function of the situation. For instance, we have built systems that learn user's driving behavior, thus allowing the automobile to anticipate the driver's actions (Pentland and Liu 1999), systems that

---

[1] This research was supported by ARPA, ONR, ARL, BT and the Things That Think industrial consortium. Portions of this paper have appeared in Scientific American, April 1996 and Dec 1998. Many of the examples and figures are drawn from IEEE, ACM, and ICASSP conference proceedings.

learns typical pedestrian behaviors, allowing it to detect unusual events (Oliver et al 1998).

Most recently we have built audiovisual systems that learn word meanings from natural audio and visual input (Roy and Pentland 1997,1998). This automatically acquired vocabulary can then be used understand and generate spoken language. Although simple in its current form, this effort is a first step towards a more fully-grounded model of language acquisition. The current system can be applied to human-computer interfaces which use spoken input. A significant problem in designing effective interfaces is the difficulty in anticipating a person's word choice]and associated intent. Our system addresses this problem learning the vocabulary of each user together with its visual grounding. We are investigating several practical including adaptive human-machine interfaces for browsing, assistive technologies, education, and entertainment.

4   Experimental Testbeds

To realize my vision of helpful, perceptually-intelligent environments I have created a series of experimental testbeds at the Media Laboratory. These testbeds can be divided into two main types: 'Smart Rooms' and 'Smart Clothes'. The idea of a smart room is a little like having a butler; i.e., a passive observer who usually stands quietly in the corner but who is constantly looking for opportunities to help. Smart clothes, on the other hand, are more like a personal assistant. They are like a person who travels with you, seeing and hearing everything that you do, and who tries to anticipate your needs and generally smooth your way.

Both smart rooms and smart clothes are instrumented with sensors (currently mainly cameras and microphones, but also sensors for physical quantities like pressure and distance, and biosensors like heart rate and muscle action), which allow the computer to see, hear, and interpret users' actions. People in a smart room can control programs, browse multimedia information, and experience shared virtual environments without keyboards, special sensors, or special goggles. Smart clothes can provide personalized information about the surrounding environment, such as the names of people you meet or directions to your next meeting, and can replace most computer and consumer electronics. The key idea is that because the room or the clothing knows something about what is going on, it can react intelligently.

The first smart room was developed in 1991; now there are smart rooms in Japan, England, and several places in the U.S. They can be linked together by ISDN telephone lines to allow shared virtual environment and cooperative work experiments. Our smart clothes project was started in 1992, and now includes many separate research efforts.

5   Smart Rooms

In this section I will describe some of the perceptual capabilities available to our smart rooms, and provide a few illustrations of how these capabilities can be combined into interesting applications. This list of capabilities is far from exhaustive; mostly it is a catalog of the most recent research in each area.

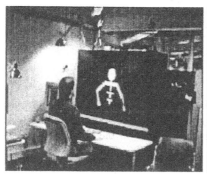

Fig. 1. The system uses 2-D observations to drive a 3-D dynamic model of the skeleton. This dynamic model uses a control law that chooses 'typical' behaviors when it is necessary to choose among multiple possible legal trajectories. Predictive feedback from the dynamic model is provided by setting priors for the 2-D observations process. It is real-time, self-calibrating, and has been successfully integrated into application ranging from physical rehabilitation to a computer-enhanced dance space.

5.1 Real-Time Person Tracking Using a Dynamic 3-D Model

To act intelligently in a day-to-day environment, the first thing you need to know is: where are the people? The human body is a complex dynamic system, whose visual features are time-varying, noisy signals. Accurately tracking the state of such a system requires use of a recursive estimation framework. The elements of the framework are the observation model relating noisy low-level features to the higher-level skeletal model and *vice versa*, and the dynamic skeletal model itself.

This extended Kalman filter framework reconciles the 2-D tracking process with high-level 3-D models, thus stabilizing the 2-D tracking by directly coupling an articulated dynamic model with raw pixel measurements. Some of the demonstrated benefits of this added stability include increase in 3-D tracking accuracy, insensitivity to temporary occlusion, and the ability to handle multiple people.

The dynamic skeleton model currently includes the upper body and arms. The model interpolates those portions of the body state that are not measured directly, such as the upper body and elbow orientation, by use of the model's intrinsic dynamics and the behavior (control) model. The model also rejects noise that is inconsistent with the dynamic model.

The system runs on two SGI machines at 20 -- 30 Hz, and has performed reliably on hundreds of people in many different physical locations, including exhibitions, conferences, and offices in several research labs. The 'jitter' or noise observed experimentally is 0.9cm for 3-D translation and 0.6 degrees for 3-D rotation when operating in a desk-sized environment.

One of the main advantages of feedback from a 3-D dynamic model to the low-level vision system. Without feedback, the 2-D tracker fails if there is even partial self-occlusion from a single camera's perspective. With feedback, information from the dynamic model can be used to resolve ambiguity during 2-D tracking. For additional information see Wren and Pentland 1997.

5.2   Self-Calibration

By collecting a set of three blob correspondences (face, left hand, right hand) over a number of frames (50--100 total correspondences) and computing the stereo calibration using a Levenburg-Marquart estimator on the batch of correspondences. The mean residual RMS error from this self-calibration process is typically about 2.25cm. The relative error of reconstruction of hand position over this trajectory is therefore about 1.8 percent. The sources of error include not only noise and modeling error, but also hand movement error, since the trajectory followed by the person was not exact and the hand shape changes. Thus only a fraction of this relative error should be counted as computational error. For additional information see Azerbayejani and Pentland 1996

5.3   Recognizing Hand Gestures

We have used the recovered 3-D body geometry for several different gesture recognition tasks, including a real-time American Sign Language reader (Starner, Weaver and Pentland 1998), and a system that recognizes T'ai Chi gestures, and trains the user to perform them correctly (Becker and Pentland 1996). Typically these systems have a gesture vocabularies of 25 to 65 gestures, and recognition accuracies above 95\%

Although we have been able to use standard hidden Markov models (HMM's) to recognize such gestures with near-perfect accuracy, we have found the training of such models to be labor-intensive and difficult. This is because use of HMMs to describe multi-part signals (such as two-handed gestures) requires large amounts of training and even so the HMM parameter estimation process is typically unstable.

To improve on this situation, we have developed a new method of training a more general class of HMM, called the Coupled Hidden Markov Model. Coupled HMM's allow each hand to be described by a separate state model, and the interactions between them to be modeled explicitly and economically. The consequence is that much less training data is required, and the HMM parameter estimation process is much better conditioned. For additional detail see Brand, Oliver, and Pentland 1997.

Fig. 2. Accurate, real-time recognition of a 40 word American Sign Language vocabulary, recognizing *and teaching T'ai Chi gestures using the Coupled HMM method*

6 Head Tracking and Shape Recovery

Because of its importance to communication and fine detail, the human head and face requires more detailed analysis than the rest of the body. We have therefore developed a system that estimates the 3-D head pose, 3-D facial structure, and skin texture at 20hz using a single SGI O2 computer. Like the body tracking system above, the system uses feedback from its 3-D structure both to guide interpretation of the 2-D features.

The system initializes itself by finding the face using a coarse model of head shape and skin-like color. A 3-D face model is then aligned to the eyes, nose and mouth and Eigenface measurements confirm and optimize the detection of a face. The system then tracks the facial features using 8 normalized correlation 2D patch trackers . While the 2-D trackers follow the face, the system continuously estimates the rigid structure that could correspond to the face using an Extended Kalman Filter (EKF). Thus the individual 2-D trackers so that they function as a single 3-D object.

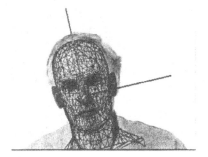 

Fig. 3. Real-time tracking of the head pose using an EKF (right) allows us to 'undo' projective effects, and make a statistical estimate of 3-D head structure directly from the intensity image data (image and estimated structure shown at right).

Having recovered 3-D pose using an EKF, we can normalize the face image by warping it in 3-D into a frontal mug-shot, analyze it using a statistical model which has been rained from a 3-D head scanner to learn to predict a full 3-D facial structure from a frontal mug-shot of any individual. Thus, we can recover in real-time estimates of the facial pose (in 3-D) as well as its texture and a full 3-D structural model. These form a very compact complete 3-D description of the face (100 bytes of data) which is recovered from live video images at over 20 Hz. For additional information see Jebara and Pentland 1998.

7 Audio Interpretation

Audio interpretation of people is as important as visual interpretation. Although much work as been done on speech understanding, virtually all of this work assumes a closely-placed microphone for input and a fixed listening position. Speech recognition applications, for instance, typically require near-field ($< 1.5m$) microphone placement for acceptable performance. Beyond this distance the signal-to-noise ratio of the incoming speech affects the performance significantly; most commercial speech-recognition packages typically break down over a 4 to 6 DB range.

The constraint of near-field microphone placement makes audio interpretation very difficult in an unconstrained environment, so it is necessary to find a solution that allows the user to move around with minimal degradation in performance. Our solution to this problem is to use our vision-based head-tracking capability to 'steer' a microphone so that it focuses on the user's head. This is accomplished by the technique of beam forming with an array of microphone. For additional information see Basu, Casey, Gardner, and Pentland 1996.

7.1 Learning in the Interface

Traditional HCI interfaces have hard-wired assumptions about how a person will communicate. In a typical speech recognition application the system has some preset vocabulary and (possibly statistical) grammar. For proper operation the user must restrict what she says to words and vocabulary built into the system. However, studies have shown that in practice it is difficult to predict how different user will use available input modalities to express their intents. For example Furnas *et al* did a series of experiments to see how people would assign keywords for operations in a mock interface. They conclude that: "There is no one good access term for most objects. The idea of an "obvious", "self-evident,' or "natural" term is a myth! ... Even the best possible name is not very useful...Any keyword system capable of providing a high hit rate for unfamiliar users must let them use words of their won choice for objects." Our conclusion is that to make effective interfaces there need to be adaptive mechanisms which can learn how individuals use modalities to communicate.

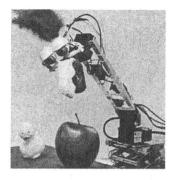 

Fig. 4. Toco the Toucan in both his robotic and computer graphics form. This computer graphics demonstration of word and gesture learning for human-machine interactions was called "the best demo at SIGGRAPH '96" by the Los Angeles Times.

We have therefore built a trainable interfaces which let the user teach the interface which words and gestures they want to use and what the words and gestures mean. Our current work focuses on a system which learns words from natural interactions; users teach the system words by simply pointing to objects and naming them. Currently training time is approximately linear in the number of terms to be learned, with only a few teaching examples required per learned term. This work demonstrates an interface which learns words and their domain-limited semantics through natural multimodal interactions with people. The interface, embodied as an animated character named Toco the Toucan , can learn acoustic words and their meanings by continuously updating association weight vectors which estimate the mutual information between acoustic words and attribute vectors which represent perceptually salient aspects of virtual objects in Toco's world. Toco is able to learn semantic associations (between words and attribute vectors) using gestural input from the user. Gesture input enables the user to naturally specify which object to attend to during word learning. For additional information see Roy and Pentland 1997, 1998 .

8   Recognizing Face and Voice

Once the person has been found, and visual and auditory attention has been focused on them, the next question to ask is: who is it? The question of identity is central to smart behavior, because who is giving a command is often as important as what the command is. Perhaps the best way to answer the "who is it?" question is to recognize them by their facial appearance and by their speech. Our speech-based speaker identification system in now in daily use to annotate the US Congressional Record; for additional information see Roy and Malmud 1996.

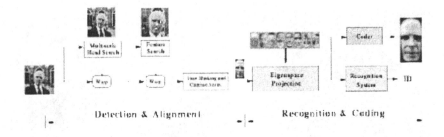

Fig. 5. Organization of our Bayesian face recognition and image coding system.

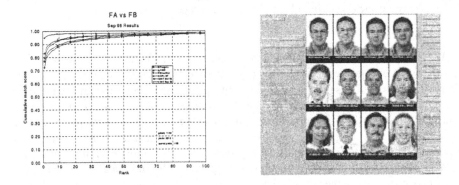

Fig. 6. The graph on the left shows cumulative recognition rates for frontal FA/FB views for the competing algorithms in the FERET 1996 test. The top curve (labeled "MIT Sep 96") corresponds to our Bayesian matching technique. Note that second placed is standard eigenface matching *(labeled "MIT Mar 95"). The curve labeled 'UMD' is the LDA or 'Fisherface' algorithm. On the left is shown typical FERET image database search result using our algorithm; the top four images are all of the same person.*

For face recognition we have developed a new Bayesian (MAP) method that may be viewed as a generalized nonlinear extension of Linear Discriminant Analysis (LDA) or "FisherFace" techniques for face recognition. The performance advantage of this probabilistic matching technique over standard Euclidean nearest-neighbor eigenspace matching is demonstrated using results from DARPA's 1996 "FERET" face recognition competition, in which this algorithm was found to be the top performer. Moreover, our nonlinear generalization has distinct computational/storage advantages over these linear methods for large databases. For additional information see Moghaddam, Wassudin, and Pentland 1997.

9 Expression Recognition

Facial expression is almost as important as who a person is. For instance, a car should know if the driver is sleepy, and a teaching program should know if the student looks bored. So, just as we can recognize a person once we have accurately located their face, we can also analyze the person's facial motion to determine their expression. The lips are of particular importance in interpreting facial expression, and so we have recently focused our attention on tracking and classification of lip shape.

Fig. 7, *The LAFTER system finds and tracks face and facial features at 30hz, feeding facial feature geometry for HMM expression recognition*

The first step of processing is to detect and characterize the shape of the lip region. For this task we developed the LAFTER system, first reported in Oliver, Bernard, Coutaz, and Pentland 1997. This system uses a on-line EM algorithm to make MAP (maximum a posteriori) estimates of 2-D head pose and lip shape, runs at 30Hz on a PC, and has been used successfully on hundreds of users in many different locations and laboratories. Using lip shape features derived from LAFTER we can train HMMs for various mouth configurations. Recognition accuracy for eight different users making over 2000 expressions averaged 96.5%

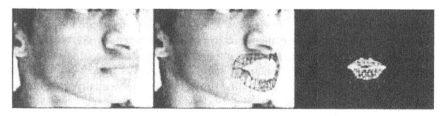

Fig. 7. Fitting a 3-D Finite Elements mesh to facial data, allowing us to extract pose-invariant 3-D lip shape.

Such a 2-D approach is not appropriate for applications which require 3-D models of the user, or where head pose can vary widely. We have therefore developed a method of estimating 3-D lip shape by use of a FEM (Finite Element Mesh) model that has been trained with 3-D data so that its motions must conform to the subspace of typical human lip motions. The figure above the 3-D tracking process. The 3-D model is fit to video data using a refinement of the LAFTER system's color and shape segmentation output, allowing us to make a local MAP estimate of 3-D lip shape despite variations in head pose. This method allows us to robustly estimate the correct lip shape by matching the distributions of the observations and those implied by the learned model. For additional information see Basu, Oliver and Pentland 1997.

10 Haptic Input

Almost every room has a chair, and body posture information is important for assessing user alertness and comfort. Our 'smart chair' therefore senses the pressure distribution patterns in the chair and classifies the seating postures of its user. Two Tekscan sensor sheets (each consisting of a 42-by-48 array of force-sensitive resistor units) are mounted to the seatpan and the backrest of the chair and output 8-bit pressure distribution data. These data are collected and the posture is classified using image modeling and classification algorithms.

The current version of the real-time seating posture classification system uses the appearance-based method developed by Pentland, Moghaddam and Starner for face recognition. For each new pressure distribution map to be classified, the "distance-from-feature-space" for each of the M postures are calculated and compared to a threshold. The posture class that corresponds to the smallest DFFS is used to label the current pressure map, except when all DFFS values exceed the threshold in which case the current posture is declared unknown. The algorithm runs in real-time on a Pentium PC, with a classification accuracy of approximately 95% for 21 different postures (e.g., seated upright, leaning forward, right/left leg crossed, etc.).

11 Smart Clothes

So far I have presented matters mostly from the smart room perspective, where the cameras and microphones are passively watching people move around. However when we build the computers, cameras, microphones and other sensors into a person's clothes, the computer's view moves from a passive third person to an active first-person vantage point. This means that smart clothes can be more intimately and actively involved in the user's activities, making them potentially an intelligent Personal (Digital) Assistant (Starner et al 1997, Mann 1997, Pentland 1998).

Fig. 9, The author, wearing a variety of new technologies. The glasses (built by Microoptical of Boston) contain a computer display that is nearly invisible to others. The jacket has a keyboard that is literally embroidered into the cloth. The lapel has a `context sensor' that can classify the user' surroundings And, of course, a computer which is not visible in this photograph.

Photo by Sam Ogden

For instance, if you build a camera into your eyeglasses, then the face recognition software can help you remember the name of the person you are looking at, by whispering their name in your ear. Or, if you build a phased-array microphones into your jacket, then our word-spotting software can remind you of relevant facts. One could imagine that if someone mentions "the Megadeal contract," the word-spotting software can project Megadeal's finances onto the display built into your glasses. If you build a Global Position Sensor (GPS) into your shoes, then navigation software can help you find your way around by whispering directions in your ear or showing a map on the display built into your glasses.

11.1 Mobile Perceptual Intelligence

The mobility and physical closeness of a wearable computer makes it an attractive platform for perceptual computing. A camera mounted in a baseball cap can observe the user's hands and feet. This allows observation of gestures and body motion in natural, everyday contexts. In addition, the camera acts as an interface for the computer. For example, the user's fingertip becomes the system's mouse pointer through tracking the color of the user's hand. Similarly, hand tracking can be used for recognizing American Sign Language. Our current implementation recognizes sentence-level American Sign Language in real-time with over 97% word accuracy on a 40 word vocabulary. See Starner, Weaver and Pentland. 1998.

Fig. 8. Stochasticks wearable billiards advisor. Left, the user. Right, what they see

By pointing the camera in the direction of the user's gaze, a sense of world context may be obtained. For example, the computer may assist the user by suggesting possible shots in a game of billiards or may provide names for the faces at a cocktail party. The figure above, for instance, illustrates an Augmented Reality system that helps the user play billiards. A camera mounted on the user's head tracks the table and balls, estimates the 3-D configuration of table, balls, and user, and then creates a graphics overlay (using a see-though HMD) showing the user their best shot. For additional information see Jebara, Eyster, Weaver, Starner, and Pentland 1997

In controlled environments, object identification is possible. For instance, if objects of interest have bar tags on visible surfaces, then a wearable camera system can recognize the bar code tags in the environment and overlays 3D graphics, text, or video on the physical world. The computer scans the user's visual field, identifies potential tags, and then applies self-consistency checks to eliminate false hits. The codes in the tags are recognized and the appropriate information is then visually linked to the object.

When 3D alignment of graphics is needed, the corners of a 2D tag are located and the camera position is estimated. Multiple tags can be used in the same environment, and users can add their own annotations to the tags through wireless contact with a annotation database. In this way, the hypertext environment of the World Wide Web is brought to physical reality. Such a system may be used to assist in the repair of annotated machines such as a photocopiers or provide context sensitive information for museum exhibits. Current work addresses the recognition and tracking of "untagged" objects in the office and outside environments to allow easy, socially motivated annotation of everyday things. For additional information see Starner *et al* 1997.

12 Conclusion

It is now possible to track people's motion, identify them by facial appearance, and recognize their actions in real time using only modest computational resources. By using this perceptual information we have been able to build smart rooms and smart clothes that have the potential to recognize people, understand their speech, allow them to control computer displays without wires or keyboards, communicate by sign language, and warn them they are about to make a mistake.

We are now beginning to apply such perceptual intelligence to a much wider variety of situations. For instance, we are now working on prototypes of displays that know if you are watching, credit cards that recognize their owners, chairs that adjust to keep you awake and comfortable, and shoes that know where they are. We imagine building a world where the distinction between inanimate and animate objects begins to blur, and the objects that surround us become more like helpful assistants or playful pets than insensible tools.

References

Papers and technical reports are available at our web site, http://www.media.mit.edu/vismod

1. Azerbayejani, A., and Pentland, A. (1996) "Real-time self-calibrating stereo person tracking using 3-D shape estimation from blob features," ICPR '96, Vienna, Austria.

2. Basu, S., Casey, M., Gardner, W., Azarbayjani, A. Pentland, A. (1996) "Vision-Steered Audio for Interactive Environments," Proceedings of IMAGE'COM 96, Bordeaux, France, May 1996

3. Basu, S., Oliver, N., and Pentland, A., (1998), "3D Modeling and Tracking of Human Lip Motions," Proceedings of ICCV'98, Bombay, India, January 4-7, 1998

4. Becker, D., and Pentland, A., (1996) "Using A Virtual Environment to Teach Cancer Patients T'ai Chi, Relaxation and Self-Imagery," M.I.T. Media Laboratory Perceptual Computing Technical Report No. 390.

5. Brand, M., Oliver, N., and Pentland, A., (1997) "Coupled HMMs for Complex Action Recognition," IEEE CVPR '97, San Juan, Puerto Rico.

6. Jebara, T., Eyster, C., Weaver, J., Starner, T., and Pentland, A., "Stochasticks: Augmenting the Billiards Experience with Probabilistic Vision and Wearable Computers," IEEE Intl. Symposium on Wearable Computers, Cambridge MA, Oct. 23-24, 1997

7. Jebara, T., Russell, K. and Pentland, A. (1998), "Mixtures of Eigenfeatures for Real-Time Structure from Texture,", Proceedings of ICCV'98, Bombay, India, January 4-7, 1998

8. Mann, S.,"Smart Clothing: The Wearable Computer and WearCam", S. Mann, Personal Technologies 1(1), 1997

9. Moghaddam, B., Nastar, C., and Pentland, A. (1997) "Beyond Eigenfaces: Probabilistic Matching for Face Recognition" M.I.T. Media Laboratory Perceptual Computing Technical Report No. 443

10. Oliver, N., Bernard, F., Coutaz, J., and Pentland, A., (1997) "LAFTER: lips and face tracker," IEEE CVPR '97, San Juan, Puerto Rico.

11. Oliver, N., Rosario, B., Pentland, A., (1998) Statistical Modeling of Human Interactions, IEEE Conference on Computer Vision and Pattern Recognition (CVPR98), Workshop on the Interpretation of Visual Motion, pp. 39-46, Sta. Barbara, USA, June 21-27.

12. Pentland, A. (1996) Smart Rooms, Smart Clothes Scientific American, Vol. 274, No. 4, pp. 68-76, April 1996.

13. Pentland, A., "Wearable Intelligence" Alex Pentland, Scientific American Presents, Special Issue on Intelligence, Vol 9, No. 4, Dec. 1998

14. Pentland, A., and Liu, A., (1999) Modeling and Prediction of Human Behavior, Neural Computation, 11, 229-242, Jan 1999

15. Roy, D., and Pentland, A., (1997) "Word learning in a multimodal environment" ICASSP '98, Seattle WA

16. Roy, D., and Pentland, A., (1998) "An Adaptive Interface: Learning worlds and their audio-visual grounding" Int'l Conf. On Speech and Language, Sydney, Austrialia, Dec. 1998

17. Roy, D., and Malamud, C., (1996) "Speaker Identification Based Text to Audio Alignment for an Audio Retreival System," M.I.T. Media Laboratory Perceptual Computing Technical Report No. 395.

18. Starner, T., Weaver, J., and Pentland, A., (1998) Real-Time American Sign Language Recognition from Video Using Hidden Markov Models, IEEE Transactions on Pattern Analysis and Machine Vision, Dec. 1998.

19. Starner, T., Mann, S., Rhodes, B., Levine, J., Healey, J., Kirsch, D., Picard, R., and Pentland, A., (1996) "Visual Augmented Reality Through Wearable Computing," Presence, Teleoperators and Virtual Environments(M.I.T. Press), Vol 5, No 2, pp. 163-172.

20. Wren, C., and Pentland, A., (1998) "Dynamic Modeling of Human Motion,' IEEE Face and Gesture Conf., Nara, Japan., also M.I.T. Media Laboratory Perceptual Computing Technical Report No. 415

Advanced Interaction in Context

Albrecht Schmidt[ᛃ], Kofi Asante Aidoo[+], Antti Takaluoma[ӿ],
Urpo Tuomela[ӿ], Kristof Van Laerhoven[+], Walter Van de Velde[+]

[ᛃ]TecO, University of Karlsruhe, Germany
[+]Starlab Nv/Sa, Brussels, Belgium
[ӿ]Nokia Mobile Phones, Oulu, Finland
albrecht@teco.edu, kofi@starlab.net, Antti.Takaluoma@nokia.com,
Urpo.Tuomela@nokia.com, kvlaerho@vub.ac.be, wvdv@starlab.net

Abstract. Mobile information appliances are increasingly used in numerous different situations and locations, setting new requirements to their interaction methods. When the user's situation, place or activity changes, the functionality of the device should adapt to these changes. In this work we propose a layered real-time architecture for this kind of context-aware adaptation based on redundant collections of low-level sensors. Two kinds of sensors are distinguished: physical and logical sensors, which give cues from environment parameters and host information. A prototype board that consists of eight sensors was built for experimentation. The contexts are derived from cues using real-time recognition software, which was constructed after experiments with Kohonen's Self-Organizing Maps and its variants. A personal digital assistant (PDA) and a mobile phone were used with the prototype to demonstrate situational awareness. On the PDA font size and backlight were changed depending on the demonstrated contexts while in mobile phone the active user profile was changed. The experiments have shown that it is feasible to recognize contexts using sensors and that context information can be used to create new interaction metaphors.

1   Introduction

Current research and development in information technology is moving away from desktop based general purpose computers towards more task specific information appliances. Mobile phones and personal digital assistants (PDAs) dominate the research landscape as their dominance grows commercially. Last year alone there was a 56% increase in the use of mobile phones across Western Europe resulting in approximately 23 million users of cellular technology. The functionality of these appliances is the crucial issue.

Users of these devices are not specialists and don't accept long learning phases. Nevertheless users like advanced functionality, but it is important that this does not compromise the ease of use for these appliances. An important challenge in competition is to develop new functionality with *added value* for the user and still keep the interaction mechanism simple and straightforward. Answers and ideas can be found in the inherent nature of mobile electronics. People take their phones and PDA's everywhere using them in various environments and situations to perform different tasks. The user's expectation towards the device also change with the situation (e.g. the user would like different ring tones for a phone in a meeting than on a noisy road). Ideally, devices that know about the situational context the devices could transparently adapt to the situation. Such devices lead to the invisible computer, discussed by Weiser [14] and is a step towards the ideal of a disappearing interface as demanded by Norman [8].

In our work we aim to prove the idea that the more the device knows about the user, the task, and the environment the better the support is for the user and the more the interface can become invisible.

To build devices that have knowledge about their situational context, it is important to gain an understanding of what context is. Current research in context-awareness shows a strong focus on location [1], [6]. An architectural approach, based on a smart environment is described by Schilit et. al. [11]. Other scenarios are using GPS and RF to determine the users location [3], [4]. The visual context in wearable computing is investigated by Starner et. al. [13]. But, as pointed out in [12] context is more than location; this is also recognized in the approach at Georgia Tech to build a context toolkit [10].

We use the term *context* in a more general way to describe the environment, situation, state, surroundings, task, etc.. To provide a view on what we understand by the term context we like to provide a definition from the dictionary as well as a number of synonyms that can be found in a thesaurus:

> **Context** *n 1: discourse that surrounds a language unit and helps to determine its interpretation [syn: linguistic context, context of use] 2: the set of facts or circumstances that surround a situation or event; "the historical context"* (Source: WordNet ® 1.6)

> **Context**: *That which surrounds, and gives meaning to, something else.* (Source: The Free On-line Dictionary of Computing)

> **Synonyms Context:** *Circumstance, situation, phase, position, posture, attitude, place, point; terms; regime; footing, standing, status, occasion, surroundings, environment, location, dependence.* (Source: www.thesaurus.com)

As it can be seen from above context is used with a number of different meanings. In our research project Technology for Enabled Awareness (TEA, [5]) we define *Context awareness as knowledge about the user's and IT device's state, including surroundings, situation, and, to a lesser extent, location.* To describe contexts we use a three-dimensional space as depicted in fig. 1, with dimensions *Environment, Self,* and *Activity.*

Context has many aspects and in the work presented in this paper we focus on physical parameters and information provided by the appliance (e.g. PDA, or mobile phone). To acquire physical parameters we use low-cost and widely available sensors. With this information we determine the user's current situational context. This approach seems complementary to the idea of smart environments as proposed by [9]. With the new generation of mobile devices having increased processing power we focus on making the devices smarter, giving them the ability to recognize and interpret their environment. However, smart devices and smart environments are not mutually exclusive, and it is easy to imagine that a combination can be used.

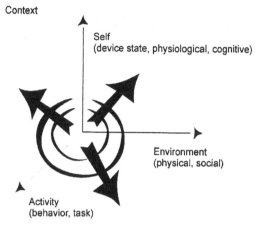

Fig. 1. 3-D Context Model

After briefly introducing the concept of context and situational awareness, we propose an architecture for context recognition. The architecture is composed of four layers, namely sensor, cue, context, and scripting. In section 3 we describe a prototypical implementation that performs the complete mapping from the real environment to awareness enabled applications on a GSM-phone and on a personal digital assistant (PDA). This proves the feasibility of the approach described here. Finally we summarize our results and discuss future directions of our work.

2 Architecture

To build a flexible and yet efficient system we introduce a layered architecture for the TEA-system. As depicted in fig. 2, the architecture consists of four layers, sensors, cues, contexts, and an application layer. In later development phases the part of the architecture that is implemented in hardware will move up, whereas in the early phases as much as possible is implemented in software to enhance flexibility.

2.1 Sensors

We distinguish between physical and logical sensors. *Physical sensors* are electronic hardware components that measure physical parameters in the environment. All information gathered from the host (e.g. current time, GSM cell, etc.) are considered as *logical sensors*.

Each sensor S_i is regarded as a time dependent function that returns a scalar, vector, or a symbolic value (X). A set (finite or infinite) of possible values (domain D) for each sensor is defined.

$S_i: t \rightarrow X_i$

t is the time (discrete), $X_i \in D_i$, i is the identification of the sensor

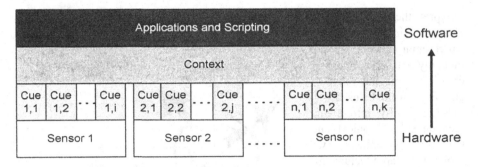

Fig. 2. Layered architecture of the TEA-system.

2.2 Cues

The concept of *Cues* provides an abstraction of physical and logical sensors. For physical sensors, introducing a layer for cues also solves the calibration problem. A cue C_{ij} is regarded as a function taking the values of a single i sensor up to a certain time t as input and providing a symbolic or sub-symbolic output Y. A set (finite or infinite) of possible values (domain E) for each cue is defined.

C_j: $S_i(t) \times S_i(t-1) \times \ldots \times S_i(t-n) \rightarrow Y_{ij}$
t is the time (discrete), $Y_{ij} \in E_{ij}$, $t \geq 0$ $n \geq 0$, j is the identifier for the cue

As seen from the definition, each cue is dependent on one single sensor but using the data of one sensor, multiple cues can be calculated.

2.3 Contexts

A context is a description of the current situation on an abstract level. The context is derived from the available cues. The context T is described by a set of two-dimensional vectors. Each vector h consists of a symbolic value v describing the situations and a number p indicating the certainty that the user (or the device) is currently in this situation. The finite set V of the symbolic values is defined.

T: $C_0(S_0, t) \times C_1(S_0, t) \times \ldots \times C_k(S_0, t) \ldots C_0(S_i, t) \times C_1(S_i, t) \times \ldots \times C_m(S_i, t) \rightarrow h$
$h = \{(v_1, p_1), \ldots, (v_j, p_j)\}$
t is the time (discrete), $v \in V$, $k \geq 0$, $i \geq 0$, $m \geq 0$, $j \geq 0$

2.4 Applications and Scripting

To provide a mechanism to include context information in applications we offer three different semantics. Basic actions can be performed when entering a context, when leaving a context, and while in a certain context. In our approach we offer the following scripting primitives[1]:

Entering a context:
```
// if the context is: T=h={(v,p)}
// if the situation v is indicated with a certainty of
// p or higher than p the action(i) is performed after
// n milliseconds, v is a situation, p is a number,
if enter(v, p, n) then perform action(i)
```

Leaving a context:
```
// if the context is: T=h={(v,p)}
// if the situation v is indicated with a certainty
// below p the action(i) is performed after n
// milliseconds, v is a situation, p is a number,
if leave(v, p, n) then perform action(i)
```

While in a context:
```
// if the context is: T=h={(v,p)}
// if the situation v is indicated with a certainty of
// p or higher than p the action(i) is performed every
// m milliseconds, v is a situation, p is a number,
if in(v, p, m) then perform action(i)
```

Beyond the defined scripting primitives the application programmer is free to use context knowledge in any part of the applications where it seems appropriate. A different approach is described by Brown et. al [2].

3   Feasibility Demonstration

The demonstrator described in this section was implemented to prove feasibility, gaining contextual knowledge using low level sensors. A main requirement for the prototype was flexibility to enable experiments with different sensors as well as a variety of recognition technologies.

The prototypical system was used in two phases. In the first phase data in several situational contexts were collected and than analyzed off-line. In the second phase the prototype was used for real-time context recognition.

3.1   Hardware

The individual sensors have been chosen to mimic typical human senses, as well as more subtle environmental parameters. An outline of the schematic is given in fig. 3.

---

[1] The parameter n indicating the time after that an action is performed is often 0 (immediate context action coupling) or positive. In certain circumstances, when future situations can be predicted (e.g. you drive your into the garage, the context 'walking' should appear soon) a negative value does make sense, too.

- The photodiode yields both a nominal light level (as experienced by humans) and any oscillations from artificial sources (not a human sense). It is sampled at a rate of approximately once per millisecond, but only for a few hundred milliseconds at a time, allowing other signals to be multiplexed in.
- The two accelerometers provide tilt and vibration measurements in two axes. Due to the limited sampling power of the current board, the signal is filtered down to 200 Hz, though the sensors are able to supply up to 1 kHz of signal.
- The passive IR sensor detects the proximity of humans or other heat-generating objects. The sensor provides a signal corresponding to the amount of IR received, possibly filtered for sensitivity to the human IR signal. This sensor is sampled at the same rate as the photodiodes.
- The temperature and pressure sensors each provide a conditioned signal between 0 and +5 volts directly, and need no amplification. These sensors are sampled a few times a second.
- Sampled at the same rate as the temperature and pressure sensors is a CO gas sensor. The PIC controls the heating and reading of this sensor.
- For sound, there is an omni-directional microphone that is directly connected to the computer.

Each of the sensors provides an analog signal between 0 and 5 volts which is read by the 8 bit, 8 channel analog-to-digital converter. The signals to the A/D converter are routed through switches that allow for off-board sensors also to be sampled. This makes the board expandable and gives the flexibility for testing new combinations of sensors.

Our first module needed to have flexibility, both in the sensors to be included on it, and the processing to be performed on the data collected. The architecture developed, whether for the first prototype or the final design, would have to follow a set protocol of development and communication that will become the standard for the duration of the project. Being a project based on sensor information the hardware architecture has to follow the basic principles of sensor based systems. The sensor information is sent as a signal to an input function. The input function prepares the signal for processing. The processing and amplification block translates the signals according to the individual sensor need and also to have uniform output signals for all sensors.

The processed signal then goes to an output function, which primes it for output reading or display. More accurately, the sensors measure conditions in the environment and translate them into analog voltage signals on a fixed scale. These analog signals are then converted to digital signals and passed to the micro-controller (PIC). The micro-controller oversees the timing of the analog-to-digital converter and the sensors as well as manipulating the data from the analog-to-digital converter's bus to the RS-232 serial line. Finally, the serial line connects to the data-gathering computer(Host).

The PIC acts as the brains of the board and executes a loop, polling the sensors through the analog-to-digital converter, and moving the data onto the RS-232 serial line. Higher bandwidth signals like the accelerometers and photodiodes are polled often, on the order of every millisecond, while slower signals like temperature are only polled once a second

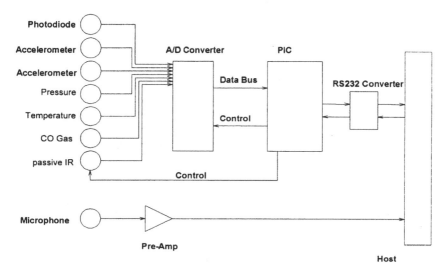

Fig. 3. Schematic of the sensor board.

Another requirement of the system is mobility. In order to simulate mobile devices the board also has to meet certain size constraints. The board is the standard Eurocard PCB size of 100mmx170 mm. At that size the board is less than half the size of a laptop. This allows for ease of movement when it comes to experimentation. The board can easily be connected, via serial cable, to a laptop for data gathering. The second phase of the project will produce an even more portable board with direct connection to the device.

3.2 Off-Line Data Analysis

As described before, the TEA sensor board sends periodically a large block of data, represent the digitized sensor outputs, through its serial port. In the experiments a portable computer is connected to this port, which makes it possible to receive and store the data. A piece of software was written for this purpose.

After this TEA reader software has made a datafile, the datafile can be analyzed to predict how a learning system could map the raw data to a context. One of the easiest and fastest methods to obtain this is by plotting the output of all sensors directly on a time scale in parallel (see fig. 4a).

This time series plot only shows the sensor values of the acceleration sensors and the light sensor in three different contexts. Initially, the TEA sensor board was placed on a table and remained there for about 100 seconds. After this period, the device was taken along and stayed in the hands of its user for another 100 seconds. Finally the TEA board was put in a suitcase for yet another 100 seconds.

The interesting thing about this plot is that the different contexts are immediately visible, while other types of plots experience problems with the high dimensionality of the data and are less clear. A phase space plot for instance, which is limited to three

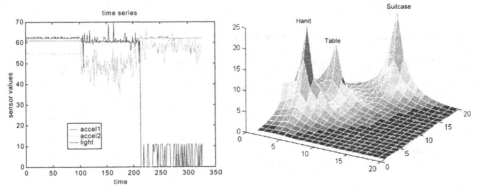

Fig. 4. a) Time series of sensor data,　　b) Kohonen Clustering of sensor readings

dimensions, is unable to visually represent the eight or more sensor values at every timestep.

The high number of sensors doesn't just cause a problem for the analysis of the sensor-outputs, it is also making the mapping phase difficult. For this reason, it is crucial to cluster the raw sensor data first, preferably with an adaptive clustering algorithm. Experiments with the Kohonen Self-Organizing Map and some of its variants show promising results. The Kohonen Map is an unsupervised neural network that is known to perform very well under noisy conditions. It clusters the values coming from the sensors onto a two-dimensional grid in an adaptive way (the cells in the grid – the neurons - 'learn' to respond better for a certain input). After the data is clustered into a low-dimensional discrete space, it has become significantly easier to process this data with symbolic AI techniques, such as predictive Markov Chains. Fig. 4b shows the clustering of a data set from our experiments is shown: the 20x20 grid depicts the Kohonen Map, while the z-axis represents the frequency of activation for every cell in the map. This way, the organization of the cells (or neurons) is visualized: three activity bubbles emerge representing the map responding to three contexts.

3.3　Online Recognition Software

Based on the experiments, methods have been developed and selected for the real-time recognition system. A set of functions to calculate cues as well as logical rules to determine contexts have been implemented.

Sensor to Cues Mapping. In the prototype the concept of cues proved to be very useful to make changes of the hardware transparent for the context recognition layer. When including new sensors with different characteristics only changes in the corresponding cues must be adapted. In our current implementation the cues are calculated on the notebook computer from the actual data read by physical sensors included in the hardware.

Cues are one way to reduce the amount of the data provided by the sensor board. In the current implementation we focus mainly on statistical functions. They can either provide a summary of the values over time or they help to extract features from the raw data that characterize the data over the last period of time. The following functions are used:

- **Average**. The average of the data items provided by a single sensor over a time frame of about one second is calculated. This is applied to data from the light, acceleration, temperature, and pressure sensor. For the acceleration sensor this value gives also the one angle of the device to the gravity vector.
- **Standard derivation**. Standard derivation for data read from the light, passive IR, and acceleration sensor is calculated over about one second.
- **Quartile distance**. For light, passive IR, and acceleration we sorted the data and calculate the distance between values at one quarter and three-quarter. This proved more reliable as using the range.
- **Base frequency**. For light and acceleration we calculate the base frequency of the signal. This provides useful information on the types of lights (flickering) and on activities such as walking (certain acceleration pattern).
- **First derivative**. For passive IR and acceleration we approximated the first derivative of data to gain an understanding of changes that happen.

In our prototypical implementation we calculate these cues in real time and provide the results in the context layer.

Cue to Context Mapping. A context is calculated on the notebook computer from the information delivered by cues. In our experiments we work with a number of context sets, all of them using exclusive contexts. Examples of these sets are:

(a) holding phone in hand vs. phone in a suitcase vs. phone on a table
(b) walking while using the device vs. stationary usage
(c) using the device inside vs. using the device outside
(d) in car vs. on a bus vs. on a train.
(e) having a phone in a stationary car vs. in a moving car

Working with exclusive contexts makes the development of the recognition algorithm easier and also simplifies the development of applications. In GSM-application we used two of the sets of exclusive contexts - (a) and (c) .

For the real-time recognition system used in the described prototype we used logical rules defined for each set of contexts to determine the current situation. In Table 1, a simplified rule set for the discrimination of situations in (a) is given. The recognition in this example is based on only three sensors: light, and acceleration in two directions (X and Y). The rules are built on observation of usage in certain contexts as well as from an analysis of the data collected in test scenarios. This data was also used to determine the constants used in the example (Dx, Dy, L, Xnormal, Ynormal, D, and Q).

```
Hand(t):-      standard_ deviation(accelX,t) > Dx,
               standard_ deviation(accelY,t) > Dy,
               % device is slightly moving in X and Y
               average(light,t)>L. % not totally dark
  Table(t):-   abs(average(accelX,t)-Xnormal)<D,
               abs(average(accelY,t)-Ynormal)<D,
               % the device is level in X and Y
               quartile(accelX,t)<Q, quartile(accelY,t)<Q
               % the device is stationary
               average(light,t)>L. % not totally dark
Suitcase(t):-      average(light,t)<L. % it is totally dark
```

Table 1. Simplified recognition rules for (a).

3.4   Initial Experimentation

We implemented experimental setups for a Palm Pilot PDA and for a mobile phone. In both cases the recognition software was running on a PC, to which both the TEA hardware and host device (GSM or PDA) are connected. Thus, the GSM setup consists of four objects: TEA Hardware, TEA Software (running on the PC), and the GSM Demo Software (running on Laptop) and the Nokia 6110 mobile phone. We performed two classes of experiments.

Experiment 1: adaptive context recognition. In the first experiment we wanted to test the robustness of the context classification when using the adaptive cue to context mapping (based on the Kohonen net). In a training phase data was collected while taking the board through a progression of contexts, related to being in the hand, being on the table, in light or in dark. The system succesfully clustered sensor reading into a two-dimensional grid in which areas of high-activation were seen to correspond to these contexts. It should be noted that parameter settings in the clustering algorithms (e.g. proximity) sometimes lead to the creation of spurious clusters. The labeling of these clusters was added by hand.

Then we tested the recognition of these contexts, when taking the board through similar (but not identical) context changes. In informal evaluation we observe a robust classification, estimated close to 90% when attempting to follow similar contexts as the ones in the training set.

Experiment 2: context-enhanced applications. In the second type of experiment we tested the full cascade of mappings from sensors to scripting, using the model-based cue to context mapping instead of the adaptive one. The context enhanced applications running on GSM or PDA received the information about the current situational context, from the recognition software. The application then decides how to adapt to this context. In the PDA scenario a notepad application was changed to adapt the fontsize to the users activity (when the user was walking a large font, small font when stationary) as well as to environmental conditions (e.g. light level). In the remainder of this section we will focus on the applications implemented for the mobile phone. Fig. 5 shows parts of the demo setup.

In the GSM scenario the profiles of the mobile phone were selected automatically based on the recognized context. Currently Profiles exist in most of Nokia mobile phones. These offer a way to personalize the behavior of mobile phone. For example, on some occasions the phone must ring as loud as possible (e.g. at Bar where is lot of noise), while in others the phone must be silent (e.g. library or movie theater). There are even cases when the phone must filter calls (e.g. a meeting where urgent home calls must get through), which can be done by using so called Caller groups, a feature that is supported when the operator provides CLI -functionality (Caller Line Identification). Profiles offer a direct and easy way to define these situations and the corresponding behaviors (what we have called scripts).

Contexts, as described in this paper, can be thought of much similar to the Profiles on Nokia phones. Profiles are currently hand selected from a menu. However, by using a device that is context sensitive and connecting that to a Nokia phone, the Profile (or Context) change can be automated. Automatic Profiles are one new type of applications that context sensitivity introduces.

For the experiment the following Profiles were defined on the Phone:

- **Hand**. When the user holds the phone in her/his hand, the audio alarm is not needed. The phone rings by vibrating.
- **Table**. Here we assume a meeting situation. The phone is almost silent. Incoming call is indicated by a very gentle sound.
- **Silent (pager)**. Phone is silent. Here we assume that the phone is put a way in a box or suitcase, and must be silent. The phone still receives calls, so that the callers' numbers can be recalled later.
- **Outside**. Here the ring volume goes as high as possible and vibra-alarm is on. All possible ways to get the users attention are used.
- **General**. General mode is used when none of the above apply.

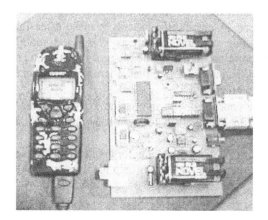

Fig. 5. Phone on a table together with the first prototypical sensor board. Phone in hand

The purpose of the demonstration was to automate the Nokia 6110 [7] Profile change, based on the cue-to-context mapping as defined in the Architecture section. The experiment was performed (in public) in a regular meeting room, by taking the TEA component from the table, in the hand, switching off the light, taking the board outside, and then in a suitcase. As expected the phone Profile followed the context of the TEA Hardware. For instance, when TEA Hardware was taken to hand the phone went to profile *Hand*. When left on the table the phone profile was *Table*.

Rule based recognition is limited by the validity of the model that it is based upon. Thus, there are at least three possible ways that recognition can fail:

1. Ambiguity. For instance, when it is very dark outside, the suitcase context may be erroneously recognized.
2. Operating close to boundary conditions. For instance, the model definition rely on threshold settings that make system behavior sensitive when operating close to them.
3. Undefined context model.

We will to tackle some of these problems in future work by combining adaptive and symbolic techniques, and by adding training and learning features to the system.

4.   Conclusion and Further Work

We proposed a layered architecture for a context-aware system based on sensors. The concepts of cue, context, and scripting are introduced. Implementing a prototype we demonstrated that it is feasible to recognize contexts with low-level sensors and that this information can be used to create new interaction metaphors. Taking the examples of a mobile phone and PDA, we showed that applications can be enhanced by context recognition.

In the next phase we will extend the recognition to more complex contexts, to context sets with a larger number of situations, and to non-exclusive contexts. We also will investigate efficient methods for the recognition process to make it feasible to include the TEA-component in mobile appliances such as PDAs and mobile phones. Currently we are developing a component that can be plugged into a phone or PDA to provide contextual information. Having a device that it is not an additional burden for the user we plan to make a usability study.

We would also like to introduce the concept of learning in the TEA-component. This will give the user the ability to induce appliances to learn individual and user specific situations.

Sensing User contexts (e.g. by bio sensors) will open doors for applications that are trying to guess user purposes. These applications may either help the user or provide additional information.

Acknowledgment

This work is founded by the project *Technology for Enabling Awareness* (TEA, [5]), situated in the European Commissions 'Fourth Framework' as part of the call 'Esprit for IT Mobility'. Many thanks to all partners in the project namely Starlab Nv/Sa (Belgium), Nokia Mobile Phones (Finland), TecO (Germany), and Omega Generation (Italy).

References

[1] Beadle, P., Harper, B., Maguire, G.Q. and Judge, J. Location Aware Mobile Computing. Proc. of IEEE Intl. Conference on Telecommunications, Melbourne, Australia, April 1997.

[2] Brown, P. J., Bovey, J. D., Chen, X. Context-Aware Applications: From the Laboratory to the Marketplace. IEEE Personal Communications, October 1997.

[3] Brown, P.J. The stick-e Dokument: A Frameowrk for creating context-aware Applications. Proc. EP'96, Palo Alto, CA. (published in EP-odds, vol 8. No 2, pp. 259-72) 1996.

[4] Cheverst K, Blair G, Davies N, and Friday A. Supporting Collaboration in Mobile-aware Groupware. Personal Technologies, Vol 3, No 1, March 1999.

[5] Esprit Project 26900. Technology for enabling Awareness (TEA). www.omega.it/tea/, 1998

[6] Leonhard, U., Magee, J., Dias, P. Location Service in Mobile Computing Environments. Computer & Graphics. Special Issue on Mobile Computing. Volume 20, Numer 5, September/October 1196.

[7] Nokia Mobile Phones. 6110 Mobile phone, http://www.nokia.com/phones/6110/index.html, 1998

[8] Norman, D. A. Why Interfaces Don't Work. The Art of Human-Computer Interface Design. Brenda Laurel (editor). Addison-Wesley. 1992.

[9] Harter, A. and Hopper, A. (1994). A Distributed Location System for the Active Office. IEEE Network, Vol. 8, No. 1, 1994.

[10] Salber, D., Dey, A.K., Abowd, G.D. The Context Toolkit: Aiding the Development of Context-Enabled Applications. In the Proceedings of CHI '99. May 1999.

[11] Schilit, B.N., Adams, N.L., Want, R. Context-Aware Computing Applications. Proc. of the Workshop on Mobile Computing Systems and Applications, Santa Cruz, CA, December 1994. IEEE Computer Society.

[12] Schmidt, A., Beigl, M., Gellersen, H.-W. There is more to context than location. Proc. of the Intl. Workshop on Interactive Applications of Mobile Computing (IMC98), Rostock, Germany, November 1998.

[13] Starner, T., Schiele, B., Pentland, A. Visual Contextual Awareness in Wearable Computing. Proceeding of the Second Int. Symposium on Wearable Computing. Pittsburgh, October 1998.

[14] Weiser, M. Some Computer Science Problems in Ubiquitous Computing, Communications of the ACM, July 1993.

Exploring Brick-Based Navigation and Composition in an Augmented Reality

Morten Fjeld[1], Fred Voorhorst[1], Martin Bichsel[2], Kristina Lauche[3], Matthias Rauterberg[4], and Helmut Krueger[1]

[1] Institute for Hygiene and Applied Physiology (IHA),
Swiss Federal Institute of Technology (ETH), Clausiusstr. 25, CH-8092 Zurich
{fjeld, voorhorst, krueger}@iha.bepr.ethz.ch
www.fjeld.ch
[2] Institute for Design and Construction Methods (IKB),
Swiss Federal Institute of Technology (ETH), Tannenstr. 3, CH-8092 Zurich
mbichsel@ikb.mavt.ethz.ch
[3] Institute for Work and Organisational Psychology (IfAP),
Swiss Federal Institute of Technology (ETH), Nelkenstr. 11, CH-8092 Zurich
lauche@ifap.bepr.ethz.ch
[4] Center for Research on User-System Interaction (IPO),
Technical University Eindhoven (TUE), Den Dolech 2, NL-5612 AZ Eindhoven
g.w.m.rauterberg@tue.nl

Abstract. BUILD-IT is a planning tool based on computer vision technology, supporting complex planning and composition tasks. A group of people, seated around a table, interact with objects in a virtual scene using real bricks. A plan view of the scene is projected onto the table, where object manipulation takes place. A perspective view is projected on the wall. The views are set by virtual cameras, having spatial attributes like *shift*, *rotation* and *zoom*. However, planar interaction with bricks provides only position and rotation information. Object height control is equally constrained by planar interaction. The aim of this paper is to suggest methods and tools bridging the gap between planar interaction and three-dimensional control. To control camera attributes, *active* objects, with intelligent behaviour are introduced. To control object height, several real and virtual tools are suggested. Some of the solutions are based on metaphors, like *window*, *sliding-ruler* and *floor*.

1 Introduction

BUILD-IT is a planning tool based on computer vision technology, with a capacity for complex planning and composition tasks [19] [20]. The system enables users, grouped around a table, to interact in a virtual scene, using real bricks to select and manipulate objects in the scene (Fig. 1). A *plan view* of the scene is projected onto the table. A perspective view of the scene, called *side view*, is projected on the wall. The plan view contains a storage space with originals, allowing users to create new objects. Object selection is done by putting a brick at the object position. Once selected, objects can be positioned, rotated and fixed by simple brick manipulation. They are de-selected, and stay put, when the brick is covered or lifted off the table. Objects brought back to the storage space are deleted from the views.

Fig. 1. BUILD-IT consists of a rack, mirror, table, chairs and a screen (top left). In addition to a high-end personal computer (PC), the rack contains two beamers, a video camera and a light-source (top right). The system offers a horizontal *plan view* for combined action and perception (bottom left), and a vertical *side view* with a perspective of the situation (bottom right).

Using the BUILD-IT system as a research platform for graspable interaction [8], our exploration takes the following path: Section 2 introduces some of the problems related to working in *real* and *virtual* environments, then indicates a few guidelines to achieve what we call *natural interaction*. Section 3 gives more details about the *interaction content*, which is configuration and planning tasks. Section 4 presents the interaction form, Augmented Reality (AR). Section 5 gives more detail on designing hand-held bricks for interaction. Section 6 presents some new implementations for three-dimensional (3D) navigation. Section 7 introduces alternative ways to control object height in the BUILD-IT system. Section 8 discusses the outcome of our design activity and suggests ways to advance the issues presented in Sections 6 and 7.

2 Working in Real and Virtual Environments

When people act, and interact, in a setting of real, tangible objects, we prefer to call this *natural behaviour*. Computer-supported group-work actually tends to bring people, physically, farther away from each other, setting them at remove from the concrete world. They interact with *virtual* objects and may even be totally engrossed in a *virtual world*. The larger aim of this project is to study ways to integrate real-world, *natural behaviour* with *computer-mediated work* in order to draw on the advantages of both these worlds.

First, we consider the characteristic features of natural behaviour. When people act in a real setting, they make *eye-contact, speak to each other* and *communicate through body language*. They can also *touch* each other and directly *manipulate* real-world objects. They may use the physical world as part of their memory and explore that world by direct interaction [25]. This fosters cooperative thinking, individual expression, and visualisation of ideas.

Using this sketch of natural behaviour as a guide, we sought feasible means of making interaction with virtual worlds more *natural*. We found it important to:

- support body motions and everyday skills [5]
- support haptic feedback [17]
- use real interaction handles with intelligent features
- connect real interaction-handles with virtual objects in a clear manner
- give consistent user feedback

Second, we chose to make the distinction between interaction *content* and *form*. *Content* refers to the kind of tasks that are being solved and the social setting under which they are performed. *Form* refers to such things as the layout of the human-computer interface, which kind of handles are being used and what kind of interaction features are offered.

Content: In this project, the kind of tasks to be solved are composition tasks with existing objects. Such objects have analogues in the real world, like chairs, machines and buildings, but neither molecules nor proteins. We study how subjects solve such tasks, both individually and in groups. The important criteria for successful task solving are given by users' task solving performance, which can be defined in various ways depending on the task.

Form: We work in the context of Augmented Reality (AR) where virtual objects and real objects are manipulated in one, coincident interaction-space. We study different ways of implementing real interaction handles and their connection to the virtual world. Also, we study different manners of navigation in the virtual word. Finally, we are interested in two-handed operations and how interaction can be designed to accommodate the dominant and non-dominant hand.

Based on the said dichotomy of content and form, we set out to explore possible implementations. The long-term aim is to determine what is a *good design strategy* for interfaces supporting *natural behaviour*. Thus we need a way to construe *natural* in terms of guidelines pertaining to interface design. Some of these *design guidelines* may be as follows:

- give visual feedback consistent with user expectation
- assure ease of navigation
- support exploratory behaviour and ensure that 'trying out' is a low risk activity
- draw on bimanual handling, adapted to dominant and non-dominant hand
- use real handles with clear explanations of their connection to the virtual world
- offer real handles as extended user memory

3 Interaction Content: Configuration and Planning Tasks

For most planning tasks in engineering and architecture systems, drawings and two-dimensional (2D) models have been replaced by Computer-Aided Design (CAD) system. This change has given raise to a range of supportive tools for drawing and information processing. However, this also entails less immediate contact among CAD users, planning experts and sales people.

First, we performed a task analysis with potential user groups for our system. We observed that they spent a great deal of time in discussions with their clients and noticed that off-line CAD support is hardly available during their sales trips. This lack of support sometimes caused misunderstandings with the designers at home, trying to communicate their solutions to the travelling sales people. Also, some of the customers were not familiar with 2D layout techniques; they were unable to imagine what an object would look like in three dimensions. Therefore, an easy-to-handle, three-dimensional (3D) planning tool proved to be attractive for planning experts and sales people. A distributed, networked system would additionally allow for interaction among users located at different sites.

Actually, modern management concepts like *simultaneous engineering* are based on dynamic interaction among cooperating experts. Simultaneous engineering goals are realised through an early involvement of different functions, like marketing and manufacturing. Many companies are forming multi-functional teams as a solution to rapid product development goals. For these teams to be significantly more successful than other organisational approaches, it is necessary to build a process around them that is appropriate for this new type of organisation structure. The process should encourage team-based cooperation rather than a one-person-one-screen set-up. Such requirements can hardly be met by existing technologies like video conferencing. Adequate solutions must offer more intuitive, natural interaction.

All of these considerations were taken into account in the designing of the BUILD-IT technology. The result was a system supporting early offering and design processes. This apparatus is not intended as an alternative, but rather as a complement to CAD systems. It allows for ready-made applications in various fields, such as machine configuration, city and urban planning, architecture and interior design.

4 Interaction Form: Brick-Based Augmented Reality

Computer-supported group work has allowed for distant and asynchronous communication between people and has helped build bridges in our global economy. This has brought about many well-advertised advantages, ranging from economic benefit to less status-oriented network communication. However, with many computer applications users hardly interact with their physical environment. They deal with virtual objects only, which is also the case for most single-user applications. Sometimes users are even embedded in a fully virtual world, unable to draw on any attributes of the tangible world. Much of the users' mental capacity is employed to adapt to the virtual world, leaving less capacity for actual task solving.

An alternative approach is to bring the *virtual* world of computers into the *real* world of everyday human activity. This approach includes aspects of natural communication which serve as mediators for mutual understanding: eye-contact, body language and physical object handling. It is *non-intrusive*, using no gloves or helmets, and thereby respects the body-space [21]. At the same time users can still draw on the advantages of a virtually enriched world, which is of particular importance to planning tasks. The activity of planning is intrinsically virtual because it involves reflecting on and modifying objects that only exist in the future. Virtual objects can be more easily changed than physical objects, can be stored in external computer memory and can be visualised for interaction purposes. Thus both physical and virtual methods have their rightful place in a planning process. A specific aim of our project is to study ways to integrate the real-world and computer-mediated activity. This is how we came to work within the tradition of AR, where computer-generated and real-world objects are handled in one workspace.

Fig. 2. AR means that a real workspace (left) is augmented, or enriched, by a virtual world (right). Even when users interact with the projected, virtual objects, they do not leave the real world context (e.g. sketching) and tools (e.g. pencil).

AR was first described by Wellner et al. [24]. The goal of AR is to "allow users to continue to use the ordinary, everyday objects they encounter in their daily work and then to enhance or augment them with functionality from the computer" [16]. According to Mackay [16], AR means that computer information is projected onto drawings so that users can interact with both the projected information and the paper drawing (Fig. 2). The first brick-based AR system was described by Firtzmaurice et al. [6] using tethered bricks. Wireless brick-based system were also described by Ishii and Ullmer [12] and Underkoffler and Ishii [22].

4.1 The BUILD-IT System

Compared with physical, model-based layout systems, BUILD-IT offers cheaper, quicker and more exact object representation. Based on a 3D multimedia framework [MET++, 1], the system can read and display arbitrary objects. Employing Virtual Reality Modelling Language (VRML), these objects are sent from a CAD system to BUILD-IT. After a planning session, the results can be sent back to the CAD system [10].

Geometry is not the only aspect of product data. With a growing need to interact in other dimensions, such as cost and configurations, the system has been engineered to send and receive numerous forms of meta-data [10]. The potential of computer-mediated work is made readily available through automatic calculation of prices and time-to-delivery. Also, animation of objects, like robots and laser welders, combined with plant configuration, allow for live simulation [9] of production cycles.

So far, the system is a multi-user, single-site interaction tool. However, the *interaction methods* realised thus far are capable of supporting distributed networking systems. Based on this system, Sections 5-7 offer a tour through some of the recent design cycles.

5 Designing and Using Bricks

In BUILD-IT mediation between users and virtual worlds follows a cyclic order (Fig. 3). Users select an object by putting the brick at an object position. The object can be positioned, rotated and fixed by simple brick manipulation. An object is deselected by covering the brick. Then, another object is selected or the brick is left idle inside or outside the plan view. It was shown that a brick-based interface is significantly easier to use and more intuitive than a mouse-keyboard-screen [18].

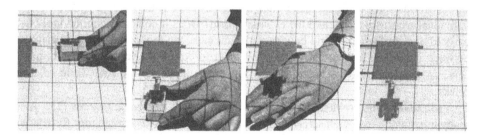

Fig. 3. The basic steps for user manipulations with the brick.

Bricks are handheld mediators linking a virtual world with the physical world. We aim for brick forms inviting users to perform manipulations like grasping, moving, rotating and covering. Since all the steps in the described cycle are reversible, the cost of making a mistake is low. Thus, exploratory epistemic and goal-directed pragmatic actions [14] are equally supported. Bricks can be left and picked up later anywhere in the plan view, serving as ubiquitous extended user memory (Fig. 2).

The detection of the brick is achieved by using infra-red light and retro-reflective paper [4]. The light is reflected by the paper, then picked up by an infra-red camera which in turn triggers an update of the computer image. There are only a few constraints on *brick size* and *shape*. For instance, the reflective area must exceed a two by three centimetre size. With such modest technical limitations, the major question is how to design bricks so that people can move real bricks and simultaneously immerse themselves in a virtual setting. We performed some exploratory brick modelling [15], based on different materials, forms and metaphors (Fig. 4, left).

The first feasible brick was the *block* (Fig. 4, right). The advantages of this shape is that users grasp the brick easily and that image detection is simple. However, due to the height of the brick, the image projected upon it is distorted. Therefore the brick is not always suited to mediate fluently between users and the virtual world.

 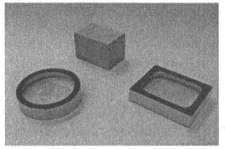

Fig. 4. In the beginning we experimented with different bricks, based on different materials, forms and metaphors (left). The first feasible brick was the *block* (right). The more recent *circular* and *rectangular* bricks (right) are based on the principle of *reduction screen*.

To solve such a problem Kaptelinin [13] suggested: "deal with two interfaces instead of one user interface, with two borders, separating (1) the user from the computer and (2) the user *and* the computer from the outside world". This situation is similar to Bateson's [3] blind man's stick dilemma: where is the boundary between the individual who uses a tool and the external world? Does it coincide with the individual-tool or with the tool-world boundary? In our case, the tool is the brick, mediating between individual and virtual worlds. We want to design a brick so that users perceive interaction with the virtual world, not interaction with the real world of the bricks.

A solution to this problem can be found by employing a *reduction screen* [23]. Already in common use, such screens are *borders* placed in front of a monitor to reduce flattening cues. The same idea can be used to make the brick like an open box with a narrow black border on the edge (Fig. 4, right). For users, the bottom of the box-like brick is indistinguishable from the table surface and image distortion is minimised.

A final aspect of using bricks, is how they actually connect with the virtual world. At the moment of selecting a virtual object with a real brick, a planar relation - in terms of position and rotation - is established between real and virtual. We call this a *locking mechanism*. A *locking mechanism* determines how a real brick and a virtual object stay connected from the moment of selection until the moment of de-selection.

For different brick forms appropriate locking mechanisms must be defined. For instance, the virtual object may align with the brick, its centerpoint may move to the centerpoint of the brick or both.

6 Spatial Navigation: Controlling Shift, Rotation and Zoom

Some basic aspects of 2D, brick-based interaction were previously explored [7]. Bimanual camera control and object manipulation in 3D graphics interfaces were also explored [2], using two mice, keyboard and screen. The innovative feature of BUILD-IT, beyond the brick-based interaction, is that the objects are part of a 3D scene. The use of the multimedia framework [MET++, 1], allows for full 3D interaction, including *shift, rotation, zoom, tilt* and *roll*. However, planar interaction with bricks provides only position and rotation information. Hence, there is a need to bridge the gap between planar interaction and 3D view control.

The exploration of an environment, or a product, is important in a range of composition and planning tasks, e.g. design of production lines, architecture and industrial design. To explore a 3D virtual world, it is essential to assume different point of views, to take an overview and to look at things in detail. This, at least, calls for a direct control of *shift, rotation* and *zoom* in *both views*.

One strategy which we considered was the use of a specialised brick, which would control a side view camera. This would require extending the properties sensed by the computer vision input. We want to explore software solutions, so this approach was not pursued. Instead, *active* virtual objects were introduced. *Active* objects feature *intelligent behaviour* and support *complex operations*.

Employing active objects, plan- and side view control were implemented. For each view, two alternative methods will be explored: GroundCatcher and FrameCatcher for the plan view, Camera and Window for the side view. Two of the methods, Ground-Catcher and Window, are based on *scene* handling. The other two, FrameCatcher and Camera, are based on what shall be called *observer* handling.

6.1 Plan View Control: GroundCatcher and FrameCatcher

One brick offers shift and rotation, a second brick adds zoom (Table 1). Zoom is given by brick movements along a connecting line; other movements give shift and/or rotation. GroundCatcher (Fig. 5) updates the scene according to user action. One quits by removing bricks. FrameCatcher (Fig. 6) updates a frame of interest according to user action. When bricks are removed, the scene adjusts to the frame. Objects have no real-world analogues.

Table 1. GroundCatcher and FrameCatcher

		Shift	*Rotate*	*Zoom*
Ground Catcher	User action	⬒→	↶⬒	←⬒ ⊙ ⬒→
	Scene	→	⌒	← →
Frame Catcher	User action	⬒→	↶⬒	←⬒ ⊙ ⬒→
	Scene	←	⌒	→ ←

⊙ = zoom fix-point

Fig. 5. GroundCatcher: Introducing, using, and removing bricks (left to right).

Fig. 6. FrameCatcher: Introducing, using, and removing bricks (left to right).

6.2 Side View Control: Camera and Window

Both these objects are fixed at the approximate height of a person's eyes, 1.6 meter above the ground. One brick offers shift and rotation, a second brick adds zoom (Table 2). Camera (Fig. 7) sets the virtual camera of the side view. Handle distance sets zoom. Window (Fig. 8) sets the side view border. Scaling it sets the zoom.

111

Table 2. Camera and Window.

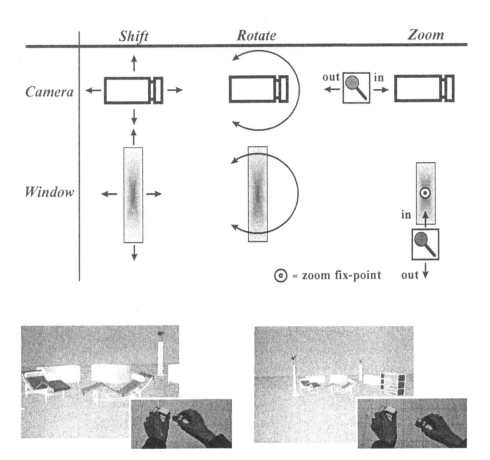

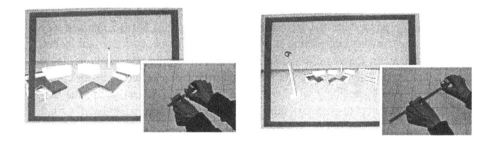

Fig. 7. Camera handling: Zooming in (left) and out (right).

Fig. 8. Window handling: Zooming in (left) and out (right).

7 Object Height Control

The need to set object height, or more generally, to handle a ground level where objects sit, is our concern for the rest of this paper. The instrument was developed from a virtual tool, used for scrolling the side view and for setting object height, to a set of real tools working on a grid-based floor, before integrating all these features into one single virtual tool.

7.1 A Virtual Prototype for Height Manipulation

Side view control was first achieved by copying a section of the side view, called *height slice*, onto the table (Fig. 9). Scrolling the side view is performed by putting a brick at the upper (scroll up) or lower (scroll down) edge of the *height slice*. When the brick is away from these edges, objects can be selected, and moved up and down.

Fig. 9. Scrolling the side view by putting a brick at the height slice corner; moving an object in the height slice; perceiving the moved object in the side view (left to right).

7.2 Using Real Tools to Control the Third Dimension

Based on real tools (Fig. 10), we explored three ways to *physically* handle object height. We tried to get closer to the principle of *coinciding action and perception spaces* [18]. *Digit*, a digital controller, works on selected objects and sets their height according to up-down buttons. *Tower* offers the same buttons but is combined with a luminous scale showing current height. The up-down buttons and the visual feedback are organized along the height axis, so action and perception are partly coincident. *Slider* is a vertical sliding-rule, where height is handled *and* indicated by an up-down handle. With *Slider*, handling and height cues are both organized along the height axis; thus action and perception are fully coincident. The actual height handling in the virtual setting is carried out by a virtual floor, which is called *Floor* and described below. The problematic aspect of this solution was that these tools require serial interfaces (RS 232, bi-directional, 9600 Baud) with the BUILD-IT system. Also, they rely on battery driven remote control. Hence, we looked for a software solution.

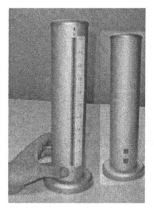

Fig. 10. Real height tools: *Digit*, a box with up-down buttons; *Tower*, a luminous scale with up-down buttons; *Slider*, a sliding-ruler with up-down handle and digital display (left to right).

7.3 Back to the Virtual: A Concept for Floor Handling

The resulting solution for placement and manipulation of objects among multiple stories is a fully virtual solution. It reuses the *height slice* from the first solution and *Floor* from the second solution. Hence, it integrates the knowledge acquired in the previous steps.

Floor is handled in the *height slice*, located along one edge of the plan view. The objects selected are all assembled on one storey. This assembly of selected objects then moves vertically as a whole when *Floor* is moved upwards or downwards (Figs. 11-12). De-selected objects are unloaded at the desired storey. Only objects at or above *Floor* are visible. To support multi-storey planning, we also offer a virtual ceiling, which is called *Ceiling*. *Ceiling* is also handled in the *height slice* and only objects below *Ceiling* are visible. Hence, by using *Floor* and *Ceiling*, objects within one storey can be *focused* and handled in the plan view. In the case of the side view, all stories are visible. *Ceiling* does not affect the side view.

A requirement for *Floor* and *Ceiling* to be developed was that the system should offer what we will call *dynamic control of clipping planes*. This technology is employed in the following way: *Floor* and *Ceiling* are each connected with a clipping plane so that only *focused* objects are visible.

When *Camera*, or *Window*, is selected, it also follows *Floor*, updating the side view content (Fig. 12).

In some cases work with a complete building where roof and walls are part of the CAD model. To see different levels, an empty *Floor* can be raised to traverse different stories of the building (Fig. 13). When *Floor* is raised *Ceiling* automatically follows.

Fig. 11. Floor and object handling in the plan view: Normal object handling; selecting *floor*; raising *floor* with selected objects (left to right).

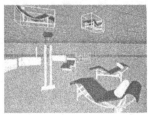

Fig. 12. Floor handling as seen in the side view: Normal object handling; raising *floor* with selected objects; raising *floor* with objects *and* Camera selected (left to right).

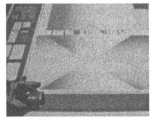

Fig. 13. Floor handling as an aid for inspection: Selecting *floor*; raising *floor* to roof-level; raising *floor* through roof-level (left to right).

8 Discussion and Perspectives

The navigation methods (Section 6) will be followed up by an evaluation of the different design strategies. First, *inspection tasks*, conducive to exploration, will be developed. With these tasks, users are offered *one* (plan *or* side view), *two* (plan *and* side view), or *alternative* (more than two) control methods. For each set-up, mean task completion time will give *quantitative data*. For *subjective evaluation*, participants will be asked to rate their preference of each method after the experiments. We conjecture that methods based on *scene* handling are better than methods based on *ob-*

server handling. Second, *composition task* experiments, following the same set-up, are planned.

Rotation with one brick requires an oriented brick form. GroundCatcher or Frame-Catcher using two bricks do not rely on brick orientation. So it may be of interest to fit *form* to *operation*, by employing rectangular and circular bricks.

Zoom may be controlled by *one* or *both* bricks, raising the topic of *asymmetry* [11]. The same applies to the functions *tilt* and *roll*. Sets of these functions, and their relation to one- or two-handed interaction, will be explored in future research. The concept of time- and space-multiplexed input [7] may prove fruitful in this regard.

The need to control object height (Section 7) was first met with a virtual method, and then triggered the realisation of real tools, before it was answered with virtual floor handling. This *cycle* may indicate a future design strategy. To evaluate the outcome of that *cycle*, usability studies must be carried out. Also, a seamless integration of Floor with the spatial navigation methods (Section 6) is required.

The structure of *scene* and *observer* handling (Section 6.1) may actually be valid for virtual floor handling as well. In the plan view, Floor and clipping-plane are connected, so scene *and* observer are handled together (Figs. 11, 13). In the side view (Fig. 12), *scene* is always handled, *observer* is only handled when Camera, or Window, is selected.

In this paper, the names of certain tools were somewhat metaphorical, such as *window*, *sliding-ruler* and *floor*. It may be of interest to know more about the consequences of using metaphors, for user behaviour *and* for our design activity.

Guided by the suggested *design guidelines* (Section 2), the tools and methods presented are subject to usability studies. At the same time, the value of the indicated guidelines may turn out clearer.

References

1. Ackermann, P.: Developing Object-Oriented Multimedia Software. dpunkt Verlag für digitale Technologie, Heidelberg (1996)
2. Balakrishnan, R., Kurtenbach, G.: Exploring bimanual camera control and object manipulation in 3D graphics interfaces. Proceedings of the CHI'99, ACM, NY (1999) 56-63
3. Bateson, G.: Steps to an ecology of Mind. Ballantine Books, NY (1972)
4. Bichsel, M.: Personal communications (1997)
5. Campbell, J.: Training design for performance improvement. In Campbell, J, Campbell, R. (eds.): Productivity in organisations. San Francisco, Jossey-Bass. (1988) 177-216
6. Fitzmaurice, G., Ishii, H., Buxton, W.: Bricks: Lay-ing the Foundations for Graspable User Inter-faces. Proceedings of the CHI'95. ACM, NY (1995) 442-449
7. Fitzmaurice, G. W.: Graspable User Interfaces. PhD at the University of Toronto, Toronto (1996) Ch. 7
8. Fjeld, M., Bichsel, M., Rauterberg, M.: BUILD-IT: An Intuitive Design Tool Based on Direct Object Manipulation. In: Wachsmut, I., Frölich, M. (eds.): Gesture and Sign Language in Human-Computer Interaction. Lecture Notes in Artificial Intelligence, Vol. 1371. Springer-Verlag, Berlin Heidelberg NY (1998) 297-308

9. Fjeld, M., Jourdan, F., Bichsel, M., Rauterberg, M.: BUILD-IT: an intuitive simulation tool for multi-expert layout processes. In Engeli, M., Hrdliczka, V. (eds.): Fortschritte in der Simulationstechnik (ASIM). vdf Hochschuleverlag AG, Zurich (1998) 411-418

10. Fjeld, M., Lauche, K., Dierssen, S., Bichsel, M., Rauterberg, M.: BUILD-IT: A Brick-based integral Solution Supporting Multidisciplinary Design Tasks. In Sutcliffe, A., Ziegler, J., Johnson, P. (eds.): Designing Effective and Usable Multimedia Systems (IFIP 13.2). Kluwer Academic Publishers, Boston (1998) 131-142

11. Guiard, Y.: Asymmetric division of labour in human skilled bimanual action: The kinematic chain as a model. Journal of Motor Behaviour, Vol. 19. (1987) 486-517

12. Ishii, H., Ullmer, B. Tangible Bits: Towards Seamless Interfaces between People, Bits and Atoms. Proceedings of the CHI'97. ACM, NY (1997)

13. Kaptelinin, V.: Computer-Mediated Activity: Functional Organs in Social and Developmental Contexts. In B. Nardi (ed.) Context and Consciousness, MIT Press, MA (1996) 50

14. Kirsh, D., Maglio, P. On Distinguishing Epistemic from Pragmatic Action. Cognitive Science, 18, (1994) 513-549

15. Lauche, K.: Personal communications (1998)

16. Mackay, W.E., Pagani, D.S., Faber, L., Inwood, B., Launiainen, P., Brenta, L., Pouzol, V.: Ariel: Augmenting Paper Engineering Drawings. Proceedings of the CHI'95, video program, ACM, NY (1995)

17. Mackenzie, C., Iberall, T.: The grasping hand. Elsevier. (1994) 15

18. Rauterberg, M., Mauch, T., Stebler, R.: What is a promising candidate for the next generation of interface technology. Proceedings of the 5th International Conference INTERFACE to Real and Virtual Worlds. EC2 & Cie., Montpellier (1996) 95-103

19. Rauterberg, M., Bichsel, M., Meier, M., Fjeld, M.: A gesture based interaction technique for a planning tool for construction and design. Proceedings of the RO-MAN'97. IEEE. (1997) 212-217

20. Rauterberg, M., Fjeld, M., Krueger, H., Bichsel, M., Leonhardt U., Meier M.: BUILD-IT: A Planning Tool for Construction and Design. Proceedings of the CHI'98, video program, ACM, NY (1998)

21. Rauterberg, M.: Personal communications (1999)

22. Underkoffler, J., Ishii, H.: Illuminating Light: An Optical Design Tool with Physical Interface. Proceedings of the CHI'98, ACM, NY (1998)

23. Voorhorst, F.: Personal communications (1999)

24. Wellner, P., Mackay, W., Gold, R.: Computer Augmented Environments: Back to the Real World. In Communications of the ACM, July, Vol. 36, No. 7, (1993) 24-26

25. Winograd, T., Flores, C. F.: Understanding computers and cognition: a new foundation for design. Ablex publishing corporation. (1986) 97

Acknowledgements

We thank Peter Troxler (peter@klapt.ch) for the photos (Figs. 1-3, 8) and Scott Stapleford (Philosophy, www.uwo.ca) for the editorial assistance. BUILD-IT is funded by The Swiss Federal Commission for Technology and Innovation (KTI), The Center for Integrated Production Systems (ZIP) at ETH Zurich, and The Institute for Design and Construction Methods (IKB) at ETH Zurich. Morten Fjeld thanks the Research Council of Norway (www.forskningsradet.no) for his Ph.D. fellowship. BUILD-IT is a registered trademark of TellWare (info@tellware.com).

Handheld Computing Predictions: What Went Wrong?

Jonathan P. Allen[1]

[1] Judge Institute of Management Studies, University of Cambridge,
Cambridge CB2 1AG, UK
jpa@eng.cam.ac.uk

Abstract. Handheld computers have been criticized as one of the most excessively hyped new IT products of all time. This paper looks at handheld computing predictions made over a 10 year period, investigating what went wrong, and what went right, with handheld computing predictions. Handheld computing predictions can be divided into three phases, depending on the product concept definition widely held at the time: handheld computers as pen-based computers, personal digital assistants, or handheld companions. While longer-term predictions were inflated in the first stage, they were surprisingly accurate in the second stage and excessively conservative in the third stage. The complaints about over enthusiasm and hype have more to do with incorrect product concept assumptions than poor guesses about the size of markets—technology directions are just as difficult to predict, or even more difficult, than technology sales.

1 Introduction

Handheld computers have been criticized as one of the most excessively hyped new IT products of all time (e.g., [3]). The disappointing market performance of the Apple Newton MessagePad was often highlighted as a symbol of computer industry hype spinning out of control, though almost all the major personal computing companies in the early 1990's (including Apple, Microsoft, IBM, Tandy, and AT&T), in addition to some well funded start-up companies (such as Go and Momenta), suffered from high-profile disappointments in this industry. The most famous prediction about handheld computing was attributed to John Sculley, then CEO of Apple Computer, who was said to have claimed the Personal Digital Assistant (PDA) market would grow to $3.5 trillion. Sculley denies ever making this overly optimistic prediction [5], but the widespread repetition of this claim indicates how disappointed many observers were with the early handheld computer industry.

This paper looks at handheld computing predictions made over a 10 year period, investigating what went wrong, and what went right, with handheld computing predictions. With the benefit of hindsight, what can be said about these predictions? How wrong were they? And did they come close to envisioning the increasingly successful handheld computer industry found today? An important idea used in this study, borrowed from studies of the history and sociology of technology, is that technologies are developed by communities with conceptions of the problem that a new technology is trying to solve, and the key performance criteria that follow from a particular product concept definition [2]. While the 'winning' technology ideas seem obvious in retrospect, it was not obvious in the early 1990's that handheld computers were better seen as companions to existing PCs than as stand-alone consumer devices, or that handwriting recognition or wireless communications would not be the most crucial technological features for market acceptance. The numerical forecasts of the size of the handheld computing market appear, in retrospect, to be surprisingly accurate, despite the complaints about hype and technology fads. What proved to be inaccurate in the early forecasts were the assumptions about product concept definition—an understanding of what exactly a handheld computer should be.

Why is examining emerging technology predictions important? There are at least two good reasons: one to do with expectations management, and another, more fundamental concern with the impact of events early in a technology's development. The expectations management problem is the issued raised by most industry observers. If a new technology is excessively hyped, disappointment inevitably follows, and development of a new technology may be slowed or abandoned. A more fundamental reason, however, for studying emerging IT predictions is the argument that events early in the life of an emerging technology have a disproportionate effect on its later development [4]. A choice of a particular standard (e.g., the QWERTY keyboard), a business partnership, or a key customer at a critical moment could, according to this argument, may have a substantial impact on what the technology eventually becomes. To the extent that visions or predictions of technology futures affect these early events, predictions are important.

2 Handheld Computing Predictions Data

Data on handheld computing predictions was taken from a search of the ABI/Inform Global article database. 2528 articles on handheld computing, pen computing, palmtops, and personal digital assistants were found in the database between 1987 and 1997. This study extracted published numerical predictions that were made three or more years into the future. This data is summarized in table 1.

Table 1. Handheld computing predictions, three or more years in advance.

Year	Projected Units	Product Definition	Source	Publication
2001	13m	handhelds	IDC	Infoworld, May 18 98
2000	2.4m	PDA, US	Yankee Group	InformationWeek, 22 Jul 96
2000	5m	handhelds	Dataquest	Ziff-Davis UK, 4 Jun 1997
1999	2.7m	handhelds	Dataquest	Guardian (London), 1 Aug 96
1999	1.6m	handhelds	Microsoft	Computer Reseller News, Apr 18 94
1999	4.84m	PDA	Forrester	Computer Reseller News, Sep 26 94
1998	5m	PDA	Link Resources	Upside, June 1994
1998	1.36m	PDA, US	BIS	Computer Reseller News, Sep 26 94
1997	1.4m	PDA	BIS	Computer Reseller News, Apr 18 94
1997	2.6m	PDA	BIS	Computer Reseller News, Feb 21 94
1995	6.1m	pen-based	Dataquest	Sales & Marketing Mgmt Feb 91
1995	2m	pen-based	Infocorp	Computerworld, June 3 91
1995	1m	pen-based	BIS	Advertising Age, Nov 11 91

1995	4m	pen-based	Dataquest	Business Week Mar 30, 92
1995	70m	PDA	Technologic	Computerworld, Aug 31 92
1994	3.2m	hand-held	Dataquest	Sales & Marketing Mgmt Feb 91

The handheld computing predictions can be divided into three distinct periods, based on the most common definition of what the product category was assumed to be. Though these products were always assumed to be highly portable, and were computing devices, the names given to them varied over time. Predictions before 1992 tended to focus on handheld computers being pen-based. Predictions made around 1994 tended to define handhelds as Personal Digital Assistants (PDAs), while predictions afterwards used the label handheld computer or handheld companion.

While longer-term predictions about the handheld computer market were inflated in the first stage (the pen-based stage), they were surprisingly accurate in the second stage (the PDA stage), and even became excessively conservative in the third stage (the handheld stage). Figure 1 plots these numerical predictions against the actual size of the world handheld computing market, as reported by Dataquest.

Handheld Computer Sales Forecasts (Units)

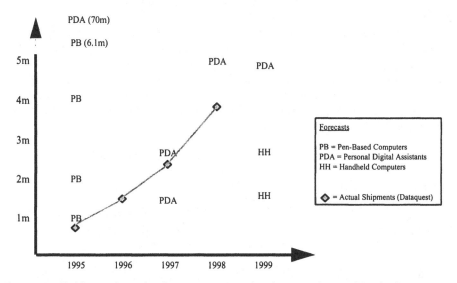

Fig. 1. Handheld computer sales forecasts appear to be almost random, unless the forecasts are classified by product concept definition. The first definition (pen-based) results in overestimates, the second definition (personal digital assistants) is not as inaccurate as often suggested, and the third definition (handhelds) is conservative

During the period when handheld computers were assumed to be primarily pen-based computers, the predictions of future market size can be fairly criticized for being both highly variable and too inflated. One prediction of 70 million PDAs by the year 1995 falls into the category of pure fantasy. Yet, by 1994, when the industry began to talk about the importance of PDAs more generally, the widely published long term predictions for the handheld computing industry were impressively accurate. By the time that industry analysts began to concentrate on the idea of handheld computers, or handheld companions, the predictions were, if anything, too conservative.

So, while handheld computing predictions could be accused of hype during the earliest years of the decade, the strictly numerical estimates appear to be reasonable in retrospect, particularly during the second and third phases. Why, then, are there so many complaints about the handheld industry making poor predictions about the future? To help answer this question, we need to look at not just the size estimates of an emerging market, but predictions about what problem the technology should be solving, and what the key performance criteria of a handheld computer should be.

3 Product Concept Definitions and IT Predictions

The complaints about over enthusiasm and hype may have more to do with incorrect product concept assumptions than poor guesses about the size of future markets. The early industry did a better job than is often supposed of predicting the size and importance of its future market. The industry did a relatively poor job with the difficult task of predicting what the key performance criteria would be for market acceptance.

If we accept the suggestion of technology historians and sociologists to look at the assumptions about the problem a new technology is trying to solve [2], we can see that the most commonly discussed assumptions about handheld computers tended to cluster around particular ideas, but were also liable to change rapidly. Table 2 summarizes the major product concept definitions found in the early handheld computing industry, taken from a more detailed analysis of the ABI/Inform database information [1].

Table 2. Product concept definitions in the early handheld computer industry.

Definition	Problem	Key Performance Criteria	Examples
Palmtop Computers	*Very small computers*	• Size • Computing power • Computer applications	Atari Portfolio (1989) HP 95LX (1991) Poqet PC (1989) Psion Series 3 (1991)
Pen-Based Computers	*Information for mobile workers and technophobes*	• Pen input (handwriting recognition) • Intelligent assistance (mass consumer)	Apple Newton MessagePad (1993) Casio/Tandy Zoomer (1993) GRiD Convertible (1992) Sharp ExpertPad (1993)
Communicators	*Portable wireless connectivity*	• Wireless link • Telephony applications • Pen input	EO Personal Communicator (1993) Motorola Envoy (1995) Motorola Marco (1995) Sony MagicLink (1994)

Handheld Companions	*Small devices that complement personal computers*	• Synchronization • Organizer applications • Computer applications	Franklin REX (1997) HP 320LX (1997) PalmPilot (1996) Sharp SE-500 (1997)

This analysis of the early handheld computing industry identifies four commonly held sets of assumptions about the problem that handhelds were trying to solve. The first commonly held definition, palmtop computers, assumed that handheld computers were supposed to be miniature versions of personal computers. The key performance criteria were size, of course, but also traditional personal computing criteria such as processor speed, RAM, and standard operating systems. The product lines that were launched during this period, mostly from the year 1991 and earlier, all share the appearance of being a very small notebook computer, with a tiny screen and a tiny keyboard.

The handheld computing predictions examined in this paper begin with the second definition of handhelds as pen-based computers. The assumptions about key performance criteria changed during this period. Pen-based input was widely seen as the defining feature of handheld computing, and both handwriting recognition and intelligent assistance were seen as critical to market acceptance. Pen-based computers were intended for mobile workers, but also for technophobes who were intimidated by computers and keyboards.

As the first generation of pen-based computers for the mass market ran into sales difficulties, the more generic idea of a Personal Digital Assistant became more widespread. Along with the PDA concept came a widely held view that the key to handheld computing would be portable wireless connectivity. While pen input remained important, communications ability became the most critical performance criteria during this period.

It was only by 1996, with the introduction of handheld computers such as the PalmPilot, that the dominant assumptions about handheld computing changed yet again in the industry. The newer definition, which was referred to as handhelds, or handheld companions, saw handheld devices as complements to personal computers, rather than replacements. Seamless synchronization and personal organizer applications became seen as the key performance criteria. Ideas about form factor and input method became more varied.

In retrospect, it appears that the difficult aspect of predicting the future of handheld computing was not estimating the overall size of the market, but predicting what the accepted product concept definition would be, and therefore what the key performance criteria would become. Early product concept definitions around pen-based input and wireless communications led many industry players to pursue the development of those technologies, at the expense of others. The PalmPilot of 1996, for example, featured only the most rudimentary handwriting recognition, little in the way of computing power, a non-standard operating system, no wireless connectivity, and assumed the user of a handheld already had a personal computer. This is what the industry found so difficult to predict.

4 Conclusion

What went wrong with handheld computing predictions? According to this analysis, predictions about the size of the market improved over time, and even became excessively conservative. This suggests that even in evolving, highly uncertain technology industries, it is possible to talk about the general importance and significance of new product categories. Where the industry fared much more poorly was in predicting the product concept definition that would become commercially dominant. Industry thinking had a tendency to lock on to product concept definitions that were eventually unsuccessful commercially.

Obviously, predicting the future of technology is extremely difficult. Being flexible about uncertain futures can be a useful strategy. And yet, in fast-moving emerging industries, there must be some level of bold and sustained commitment to a new technology, based on educated guesses about the future. The first step towards understanding and improving how people think about technological futures is to look at past performance: what was predicted relatively well? What was predicted relatively poorly? And what were the common pitfalls or traps? This research argues that in the early handheld industry, predictions about the significance of a broad technological area were much better than predictions about which key performance criteria would become the most important. Beliefs in the industry about the appropriate definition of a handheld computer changed substantially, rapidly, and certainly more than once, over a 10 year period. One possible implication is that participants in an emerging industry should be more confident about the potential of new technology areas, while at the same time be more flexible about specific product concept definitions and application areas.

Before the process of predicting technology futures can be improved, however, we need to know much more about how companies and industries form their understanding of appropriate product concept definitions. This would require an analysis of the interaction between producer, expert, investor, and consumer understandings of a technology in wider communities [4], forcing researchers to look beyond the usual interest in the internal connection between product development and marketing in individual companies. Clearly, the companies who have had the most influence over this industry to date have not been the biggest, or possessed the most leading-edge technology, but they certainly have been successful at identifying product concepts and redefining the vision around new technologies.[1]

References

1. Allen, J.P.: Who Shapes the Future? Problem Framings and the Development of Handheld Computers. Computers and Society, June (1998) 3-8
2. Bijker, W.E.: Of Bicycles, Bakelite, and Bulbs. Toward a Theory of Sociotechnical Change. MIT Press, Cambridge Massachusetts (1995)

---

[1] This research was supported by the UK Economic and Social Research Council 's (ESRC) Virtual Society? programme. More information about the Virtual Society? programme can be found at http://www.brunel.ac.uk/research/virtsoc.

3. Dvorak, J.C.: Dvorak Predicts. An Insider's Look at the Computer Industry. Osborne McGraw-Hill, Berkeley (1994)
4. McLoughlin, I.: Creative Technological Change. The Shaping of Technology and Organisations. Routledge, London (1999)
5. Sculley, J.: Open Letter. The Red Herring, September/October (1994)

The Open-End Argument for Private Computing*

Tage Stabell-Kulø, Feico Dillema, and Terje Fallmyr

Department of Computer Science, University of Tromsø, Norway
{tage,feico,terje}@pasta.cs.uit.no

Abstract. A truly personal machine, called a private machine and implemented as a Personal Digital Assistant (PDA), is fundamentally different from traditional machines. It is *personal* and *private* in an unprecedented manner, and its modus operandi is such that network and power failures will not be rare. Designing distributed systems where PDAs are treated as "first class citizens" is a challenge.

Furthermore, private assets (electronic money, keys for authentication and opening doors) will be stored in PDAs. Ownership and control of these assets and the media that store and communicate them should remain with the user. This must be reflected in the design of systems for private computing.

We introduce the "open-ended argument" to describe the design strategy we used for designing a system that is designed to reveal information to the user (as opposed to hide it). We argue and show that when systems are designed this way, the user (a human) is better able to control the system and his personal data, as he can make better decisions than the system itself based on *qualitative assessment* of the provided information. The system we have designed and implemented under this design guidelines is presented and discussed.

1   Introduction

"Private information is practically the source of every large, modern fortune."
Oscar Wilde, "An ideal husband", act two.

We have designed and implemented a system around the use of Personal Digital Assistants (PDAs). While designing the system, we came to realize the need for attention to where decisions are taken as the system is operating. Users' ability to exercise control depends on whether the system is structured so that no important decision is taken without first consulting them. Moreover, important information for making decisions should be made available in spite of the engineering tradition of information hiding. A traditionally layered system shields the user from the intrinsic details of the system, and does not require him to be

---

* Funded by the GDD project of the Research Council of Norway (project number 112577/431).

competent to act according to the information the system might present about its internal state. Removing such requirements from the user is generally considered as an advantage, in particular in order to make the system user-friendly. Systems based on this model are designed to be transparent. The "transparency design principle" states that users should be shielded as much as possible from the inner workings and state of the system they are using (see, for example [5]). This principle is not only applied to end-systems, but also more generally to layers of abstraction inside the system. While this design principle is important for building abstractions and has been applied successfully to many system designs, its rigid application suffers from some serious problems.

The end-to-end argument [15] argues against placement of functional components and services at low levels of abstraction in a computer system. A function or service should only be implemented at a (low-level) architectural layer if it is needed by all clients of that layer and if it can be completely implemented by that layer. In general, a layer cannot handle all types of errors, and will in some situations enter undesired states, such as for instance by blocking or even failure by crashing. Such errors or exceptional events in one layer require intervention from the layer above, where the peer entities may utilize their position to resolve the situation below. This may propagate up through the layers until it reaches the topmost layer, which implements the interface towards the user. In the end, the user is confronted with a malfunctioning system.

With the advent of truly personal and mobile computing and communication devices, we believe the system and user model as described earlier is rendered ineffective, for at least three reasons:

• We believe that "real world" private assets will be stored in PDAs, owned and controlled by individual users. Such assets can be diaries, keys for authentication and/or access control, and possibly electronic money. Users will want zealous control over such resources; before valuables are handed to the system, a user needs to be able to trust it. Trust and trust relations are crucial components in any secure system. Trust is a *feeling*, based on personal experience, social context and personal perception. It can not be measured or quantified by the system in any way, and it is often difficult or impossible for a user to quantify (and specify to the system) *a priori*. Hence, it can not be used in algorithmic computations by the system for making decisions and evaluations. In essence, acknowledging the non-computability of trust implies that systems designed with the traditional system and user model, cannot support the user's perception of trust and cannot make decisions based on a user's trust and trust relations.

• The user will view the system as providing him with a set of services for processing, storage, retrieval and communication of (private) data. Traditionally, the system decides for the user how such services treat the user's data. In addition, the system is often the only designated authority when it comes to making qualitative judgments (based on policies specified by the system maintainer/owner). This makes sense in traditional environments where no part of the system is really owned by the actual user and the user's data is not considered (at least by the owner of the system) as his private property. When systems are to process a user's truly private data, the user will want to be in control of the system rather than being "just a user".

- PDAs often operate at the limits of what can be achieved by current technology and operational problems due to resource shortage must be considered part of normal operation. Since PDAs typically are powered by batteries, communicate over wireless links and may roam in hostile environments, several types of failure are likely to occur much more frequently than in non-PDA based systems. Almost all failures will occur in what is normally considered as "infrastructure", and users are not supposed to interact with problems at such a low level. However, when operating a PDA each and every user must be involved also in these issues in order to keep the system usable even when parts of the system fail as part of almost normal daily operation.

There is a common denominator in these three aspects. Distributed systems are designed as layers of abstraction, with peer entities communicating with each other over the network. The user, however, often has no peer in computer systems (in the "other end" so to speak) that can replace the user for making certain decisions. We have an *open-ended* setting when the users rôle is controlling rather than just using the system.

Taken together, systems that encompass PDAs do not fit elegantly into the classical model of distributed systems design, where computation may be distributed, but where authority and competence to make decisions is centralized. Based on our experiences, we propose a new design principle, named the "open-end argument". In the following section, Section 2, we argue for and describe this "open-end argument" for systems design. An implementation of a system designed with this argument as guideline — our research vehicle — is described in Section 3, followed by examples from other systems that contrast our approach in Section 4. Conclusions and future work is offered in Section 5.

2   The Open-End Argument

Rigid application of the transparency design principle tends to structure the design in ways that causes two problems:

- A quest for transparency tends to push complexity down into the lower layers because more functionality is needed to handle ever more exceptions. As a consequence, hiding the state of the system from users may in itself result in increased system complexity. Increased complexity often leads to more complex failure modes of the system at large, which in effect may be increasingly difficult to hide from users, and so on. For example, NFS (Network File System [16]) tries to shield users from the fact that some files are remote. It provides location transparency, and users are presented with a uniform interface for local and remote files. However, an application that issues a write operation on what seems to be a local file can get in return an error message like "Remote Host Unavailable", or simply block (depending on implementation details). Maintaining transparency over failures like this would require the addition in the system of significantly more (and more complex) machinery, like (write) caching and consistency control and so on.

• Application of the transparency principle seems to structure the system such that the control users have over the system is reduced. This is especially true when it is combined with a rather pessimistic user model in which users are not assumed to be competent to make any decisions based on the state of the system. In such systems, problems that the system cannot handle transparently and which the typical user of the system is not assumed to be able to handle either, are left to be resolved by the more knowledgeable system manager or help-desk support personnel. The position of the user in the system can then be said to be on the "edges" of the system. When the user is placed at the edge of the system, avoiding the potential confusion caused by strange error messages in NFS (example above), is no requirement for the system design. However, proper handling of failures is of greater concern in PDA-based systems as argued in the introduction of this paper.

End-to-end and similar style arguments have led to the idea of "stupid operating systems", "stupid networks" and "stupid processors" [14]. We introduce the idea of "stupid PDAs" in order to discuss the structure of systems that support owners of such machines. A stupid PDA is designed to be simple enough for its owner to feel confident he understands how the PDA operates (on his behalf!) and for him to feel able to control the PDA. It keeps its owner well-informed about relevant aspects of its (internal) state at all times, rather than hiding it from him. The essence of what is known about the state of the system should be communicated. Only then is it possible for the user to understand what is going on, and intervene if necessary. Moreover, to aid understanding and control, it is a design challenge to reduce the number of visible and thus important states in the system, while at the same time convey as much information as is required.

Although PDAs can be viewed as just another access point to distributed systems, treating them as such in systems design ignores many important properties. The most important property of a PDA is that its user (and owner) exercises physical control over it. This might seem obvious, but it is the main discriminating factor between a PDA and a desktop PC or workstation. This property, when properly exploited by the systems' design, yields a computing and communication device that none but its user controls. This facilitates *private computing*[1] Private computing implies that the owner of a private computer is in full control of it. For the owner to be confident that he fully controls the activities of and access to this private computer, systems need to be explicitly designed for it. "User friendliness" achieved only by applying the transparency design principle is insufficient or even inappropriate for such systems. Hiding the true activities and state of the system from the owner inevitably result in reduced confidence on his ability to control his private machine.

Confidence is a human feeling and is therefore difficult or impossible for others to quantify. Like concepts such as "trust" and "competence" it is defined by a

---

[1] In order to avoid confusion with "personal computing" denoting one (desktop) machine per user (PC), we will use the term *private computing* instead.

user's beliefs, experiences and personality (amongst others). These notions are inherently qualitative in nature and must be quantified in a meaningful way in order to be used in a computation. The notion of trust can serve as an example. Alice might trust Bob in some circumstances, but not in others. Furthermore, whether she trusts Bob depends on the credentials he conveys with his requests to Alice. She may accept an authentication performed by a Kerberos server for access to her work-related documents [18], but require a completely different set of credentials for access to private documents [11]. Alice makes a qualitative assessment of the information presented to her. For example: Is this signature 'better' than the other, and do I find it 'sufficient' for this particular request?. Such assessments are well known in "the real world", where different credentials (i.e. papers) are needed for different purposes; a passport is needed in some situations, an ID card suffices in others. Different papers that "say" essentially the same thing, but with different quality. Again, it is the notion of private computing using PDAs that introduces such qualitative assessments into the system. This forces the designer to either ignore the user, or ensure that the user can control the system.

Often a system is considered easy-to-use if it requires little a priori knowledge and little training from the user. Even though competent users can not be assumed for many system designs, we may assume that even ignorant users have the ability to learn. Unfortunately, many system designs hide much of their inner workings (by design), so that it is very difficult for a user to learn how to control and manage it better. We argue that especially in the context of private computing, a system that is not designed to let a users learn to control and manage it, can not be considered easy-to-use as users are prevented to learn how to deal with situations the system itself can not resolve transparently. In order to support user learning and user control, a private computing system should provide the user with all the system information he needs and/or desires.

We believe that a different approach is required when designing systems to support private computing. In addition we argue that only the user can and should be the arbiter of what is important for him to control. This can not be left for the system to decide. We call this line of argument *the Open-end argument*:

Open-end argument: The system should be designed in such a way that in all situations where qualitative assessment of information is needed to make a decision, the user is informed and consulted.

This argument guides a system designer in deciding when to follow the transparency design principle and when to violate it by informing and consulting the end-user. The remaining of this article describes a system designed under guidance of the open-end argument, which we then contrast with other systems to clarify its properties.

3 The Research Vehicle

The open-end argument concerns the design of systems which are to include private computers as "first class citizens". In order to gain experience with the argument, we have designed and implemented a system under its guidance. This system is called the File Repository (FR); it supports users who are expected to have (and use) private machines in concert with their workstations at home and at work. FR is our research vehicle; we use it to investigate the design and implementation of distributed systems supporting private computing.

3.1 Features

The primary task of FR is to store files and information about files. FR consists of clients and servers that interact with each other using a custom-designed protocol FRTP [17]. The unit of operation in FR is a file, a sequence of bytes. Hence, FR is not aware of file formats nor is it aware of logical relations that might exist between different files; FR thus does not provide the functionality of version control systems such as RCS, SCCS or CVS. Increased availability of files is achieved by replication. FR provides the mechanisms *replication* and *shipping* and provides machinery for implementing flexible *access control policies*.

FR provides users with high availability of files by means of replication[2] even when connectivity is poor (low bandwidth and/or relatively high chance of disconnected operation). Users can instruct FR to replicate files over multiple servers. These servers maintain consistency between the replicas by means of a server-to-server protocol [12]; this protocol is based on two-phase commit. FR-servers maintain consistency between multiple copies of a file on a best-effort basis.

Files can also be *shipped* from one FR server (site) to another. Shipping is replication under explicit user control. Before a user travels to another site, he can delegate access rights for his own files to himself in the rôle of visitor at the remote site. FR will then ship the files, and make them available to him there. The rationale for doing so is that it alleviates the need for substantial amounts of storage space on PDAs when traveling.

FR runs entirely in user space, and users are free to install one or more instances of FR on any machine at their disposal. Every user decides for himself which servers he trusts and believe is reliable.

3.2 Concurrency control

A lock might be set on a file to ensure consistency. Locking is the ultimate pessimistic concurrency control regime. In FR, however, a lock on a file is not absolute, in that any user might ignore any lock at will. The semantics are

---

[2] The term *copy* has to do with distribution in space, while *version* implies changes over time. Replication ensures that all copies of a file have the same version, and a *replica* is a copy which is kept up-to-date.

that when a locked file is extracted from FR, a warning is issued, and if a user attempts to write data on a locked file, the data is redirected onto a "shadow" of the original file. No scenario causes the loss of data. The important issue is that the user might ignore a lock because he has extra-system information; a conversation or phone call with a co-worker ("Are you editing this file at the moment?") are typical examples of channels for information outside the system.

There are two additional features related to locking. The first is that each lock is identified by what might be called a capability [3]. By sharing a capability with another user, the lock can be released by any one of them. This usage of capabilities resembles the way Amoeba used them as a form of shared secret [19]. The important issue is that *the user* decides the lifespan and semantics of the locks he holds. The second feature is that if data is written optimistically on a locked file, the holder of the capability can later use it to upgrade the shadow to the valid file.

Denying a user service is avoided in FR, even in case that would preserve correctness from the systems point of view. Consequently, a server does not deny read access to a write-locked file. Rather, the requester is informed about the existence of the lock, and will have to decide whether it is safe to proceed, based on extra-system information (or by taking his chances). A user may, for instance, extract a file optimistically even though some other user already has extracted it pessimistically (i.e. locked). However, the former will not be able to insert the file (i.e. change it) before the lock is released (or expired) without his data being diverted into a shadow of the current file.

During a network partition it is impossible to know from within the system and/or application in the minority partition, whether it is safe to proceed with a task that alters shared data [4]. In fact, it is even impossible to know whether a datum has become shared. The user, on the other hand, may be capable of understanding the situation and *evaluate* the risk, and, more important, understand the consequences of his actions. Also, as mentioned above, the user might use channels outside the system to gather information for understanding and evaluation.

In a scheme where users have the opportunity to decide, progress is always possible but can obviously lead to situations where copies of files become inconsistent. The FR has machinery to handle such situations, instead of merely labeling them as "incorrect". In fact, it is not incorrect for a user to overwrite his own files with new data, the opposite is true. The issue is who decides which copy is up-to-date. According to the open-end argument, the user is to decide.

For example, consider the user Alice, who has a computer in her office, on which the latest up-to-date copy of a file is stored; Alice is at home. During the evening she decides to edit the file, but her requests for an up-to-date copy can not be fulfilled due to a network partition, that is, she is unable to contact the FR. Alice is now left to *decide* which actions the system shall undertake on her behalf. It is obvious that she can safely proceed working at home, if she knows the state of the file, and can refrain from altering those sections where she knows her out-of-date copy differs from the more up-to-date version at work. By exploiting her understanding of the situation she is able to take the "correct" action even though seen from the systems' point of view, she has created two inconsistent copies of the file. When the network becomes operational again, the copy in Alice's office is augmented with a "shadow". The shadow contains her updates, and she can either merge the two, replace one of them, or create a new file. The point is, *the system* did not force her to try to circumvent the system services, but rather made it possible for her to obtain progress even when she was in a minority partition. She obtained progress at the risk of conflicting updates, but at her discretion. This is in accordance with the open-end argument.

But FR can also be employed by different users wanting to share data. Consider the following scenario: Alice and Bob are sharing a file; they are employed at different sites. On one fine Sunday afternoon Alice decides to write, she contacts her local FR and requests a write-lock on the file. The response is that a copy of the file is available (after all, it is replicated) but the network is partitioned (between the sites of Alice and Bob) so that no guarantees regarding neither consistency nor correctness can be given by the system. Alice is left to make the decision how to proceed based on her extra-system knowledge, e.g. about the work habits of Bob and the amount of work involved in merging possible conflicts later. It is obvious that she has no guarantee from the system whatsoever, but *she* decides whether to proceed or not. She might use the telephone to establish a de facto lock by means of social engineering, for example, to reduce the risk of inconsistencies. Also in this scenario, FR supports smooth integration when connectivity is restored; in whatever state the file is in. This example highlights the prudence in permitting users to achieve progress at their own risk, when they desire.

3.3 Security

Users are known by their public keys, and a user is represented in the system as a delegation from a key to some form of authenticated channel; access control is based on access control lists (ACLs) [10, 11]. The system's rôle is to implement the policy set by the user. In particular, FR has no business in authenticating users, but should only validate requests.

FR protects the interest of users by implementing whatever policy the user wants. A user can, at any time, create a certificate that will give another user access to a file in FR. That other user need not be known to FR in advance; the importance of this will be discussed in the context of Kerberos in Section 4.2. When the user decides what credential should be sufficient for access to his files, useful services such as offline delegation become feasible [6]. That is, a user (with his PDA) is able to grant access to his own files without having to interact with FR. Delegation certificates generated offline have the same "value" as those generated in cooperation with the FR, since the user is the focal point in the system. Offline delegation is required for the smooth integration of private machines in a distributed system; we know of no other system that supports offline delegation.

3.4 Summary

It is a challenge to design and implement a system in accordance with the open-end principle as well. Mainly, it is hard to identify the states where sufficient information about the system is available, and then to capture the essence of the situation in such a way that it can be presented to the user. However, these are (only) engineering problems. In other words, there is no need to (try to) predict neither what users will actually do nor guess what is taking place in other parts of a partitioned network. By promptly leaving such impossible tasks to the user —who will ultimately have to resolve any conflicts anyway— the system's complexity becomes far less daunting. And as a consequence of a less complex system, its users can more often grasp the implications of the information the system provides, hence making it feasible for the user to make use of all options available even when the system itself can not.

At an abstract level we can view the inclusion of the "user in the decision loop" as providing the means for the user to decide at each junction which design cut to make, rather than to decide on one single cut through the different design choices concerning the division of responsibilities between user and system at the time the system is designed. The system appears to be dynamic, in that the user can choose to have powerful services with fixed "guarantees", or just information to facilitate his own decision making.

Regarding security, FR mainly makes machinery available to users; they implement their own policy.

4 Examples

FR has been designed in compliance with the open-end argument. As explained above, the end-to-end argument is similar in appearance and, on the surface, FR has properties that makes it resemble other systems. However, because it was designed with a different strategy in mind, FR is different in important areas.

The challenges of systems that contain small mobile nodes have been addressed in several other projects, and many systems address the problem of variable supply of resources in mobile computers. The duality of system and application control, captured in the term application aware adaption is addressed in projects like Odyssey [13], Rover [7] and Barwan [2]. Projects like INRIA's Project SOR [1] target at minimizing user annoyance when disconnected, and seek solutions in providing transparency to mobility by identifying and using locally available resources. In general, the projects tend to address problems related to system issues and how to minimize user annoyance when resource supply becomes insufficient. We are not aware of any project that addresses the issue of providing the user with proper information about internal state and the ability to fully control the mobile machine. The remainder of this section contrasts FR with the two well-known classic systems Coda and Kerberos to highlight the specific characteristics of FR.

4.1 Coda

It might seem as if FR has striking similarities with Coda [9,8]. However, the design philosophies behind the two systems are almost antithetical, and this becomes visible when parts of the system fail. In the following we will discuss the main ideas in Coda and how they are realized, and contrasting Coda to FR.

The most important observation underpinning the design of Coda, is that conflicting updates on files are rare. That is, if a file is taken offline for a day or two, chances are overwhelmingly large that a modified version can be copied back in place without any conflict. In fact, the authors report that within a week, the probability that two different users modify the same file is less than 0.2% [8]. The smooth working of Coda relies on this being true. Coda is designed after a model where the "laptop" is in focus. Users have copies of their files on the laptop and bring the machine home in the afternoon. It is to be expected that files in user's home directory remain unaltered. If, however, both copies of a file are updated, Coda does not resolve the conflict. In fact, since Coda does not have any knowledge about the files' contents it *can not* resolve the conflict. Instead, Coda generates an archive containing both files; it left as a task for the user to decide what to do afterwards (how to merge the files).

In a system with private machines and where each user owns several machines, the assumption that conflicts do not occur will inevitably lead to failures. In fact, we *assume* that conflicting updates will be common rather than the exception. In accordance with the open-end argument, FR strives to detect potential conflicts (and report these to the user) rather than hide potential risks (as Coda does). In fact, in [9] it is noted that *involuntary* disconnection caused by failures are no different than *voluntary* disconnections, but that users expectations and extent of user cooperation are likely to be different. There is a fundamental difference between Coda and FR in that FR will try its outmost to inform users about the state of the system while Coda does the opposite.

Furthermore, Coda explicitly denotes the copy on a users' machine as second-class, while denoting the copy on the server as first-class. In FR, the open-end argument tells us that when *the user* owns the file, the copy the users chooses to denote as the "first class" version, by definition it is just that. In our view, it is inappropriate to overrule a decision made by the user rather than trying to implement it. These differences between Coda and FR are explained by the different system and user models each has been designed for.

4.2 Kerberos

The open-end argument has applications other than consistency control. As an extreme example, in Kerberos it is impossible for a user to delegate access to another user, unless that user is recognized by Kerberos [18]. That is, it is impossible to generate credentials outside the realm of Kerberos that will be valid within. The users are not trusted by the system, not even to control access to their own files. Notice that this is inherent in the design of Kerberos, rather than an artifact of the type of cryptography used (shared or public key). Furthermore, in order to log in, the user must release his password for the system to authenticate him. The reverse, the user authenticating the system (against, for example, a man-in-the-middle attack) is not possible. In other words, it is a highly system-centric design.

In the examples related to consistency, there exists a "correct" solution (an algorithm) for all situations [4]. In contrast, many situations where PDAs will be employed, algorithmic solutions are not possible. We mention but a few examples here:

- Is this encryption key "good"?
- Is this machine trustworthy?
- Can I safely type my PIN on this keyboard?

It is the use of private machines that makes it necessary to answer questions where the answer depends on the "quality" of some object. In centralized systems (such as Kerberos) the answers were given at the time when the system was designed. According to the open-end argument, the user should be left to decide.

5 Conclusions

Personal Digital Assistants are becoming commonplace, and they will become more resourceful and can be used in an increasing number of ways. A machine that is trusted can be part of daily life, and their owners will soon come to depend on them for their real-life daily activities. Successfully including such machines in a static infrastructure requires that the design acknowledges the special properties PDAs have, and the special way PDAs can and will be used. We have defined and discussed the open-end argument. It states that whenever assessing quality of information is required for making a decision, the user should be consulted. We claim that systems structured in accordance with the open-end argument will be different than systems targeted at support for static systems only. Or, with other words, systems that aims at encompassing PDAs should be designed with extra care. Decentralization of control, management and authority inevitably leads to new semantics of terms such as "conflicting updates" and "trusted". Discussing this in a setting with concurrency control reveals that an open-ended system shows different characteristics than systems designed using more traditional system design guidelines. We argued and showed that this also applies to security issues like access control.

We presented the File Repository. It serves as a research vehicle for investigation of the open-end argument and its effect and usefulness in systems design. By firmly placing the user in the control of the system, the File Repository has been designed to gracefully support users with PDAs.

The security infrastructure built to support users using FR is currently being used to monitor access to other objects than files. In particular, we are designing and building a system for access control (to a physical location) based on the assumption that users have private machines at hand. The design is guided, naturally, by the open-end argument.

Acknowledgments

Frode Fjeld, Åge Kvalnes and the anonymous referees gave us feedback that has improved the presentation. Arne Helme participated in the work on offline delegation. Working in the "PASTA laboratory" is very stimulating.

References

1. A. Baggio. System support for transparency and network-aware adaptation in mobile environments. In *ACM Symposium on Applied Computing special track on Mobile Computing Systems and Applications*, Atlanta, Georgia, USA, February 1998. Also available as a research report: INRIA Research Report 3408, April 1998.
2. E. Brewer, R. H. Katz, E. Amir, H. Balakrishnan, Y. Chawathe, A. Fox, S. Gribble, G. Hodes, T. Nguyen, V. Padmanabhan, M. Stemm, S. Seshan, and T. Henderson. A network architecture for heterogeneous mobile computing. *IEEE Personal Communications Magazine*, 5(5):8–24, October 1998.
3. J. B. Dennis and E. C. van Horn. Programming Semantics for Multiprogrammed Computations. *Communications of the ACM*, 9(3):143–155, March 1966.
4. D. K. Gifford. Weighted voting for replicated data. In *Proceedings of 7th SOSP*, pages 150–62. ACM Press, 1979.
5. A. Goscinski. *Distributed Operating Systems, The Logical Design*. Addison-Wesley, 1991.
6. A. Helme and T. Stabell-Kulø. Offline delegation. In *Usenix Security Symposium*, 1999. Accepted for publication.
7. A. D. Joseph, J. A. Tauber, and M. Frans Kaashoek. Mobile computing with the Rover toolkit. *IEEE Transactions on Computers: Special issue on Mobile Computing*, pages 337–352, March 1997.
8. J. J. Kistler. *Disconnected operations in a distributed file system*, volume 1002 of *Lecture Notes in Computer Science*. Springer Verlag, 1996.
9. J. J. Kistler and M. Satyanarayanan. Disconnected operation in the Coda file system. *Transactions on Computer Systems*, 10(1):3–25, February 1992.
10. B. Lampson. Protection. In *Proceedings of the Fifth Princeton Symposium on Information Sciences and Systems*, pages 437–443, Princeton University, March 1971. Reprinted in Operating Systems Review, 8, 1, January 1974, pp. 18–24.
11. B. Lampson, M. Abadi, M. Burrows, and E. Wobber. Authentication in distributed systems: theory and practice. *ACM Transactions on Computer Systems*, 10(4):265–310, November 1992.
12. G. Moxnes. Design og implementasjon av replikering i file repository (in Norwegian). Masters thesis, Department of Computer Science, University of Tromsø, Norway, April 1997.
13. Brian D. Noble, M. Satyanarayanan, D. Narayanan, J. E. Tilton, J. Flinn, and K. R. Walker. Agile application-aware adaption for mobility. *ACM SIGOPS Operating Systems Review*, 31(5):276–287, Dec. 1997. in: SIGOPS '97. Proceedings of the sixteenth ACM symposium on Operating systems principles, pages 264-275.
14. D. P. Reed, J. H. Saltzer, and D. D. Clark. Active networking and end-to-end arguments. *IEEE Network*, 12(3):69–71, May 1998.
15. J. H. Saltzer, D. P. Reed, and D. D. Clark. End-to-end arguments in system design. *ACM Transactions on Computer Systems*, 2(4):277–288, November 1984.

16. R. Sandberg, D. Goldberg, S. Kleiman, D. Walsh, and B. Lyon. Design and implementation of the Sun Network Filesystem. In *Summer conference proceedings, Portland 1985: June 11-14, 1985, Portland, Oregon USA*, pages 119–130. USENIX, Summer 1985.

17. T. Stabell-Kulø. File repository transfer protocol (frtp). Technical report, Department of Computer Science, University of Tromsø, Norway, February 1995.

18. J. G. Steiner, B. G Neumann, and J. I. Schiller. Kerberos: An Authentication System for Open Network Systems. In *Proc. of the Winter 1988 Usenix Conference*, pages 191–201, February 1988.

19. A. S. Tanenbaum, R. van Renesse, H. van Staveren, G. J. Sharp, S. J. Mullender, J. Jansen, and G. van Rossum. Experiences with the Amoeba distributed operating system. *Comunication of the ACM*, 33(12):46–63, December 1990.

Integrating PDAs into Distributed Systems: *2K* and PalmORB *

Manuel Román **, Ashish Singhai ***, Dulcineia Carvalho, Christopher Hess,
and Roy H. Campbell

Department of Computer Science
University of Illinois, Urbana, IL 61801
E-mail: {mroman1,singhai,dcarvalh,ckhess,rhc}@cs.uiuc.edu
Web: *http://choices.cs.uiuc.edu/*

Abstract. In this paper we describe an application model for seamless mobile data access using handheld devices and wireless links. We go beyond the current model in which handhelds are used as smart organizers augmented with stripped down versions of popular desktop programs. Instead, we propose to integrate handheld devices seamlessly in a distributed computing environment. Componentized applications, adaptable middleware frameworks, and standardized protocols play a significant role in this new paradigm. We also describe an implementation within this paradigm using PalmORB, a CORBA client for the 3Com Palm devices.

1 Introduction

The current distributed system organization is machine centric. Users have different accounts, passwords, and software on different machines. This organization has sufficed for the computers to users ratio of one or less. However, with a larger computers to users ratio, afforded by smaller devices and cheap wireless connectivity, the existing model breaks down. The challenge is to provide the users with a seamless image of a distributed system irrespective of the device used to access the system. Previous attempts to provide a consistent system image using clusters (e.g., NOW [1]) and distributed file systems (e.g., NFS [6]) are applicable only for LAN based distributed systems.

The *2K* distributed system, currently under development at the University of Illinois proposes a user centric organization of a distributed system. Users view the system as a collection of resources that they can use regardless or their location.

In this paper, we consider the issues related to incorporating handheld devices in a distributed system. We describe the challenges in doing so and our solutions to them.

---

* This research is supported by a grant from the National Science Foundation, NSF 98-70736
** Supported by a Fulbright-Ramon Areces Fellowship
*** Supported by an IBM Graduate Fellowship

1.1 The Issues We Consider

Small mobile devices are restricted in terms of bandwidth, CPU and the amount of memory and storage availability. Thus they cannot be treated as workstations or PCs when integrating them in a distributed environment. Each scenario must be analyzed independently in order to customize the system and achieve the best possible performance.

All the issues we will discuss in this paper can be applied to any small mobile device (Palm Computer, HandHeld, wearable...). However, for the sake of concreteness, we will focus on the Palm Pilot only. To refer to all of them as a set we will use the term PDA (Personal Digital Assistant).

Current PDAs cannot be considered as mere schedulers or devices to store telephone numbers anymore. They offer enough functionality to be used in sophisticated environments. This paper describes an infrastructure that integrates PDAs in distributed environments based on the *2K* operating system. Thus, instead of using PDAs as isolated entities, users will be able to use them as an enabling bridge to a collection of distributed resources and services.

One of the more interesting integration issues is how to offer a consistent view of a distributed system from a PDA. If we only take into consideration the screen size, it seems clear that it is difficult to offer the same interaction interface in a PDA than in a 21 inch monitor. However *2K* OS offers an object oriented vision of every single resource and service. This allows us to consider the interaction interface offered to the user as an object container. Therefore, in a big powerful monitor we represent every resource as a graphical icon whereas in a Palm Pilot we could simply use a list of names. In this way, the concept of interacting with components (objects) is preserved, no matter which device is used. However, the way those components are presented to the user is likely to change according to the device being used (the approach extends for example to a voiced controlled PDA that includes no screen). The interaction interface offered to the user is therefore polymorphic as it offers the same functionality through specialization of the interface according to the device.

One of the design features of *2K* is that the operating system resides in a computer network and not in a specific machine. Therefore, it is possible to access the operating system from different devices and locations while keeping a consistent view of the system. This is achieved by using object oriented and component concepts. For example, a user can log in to a login component of the system which may reside in a disconnected PDA. When the PDA is connected to the network, the operating system services are instantiated in the device being used. The state associated with the user attributes is kept in the distributed environment. Sessions may be transfered from one device to another. For example, it will be possible to start a videoconference in a desktop and transfer the videoconference to a PDA. The transition from the desktop to the PDA must be smooth and must not require any user intervention. The system will automatically adapt and synchronize itself to the new environment. If the PDA is disconnected, the session should be reestablished automatically on reconnection.

There is a wide range of PDAs, and each one of them can greatly vary in terms of resource availability. This requires an infrastructure able to deal with every different kind of device. Therefore we propose the use of adaptable proxies, which will alleviate the PDA from the execution of computation intensive software. The decision about what should be done at the PDA and what at the proxy should be determined according to the hardware capabilities of the PDA. Moreover, it should be possible to modify that decision dynamically, by monitoring techniques.

1.2 Organization of the Paper

Section 2 introduces the *2K* distributed operating system which is the enabling infrastructure. Section 2.1 provides a more detailed description of *2K* environments which are fundamental for the integration of PDAs into the *2K* distributed system. Next section, section 3, describes the challenges associated to integrating HandHeld devices into a distributed system. Section 4 explains the design and implementation of PalmORB which is the core component that provides PDAs with CORBA capabilities. Section 5 presents two applications: PalmShell, a *2K* shell for PalmPilots (section 5.1) and Video Streaming Proxies (section 5.2) which brings video to the PalmPilots by using the dynamic architecture of *2K*. Section 6 offers some information about the performance of PalmORB and PalmShell. Section 7 describes two related approaches, and finally, section 8 concludes the paper and describes our future work.

2 Brief Overview of the *2K* System

2K is a distributed operating system currently under development at the University of Illinois. It offers a reflective architecture that can be modified on the fly. The operating system is built on top of CORBA and the reflective behavior is offered at the ORB level. The ORB that we are using is a modified version of TAO [12] called dynamicTAO [11], which is built on top of the ACE toolkit [4]. The ACE toolkit runs on top of several platforms, therefore, *2K* can run on every platform where ACE has been ported. The main platforms we use for development are Windows NT and Solaris, and we are also working on the design of a customized microkernel called Off++ [2]. *2K* is based on the principle of *What You Need Is What You Get*, which means that the system can dynamically adapt itself to the requirements specified by the user, thus providing a customized execution framework for every application. The main issues associated with *2K* are: architectural awareness, adaptability and network and user-centrism.

Users become active entities within the system and specify what resources they want and how they want to use those resources (QoS requirements). All this information is stored persistently in an object called an environment, which is associated with the user's instantiation within the system.

Network centrism plays a key role in *2K*. The network becomes a single pool of resources managed by *2K* according to the QoS specified by users. Dependencies between resources (local and distributed) are reified by the Component Configurator [8], a *2K* fundamental core component.

A *2K* user is unique within the whole system, it can access to *2K* from different platforms (Windows NT, Solaris, PalmOS) and during a session, resources from different machines can be used. A dynamic security policy mechanism based on the Cherubim project [3] can be attached at runtime to specified dynamicTAO ORBs.

2.1 *2K* Environments

A *2K* environment is a container of components, devices and configuration parameters and provides an execution context for users within the *2K* distributed system. The environment is responsible for managing groups of components as a collective entity, and for facilitating the interface of the components with the *2K* operating system.

Environments are persistent objects that are created and managed by the *2K* Environment Service. When a new environment is created on behalf of a principal, the Environment Service locates a profile of that principal describing default components and devices, as well as resource requirements for that environment. Typically, principals have default profiles that can be customized depending on the location of the principals, their role and the components they execute.

When an environment is created the system must assure that the resource requirements of the profile are satisfied. Moreover, as components execute, their potentially variable QoS requirements must be understood and satisfied by the system. This is accomplished by the interaction with the Resource Manager and the QoS Monitor, two of the *2K* core components.

As activity in the environment proceeds, the own environment contacts all the components and devices it requires, either by reusing existing components or by creating new ones.

3 Challenges in Integrating a Hand Held Device in a Distributed System

One of the major challenges is to discover all the new possibilities offered by the integration of PDAs in distributed environments.

The main use of a PDAs nowadays is personal information management. However, with the incoming era of wireless communications, it will be possible to introduce the concept of "Everything, everywhere, anytime computing". Users will be able to access every single resource from every possible device and at any moment.

There are many issues that must be studied carefully in order to provide a minimum computing environment. Connecting to some kind of network is crucial in order to guarantee resource availability, but currently, in most of the cases, the bandwidth offered for PDAs is low. Therefore, it is a priority to offer some kind of optimized transport protocol or use proxies that minimize the communications required with the PDA. By using the adaptation capabilities of *2K*, we can address some of the limitations of the PDAs by locating computation intensive tasks of the user's in PDA accessible self-adaptable proxies.

Users are registered within the *2K* environment, not within a particular device or domain. This translates into a single login mechanism. As it will be explained in next sections, when the user logs in, the login mechanism will contact the Environment Service. This will receive the request and will grant or deny the user to start the session.

The PDA caches the state of the user's environment. This caching allows disconnected operation mode and in most cases reduces the amount of data that the distributed system sends to the PDA each time a log in session is started.

An important issue when offering a unique system view is to find some kind of application user interface that can be used from different architectures and OSs. The ideal would be to provide a single interface instead of one for each platform. We are studying the feasibility of using XML to describe the application interface, and different data style sheets, one for each platform.

Mobile computing combined with distributed environments offer a large number of benefits. However it also introduces some interesting challenges. When working in a distributed system, security becomes an issue of particular importance. It affects several aspects: login authentication, information encryption, privacy, key sharing and proxies. Confidentiality must be guaranteed by protecting users' data from other users. Since it is likely that PDAs will use proxies in some situations, a security delegation mechanism will be required. The initial authentication mechanism sends information about the user to the Environment Service. This information must be protected to avoid a third party intercepting the information and using it later to impersonate the original user. Finally, there is another level of security that should be considered and that is related to the device itself. Because of the size of PDAs they can be easily stolen or lost. In both cases, there must exist a mechanism to guarantee that nobody but the legitimate user can initiate a session or access confidential data stored in the device.

Using the *2K* operating system and the Cherubim project [3] developed by the Software Research Group of our CS department, we can deal with user validation. By attaching the Cherubim Security strategy to a running dynamicTAO ORB, we can allow or deny the execution of methods on objects, according to the identity of the principal issuing the request. Besides user validation, the Software Research Group is also working on other security aspects that we plan to include in *2K* and PDAs applications.

4   Design and Implementation of the PalmORB

Our *2K* Distributed Operating System is based on CORBA. Therefore any device capable of generating IIOP requests can take benefit of the services that *2K* offers. This was the reason that lead us to the development of PalmORB, a small client side ORB for Palm Pilots that offers a subset of the CORBA functionality.

Most of the existing ORBs (commercial and freely available) are not suitable for embedded systems. In most cases, their monolithic design restricts their applicability to PDAs. Their size is too big to be ported to a memory limited device item, offer features that will never be used in a PDA and in some the cases, the client and server side functionality are combined in a single library.

In the case of a PDA, the execution environment greatly varies from the one of a PC or a Workstation. PDAs are not likely to use all the features offered by a standard ORB. Therefore, offering the whole CORBA functionality by default implies, at least at first glance, a waste of memory for properties that will rarely or never be used.

PalmORB was designed having in mind the restrictions of the platform on which it was going to be used. It has been implemented by using the freely available source code from SUN, though the code has been modified to offer only what is required. The current implementation is CORBA 2.0 compliant (at least the functionality provided) and follows the GIOP 1.0 protocol (the IIOP implementation).

All the server side functionality has been removed, and at the client side, only the Dynamic Invocation Interface and the ORB interface is provided. We decided to remove the server side functionality because we consider that the Palm Pilot will be used mostly as a client that uses CORBA objects' services. We do not discard, however, adding minimal server side functionality in the future.

Our current version of PalmORB cannot be customized on the fly. However, by taking benefit of *2K*, we can customize the remote server to optimize the interaction between the PalmPilot and the server.

4.1 Implementation Overview

PalmORB is implemented in C++ by using CodeWarrior Release 5 for Palm Pilot. It has 6000 lines of code and uses around 50Kb of memory. If we consider a PalmPilot III which has 2Mb of RAM, the percentage of memory required to enable CORBA capabilities is 2.5%.

PalmORB runs on any PalmOS compatible architecture with the network library. Current implementation is a static library though in the future we will change it into a dynamic library.

We have been testing PalmORB by sending requests from a PalmOS application to a CORBA object running on a Windows NT machine and another one running on a Unix machine. For the tests we have been using the PalmOS emulator (version 21d25) as well as a Palm III device connected to Internet through a PPP connection by using a serial cable (figure 1).

Our final objective is establish a wireless connection between a Palm Pilot and a PPP server.

5 Sample Applications

This section describes two applications. The first is based on the PalmORB and in the services provided by *2K*. The second one does not use PalmORB, but takes benefit of the adaptive and architecture awareness capabilities inherent to *2K*.

5.1 PalmShell

The PalmORB library introduced in the previous section, allows palm devices to interact with CORBA objects. On the other hand, *2K* offers a set of adaptable,

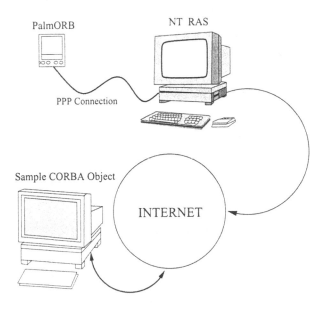

Fig. 1. PPP Connection

customizable CORBA based services and resources. However, there is a gap that must be filled to connect both sides.

We introduce here the PalmShell, an application that allows palm devices to be integrated in *2K*. PalmShell creates a *2K* environment customized for the PalmPilot, based on the user's profile that is stored in the distributed system.

Figure 2 illustrates all the components involved in the application as well as all the steps required to establish a *2K* session.

Whenever a device starts a session, it must contact the environment service to request the activation of the user's environment (1). When the request gets to the Environment Service, the security strategy checks whether the principal that is issuing the request is authorized to invoke that method on that object (2). If the request can proceed (the user has been authenticated), the environment service contacts the profile server (3) and retrieves the profile associated to the user (4). Based on the information contained in the profile, the environment service activates an instance of an environment in a *2K* host (5) (PalmPilot will interact with it remotely) and returns its reference to the PalmShell (6). If the user logged from a PC, for example, the environment could have been instantiated in the PC. The Palmshell will retrieve the list of components contained in the environment and show it to the user (7). The user can add new components to the environment by contacting the implementation repository (8), which will return a list of different categories available (9). When the user selects a category, PalmShell sends a request to the implementation repository, asking for all the components that belong to that category.

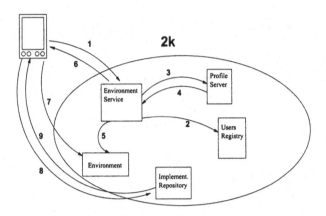

Fig. 2. PalmPilot Login

The PalmShell displays a list with all the components stored in the environment. The user can then interact with those components by means of CORBA requests. Since the user can dynamically add and remove components from the environment, there is an important issue to be considered: how can the user interact with those components? The problem is that we do not know the programmatic interfaces of those objects, neither what their user interface should look like. The first issue, the one related to the programmatic interfaces of the objects, can be solved by using the interface repository. It contains information about the methods offered by interfaces as well as the parameters required. For the second issue, we are considering two different approaches. On one hand we are working on downloading native applications to the Palm Pilot (which can be obtained from the implementation repository). This solution makes it possible for the user to create customized graphical interfaces. However, these graphical interfaces will be specific for PalmOS devices. The second approach will use XML pages to define the graphical interfaces associated to the components. These XML pages will contain information about the graphical interface, information about different methods associated to the object, and information about how to issue dynamic method calls.

The advantage of this last option (XML pages) is that the component creator will have to define the XML page once, and different filters (data style sheets) will be responsible for making the appropriate changes for every different device.

Figure 3 shows the screenshots of the current PalmShell. The leftmost picture is the login screen. Once the username and password have been introduced, the Environment Service is contacted and if the user is validated, it returns the Environment IOR see the middle form on figure 3. The rightmost form is the Object Browser that allows choosing new components to be added to the environment from a *2K* Implementation Repository.

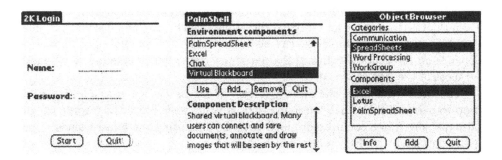

Fig. 3. PalmShell

5.2 Video Streaming Proxies

As mentioned earlier, proxies are used in the *2K* environment to alleviate some of the computational burden from palm devices. Since the processing power of these devices is quite limited, certain computations may be performed at the proxy and the results sent to the PDA. We have used this approach in streaming video to the Palm Pilot. The decompression of video frames requires significant amounts of CPU cycles and memory and is better off-loaded to a proxy. In addition, frame size and rate should be reduced to accommodate the small screen size and limited bandwidth to the device. The reduced color depth of the Palm Pilot also provides room to reduce the number of bits sent. Palm Pilots currently only support 4 colors. Therefore, there is no need to send frames with full color; the extra unusable color information should be removed.

We have implemented a video proxy that filters video streams on the fly, allowing the Palm Pilot to view the video sequence. These streams may be stored on disk or may be a live feed. Our proxy currently filters MPEG-1 video and system streams and transforms them to compressed bitmaps.

The proxy first decodes the MPEG stream using a modified version of the MPEG Software Simulation Group's *mpeg2play* [10]. A small decoding engine was created with an object-oriented interface. The interface allows different data sources to be easily plugged in, allowing the decoder to read from the network, files, buffers, etc. For example, to send MPEG files stored on disk, a simple file input stream can be plugged in. The proxy decodes frames into an array of 8 bit pixels and reduces it to 2 bits using a simple lookup table. This produces a grey-scale version of the frame. Next the frame is reduced in size if necessary. We currently reduce images by factors of 2 in both dimensions. For example, a 160x120 image can be reduced to 80x60. This is accomplished by averaging blocks of pixel values. Although frames of 80x60 are small, it is still possible to clearly view the image. The Palm Pilot screen is actually able to view 160x120 frames. However, if a greater frame rate is desired, scaling of the images is necessary. During testing, we were able to view 3 frames per second at 80x60 quite well. The "ghosting" effect that is inherent to the Palm Pilot LED screen was not noticeable.

After the image has been scaled down, it is runlength encoded and sent. The Palm Pilot is responsible for receiving the compressed bitmap and decoding it. The decoding algorithm is simple and can be done quickly. The amount of compression depends on the characteristics of the particular frame, but was found to be good for most of the frames tested.

The proxy can filter the stream further if necessary. For example, it could drop frames if it finds that too much data is being sent. Since the frames are all bitmaps, any frame could be dropped without disrupting the other frames. This is in contrast to MPEG frames which depend on each other. The side effect of removing inter-frame dependencies fits well into our model of streaming video to the Palm Pilot.

Different policies in the proxy may be employed when streaming video to a disparate set of devices. For example, streaming to a desktop workstation on a LAN may require no filtering at all, while if the workstation is connected via a dial-up line, some degree of filtering may be required to compensate for the limited bandwidth. This allows different devices to view the same video stream, with the quality adjusted appropriately for the particular device.

Fig. 4. PalmMPEG

6 Performance of Our System

In this section we will discuss the performance of PalmORB and PalmShell. For information related to the *2K* distributed operating system, check [9].

PalmShell is implemented in C++, has around 1300 lines of code and uses 10Kb of RAM. If we consider a PalmPilot III with 2Mb of RAM, the percentage required for the PalmShell is 0.5%. If we add also the PalmORB which will allow the integration of the PalmPilot into the *2K* distributed system, the total percentage of memory required is 3%.

To initiate the session in a PDA, the PalmShell contacts a Name Service and obtains the references for the Environment Service and the Implementation Repository. Then it sends a request to the Environment Service and obtains the reference of an Environment that will be associated to the user. PalmShell sends a request to the Environment and retrieves the list of components stored in the environment. For this particular test, we will assume that four components are returned. Each component returned consists on a name and an IOR. The amount of information received during the log in is around 2Kb, without counting the CDR extra stuff.

The average time required to establish a log in session in a Palm Pilot is 1.95 seconds (average time after loging in ten times). From the users point of view, this is the time it has to wait since it enters the login and password and clicks on start, until the shell with the list of components is displayed on the screen.

To calculate the overhead we used a Palm III device and established a PPP connection with a Linux machine using a serial cable at 38400 bps. We started two CORBA objects, the Implementation Repository running on a NT box and the Environment Service on a Solaris machine running Solaris 2.7. The Environment object was instantiated by the Environment Service in the same Solaris machine.

7 Related Work

There are some projects that focus on some of the issues discussed in this paper. The ones that will be discussed in this section are: Adaptive Middleware Proxy and the TACC programming model [5], and Rover [7].

The first project, AMWP (Adaptive Middleware Proxy), provides an infrastructure for developing applications for "thin" clients, that is, clients with limited hardware resources. The infrastructure provides a set of resources for developing proxies, which alleviate those thin clients from computation expensive tasks. The main idea behind this approach is to offer some building blocks and programming interfaces for developing TACC modules (Transformation Aggregation Caching and Customization). These modules preprocess data before sending it to the client. Therefore, the amount of work that the client has to do on the data is minimized. Examples of Transformations are filtering, re-rendering and encryption. Aggregation refers to collecting and collating data from several sources. Caching is used to store post-transformed data, so it does not have to be transformed everytime. Finally customization is related to the configuration of shared services, so that every client gets exactly what it needs. Different TACC modules execute independently and the output of one of them can be redirected to the input of another one. They can also be easily changed or updated. However, specific aspects of a TACC module cannot be dynamically customized; instead they whole module must be replaced by a new one that provide the required functionality.

The Rover Toolkit is an object oriented platform that offers a set of tools to develop mobile applications. It is mainly based on two fundamental ideas: relocatable dynamic objects (RDOs) and a queued remote procedure call (QRPC).

Relocatable dynamic objects can be loaded dynamically into client devices from server computers. Therefore, the execution environment characteristics (bandwidth, properties of the client device, etc.) will dictate which RDOs must be sent to the client and which ones must remain in the server. This decision can be modified later on according to how the execution evolves.

Disconnected operation mode is supported by means of the queued remote procedure call. When the system detects a network disconnection, it stores incoming RPC requests in a log file; as soon as the connection is reestablished, the log file is replayed

The infrastructure offered by *2K* is similar to the Rover approach at the dynamic adaptation level. However the idea introduced in *2K* of extending the whole OS to mobile devices is new. Neither AMWP nor Rover contemplate that possibility.

8 Conclusion and Future Work

The infrastructure introduced in this paper extends the OS to every kind of device, providing a unique and seamless image of the system. The user can interact with the system from different locations, scenarios and by using different devices. The *2K* distributed operating system creates a customized execution context for each user. This context is defined in *2K* as an Environment, and it is persistent and independent of the device being used (workstation, PDA, PC).

Using CORBA as the standard *2K* underlying object bus provides a uniform way for interacting with every single service and resource offered by the system. This feature is exploited by PalmORB to offer sophisticated services to the Palm Pilots.

Adaptable *2K* proxies are useful tools for alleviating the hardware limitations of PDAs. They can provide users with functionality similar to the one offered in Workstations or PCs.

The *2K* distributed operating system introduces the concept of "Everything, everywhere, anytime computing", which introduces new possibilities in the field of information accessibility.

As part of our future work we plan to introduce several changes as well as new services and features. We will port our PalmORB to other PDA platforms though we will introduce changes in its design. We are interested in breaking the PalmORB into different components. These components will be added, updated and removed dynamically according to what is required by the execution environment. Our experience with a reflective ORB (dynamicTAO) has proved to be a useful mechanism to cope with dynamically changing environments. We will also redesign the Palm Pilot shell to add the new functionality. By adopting this approach there will not be any difference, from the user's point of view, when accessing local Palm Pilot applications and remote *2K* components.

References

1. Thomas E. Anderson, David E. Culler, David A. Patterson, and the NOW Team. A case for networks of workstations: Now. In *IEEE Micro*, February 1995.
2. Francisco J. Ballesteros, Fabio Kon, and Roy H. Campbell. A Detailed Description of Off++, a Distributed Adaptable Microkernel. Technical Report UIUCDCS-R-97-2035, University of Illinois at Urbana-Champaign, August 1997. Also available at `http://choices.cs.uiuc.edu/2k/off++`.
3. Roy Campbell and Tin Qian. Dynamic agent-based security architecture for mobile computers. In *Second International Conference on Parallel and Distributed Computing and Networks (PDCN'98)*. IASTED, December 1998.
4. Schmidt Douglas C. The ADAPTIVE Communication Environment. In *Proceedings of the Sun User Group Conference*, San Jose, California, December 1993.
5. Armando Fox, Steven D. Gribble, Yatin Chawathe, Eric A. Brewer, and Paul Gauthier. Cluster-based scalable network sevices. In *Proc. 1997 Symposium on Operating Systems Principles (SOSP-16)*. ACM, October 1997.
6. Network Working Group. Nfs: Network file system protocol specification. In *rfc 1094*. March 1989.
7. Anthony D. Joseph and M. Frans Kaashoek. Building reliable mobile-aware applications using the rover toolkit. In *Proceedings of the 2nd ACM International Conference on Mobile Computing and Networking*, November 1996.
8. Fabio Kon and Roy H. Campbell. Supporting Automatic Configuration of Component-Based Distributed Systems. In *Proc. 5th USENIX Conference on Object-Oriented Technologies and Systems (COOTS'99)*, San Diego, CA, May 1999.
9. Fabio Kon, Ashish Singhai, Roy H. Campbell, Dulcineia Carvalho, Robert Moore, and Francisco J. Ballesteros. 2K: A Reflective, Component-Based Operating System for Rapidly Changing Environments. In *ECOOP'98 Workshop on Reflective Object-Oriented Programming and Systems*, Brussels, Belgium, July 1998.
10. mpeg2play. `http://www.mpeg.org/MPEG/MSSG`.
11. Manuel Román, Fabio Kon, and Roy H. Campbell. Design and Implementation of Runtime Reflection in Communication Middleware: the *dynamicTAO* Case. In *Proc. ICDCS'99 Workshop on Middleware*, Austin, TX, June 1999.
12. Douglas Schmidt. Tao overview. `http://siesta.cs.wustl.edu/~schmidt/TAO-intro.html`.

Designing Information Appliances Using a Resource Replication Model

Mário J. Silva, Ana Paula Afonso

Departamento de Informática
Faculdade de Ciências da Universidade de Lisboa
Campo Grande, 1700 Lisboa – Portugal
Phone: +351.1.7500153, Fax: +351.1.7500084
{mjs, apa}@di.fc.ul.pt

Abstract. We discuss the design of new network applications that collect and manage data and interface with users through portable devices. These applications maintain data pipelines that interact with network information servers and distill information into reduced data models that may be queried and replicated effectively through wireless networks to computing devices of very small size. We present initial design considerations for applications of this class.

1. Introduction

JINI has been recently announced as a new class of middleware for building distributed software applications that may run from small portable devices and then locate and interact with network services [11]. The designers of JINI announce a generation of new applications, built on this model, which will let users invoke coordinated sequences of actions from these devices to be executed in the distributed environment. Examples of the typical scenarios used to demonstrate the new mobile device capabilities include the use of digital cameras that dispatch captured pictures to handheld computers that send them in turn by email through a mobile phone.

However, we believe that this view of the application domain of this new class of middleware is too much control-oriented. As portable computing devices become more ubiquitous and familiar to users, a trend to a more data-centric view of their operation can be expected. The new devices will be selected not only by their computing power or that of installed applications, but by the value of the information they give to their users. Norman argues that the proper way to establish this new paradigm is through the development of human technology appliances, simple task-specific devices, called *information appliances* [14]. This view brings a new perspective to the ubiquitous computing paradigm previously developed at Xerox PARC [19]. In this new perspective the complexity of the computer disappears, becoming invisible. The emphasis of the design is on the human activity the appliance is meant to serve.

We have been inspired on the *information appliance* concept to refer to the new class of new applications that bring data to users' hands to help them in completing well-defined tasks. We see the PalmPilot as a first example of the information appliance concept [17]. Its owner sees the device as a handy portable database repository for personal data. The device is not really viewed by users and programmers as a distributed application or a distributed database with support for disconnected operation, but rather as a database management system that is occasionally synchronized with other databases (which may or not be replicas). Communication takes place when a user requests its Palm database to synchronize with another database.

The popularity of the PalmPilot and others that followed its operating model motivates the extension of the information appliance paradigm to other types of information processing applications. However, the PalmPilot works well as an information-processing platform only when the nature of the data to be manipulated is of relatively small size, infrequently updated with relatively small changes. When the nature of the data differs significantly, palm-based applications do not perform as well. For instance, Web browsers have been developed for palm computers, some with the capability to pre-load web pages. However, a desktop web browsing experience is radically different from that of reading the web from a palm-based computer. We cannot provide the type of interaction that is best adapted to this type of devices with web-style distributed applications. In wireless networks, short bandwidth, frequent fadings and intermittent connectivity, severely affect web access usability.

In recent years, we began witnessing that the Web itself is evolving from a distributed hypertext system into a collection of databases of information, which may be not only browsed directly, but also queried and downloaded for local processing. Formats such as XML and RDF are examples of standards supporting this direction.

We believe that this trend and the popularization of portable computing devices of many forms will generate a more heterogeneous environment than we have today. In the new environment, specialized devices and browsers for specific "web data types" will become more common. These browsers will be specialized in managing local databases and synchronizing with external data sources.

We see the process of development of information appliances as the creation of data pipelines that feed from network information servers and distill data into reduced data models for personal use. These may be activated to deliver information effectively through wireless networks.

A key requirement for information appliances will be a synchronization framework that will be able to manage replicated data sets in this environment at variable levels of consistency as data steps through various stages until reaching users' devices. We call this framework the Resource Replication Model.

The remainder of this paper is organized as follows: in Section 2, we discuss related works. In Section 3, we present our approach for the development of information appliances. Finally, in Section 4, we discuss our future work and present concluding remarks.

2. Related Work

The Resource Replication Model is inspired on concepts from network proxies and middleware services, materialized views maintenance, file/data synchronization, web information systems and information dissemination models.

Network Middleware

Network proxies have been proposed and used successfully as a mechanism for adaptation of mobile applications that access information services through wireless networks [24]. In addition to hiding from existing distributed applications the new protocols and services that are required for operation on mobile networks, proxies can be used to translate data into formats that are better adapted to the requirements of mobile users that access the network using resource limited devices [7].

Proxies are examples of software frameworks for building mobile distributed applications, also called mobile computing middleware. These provide a set of objects that hide all the networking details and offer a set of interfaces at an higher level of abstraction, for replicating objects and invoking methods, independently of the characteristics of the underlying network infrastructure [5]. In the Mobiware project, the use of open (CORBA) interfaces for its middleware components enabled the creation of applications that combined the networking specific service objects with other objects [4].

More than the hiding of many of the complexities of networking in mobile wireless environments, we are interested in the use of these systems as the basis for enabling user spontaneous composition and activation of personalized information services.

Materialized Views Maintenance

The role of materialized views and view maintenance as a caching schema has been studied in the context of mobile database applications. In this perspective, information stored in portable computers can take the form of materialized views that can be maintained as caches in distributed systems [3]. A survey of materialized views concepts can be found in [20].

The intrinsic characteristics of mobile computing devices and wireless networks, such as limited resources and limited bandwidth, require a customizable view maintenance mechanism. Wolfson *et al.* discuss the problems associated with view maintenance and propose possible solutions [22]. First, a view can contain continuously changing location and time dependable data. Second, there is a need to dynamically switch between broadcasting and point-to-point transmission of updates to materialized views. Finally, another important issue to be addressed is the predictable/voluntary disconnections in mobile computing environments. Another approach considers the development of a mechanism in the form of a proxy within the fixed network, providing customizable and client oriented data-warehouses [12].

With the above extensions, materialized views provide a good framework to collect and extract information from several data sources. In our Resource Replication Model we also consider an approach based on software agents that extract data for information appliances.

File and Data Synchronization

Replicated storage systems are a solution to get improved availability, scalability and performance in distributed systems [6]. In mobile computing environments, data replication is a method for supporting disconnected operation. The process of data replication may be provided either transparently or in a user-aware mode. Examples of the first approach include replication models of distributed file systems that use caching, such Coda [13], and models for database reconciliation, such as Bayou [6]. In a user-aware approach, users must know what files are replicated and explicitly specify the replicas management policy [2]. This later model is adapted to the operating mode used in portable devices, as it supports discrete points of synchronization, lazy reconciliation and immediate update propagation. In Oracle's symmetric replication, it is possible to replicate data between a relational database and portable computers at a smaller level of granularity, using specific knowledge of the structure of the files [16].

Web Information Systems

The web is a natural context for replication with its increasing scalability and performance demands. We can view the web as a very large heterogeneous distributed information system, evolving from a collection of hyperlinked documents to dynamic contents generated from database sources, document libraries and others information sources. We believe that new standards like XML (Extensible Markup Language) [23] and RDF (Resource Description Framework) [15] will provide good support for the integration of web data sources. They contribute to define standardized conventions to represent the information and provide a foundation for processing metadata in the web. XML vocabularies and automated conversions to other vocabularies provide compatibility between web integration methods, maximizing interoperability between independent servers and clients.

Information Dissemination Models

In our previous work, we studied the use of push models for disseminating information to mobile users and implemented *Ubidata*, a general and adaptable framework for mobile computing dissemination systems [1]. We added an adaptation capability to channels, where the update frequency and priority of information items changes dynamically as the users change their location. This is an extension to the conceptual models for information channels (publish/subscribe model) and a hybrid schema of information dissemination [8].

Our information dissemination model revealed some limitations of this approach in our application domain, such as the impossibility to maintain many replicas with bi-directional updates. In this work, we want to extend this paradigm, providing a model of replication that will support bi-directional synchronization between the data in portable devices and other databases.

3. Resource Replication Model

In our perspective, the elaboration and construction of an information appliance consists in creating and customizing a user agent that will act as a proxy of the information appliance (see Figure 1). User agents live on the fixed network and may track the associated portable devices. In addition, they cooperate with other agents and request data from network services to build the appliances' databases.

We envision the development of mobility-aware information appliances as follows:

- *Design of conceptual user data models* (personal user models). Information appliances running on portable devices will download information by connecting periodically with the associated user agent. Each appliance' agent has a specific conceptual model that holds the manipulated information. This could be represented as a relational or object-oriented data-model.
- *Design of the application interfaces.* This may include development of an interface to interact with the user agent in addition to the interface that will be used from the portable device.
- *Specification of the data extraction mechanism for model maintenance.* Once the model is created, the user agent database will be filled with data extracted from network web services. We see the user agents databases as appliances' data-warehouses.
- *Synchronization between databases.* We specify the data synchronization policy matching the application requirements regarding disconnected operation, availability of points of synchronization, and networking possibilities and cost trade-offs.

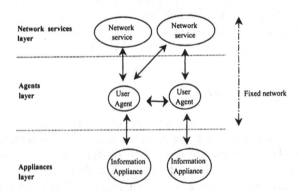

Figure 1 The environment of information appliances

To maintain the data held at each model we can use a triggering mechanism, so that the data sources notify user agents whenever a data change occurs. This option usually depends on the trigger functionality of the data sources and the ability of keeping track of the user agents that are interested in their changing information. Alternatively, we also support the definition of monitoring mechanisms, so that the user agent periodically monitors the data sources and detects possible changes.

We assume that data is available in XML and that RDF descriptions are available to provide the download and representation of the information stored in network services. As the use of these formats is disseminated we expect to be able to integrate many data sources from a large number of heterogeneous and autonomous web data sources. Meanwhile, we can integrate existing web data by using systems such as W4F [18], which fit in our environment as agents that can convert unstructured web sites into data sets that could be joined with other data to create the personal data models required by information appliances.

In our model, the users can construct data replication services dynamically. A new service is defined by specifying the information sources and data transformations to perform. The system then instantiates the required services and creates the necessary connections between the used components. To compose a replication service, we pipe data through proxies and have it transformed by objects with exportable interfaces using the Java technology [10], [11].

The power of network proxies as a paradigm for coping with mobility comes fundamentally from their capability of being inserted transparently in the data pipes that flow between communicating peers in mobile networks. As proxies change data, not the protocols or data formats, they can be composed to perform complex transformations on the data. As on the Unix system, these software pipes can be the basis for reusability of programs.

4. Summary and Future Research

We have introduced the need for rapid creation of information appliances run from portable devices and presented an approach based on the Resource Replication Model. We have described the initial architecture and the roles assumed by user agents responsible for the consistency of reduced data models, collected from web information systems into portable devices.

We intend to elaborate these initial ideas and develop a specification of a prototype that will demonstrate these concepts. The prototype will be an information appliance of events related to leisure activities. We recently developed a database and information service that publishes this information on the web [9]. To make this service available to our users while disconnected, we will offer it on small footprint devices, following the information appliance model described in this paper.

The appliance will run on palm computers and we intend to evaluate WAP devices as an alternative [21]. The devices will be used to view data that they receive from user agents when they reconnect to the fixed network.

User agents are java programs that can be configured to communicate with other software agents that perform specialized data processing, such as information filtering of news information or data conversion from external web sources.

Building a software system with the described functionality is not the main challenge. We anticipate that the hardest part will be the design of a usable interface that conveys not only the information to be presented but also shows, in an intuitive way, how, when and where data was obtained.

Acknowledgement

We thank the anonymous reviewers for their comments and suggestions for improving this paper.

References

[1]   A.P. Afonso, F.S. Regateiro, and M.J. Silva, UbiData: An adaptable framework for information dissemination to mobile users, in S. Demeyer e J. Bosch editors, *Object-Oriented Technology, ECOOP'98 Workshop on Mobile Computing and Replication*, volume 1543 de Lecture Notes in Computer Science, Springer-Verlag, July 1998.

[2]   S. Balasubramaniam and Benjamin C. Pierce, What is a File Synchronizer, *Proceedings of the ACM/IEEE MOBICOM' 98 Conference*, pp.98-108, October 1998.

[3]   D. Barbara and T. Imielinski, Sleepers and Workaholics: Caching Strategies in Mobile Environments, *Proceedings of the ACM SIGMOD, International Conference on Management of Data*, May 1994.

[4]   A.T. Campbell, H.G. De Meer, M.E. Kounavis, K. Miki, J. Vicente, and D. Villela, A Survey of Programmable Networks, *Computer Communications Review*, April 1999.

[5]   Daedalus Web Page, http://daedalus.cs.berkeley.edu/.

[6]   A. Demers *et al.*, The Bayou Architecture: Support for Data Sharing among Mobile Users, *Proceedings IEEE Workshop on Mobile Computing and Applications*, December 1994.

[7]   A. Fox and E.A. Brewer, Reducing WWW Latency and Bandwith Requirements by Real-Time Distillation, *Proceedings of the 5th International World Wide Web Conference*, May 1996.

[8]   M. Franklin and S. Zdonik, A Framework to Scalable Dissemination-Based Systems, *ACM OOPSLA Conference* (Invited Paper), October 1997.

[9]   Guia do Lazer, http://lazer.publico.pt/.

[10]   JavaBeans Specification, http://java.sun.com/beans/docs/spec.html.

[11]   JINI Technology, http://www.sun.com/jini/.

[12]   S. W. Lauzac and P. K. Chrysanthis, Programming Views for Mobile Database Clients, *Proceedings of DEXA'98 the Ninth International Workshop on Database and Expert Systems Applications*, pp. 408-413, August 1998.

[13]   J.J. Kistler and M. Satyanarayanan, Disconnected Operation in Coda File System, *ACM Transactions on Computer Systems*, 10(1): 3-25, February 1992.

[14]   Donald A. Norman, *The Invisible Computer*, MIT Press, 1998.

[15]   E. Miller, An Introduction to the Resource Description Framework, *D-Lib Magazine*, May 1998. http://ww.dlib.org.

[16]   Oracle Lite for Handheld Devices Release 3.5, Oracle Corporation, 1998.

[17]   Palm Pilot Web Page, http://www.palm.com.

[18]   W4F Web site, http://db.cis.upenn.edu/W4F/publi.html.

[19] M. Weiser, The Computer for the 21st Century, *Scientific American*, 265(3): 94-104, September 1991.

[20] J. E. Widom, Special Issue on Materialized Views and Data Warehousing, *Data Enginnering Bulletin*, IEEE Computer Society, 18(2), June 1995.

[21] Wireless Application Protocol Homepage, http://www.wapforum.com/.

[22] O. Wolfson, P. Sistla, S. Dao, K. Narayanan, and R. Ray, View Maintenance in Mobile Computing, *ACM Special Interest Group on Manangement of Data*, 24(4), December 1995.

[23] XML W3C Homepage, http://www.w3.org/XML.

[24] B. Zenel, D. Duchamp, A General Purpose Proxy Filtering Mechanism Applied to the Mobile Environment, *Proceedings of the ACM/IEEE MOBICOM' 97 Conference*, pp.248-259, September 1997.

ACTIVEMAP: A Visualization Tool for Location Awareness to Support Informal Interactions

Joseph F. McCarthy, Eric S. Meidel

Center for Strategic Technology Research (CSTaR)
Andersen Consulting
3773 Willow Road
Northbrook, IL 60062 USA

mccarthy@cstar.ac.com, eric.s.meidel@ac.com

Abstract. ACTIVEMAP is a visualization tool that enables users to gain greater awareness of the location of people in their workplace environment, increasing each person's ability to seek out colleagues for informal, face-to-face interactions. Our initial implementation of the tool places images of each person's face on a map of the building. We have explored variations on how to best represent a range of features: the "freshness" of location information, groups of people in a single office, and the movement of people throughout the environment. We describe the context of the environment in which the tool is used, the features embodied in this tool, variations we have implemented for representing location and movement information, and some potential extensions for future versions of the tool.

1. Introduction

Informal interactions constitute a frequent and crucial aspect of accomplishing work [Isaacs, *et al.*, 1993]. A number of other researchers have explored issues of awareness [Dourish & Bellotti, 1992] and how video and audio technology can be used to provide interaction capabilities for *distributed* workgroups [Dourish & Bly, 1992; Fish, *et al.*, 1993; Tang, *et al.*, 1993; Hudson & Smith, 1996; Nakanashi, *et al..*, 1996; Lee, *et al.*, 1997]. The developers of all of these systems acknowledge and seek to address the problem of users' perceptions of privacy invasion that often accompanies the deployment of cameras and microphones in the workplace.

People are generally willing to sacrifice some amount of privacy for commensurate benefits, as is evidenced by the widespread use of credit cards. For *distributed workgroups*, the benefits of the awareness provided by cameras and/or microphones may well outweigh the potential privacy costs. In contrast, we are primarily interested in exploring how ubiquitous – but less invasive – technology [Weiser & Brown, 1997] can be used to better support *physically proximate workgroups*. Although people in adjacent offices often have a high level of awareness of the location of their neighbors, people in non-adjacent offices experience a horizon effect and do not have much awareness of their physically distant colleagues. The degree of awareness is often mirrored in the number of interactions: people tend to interact more with their neighbors than with people further away [Kraut, *et al.*, 1990]. By expanding the sphere of awareness, we hope to expand the scope of regular interactors.

ACTIVEMAP is a tool that enables users to visualize the location and movement of all people within a workplace environment, providing large-scale, real-time awareness of that environment with minimal need for explicit interaction: *awareness at-a-glance*. The tool displays a window with a background showing a map of the physical layout of the workplace. In the foreground, images of the faces of people in that workplace are superimposed over the locations in which they were last seen.

Researchers at Xerox Palo Alto Research Center developed a program named "locations" that also superimposed images over a background of a map of their workplace [Spreitzer & Theimer, 1993]. However, few details were reported on this program, which was part of a larger research effort into developing a mobile and context-aware computing infrastructure [Schilit & Theimer, 1994]. In particular, very little was reported with respect to how the program represented different aspects of location information.

In contrast, our focus is on how best to visualize location information, given an existing infrastructure for providing location information. ACTIVEMAP provides users with a set of parameters that specify how to represent the freshness (or recency) of location information, how to represent collocated groups of people, and whether and how to represent movement of people throughout the workplace environment. We want to investigate how useful these representations are by finding out how people use them, which we are learning through both interviewing users and examining logs that show how users set these parameters.

Our larger goal is to investigate what effect this tool has on interactions in the workplace. By providing greater awareness of where people are, and who is with them, we create more opportunities for face-to-face interactions. Using the taxonomy proposed by Kraut, *et al.*, [1990][1], we believe that the use of ACTIVEMAP will allow people to engage in more *intended* interactions, possibly while creating the appearance of *opportunistic* or even *spontaneous* interactions.

This paper will describe our ACTIVEMAP tool. We first describe the context within which ACTIVEMAP operates; we next describe some of the basic features of the tool; we then present the different methods we have implemented for visualizing information about the location and movement of people; we report on some initial user expe-

---

[1] The four types of interpersonal communication are *scheduled* (planned by both parties), *intended* (planned by one party who seeks out the other), *opportunistic* (unplanned interaction regarding a planned topic of discussion), and *spontaneous* (unplanned interaction regarding an unplanned topic) [Kraut, *et al.*, 1990].

riences with ACTIVEMAP; we conclude with a discussion of some of our plans for extending the tool.

2. Environmental Context

The environmental context in which we have designed and built the ACTIVEMAP is the physical space occupied by the Center for Strategic Technology Research (CSTaR®), a 16,000 square foot section of the second floor of Andersen Consulting Technology Park, in Northbrook, IL, USA. The CSTaR area includes 30 individual offices, four laboratories, two large conference rooms (the Group Discussion Lab, or GDL, and a Videoconference room), two small conference rooms, a break area with kitchenette and vending machines, three furnished open areas used for informal meetings and numerous hallways. There are approximately 30 members of the CSTaR group in Northbrook,[2] including researchers, programmers, technical writers and administrative staff.

We have installed an ArialView™ Awareness System [Arial Systems Corp.] within the CSTaR area, consisting of a network of over 70 ceiling-mounted nodes, each housing an infrared sensor, radio frequency receiver and audio speaker, and a set of badges that transmit infrared identification signals every two seconds.[3] In addition to this hardware, the ArialView system includes components to process the signals and maintain badge location information in a Microsoft SQL Server 6.5 database, and a web browser interface for accessing and administering this information.

Some members of CSTaR have voiced privacy concerns about wearing a badge that allows them to be located in real-time or tracked over a period of time. Fortunately, we work in a profession in which our location does not reveal a great deal about our work (or play) activities: time spent in a colleague's office could represent an intensive exchange of project-related ideas, or a heated debate over whether a president committed impeachable offenses. One of the nice things about a badge system, is that anyone who objects to being located or tracked can simply not wear a badge, although this admittedly may not be the case in other professions. Ubiquitous cameras and microphones are not so easy to avoid (though one can presumably at least control the devices installed in one's office).

We believe that most people are willing to relinquish some degree of privacy for what they perceive as a compensating benefit. For example, most people in the United States are willing to let grocery stores track their purchases via some kind of

---

[2] There are six members in another CSTaR group in Palo Alto, CA, USA, but their workspace is not yet incorporated into the environment(s) served by ACTIVEMAP.

[3] The ArialView system is similar in many respects to the Olivetti Active Badge System [Want, et al., 1992; Harter & Hopper, 1994], except that the current ArialView badges have a single two-position slider switch rather than two buttons, and the ArialView sensor nodes include RF receivers and speakers.

preferred shopper's card in exchange for small discounts received when they present the card to the cashier. It remains to be seen whether the members of CSTaR will perceive enough benefits from ACTIVEMAP and other tools within our suite of active environment applications (e.g., EventManager [McCarthy & Anagnost, 1999]) to warrant their continued wearing of badges.[4]

3. The ACTIVEMAP Tool

ACTIVEMAP provides at-a-glance awareness of the location and movement of colleagues within a workplace environment by superimposing an image of each person over the location in which that person was last seen.[5] The tool runs under Windows 95/98/NT and has been installed on over 30 different laptop and desktop computers, which communicate with the ArialView servers via TCP/IP.

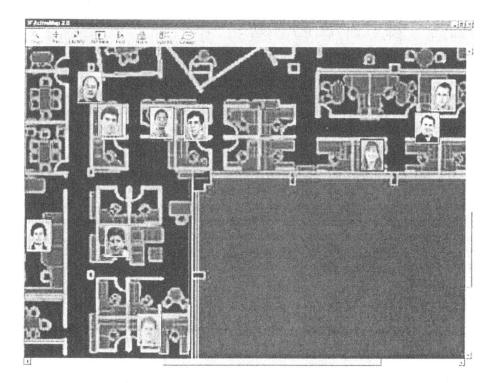

Figure 1: ACTIVEMAP displaying a region of the CSTaR workspace.

---

[4] See Harper [1992], for a more thorough discussion of acceptance issues with respect to the use of badges in a research lab context.

[5] More precisely, the location in which that person's badge was last detected by the ArialView sensors.

Figure 1 shows a snapshot of ACTIVEMAP depicting 11 people in a small region of the CSTaR area; this snapshot illustrates a number of representational features we have implemented in the tool. The following sections describe these features in greater detail.

3.1. Representing Information Freshness

ACTIVEMAP shows where each person's badge was last seen. However, a variety of factors can prevent the ArialView system from seeing a badge: a badge may be occluded by a body part or article of clothing (including a person's pocket); a person may be moving through (or stopped at) a "blind spot" not well covered by any sensor; or the person may have left the area covered by sensors.[6] Note that in the first case, the person is still in the location he or she was last seen, in the second case he or she may be close to the location last seen, and in the third case he or she may be long gone. In all three cases, the location information for a person is out-of-date, and we provide two different mechanisms for representing how fresh the information is for each person: image fading and frame shading.

Image Fading. One mechanism for representing freshness is to reflect the quality of the information in the quality of the image – clear images indicate people who have been sighted recently, faded images indicate people who have not been seen in a while. The intuition behind this metaphor is that a quick glance at ACTIVEMAP shows clearly who is currently located by the system; if you have to look closely at an image, it may be due to that person not being in the last seen location.

The user specifies a time interval over which fading will occur, between 1 and 24 hours, and selects a fading scale, either linear or [decaying] exponential. For the linear scale, we divide the total number of minutes in this interval by 256 to determine a fading change interval, and lower the brightness value (using the Hue, Saturation and Brightness, or HSB, color scheme) used to display the image by one for each elapsed interval value. For the exponential scale, we use the following darkening formula to adjust brightness:

$$\left[\frac{1}{1-e^{-2}}\right] \cdot \left(e^{-2t} - e^{-2}\right)$$

where t is the normalized time interval. At the upper limit of the user-specified fading period, the image will have faded to black.

Frame Shading. A drawback to using the image quality to represent information quality is that images that are faded may in some cases represent people who are still at the location they were last seen, i.e., the location information is still valid even though their badges have not been detected recently. We therefore created an alter-

---

[6] For simplicity of exposition, we will often speak of "a person being seen" rather than "a person's badge being detected by a sensor," even though the latter description is technically more accurate.

native view option that does not degrade the image quality but uses differential shading of the frame around an image to indicate information quality. White frames indicate people who are currently seen by the system. As time passes since the last sightings, these frames are progressively darkened, using the same formulae as in the image quality representation, until they appear black after the maximum length of time has passed.

In Figure 1, the frame shading option was selected, with an interval setting of one hour. The person in the far right portion of the picture (white frame) is being seen right now; the person immediately below and slightly to the left (gray frame) was last seen 20 minutes ago; and the next person below and to the left (black frame) has not been seen for over an hour.

Users also have the option of specifying a maximum lapse of time (between 1 and 24 hours) for considering a person "here" – after a person's badge has not been sighted for that period of time, the person is considered "not here" and his or her image is displayed in a separate "Not Here" window pane. Mousing over the images in the "Not Here" window will bring up tool-tip windows showing the names and times last seen, just as within the main ACTIVEMAP window.

3.2. Representing Groups of Inhabitants

One of our design goals was to create a visualization tool to facilitate awareness-at-a-glance, i.e., one look at ACTIVEMAP would provide information about all the inhabitants within the intelligent environment. However, we also wanted ACTIVEMAP to scale gracefully from small physical spaces to large ones, and to accommodate varying levels of magnification (zooming). One area in which a conflict arose between these two goals was in our representation of groups of inhabitants gathered together in a single location. We provide the user with two options for representing collocated groups: tiled and stacked. In Figure 1, the tiled representation was used; however, Figures 2a and 2b illustrate why we have provided both alternatives.

Tiled Groupings. The tiled representation places images of inhabitants around the center point of the location in which they are located; they are separated by as much space as possible, maximizing the difference between their respective angles from the center point of that location. The advantage of this representation is that it exposes as much of the images as possible; the disadvantage is that for locations with little space, such as individual offices, it is sometimes difficult to discern exactly where a person is located, since images sometimes overflow into adjacent offices or hallways.

Figure 2: Groups in (a) Tiled representation and (b) Stacked representation

Stacked Groupings. The stacked image representation, in which multiple collocated images are stacked on top of one another in decreasing order of recency (the topmost image is of the person who was most recently seen), represents the reverse tradeoff. With a stack of images, only the topmost image is clearly visible, but since the bottommost image is centered in the location, it is easy to see how many people – though not which people – are in a given location. Although moving the mouse to that location will reveal all the people currently there in a tool-tip window, the interaction requirement diminishes the "at-a-glance" functionality we desire.

3.3. Representing Movement

We wanted to represent movement on ACTIVEMAP to help provide some context: when one or more images suddenly shift from one location to another on the map, it is often difficult to discern which image(s) moved. By adding movement into the representation scheme, we hoped to differentiate stationary people from those who are moving or have recently moved. However, we wanted to minimize the risk that inhabitants would feel they were being "tracked" by the system – concerns over privacy are likely to be heightened if the system maintains (and displays) a history of movement rather than an instantaneous snapshot of current locations. We also wanted to avoid cluttering the display, a situation that might arise by representing the movement of many people over a considerable amount of time.

Our initial representation for movement in ACTIVEMAP simply distinguishes images that have moved from those that have not by coloring the frames of recently moved images bright green. Users can specify a maximum elapsed time to allow since the most recent movement – in the range from 0 to 60 seconds – so that they can define "recent" for themselves.

We also provide an option that allows a user to hear audio cues that represent movement. One sound indicates that someone has been sighted for the first time that day, another sound indicates that there has been some movement by one or more people. These audio cues can be independently enabled and disabled.

3.4. Interaction through ACTIVEMAP

Although the primary purpose of ACTIVEMAP is to provide hands-free at-a-glance awareness of people in the workplace, we have provided a number of ways that users can interact with the system. ACTIVEMAP users can shift the view in any direction by using the mouse to drag the map. Users can also zoom the view in or out to one of eight levels of magnification. Moving the mouse around the map can generate "tool-tip" style windows (such as the balloon help windows that are used in Windows 95/98/NT) that label information on the map: placing the mouse over an office or meeting room on the map pops up a window that labels that location; placing the mouse over an image on the map pops up a window that lists the people in that location.

A "Find" button pops up a list of people known to the system, and then re-centers the map over the image of the selected person wherever he or she was last seen. We also provide a "Home" button (and an option to "Set Home" position) so that users can easily revert to their "normal" view of the map.

The ArialView system provides a capability to send *directed audio* messages to people in the environment: a user types in a text message, which is then processed by a speech synthesizer and the resulting output is sent to an audio speaker in the Arial-View ceiling node closest to the person to whom the message is directed. ACTIVEMAP provides an interface to this capability by popping up the text message window whenever a user double-clicks on the image of a person.

4. Initial User Experiences

ACTIVEMAP has been available to members of CSTaR for only a short time. While we have solicited feedback from a few people about the utility of various features, we have not yet conducted extensive interviews to learn how or why people are using these features. We also have a log of what settings people are using, so that we hope to conduct a quantitative analysis of features based on how people are really using the tool (which may be slightly different than how they say they are using it). This section highlights some of the early feedback we have received.

4.1. How, When and Where ACTIVEMAP is Used

We have installed ACTIVEMAP in a kiosk machine in a heavily trafficked hallway of the CSTaR workspace. It turns out that this installation of the program is accessed *far* more frequently than copies installed on individual desktop and laptop computers. Many individuals report accessing ACTIVEMAP on this kiosk several times per day, and people outside of the CSTaR group have been observed using ACTIVEMAP on the kiosk to locate people on numerous occasions. In contrast, only two individuals report accessing ACTIVEMAP on their personal computers more than a few times per week. One of these frequent users (who coincidentally happens to be one of the authors) has ACTIVEMAP running all the time on a second desktop machine in his office, almost as a screensaver type of application. This user also reports running ACTIVEMAP all day whenever he is working from a remote location, as it provides a significant degree of awareness of what is happening on-site. The other frequent user reports accessing ACTIVEMAP on his single desktop computer at least five times daily.

The lack of more widespread frequent use on personal computers may be due a number of different factors. We have released several versions of the tool, and unsatisfactory experiences with early releases may have led to a lingering image problem. Due to the pace of new versions being developed and tested, the application is a moving target, and so we have not expended much energy [to date] in marketing the application and training people how to use it effectively. Finally, our research group also produces a screensaver application that is used by most members of the research group (and several thousand people throughout the rest of the organization); while we believe that ACTIVEMAP might make a nice screensaver type of application, at this point we don't want to compete with our colleagues for screen real estate and attention.

4.2. Option Preferences

We have referenced a number of different options or parameters that users can vary to adjust the visual or aural aspects of ACTIVEMAP. In informal discussions with some of our users, we detected certain trends in how people like (and don't like) to visualize the information.

ACTIVEMAP displays the names and times last seen in tool-tip windows that popup during mouseover events. One option was to depict time last seen as absolute time (e.g., Joe McCarthy; 01:49PM) or elapsed time (Joe McCarthy; 1 minute ago). Different people expressed different preferences for displaying this information; no clearly preferred option emerged.

There was a clear tendency among users to prefer frame shading to image fading in representing information freshness. Users also tended to prefer stacked groupings to tiled groupings (but one suggested using tiled groupings in rooms that were large enough to accommodate multiple images, such as meeting rooms and open areas). Most users use the logarithmic falloff option for representing time since last seen – the difference between someone not being seen in 5 vs. 10 minutes is often not interpreted the same as the difference between someone not being seen in 65 vs. 70 minutes – with a falloff range starting from 0-15 minutes up to 1-2 hours.

Sounds emanating from ACTIVEMAP were generally perceived as distracting. Only one person enabled the audio cues to indicate any movement by anyone throughout the workplace, though a few users enabled the audio cues that represent the initial arrival of people at the workplace.

5. Future Work

We are considering extending the capabilities of ACTIVEMAP in a number of directions: alternate representations of time, movement through space and collocated groups of inhabitants; new sources of information to supplement the location information provided by our badge system; and new mechanisms for interacting with inhabitants through the tool.

5.1. Alternate Representations of Freshness, Movement and Groups

The progressive darkening of the image to represent freshness is probably not the best way to degrade image quality. We plan to experiment with other mechanisms for representing freshness in the image quality that still permit recognition of images of people who have not been seen in a long time, e.g., inserting lines of varying thickness at regular intervals across the image.

We would like to represent movement using slime trails – a notion borrowed from turtle graphics, wherein a line (usually, with some maximum length) trails behind an object as it moves about on the screen – to show each person's movement over the course of the last 0 to 60 seconds. We believe that this range of settings provides sufficient context while minimizing screen clutter, and we do not believe that the addition of this small amount of movement history will be perceived as unduly invasive.

The two methods we use for representing groups of people in the same location – tiling or stacking – each has disadvantages, both of which stem from the fixed size of locations within the map. We plan to investigate the use of non-linear magnification techniques [Keahey & Robertson, 1996] to see if we can relax the rigidity of location boundaries without compromising the ability to easily interpret the map.

5.2. New Sources of Activity Information

We have found that providing simple awareness of the location of people throughout the workplace environment to be useful. However, for reasons outlined above, the accuracy of the infrared badges and sensors is not perfect. We would like to incorporate other kinds of information to augment the information provided by our badge system, to help compensate for inaccuracies and provide more information about the potential availability of people in the environment. Other sources of information we are considering include motion or noise detection within offices, detection of whether the telephone in an office is currently in use, and keyboard/mouse usage monitoring (similar to the awareness provided by AOL's Instant Messenger (AIM) application).

5.3. New Interaction Mechanisms

Our initial implementation of ACTIVEMAP provides only one mode for interacting with inhabitants: sending a directed audio message by double-clicking on a person's image. We would like to add additional capabilities, e.g., initiating a telephone call directed to the closest telephone to the person viewed in ACTIVEMAP, or perhaps linking to EVENTMANAGER [McCarthy & Anagnost, 1999], a tool that allows users to notified of the occurrence of specified events based on people and locations, so by clicking on Ted's image I can ask to be notified "when Ted returns to his office."

5.4. Speech-Enabled Interface (Kiosk)

One of the machines running ACTIVEMAP is a public kiosk machine with a large display. This kiosk has an infrared keyboard and touchpad, but the physical layout of the kiosk space makes it awkward to use direct manipulation of the ACTIVEMAP interface. We plan to enable ACTIVEMAP to accept spoken commands, so that someone viewing ACTIVEMAP from the kiosk can tell the application to "Zoom In" or "Shift Left." We also plan to enable a kiosk user to ask "Where is Eric" and have the ACTIVEMAP zoom in to the location where Eric was last seen, or to "Send an audio message to Eric" to invoke the directed audio capability.[7]

6. Conclusion

ACTIVEMAP is a tool that provides real-time at-a-glance awareness of the locations of people throughout the environment based on information provided by a system of infrared badges and sensors. Our initial implementation of the tool incorporates several features for representing location information freshness, movement and groups of people. We plan to investigate the perceived utility of these features, explore other possible representations, and incorporate other sources of information in future releases of the tool.

Our goal for the tool is to facilitate more informal, face-to-face interactions among workers within the same physical workplace, while minimizing the intrusiveness of the technology we use to accomplish this goal – essentially providing the maximum social benefit for the minimum privacy cost. While the authors have experienced an increase in such interactions, further research will be required to determine whether the CSTaR user population as a whole, experiences similar benefits, and whether the tool provides other, unanticipated functionality with respect to the interpersonal relationships and communications within the group.

---

[7] Though obviously, in this case, we'd record a spoken message directly into a WAV file and send it, rather than using speech recognition to translate the spoken words into a text file, and then using the text-to-speech synthesizer to translate the text into a WAV file before sending it.

Acknowledgements

The authors wish to thank Ted Anagnost, another member of the CSTaR Active Environments research group who contributed several ideas to the development of ACTIVEMAP; Andy Fano, for feedback both on the ACTIVEMAP application and this paper; Tony Costa and Ed Gottsman, for suggestions regarding a number of aspects of the application; and the anonymous reviewers for their careful reading and useful suggestions for improving this paper. The authors, of course, assume full responsibility for any remaining shortcomings in the document.

References

1. Arial Systems Corp. ArialView™ Awareness System. http://www.arialsystems.com.
2. Sara A. Bly, Steve R. Harrison and Susan Irwin. 1993. Media Space: Bringing People Together in a Video, Audio, and Computing Environment. *Communications of the ACM*, 36(1), January 1993, pp. 28-47.
3. Paul Dourish and Victoria Bellotti. 1992. Awareness and Coordination in Shared Workspaces. In *Proceedings of the ACM 1992 Conference on Computer Supported Cooperative Work (CSCW '92).* 330-337.
4. Paul Dourish and Sara Bly. 1992. Portholes: Supporting Awareness in Distributed Work Groups. In *Proceedings of the ACM 1992 Conference on Human Factors in Computer Systems (CHI '92).* 541-547.
5. Robert S. Fish, Robert E. Kraut, Robert W. Root and Ronald E. Rice. 1993. Video Informal Communication. *Communications of the ACM*, 36(1), January 1993. 48-61.
6. Richard H. R. Harper. 1992. Looking at Ourselves: An Examination of the Social Organisation of Two Research Laboratories. In *Proceedings of the ACM 1992 Conference on Computer Supported Cooperative Work (CSCW '92).* 330-337.
7. Andy Harter and Andy Hopper. 1994. A Distributed Location System for the Active Office. *IEEE Network* 8(1): 62-70.
8. Scott E. Hudson and Ian Smith. 1996. Techniques for Addressing Fundamental Privacy and Disruption Tradeoffs in Awareness Support Systems. In *Proceedings of the ACM 1996 Conference on Computer Supported Cooperative Work (CSCW '96).* 248-257.
9. Ellen A. Isaacs, Steve Whittaker, David Frohlich and Brid O'Conaill. 1997. Informal Communication Re-examined: New Functions for Video in Supporting Opportunistic Encounters. In *Video-Mediated Communication.* Kathleen E. Finn, Abigail J. Sellen and Sylvia B. Wilbur (eds). Lawrence Erlbaum. 459-485.
10.T. Alan Keahey and Edward L. Robertson. 1996. Techniques for Non-linear Magnification Transformations. In *Proceedings of the IEEE Symposium on Information Visualization, IEEE Visualization.* 38-45.
11.Alison Lee, Andreas Girgensohn and Kevin Schlueter. 1997. NYNEX Portholes: Initial User Reactions and Redesign Implications. In *Proceedings of the ACM 1997 International Conference on Supporting Group Work (GROUP '97).*
12.Joseph F. McCarthy and Theodore D. Anagnost. 1999. EVENTMANAGER: Support for the Peripheral Awareness of Events. Submitted.

13. Hideyuki Nakanashi, Chikara Yoshida, Toshikazu Nishimura and Toru Ishida. 1996. FreeWalk: Supporting Casual Meetings in a Network. In *Proceedings of the ACM 1996 Conference on Computer Supported Cooperative Work (CSCW '96)*. 308-314.
14. Bill N. Schilit and Marvin M. Theimer. 1994. Disseminating Active Map Information to Mobile Hosts. *IEEE Network* 8(5): 22-32.
15. Mike Spreitzer and Marvin Theimer. 1993. Providing Location Information in a Ubiquitous Computing Environment. In *Proceedings of the 14th ACM Symposium on Operating Systems Principles (SIGOPS '93)*. 270-283.
16. John C. Tang, Ellen A. Isaacs and Monica Rua. 1994. Supporting Distributed Groups with a Montage of Lightweight Interactions. In *Proceedings of ACM 1994 Conference on Computer Supported Cooperative Work (CSCW '94)*. 23-34.
17. Roy Want, Andy Hopper, Veronica Falcao, and Jonathon Gibbons. 1992. The Active Badge Location System. *ACM Transactions on Information Systems* 10(1): 91-102.
18. Mark Weiser and John Seeley Brown. 1997. The Coming Age of Calm Technology. In *Beyond Calculation: The Next Fifty Years of Computing*. Peter J. Denning and Robert M. Metcalfe (eds). Springer Verlag. 75-85.

Close Encounters:
Supporting Mobile Collaboration
through Interchange of User Profiles

Gerd Kortuem, Zary Segall, Thaddeus G. Cowan Thompson

University of Oregon, Department of Computer Science
Eugene, OR 97403, USA
{kortuem,zs}@cs.uoregon.edu, tcowanth@gladstone.uoregon.edu

Abstract. This paper introduces the notion of *profile-based cooperation* as a way to support awareness and informal communication between mobile users during chance encounters. We describe the design of *Proem*, a wearable system for *profile-based cooperation* that enables users to publish and exchange personal profile information during physical encounters. The *Proem* system is used to initiate contact between individuals by identifying mutual interests or common friends. In contrast to most previous research that concentrates on collaboration in well-defined and closed user groups, *Proem* supports informal communication between individuals who have never met before and who don't know each other. We illustrate the benefits of profile-based cooperation by describing several usage scenarios for the Proem system.

1   Introduction

During the course of a day we encounter and meet a large number of people, some of whom we know personally and some of whom we never met before. In everyday language we use the verb "to meet" to describe many different situations. To meet someone can mean to have a face-to-face conversation or to be introduced to someone. On the other extreme, it can simply describe a situation where we are in someone's physical presence without communicating. In contrast to a meeting, an *encounter* describes a situation where we meet someone unexpectedly, for example in a hallway or an elevator. Such an encounter with another person is a chance for striking up a conversation and for exchanging information. It has been realized that unexpected and unplanned encounters between co-workers play an important role in collaboration and coordination of work activities.

Encounters can also be virtual. Visitors can encounter each other in virtual-reality environments and online chat rooms. Similarly, web-based on-line communities like SixDegrees [SixDegress 1999] support the notion of co-presence by informing visitors who else is online. Often, online communities require members to describe their online personality in form of user profiles, a more or less truthful description of who they are or want to be, what they like and what they don't. By giving users access to other members' profiles, online communities are able to foster communication between users who have never met before in real life. In this way, encounters in virtual worlds or on the Internet can serve a purpose similar to real-world encounters: they promote informal communication by increasing awareness and they are a chance for one-on-one conversations through direct messaging.

Today's mobile technology provides the means to apply the concept of user profiles to real-world encounters between individuals. On the one hand, there is a rapidly growing acceptance of palm-size, handheld and wearable computers, and on the other hand there is the imminent arrival of ubiquitous wireless communication. Based on this background we investigate how the concept of user profiles and online identities can be used to support cooperation during physical encounters of individuals who congregate in groups or large crowds, such as at indoor/outdoor meetings, conferences, and trade-show events.

This paper introduces our notion of *profile-based cooperation* as a way to support awareness and informal communication between mobile users during chance encounters. We also report on the design of a mobile system called *Proem* that we are building as a testbed for our ideas. Proem provides the infrastructure for mobile users to publish and exchange personal profile information during physical encounters. Proem can be seen as an extension of the Inter-Personal-Awareness Device (IPAD) idea introduced by [Holmquist 1998; Holmquist et al 1999] and exemplified by the Hummingbird mobile device.

In the following sections, we will introduce our concept of *profile-based cooperation* and describe the design of the Proem system.

2   Profile-Based Cooperation

We are interested in the question of how mobile devices (handheld and wearable devices) can be used during chance encounters to support cooperation. In particular and in contrast to most previous research, we are interested in how mobile technology can be used during *encounters of people who have never met before and who don't know each other*. We have developed the notion of *profile-based cooperation* as a means to support awareness and informal communication between mobile users. Our idea is based on four fundamental concepts:

1. *User Profile*: a collection of personal data stored on a mobile device that describes the user.
2. *Encounter*: a situation of physical proximity of two or more individuals.
3. *Profile Exchange*: the transmission of personal data between two or more mobile devices during an encounter.
4. *Rules of Encounter*: predefined behaviors that are triggered as side effect of a profile exchange.

We will now discuss these concepts in more detail.

2.1   Profiles

A profile is a description of an individual – his or her personal tastes, interests, expertise, and opinions. What is and isn't in a profile depends on the specific context. A profile is defined by the individual that it describes with the express purpose of sharing this information with others, friends as well as colleagues and strangers. A profile can contain any information whose exchange with others might be beneficial to either the sending or receiving party.

Typical information that could be part of a profile includes: name and address; phone, fax numbers and email addresses; company affiliation; calendar information and appointments; a list of to-do tasks; a list of friends and relatives; health-related and emergency information; a list of the user's favorite web sites; an assumed name or user id; a collection of favorite poems; classifieds the user placed in last week's newspaper; the title and author of every single book the user owns; model and year of the user's car; a list of favorite recipes; a list of the user's publications; keywords indicating the user's research interests.

A profile is similar to a vCard [vCard 1996] in that it is intended for automated exchange of personal data. But a profile goes beyond mere contact information and may include a much more detailed description of the user.

In order to make sense of profile information, users must share a common understanding of the types of information contained within profiles. Users must agree on the meaning and purpose of an attribute such as `interest`, or else they can not successfully exchange profile data.

Profiles should be extensible: individual users should be able to add additional information categories at any time. This requires a semantic foundation for profiles that is similarly flexible.

2.2 Encounters

The purpose of maintaining a profile is to exchange it with other users during an encounter. We define an *encounter* between individuals as a situation
1. where these individuals are in close physical proximity to each other,
2. the mobile devices of these individuals have discovered each other's presence and
3. these devices are able to communicate.

This definition does not say anything about how devices discover each other, nor how close they have to come in order to do so. Many different technologies have been used in the past for discovering nearby devices, including infrared transmitters and near-field radios. Similarly, this definition does not say whether discovery and communication are independent functions or can be combined into one, as would be possible with wireless ad hoc networks, future short-range wireless networks like Bluetooth and Home RF, or Personal Area Networks [Zimmerman 1996].

Encounters have several important properties:
- Encounters can occur between two or more individuals.
- Encounters are asymmetrical: it is possible that user A encounters user B, but not vice-versa.
- Encounters are situations with a time duration, not momentary events: encounters can be short, lasting only a few seconds, or they can be long-lasting, going on for hours. For example, the encounter between two individuals passing each other in a hallway might last just a few seconds. On the other hand, two or more people in a lengthy meeting encounter each other for the full duration of that meeting.

- Encounters are nontransitive: if user A encounters user B, and users B encounters user C, then user A does not necessarily encounter user C.
- An encounter occurs even if no data is transferred between the involved parties.

2.3 Profile Exchange

An encounter between individuals is a chance for an exchange of profile data. There are two parties involved in an exchange: the *owner* is the individual who is described by a profile; the *reader* is any individual who accesses another user's profile.

We define the following principles for the exchange of profiles:

- *Owner control*: access to profile data should be controlled by its owner; that includes control over what information to include, with whom to share it, and when to share.
- *Reader selection*: dissemination of profile information should be controlled by the reader, not the owner. In other words, profile data should not be pushed onto devices of unsuspecting users, but required to be pulled by readers.
- *Reciprocity*: owners should be able to restrict access to their data to individuals which themselves are willing to share their data.

Other requirements we see as important are:

- Support for multiple privacy levels with the effect that owners are able to deny strangers access to data which they are willing to share with friends.
- Support for anonymous as well as authenticated exchange: on the one hand, users who wish to do so should be able to hide their true identity, using an assumed identity instead. On the other hand, trusted and secure exchange between authenticated parties should be supported as well.

2.4 Rules of Encounter

Every day we meet and encounter so many people that it wouldn't be viable to manually scan profiles of all these people in the vague hope of finding some bit of information that catches our interest. Our concept of profile-based cooperation thus contains as integral part the notion of software agents that on behalf of the user scan profiles for user-defined patterns. These agents not only should know what to look for, but also what to do once they discover it. Such software agents embody 'rules of encounter' between individuals.

The tasks these agents perform can range from very simple ones to very complex ones. Agents could inform the user that something interesting has been found, they could collect data over a longer time period or they could even perform automated negotiations with agents of other users. Some simple examples include:

- "Alert me when I meet a friend of mine."
- "Alert me when I meet someone who sells an IBM PC110."
- "Alert me when I meet someone who went to my junior high school."
- "Save a record of everyone I meet who is interested in wearable computing."

2.5   Usage Scenarios and User Benefits

In order to highlight the benefits of publishing and exchanging profiles we introduce the following three usage scenarios:

The first usage scenario is a scientific conference or trade show where encounters between people who don't know each other occur often. Typically, at a conference or workshop we only know a handful of people personally, have seen or informally met a large number of other people, but have never met nor spoken to the majority of participants.

The second usage scenario is a swap meet, a flea market-like event where people come together in order to buy and sell rare and unusual items. One of the difficulties of swap meets is to find the person who sells the item that one is interested in.

The third usage scenario is a meeting between a small group of people, such as a visit to a construction site by architects, contractors, and owners.

In these scenarios profile-based cooperation can occur in a variety of ways. A device that implements the functionality as described above could serve multiple purposes:

- As *awareness tool* it could enable us to know the names and company affiliations of other people in a meeting.
- As a *reminder* it could alert us to the presence of people we want to meet or talk to in person ("When I meet Howard, remind me that I need to get the key from him.)"
- As a *diary* it could keep a record of all individuals we meet during the course of a day. This could be particularly useful when we meet a lot of potentially interesting people we don't know yet, but might want to contact later on, such as during a conference or trade show ("Tell me who I met today.")
- As a *matchmaker* it could alert us to the presence of some yet unknown person we might want to meet based on a description we defined. For example, during a swap meet we could be alerted to the presence of someone who sells a precious item we have been looking for for a long time. Similarly, we could set up our device to advertise items we want to sell so that other people can become aware of us. ("Let me know if someone around here sells a head casket for a 1967 Jaguar E-Type.")

Many more uses are possible within the framework of profile-based cooperation.

3   The Proem System

To explore our concept of profile-based cooperation we are developing the *Proem*[1] system. Proem is an experimental prototype that is currently under construction. It consists of several mobile computers with access to a Metricom wireless campus-wide network and a WaveLAN wireless indoor network. We use regular laptop computers as well as wearable computers. One of them is a commercial Via wearable computer, while the other is a self-built wearable computer we constructed from components of a laptop computer (Figure 1). Both computers are described in more detail elsewhere [Bauer et al, 1998; Kortuem et al, 1998; Kortuem et al, 1999a].

---

[1] A 'proem' is a brief introduction.

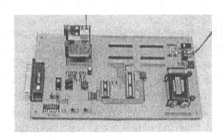

Fig. 1. Wearable Computer and Proem Radio Beacon

Each of these computers is equipped with a simple radio transmitter that sends out and receives beacon signals. These signals can be used to determine which other devices are in the immediate vicinity (the transmission range is about 6-10 feet). The radio transmitters are constructed from radio packet controllers from Radiomatrix [Radiomatrix 1998]. Figure 1 shows an early prototype without case. The final design is much smaller, fitting comfortably in a pager case including 9V battery.

Each Proem device runs software that is implemented in Java and is divided up into three layers as shown in Figure 2.

- The lowest layer is the service layer. It is based on Jini, Sun's network plug-and-play architecture [Sun 1998]. The main function of the service layer is to interconnect two devices during an encounter.
- The middle layer is divided up into three components: the profile, a profile cache for storing other user's profiles, and a rule base that contains the 'rules of encounter'

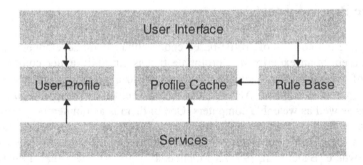

Fig. 2. Proem System Architecture

- The top layer is the user interface and contains functions for profile and rule editing.

In the following sections we will give a brief run down of the overall Proem design from a user's perspective before we explain the service component in more detail.

3.1 Profile Editor

The profile editor (Figure 3) allows users to define their profile.

The profile is a tree-like data structure containing personal information about the user. The leaf nodes of a profile are attribute-value pairs. Interior nodes represent named profile sections. Attribute values are untyped; they are either strings or comma-separated lists of strings. For example, the attribute `fullname` has a simple string value like `'James Joyce'`. The value of the attribute `interests` is a list of strings like `'wearable computing, CSCW, rock climbing'`.

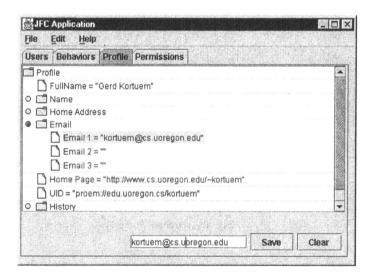

Fig. 3. Profile Editor

Several profile sections require special mentioning:

- The unique user id (`UID`) attribute stores the owner's global unique user id. We use a syntax for `UID`s that follows the Unique Resource Identifier specification [URI98]. A `UID` is a string consisting of a protocol part, a domain part and a user part. For example, `proem://edu.uoregon.cs/kortuem` identifies the user `kortuem` in the domaic.uoregon.edu.
- The friend section of the Profile contains three separate attributes: `FirstDegree`, `SecondDegree` and `ThirdDegree`. The value of each of these attributes is a list of `UID`s representing friends of the first degree, second degree and third degree. Friends of the first degree are immediate friends of the user. Friends of the second degree are friends of friends of the user, and friends of the third degree are friends of friends of friends of the user. The user only has to

specify immediate friends of the first degree. The values for second degree and third degree friends are automatically gathered during encounters from the profiles of friends and friends of friends.

3.2 Awareness Tool

The awareness tool is displays the names of all Proem users who are physically close (Figure 4). A time stamp counts the number of time units the respective user has been present nearby. After selecting a name from the list, the user can view or save the entire profile, or take a snap shot of everyone in the immediate vicinity.

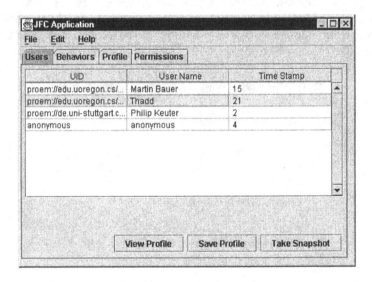

Fig. 4. Awareness Tool

3.3 Rule Editor

The rule editor (Figure 5) allows users to define 'rules of encounter', that is automatic system behaviors that are executed whenever certain conditions are met. Each rule consists of two parts. The *rule action* specifies which behavior will be executed, while the *rule condition* defines when an action is triggered. Rules are executed once for each encountered user.

The syntax for conditions is as follows:

```
<cond>    ::=   <term> <op> <term>
<op>      ::=   ==  |  contains  |  is_in
<term>    ::=   <attribute>  |  <value>
```

The == operator tests for equality of two strings; the operator contains tests if the second argument is a substring of the first argument; the operator is_in tests if the first argument is a substring of the first argument.

There are two built in actions that can be used in rules: alert brings up a dialog box and is used to inform the user that a condition was met; call allows users to specify the name of a Java procedure that will be called whenever the condition is true.

Using these simple rules, the user can define a variety of interesting and useful behaviors. The following are some examples:

- Alert me if I meet someone with my last name
  ```
  (lastname == "kortuem" -> alert)
  ```
- Alert me if I meet someone who sells an IBM PC110
  ```
  (sell contains "PC110" -> alert)
  ```
- Alert me if a meet a friend of mine.
  ```
  (uid is_in /Friends/FirstDegree -> alert)
  ```
- Save a record of everyone I meet who is interested in wearable computing
  ```
  (interest contains "wearable computing" -> call "save")
  ```

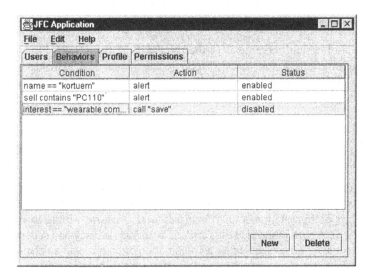

Fig. 5. Rule Editor

3.5 Device Discovery

The main function of Proem's service layer is to give devices mutual access to each other's profiles. Our solution for connecting Proem devices in an ad hoc manner is based on Jini, Sun's network plug-and-play architecture. Jini provides simple mechanisms to plug devices together to form an impromptu community - a community put together without any planning, installation, or human intervention.

Each Proem device implements a Jini service ReadProfile() which when called returns the complete profile. Using standard Jini procedures this service publishes its capabilities and availability by registering a *service advertisments* with the *lookup service* which is Jini's version of a service trader. The Service advertisement contains a *service handle* and an *offer descriptor*.

A Proem device (the client) that wants to gain access to ReadProfile() services of co-located devices (the servers) has to follow a two step procedure. The first step consists of locating the lookup services of all co-located devices. In Jini, this is done by broadcasting a multicast request throughout a network. In turn, lookup services of all devices that receive such a request answer back to let the client know that they are able and willing to provide information about services that have been registered with them. The client now queries each device lookup service by supplying a *service template*.[2]. In response, it receives a collection of matching *service proxies*. These service proxies, which are moved dynamically across the network, are then used to call the remote services.[3]

Since users and their devices constantly move around in space, Proem devices do not form long-lasting stable configurations. Thus, having discovered a service and having gained access to it through its service proxy is not a guarantee that a service is *usable*. In between the time a service was discovered and the time a client attempts to access it, the distance between both devices might so large that they are out of range. If this is the case and the service cannot be reached, the service proxy is simply discarded.

The role of client and server as described above is not fixed. Each Proem device is at the same time client and server. Upon request each device makes its service available to other devices, and each device also requests other access to remote services.

3.5 Privacy and Security

Since profiles can contain sensitive information, there is a potential threat to individual privacy that might make Proem users wary of sharing any information. However, the Proem system can only be effective if users are willing to freely share personal data with each other. It is thus critical to address privacy and security issues.

Personal privacy can be secured by a combination of control and awareness:

- The user must be given control over the release of their information, i.e. control over which information is released to whom and when.
- The user should be aware of who accesses his or her profile, i.e. the user should be able to track the exchange and usage of their personal profile.

Our solution for privacy protection is based on a combination of *access control lists* and *user authentication*.

Simply speaking, user can protect selective parts of their profile by an *access control list*. Whether access to a section is granted depends on the contents of an access control list associated with each profile section. An access control list specifies which users have and have not access to that particular profile section. Proem knows four built-in access control lists. While the meaning of these access control lists is built-in, membership is determined dynamically:

---

[2] The client filters out responses from devices that are not in the immediate vicinity using the information from the radio transmitter. This step would not be necessary if we used a true short-range wireless network.

[3] The ability of moving service proxies, i.e. compiled Java code, across the network on-demand, distinguishes Jini from other static trader architectures.

```
<?xml version="1.0" encoding="UTF-8"?>
<profile version="1.0">
  <uid access="all">proem://edu.uoregon.cs/kortuem</uid>
  <fn access="all">Gerd Kortuem</fn>
  <n access="all"><family>Kortuem</family>
    <given>Gerd</given>
    <middle>Werner</middle>
  </n>
  <tel tel.type="WORK" access="all">+1-541-346-1381</tel>
  <adr access="degree3">
    <organization>University of Oregon</organization>
    <street>1333 E 13th</street>
    <locality>Eugene</locality>
    <region>OR</region>
    <pcode>97403</pcode>
    <country>US</country>
  </adr>
  <email access="all">kortuem@cs.uoregon.edu</email>
  <email access="all">kortuem@grafikarchive.com</email>
  <homepage access="all">
    http://www.cs.uoregon.edu/~kortuem</homepage>
  <weblinks access="all">
    <url>http://wearables.gatech.edu</url>
    <url>http://www.cs.uoregon.edu/research/wearables</url>
    <url>http://wearables.www.media.mit.edu/wearables</url>
    <url>http://www.hitl.washington.edu</url>
    <url>http://www.cs.purdue.edu/research/cse/mobile<url>
  </weblinks>
  <friends access="degree3">
    <degree1>proem://edu.uoregon.cs/suruda,
             proem://edu.uoregon.cs/jay</degree1>
    <degree2>proem://edu.uoregon.cs/zary,
             proem://de.uni-stuttgart.cs/mabauer,
             proem://edu.washington.hitl/grof</degree2>
    <degree3>proem://de.uni-stuttgart.cs/peterh</degree3>
  </friends>
  <research access="all">
    wearable computing, mobile computing, CSCW,
    augmented reality, wireless networking</research>
  <hobbies access="all">rock climbing, scuba diving, soccer,
    movie posters</hobbies>
  <classifieds access="all">
    <sell>http://sar.classifiedwarehouse.com/search.cw1?t
        =2&lc=news&cat=bst&cp=atv2_&news=news_reg</sell>
  </classifieds>
</profile>
```

Fig. 6. XML-encoded profile with access modifiers (partial)

- *Degree1* contains those users who are explicitly named in the 'Friends/Degree1' section of the profile. Thus access to a profile section with associated access control list *Degree1* is granted only to those users who are explicitly named in the 'Friends/Degree1' section of the profile.

- *Degree2* grants access rights to all friends of friends of the user, that is, to all users who are named in the Friend/Degree2 section.

- *Degree3* grants access rights to all friends of friends of the user, that is, to all users who are named in the Friend/Degree3 section.
- *All* grants access to all users.

As explained above, the Friend/Degree2 and Friend/Degree3 attributes are updated whenever the user encounters a friend or 2nd degree friend.

User authentication is performed on the service level. The calling client has to provide its guid as first argument of each service call.

3.6 Communication Encoding

Proem profiles are encoded as XML documents (Figure 6). The internal representation of profile information on the device is left to the implementation. Different Proem implementation can use different internal representation formats for profiles.

4 Discussion and Related Work

Profile-based cooperation is a way to support awareness and informal communication between mobile users during chance encounters. Our work has precursors in many areas.

More recently researchers have started to understand how important informal communication and awareness is for effective workplace collaboration. Several researchers [Dourish and Bly 1992, Greenberg 1996, Tollmar et al 1996; Whittaker 1994; Whittaker 1997] investigated the role of informal communication in office settings, while others [Belloti and Bly 1996] studied the same question in settings where people are mobile within an office. Most of this work, however, focuses on creating awareness between people who know each other, for example co-workers. In contrast, our work is motivated by the question in how mobile technology can be used for awareness and informal communication between people who have never met before or don't know each other very well.

At first look Proem fits the description of an Inter-Personal Awareness Device (IPAD) laid out in [Holmquist 1998;Holmquist et al 1999] and exemplified by the Hummingbird. It can initiate contact between individuals – for example by identifying mutual interests or friends, but it is not used for a sustained actual communication. Like the Hummingbird, Proem devices are not designed to carry on sustained communication or to replace actual face-to-face conversations. Proem, however, differs from Hummingbirds in several respects. Most importantly, Proem supports informal communication between individuals who have never met before and who don't know each other. Hummingbird only supports inter-personal awareness among members of a well-defined and closed user group. In that respect, Proem is similar to the Lovegety [Iwatani 1998], a popular Japanese toy that functions as matchmaker between users of the opposite sex. The success of the Lovegety is a hint that anonymous exchange of preferences and interests can be useful even on a relatively shallow level.

More elaborate profiles have been used in the Groupwear system that is based on interactive nametags (called "thinking tags") that assist conversation between people by informing users how much they have in common with regard to a set of precompiled background information [Borovy 1996; Borovy et al 1998a; Borovy et al. 1998b]. Our concept of profile-based cooperation differs from Groupwear in two important respect. First, GroupWear requires and supports only face-to-face conversations while Proem allows two users to exchange their profiles whenever they are physically close, regardless of whether they talk to each other or not. Second, Groupwear relies on a predefined profile structure. Users have no real control over the content of their profile, they cannot change it or add to it, nor can they decide to hide certain information from other users.

One of the most important differences to the works quoted above is Proem's ability to create a record of the user's encounters. As such Proem is less of an awareness device than it is a memory aid or electronic diary. Thus Proem's function extends well beyond the actual time of an encounter. Whether or not two users' preferences match can be determined well after the actual encounter occurred. Users might or might not have been aware of the data exchange at the time it happens.

Another source of inspiration for our work was the growing body of research on web-based online communities and personalized delivery of web content. The Open Profiling Standard (OPS) introduced by Firefly defines a framework for the trusted exchange of profile information between a web site and its visitors [Firefly 1997a;Firefly 1997b;Firefly 1997c]. The Firefly Passport is an individual's trusted identity and personal profile that stores information about who people are, what people like, and what they don't. OPS emphasis on trust and security reflects the primary intended application of OPS, which is e-commerce. Our domain of interest does not seem to require the same level of trust and security. We see, however, a need to provide ways to grant or deny access to a profile section based on the readers identity. For example, most people do not want to give out their address to anyone who happens to pass by, but they might not care whether a friend or colleague gains access to it. Similarly reservations can be expected for other types of information as well.

5   Conclusion

In the preceding sections we have done two things: we have laid out a framework for what we call *profile-based cooperation* of mobile users, and we have described the design of *Proem*, a system that exemplifies some of our ideas. We see profile-based cooperation as a way to support awareness and informal communication during chance encounters of mobile users who have never met before or don't know each other very well. We discussed some principles such as *owner control, reader selection* and *reciprocity* that we believe should guide the exchange of profile data.

While the first experiences with the prototype are encouraging from a technical point of view, we have limited insight into the social issues of exchanging personal profile data. A systematic evaluation is made difficult by the limited availability of the current system and the small size of the user population.

We are now pursuing continued research in the directions discussed in this paper. In particular, we investigate the use of negotiation protocols for further automating the exchange of profiles [Kortuem et al, 1999b].

References

[Belotti and Bly 1996] Belotti, V. and Bly, S. (1996) Walking Away from the Desktop Computer: Distributed Collaboration and Mobility in a Product Design Team. In *Proceedings of CSCW '96,* ACM Press.

[Bauer, 1998] Martin Bauer, Timo Heiber, Gerd Kortuem, Zary Segall. *A Collaborative Wearable System with Remote Sensing.* Proceedings Second International Symposium on Wearable Computers, Oct 19-20, 1998, Pittsburgh, PA

[Borovoy 1996] Borovoy, R. MacDonald, M. Martin, F. and Resnik, M. Things that blink: Computationally augmented name tags. IBM Systems Journal 35, 3 & 4, 1996.

[Borovoy 1998a] Borovoy, R., Martin, F. Resnick, M. and Silverman, B. (1998a) GroupWear: Nametags that Tell About Relationships. *CHI '98 Summary,* ACM Press.

[Borovoy 1998b] Borovoy, R., Martin, F., Vemuri, S., Resnick, M., Silverman, B. and Hancock, C. (1998b) Meme Tags and Community Mirrors: Moving from Conferences to Collaboration. In *Proceedings of CSCW '98*, ACM Press.

[Dourish and Bly 1992] Dourish, P. and Bly, S. (1992) Portholes: Supporting Awareness in a Distributed Work Group. In *Proceedings of CHI 92,* ACM Press.

[Firefly 1997a] Firefly 1997. "Open Profiling Standard OPF" www.firefly.net, 1997

[Firefly 1997b] Firefly 1997 "Implementation of OPS over HTTP: www.firefly.net, 1997

[Firefly 1997c] Firefly 1997 "Standard Practices for OPS Systems" www.firefly.net, 1997

[Greenberg 1996] Greenberg, S. (1996) Peepholes: Low Cost Awareness of One's Community. In *CHI '96 Companion,* pp. 206-207, ACM Press.

[Holmquist 1998] Holmquist, L.E. *Supporting Group Awareness with IPAD:s - Inter-Personal Awareness Devices.* Workshop paper, Workshop on Handheld CSCW, ACM CSCW '98 Seattle, USA.

[Holmquist et al 1999] Holmquist, L.E., Falk, J. and Wigström, J. *Supporting Group Awareness with Inter-Personal Awareness Devices.* In Journal of Personal Technologies, Special Issue on Hand-Held CSCW, Springer Verlag, 1999.

[Kortuem et al, 1998] Gerd Kortuem, Zary Segall, Martin Bauer. *Context-Aware, Adaptive Wearable Computers as Remote Interfaces to 'Intelligent' Environments.* Proceedings Second International Symposium on Wearable Computers, Oct 19-20, 1998, Pittsburgh, PA.

[Kortuem et al, 1999a] Gerd Kortuem, Martin Bauer, Timo Heiber, Zary Segall. *Netman: The Design of a Collaborative Wearable Computer System.* ACM/Baltzer Journal on Mobile Networks and Applications (MONET), 1999.

[Kortuem et al, 1999b] Gerd Kortuem, Jay Schneider, Jim Suruda, Steve Fickas, Zary Segall. *When Cyborgs Meet: Building Communities of Cooperating Wearable Agents.* Proceedings Third International Symposium on Wearable Computers, Oct 18-19, 1999, San Francisco, CA (forthcoming).

[Iwatani 1998] Iwatani, Y. (1998) Love: Japanese Style. In *Wired News,* 11 June 1998. URL: http://www.wired.com/news/culture/story/12899.html

[Radiomatrix 1998] http://www.radiomatrix.co.uk

[Rhodes 1997] Rhodes, B. The wearable remembrance agent: A system for augmented memory. Proceedings of the First International Symposium on Wearable Computers (ISWC'97), Cambridge, MA, October 1997.

[SixDegrees 1999] www.sixdegress.com

[Sun 1998] www.javasoft.com/products/jini

[Tollmar et al 1996] Tollmar, K., Sandor, O and Shömer, A. Supporting Social Awareness @Work, Design and Experience. In *Proceedings of CSCW 96,* ACM Press.

[vCard 1996] VERSIT Consortium, "vCard - The Electronic Business Card Version 2.1", http://www.imc.org/pdi/vcard-21.txt, September 18, 1996

[Want et al 1992] Want, R., Hopper, A., Falcao, V. and Gibbons, J. The Active Badge Location System. In *ACM Transactions on Information Systems,* Vol. 10 (1), 1992

[Whittaker 1994) Whittaker, S., Frohlich, D. and Daly-Jones, O. Informal Workplace Communication: What Is It Like and How Can We Support It? In *Proceedings of CHI 94,* ACM Press.

[Whittaker 1997] Whittaker, S., Swanson, J. Kucan, J., and Sidner C, "TeleNotes: managing lightwieght interactions in the desktop," ACM Transactions on Computer-Human Interaction, Vol 4, No.2 (June) pp137-168.

[Zimmerman 1996] T. G. Zimmerman. Personal Area Networks: Near-field intrabody communication, IBM Systems Journal, *Vol. 35, No. 3&4, 1996.*

A Digital Photography Framework Supporting Social Interaction and Affective Awareness

Olivier Liechti, Tadao Ichikawa

ISL, Hiroshima University, 1-4-1 Kagamiyama, Higashi-Hiroshima, Japan 739
{olivier,ichikawa}@isl.hiroshima-u.ac.jp

Abstract. Photographs have significant social roles. For example, they help families and friends to preserve an affective link and provide support for communication. The increasing popularity of digital photography, combined with global networking, is likely to emphasize this function as sharing photographs will become cheaper, faster and easier. Based on this observation, we propose a framework that allows people to maintain mutual awareness by exchanging and annotating photographs. The framework components include digital cameras running specific software, a distributed communication and storage infrastructure, tools for watching and annotating photographs. The framework also includes tools for notifying photographers when their pictures are accessed.

1 Introduction

When it comes to illustrate the emergence of information appliances, handheld computers, smart phones and other PDA's are often cited first. Here however, we look at another kind of device, which integrates hardware components with an operating environment, communication capabilities and a user interface: the digital camera. The purpose of a digital camera indeed is to produce, process and temporarily store information. Not only graphical information, but also contextual metadata such as the time, location or title of a photograph. As we will see, some digital cameras also integrate a programming environment, which makes them a unique platform for innovative photo-centric applications. Real estate, insurance and medicine are some of the professional fields that will benefit from these applications, particularly because they will enable automatic classification and efficient retrieval.

But digital cameras are also very popular in the home consumers market, and it seems important to find out what applications could emerge in this segment. It is this question that we are trying to answer in this article, by proposing the idea of using digital photography to support new forms of social interaction. In the vision we would like to share, the digital camera becomes one component in a distributed communication system, which allows people to maintain social relationships with their peers, in a very affective and little demanding fashion. The idea of using both photographs and the activity of sharing photographs to support social interactions comes from two observations.

The first observation is that photographs have played a social role for decades. Why do people take photographs? Why and how do people share photographs with others? These are some of the questions that ethnographers and anthropologists are interested in [1, 11]. Think of a grandmother receiving a picture of her grandchildren, or of a group of friends commenting on a photo album. The first situation illustrates how photographs are a very affective and effective mechanism for connecting people to each other. The second situation reveals that the activity of sharing photographs provides a support for people to communicate and share emotions. How will digital photography affect these functions? We would argue that it will probably amplify them, as the cost, time and effort necessary to share photographs will be reduced in a dramatic way by the nature of digital media. As a result, people could end up taking more photographs and sharing them more frequently with their families and friends. But this will require the careful design of proper infrastructures, mechanisms and tools.

The second observation is that despite the large acceptance of electronic mail and Web technologies by home users, radically different human-to-human interaction modes are still needed. One problem with existing technologies is that they often require too much time and effort and are not designed to support lightweight, spontaneous interactions. Writing daily emails or updating personal Web pages are more demanding activities than, for example, casually chatting with a friend. As a consequence, people often reduce either the frequency (e.g. from daily to weekly) or the quality (e.g. limit to state weather information) of their messages. These apparently insignificant messages are, however, far from being useless. In many cases, what is important is not so much the content of the message, but rather the simple fact that the message has been sent. The message, by its mere transmission, *connects* the sender to the recipient. Sending an email is in some cases very similar to waving or smiling at someone. But our argument is that sharing digital photographs might provide a better basis to support this kind of interactions, being at the same time less demanding and more engaging.

After reviewing some related work, we will illustrate these ideas with the design of the KAN-G framework, that integrates components supporting the capture, distribution, observation and annotation of photographs. We will explain how the specific software running on digital cameras allows people to easily share photographs with their peers. We will also explain where and how these photographs are stored and how they can be accessed by others. Finally, we will explain how an important aspect of the system is that it tracks the activity of people commenting and expressing their emotions when they watch the pictures, and that it then notifies this activity back to the photographers. As a result, there is not only a communication flow from photographers to watchers, but also back from watchers to photographers.

2   Inspiration and related work

Ultimately, our goal is to propose a new method for people to keep in touch with their families and friends. In many ways, distributed families encounter similar problems as those met by distributed working groups. A common issue is the difficulty to maintain a context for communication. Hence, some of the findings in Computer Supported Cooperative Work (CSCW) literature might very well apply in home settings. The notion of *awareness*, extensively discussed in CSCW literature, is very relevant to this work. This is particularly true for the more specific notion of *peripheral awareness*, supported by media spaces and ambient media systems [6, 10, 12]. Because such systems generally rely on high-speed networking, they have long been confined to office settings. But high-speed internet connections are becoming a reality for home users. It will thus be very interesting to evaluate how these systems can be used to seamlessly connect dispersed families and friends.

Another source of related work comes from wearable computing systems, which sometimes integrate digital cameras, for example in [5]. The camera, however, is sometimes used as a sensor and not to take snapshots shared with other people. A system particularly relevant to this work is the wearable webcam [9].

A number of commercial services already support the storage and exchange of digital photographs on the WWW [4, 7]. The framework proposed in this article partly overlaps with these systems, but also extends them in different ways. First, it integrates digital cameras and really uses them as programmable information appliances. Second, it supports the notion of mutual awareness. In our approach, people watching snapshots may comment them and express their emotions. The photographers are then made aware of this activity with various tools and thus receive some feedback from the system. Also, we propose to go beyond the WWW, by displaying photographs not only in Web browsers, but also on all sorts of displays.

An other important inspiration is our daily observation of the Japanese popular culture. In this respect, we could talk about a lot of different products, especially about the new generation of mobile communication tools. But we should also mention the tremendous success of print clubs (pronounced "puricura"). Located on every street corner, these machines are used by high school students to take photographs of their smiling faces, later decorated with cute drawings and printed on small stickers. These stickers are then exchanged among friends and organized in large collections. What is interesting about print clubs, is that they are computing devices that stress the social function of photographs. The various "socialware" products tremendously popular in Japan are a good illustration that entertainment and fun will also be affected by the emerging ubiquitous computing environment [2].

3   The KAN-G framework

To illustrate the ideas introduced before, we now describe a framework, named KAN-G after the Japanese word "kanji" meaning "emotion". The goal of KAN-G is to support different processes that allow people maintaining mutual awareness by sharing photographs and comments. Social interaction in the framework is driven by the following observations:

- "Receiving and watching a photograph from a person *connects* me to that person."
- "Knowing that a person is watching my photographs *connects* me to that person."

There are two categories of KAN-G users: photographers and watchers. Photographers use digital cameras to take snapshots that they distribute to their friends, via a distributed communication and storage infrastructure. Watchers receive and observe these snapshots with different tools, which they also use to make comments and express emotions (e.g. laugh at a photograph). This activity, i.e. accessing and annotating photographs, is captured by the system and notified to the photographers with various tools, called *awareness monitors*. In other words, it is possible for photographers to virtually hear their friends laughing or crying when they observe their pictures. In this scenario, there is no direct communication between people. We nevertheless believe that an affective link has been created between them.

Another aspect of KAN-G is that it is based on the idea of channels. Photographers may specify several topical channels (e.g. "Family", "Funny pics", "Food"), and can decide to distribute a particular photograph to one of these channels. Symmetrically, watchers might be interested to subscribe to only some of the channels. The motivation for using channels, as opposed to large photo collections that continuously grow, is to make the system more dynamic. Because channels are limited buffers where photographs are successively pushed, it is likely that changes will be noticed more easily. This should make the system more interesting for watchers. Note, however, that channels are implemented on top of complete collections, which remain accessible. We now introduce the different framework components.

3.1 Programmable digital cameras

One of our main requirements was that initiating the distribution of photographs should be as effortless as possible. Otherwise, people would not do it regularly (this is very similar to the problem of updating personal Web pages). Having said that, there are at least two reasons for which to implement this function directly on the camera. First, the task can be performed in context, i.e. when the snapshot has been taken and with a single task-oriented tool. Second, the task can be performed very rapidly, in a matter of seconds (no need to find a PC and to wait for it to boot up).

Most of the currently available digital cameras offer a limited number of functions, accessible via a user interface generally composed of an LCD display, a few buttons and a few switches. More interesting are the cameras, currently including models from Kodak and Minolta, that use the Digita operating system [3]. Digita is a proposed standard OS for imaging devices. It includes a menu-driven user interface, various sub-systems and most interestingly a scripting language. Using this language, it is possible to extend the functionality of the camera and to implement interesting applications. Digita scripts can control the hardware (e.g. zoom in and out, take a shot), write text files (but unfortunately not read them) and control GUI widgets (e.g. option lists, informative messages, text input). They also have R/W access to a number of data fields storing metadata for each picture (e.g. location, title). The scripts are organized in hierarchical menus, which can easily be accessed by the user with a four arrow keys button.

As part of the KAN-G framework, we implemented two Digita scripts that run on Kodak DC260 camera. These are used to indicate which pictures should be published, and to which KAN-G channels they should be distributed. The first script, "Set channel", lets the user select one or more photographs, and choose one of the available channels in a scrolling list. When this is done, the script traverses the list of selected pictures. For each of them, it updates a metadata field with the reference of the selected channel. The second script, "Publish" traverses the list of all photographs stored in the camera and checks the content of the metadata field updated by the "Set channel" script. Accordingly, the script generates an XML document that describes what pictures should be published, and to which channels they should be distributed.

3.2   Servers, channels and kiosks

In the KAN-G framework, pictures are not sent directly from photographers to watchers (as opposed to email). Instead, they are published on *channels* managed by *servers*. Photographers push information on these channels, to which watchers may subscribe. Accordingly, every photographer must be registered and have an account on a server. KAN-G servers essentially have two functions. On one hand, they must accept photographs and maintain the state of channels. On the other hand, they must handle requests from watchers and give them access to the channels. Essentially, they are HTTP servers running different Java servlets. It seemed very important to integrate KAN-G to the WWW, in order to make it easily accessible.

In the future, it is likely that digital cameras will be equipped with a wireless network connection. It will thus be possible to send the pictures directly from the camera to the server. But because this is not the case yet, we introduced *kiosks* in the architecture. After initiating the publication of photographs, i.e. after running the two Digita scripts, the user simply has to extract the storage media from the camera and to insert it in a kiosk. In our prototype, the kiosk simply is a PC with a PCMCIA card reader. The software running on the kiosk reads the XML document generated by the script, which specifies what photographs to fetch. It also reads a special file stored on the picture card, that describes on which KAN-G server the user owns an account. Finally, a connection is established with the server and the photographs listed in the XML document are pushed to the specified channels. Although it introduces an extra step and some delay, the kiosk still keeps the publishing process simple and does not require much effort from the user (all necessary information has been gathered before, directly on the camera).

3.3   Clients for watchers

Because KAN-G servers are HTTP servers, standard Web browsers can be used to observe photographs published in KAN-G channels. The HTML documents generated by the servers not only contain photographs. They also include various GUI widgets and JavaScript code. The purpose of this code is to capture the activity and gather feedback from people watching the photographs. For example, push buttons placed under a photograph can be clicked by watchers to express a sentiment or make a comment. The problem of capturing activity on the WWW and then to notify it to interested parties has been discussed in [8].

While browsers provide a practical solution to access KAN-G channels, it would be interesting to develop other kinds of clients. Nowadays, our working and living environments are increasingly populated with diverse displays. These include televisions, computer displays, but also screen phones, wall-mounted panels, smart boards, etc. These displays often are used punctually for a specific purpose, but are often inactive for long periods. As a consequence, there seems to be a waste of interactive display real-estate, which could for example be used to display photographs and other kinds of artistic creations. One can imagine dynamic photo frames, that would periodically display a new photograph. If such devices were built, they might even capture the emotions of the watchers without their intervention (e.g. a microphone could capture their laughter).

3.4 Awareness monitors for photographers

The previous components make it easy for users to distribute their pictures and for their peers to access them. They thus enable a communication flow from the photographers to the watchers. One of the original aspects of KAN-G, however, is that it also supports a communication flow in the other direction. As we already mentioned, the activity of people observing and commenting on photographs is captured by the system. It can then be integrated and notified to the photographers. For that, it simply means that appropriate hardware and software must be provided, tot receive notifications and make them perceptible in some way. We call these tools awareness monitors.

There are many ways to implement awareness monitors, using a combination of audio, visual and tangible signals. It seems a good idea to encourage aesthetic solutions and to give emphasis to peripheral awareness. We implemented a few prototypes taking advantage of the new 2D imaging Java API, which in particular supports semi-transparency. In one monitor, accessed photographs fade in (with a legend indicating the identity of the watcher) while sounds are played (e.g. laughter if the watcher has pressed the "laugh" button in the browser). After a while, they fade out and disappear. It could be nice to place such dynamic, multi-modal paintings in our living rooms and thus to be able to "feel" in contact with families and friends looking at our pictures.

4 Conclusion

Sharing digital photographs on computer networks has been proposed as a new way for people to maintain social relationships, at the same time demanding little effort and being very affective. We have discussed this idea and illustrated it with a framework supporting the capture, distribution and annotation of digital photographs. The framework highlights that digital cameras truly are information appliances, for which special software can be created. It also illustrates the idea of mutual awareness, as photographers are notified when people watch their pictures express their feelings. Prototypes for the different framework components have been implemented. They however still have to be improved and properly evaluated, which will be the object of our future work.

Acknowledgements

This work was partly supported by the Japanese government with a Monbusho scholarship awarded to the first author. The authors are thankful to Eastman Kodak for providing them with the Digital Science DC260 digital camera used to implement the prototype system. The authors would also like to thank Mark Sifer for his helpful comments.

References

1. R. Chalfen, "Japanese Home Media as Popular Culture", presented at Japanse Popular Culture Conference, Victoria, British Colombia, CA, 1997.
2. G. Davenport, L. E. Holmquist, M. Thomas, and F. o. F. W. Participants, "Fun: A Condition of Creative Research", in *IEEE Multimedia*, 1998, pp. 10-15.
3. Digita, "Digita Operating System for imaging devices", http://www.flashpoint.com.
4. FujiFilm, "FujiFilm.net", http://www.fujifilm.net.
5. J. Healey and R. W. Picard, "StartleCam: A Cybernetic Wearable Camera", presented at IEEE International Symposium on Wearable Computers, 1998.
6. H. Ishii and B. Ullmer, "Tangible Bits: Towards Seamless Interfaces between People, Bits and Atoms", presented at CHI'97, Atlanta, 1997.
7. Kodak, "Kodak PhotoNet Online", http://kodak.photonet.com.
8. O. Liechti, M. Sifer, and T. Ichikawa, "A Non-obtrusive User Interface for Increasing Social Awareness on the World Wide Web", *Personal Technologies*, Volume 3, Issue 3, 1999.
9. S. Mann, "An historical account of the 'WearComp' and 'WearCam' inventions developed in 'Personal Imaging'", presented at IEEE International Symposium on Wearable Computers, 1997.
10. E. R. Pedersen and T. Sokoler, "AROMA: abstract representation of presence supporting mutual awareness", presented at CHI'97, Atlanta, 1997.
11. J. Ruby, "Seeing Through Pictures: the Anthropology of Photography", *Camera-Lucida: The Journal of Photographic Criticism*, pp. 19-32, 1981, http://www.temple.edu/anthro/ruby/seethru.html.
12. M. Weiser and J. S. Brown, "Designing Calm Technology", *PowerGrid Journal*, vol. Version 1.01, July 1996, http://powergrid.electriciti.com/1.01.

The Role of Connectivity in Supporting Context-Sensitive Applications

Keith Cheverst, Nigel Davies, Keith Mitchell and Adrian Friday

Distributed Multimedia Research Group,
Department of Computing,
Lancaster University,
Lancaster, LA1 4YR.
e-mail: kc,nigel,mitchelk,adrian@comp.lancs.ac.uk

Abstract. This paper considers the role of network connectivity in supporting context-sensitive applications. A range of context-sensitive applications are analysed with respect to connectivity. Following this analysis a design space is constructed which enables the positioning of context-sensitive applications depending on their reliance on network connectivity and their reliance on local storage. Further consideration of the role of connectivity is achieved through a study of the GUIDE system which has been developed to provide context-sensitive information to visitors to the city of Lancaster. The current GUIDE system utilises a cell-based wireless network infrastructure to provide both location information and dynamic information to mobile GUIDE units. However, coverage throughout the city is not complete and this raises a number of design implications, including how to maintain a visitor's trust in the system when outside of cell coverage.

1 Introduction

Context-sensitive applications [1][2] utilise contextual information, such as location, display medium and user profile, to provide tailored functionality. For example, the PARCTab [3] developed by Xerox utilises a user's location to trigger events such as notifying the user to collect a document when walking past the printer room. Context-sensitive systems, such as the PARCTab, tend to be personal and therefore highly mobile devices. This paper focuses on context-sensitive systems that are designed for use in a mobile environment, in which the user's location is a significant and dynamic factor affecting the information presented to the user.

This class of location-aware context-sensitive system must either store information locally, receive information from a remote source or some combination of the two. There are three reasons why it might be necessary to receive information from a remote source. The first reason is that the system could have insufficient memory to store the quantity of information required locally, e.g. detailed information on all the possible attractions in a major city. The second reason is that the system might receive contextual information (e.g. location information or weather forecasting information) via the network. This information could be in addition to context information sensed locally but not necessarily so. Furthermore, the context information required by the system could be received by polling some kind of remote sensor and/or received via some form of context notification server [4]. The third reason is that the system may need to receive dynamic information. For example, information on a recently opened attraction may need to be downloaded by a context-aware tour guide or a restaurant's 'specials' menu may need to be received.

Mobile context-sensitive systems that receive information from a remote source do so via some form of wireless communications channel. Unless ubiquitous network connectivity is available, the fact that users are mobile implies that they are likely to roam into and out of areas of network connectivity. This paper considers the role of network connectivity in supporting context-sensitive applications and the implications that arise from systems that must tolerate intermittent connectivity. In particular, this paper studies the implications that arise in the context-sensitive GUIDE system.

1.1 A Design Space for Modelling the Role of Connectivity in Context-Sensitive Systems

Analysing the current range of location-aware context-sensitive systems reveals interesting differences in reliance on network connectivity. For example, the functionality of the Hummingbird wearable device [5] relies absolutely on the role of connectivity. Hummingbird is designed to provide members of a group with an aural awareness when other group members are nearby. In the current system, the term nearby depends upon tweaking the range of the unit's radio transceiver which can vary between 20 and 200 metres. Connectivity with another Hummingbird's transceiver implies that its wearer is nearby whilst no connectivity implies that its wearer is at a distance.

The Olivetti Active Badge system [6] provides a technology for locating people and equipment indoors. The actual Active Badge is engineered using an infrared transponding computer with a unique ID. These communicate with an arrangement of infra-red sensors, usually one per room. Two way communication is supported, enabling the badge to receive and interpret messages and also to act as a signalling device. A variety of location-aware applications have been developed that utilise this technology. One example is an application that allows a badge to behave as a simple audible pager that notifies the wearer when new e-mail arrives, but only when the system senses that the wearer is away from his or her office. The Active Badge system has an absolute reliance on network connectivity for its function but, interestingly, the wireless networking technology used is inherently unreliable. This means that users must temper their faith in the system with the knowledge that the transmission from an active badge (e.g. an acknowledgement to a paging notification) or a transmission to a badge (e.g. a new e-mail notification) may need to be retransmitted several times before being received. The implications that arise from having a reliance on (intermittent) connectivity is a central theme of this paper.

The PARCTab device is another example of a system that relies strongly on network connectivity in order to provide useful functionality. The PARCTab utilises the Olivetti Active Badge infrastructure for obtaining positioning information and for the transmission of data, such as e-mail. Without connectivity the PARCTab can do little more than provide simple note-taking functionality (using its built-in Unistrokes handwriting recognition software) or allow the browsing of files (e.g. e-mail messages) previously downloaded from the network and stored in its relatively small 128 Kb memory. For this reason, the intended operating environment for PARCTabs is within a suitably configured office building that provides ubiquitous connectivity.

The Cyberguide system, is a location-aware tour guide system that has been developed by the Future Computing Environments (FCE) group at the Georgia Institute of Technology. The initial Cyberguide system [7] did not utilise two-way wireless communications and thus provided no support for sharing information or context. However, the indoor version of this system did utilise wireless transmissions to detect a tourist's position and orientation using a collection of IR beacons. These beacons transmitted unique IDs that could then be translated into a map location and orientation. Alternatively, the outdoor version of the system utilised Global Positioning System (GPS) data directly. The fact that mapping information (for the small area covered) was stored locally allowed the system to offer touring functionality even when the system's wireless networking capability was not available. A later version of the Cyberguide system (referred to as Cyberguide II) [8] was developed to support demonstration days. This system utilises wireless connectivity in order to enable users to observe the location of other users in the local area and to share comments with them.

The Conference Assistant application [4] also developed by the FCE group is designed to support conference attendees by providing them with appropriate context-aware information and collaborative tools via a PDA or wearable computer. The conference assistant was developed using a distributed architecture that relies on fully connected operation in order to communicate changes in context and presentation information between the various components of the architecture. The application is thus designed to operate in a fully connected environment, i.e. a conference building with RF connectivity and location sensors in every room. Given this environment, the application provides users with context-sensitive information as they navigate conference rooms. In addition, when wishing to ask a question regarding a particular slide, the application enables the user to control a presenter's display via his or her own PDA.

The GUIDE system [9][10] is another system developed for providing context-aware information to tourists. However, in common with the PARCTab system, GUIDE utilises a wireless communications infrastructure for both the transmission of data and for obtaining location information. The system can store information locally and (with a little cooperation from the tourist) is still capable of providing useful functionality when operating without network connectivity.

By considering the reliance of the aforementioned context-sensitive systems on both local storage and network connectivity the systems can be placed in the design space as shown below in figure 1.

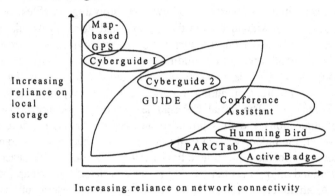

Fig. 1. A design space for considering the role of connectivity in context-sensitive systems.

Consideration of the design space raises some interesting questions. For example, is a standard GPS, i.e. one that simply displays a user's current geographic co-ordinates in reaction to the unit's location, a context-sensitive application? However, the classification becomes substantially easier when one introduces information into the system. For example, Magallen have recently released a GPS compass (the GPS 320 model) [11] that can store map-based information and allows its current position to be displayed on an appropriate map. In common with many of the car navigation systems currently available, this type of compass can certainly be considered as context-sensitive and is shown positioned in the design space. In this case, the compass has no reliance on network connectivity for receiving information but has an absolute reliance on its local storage (and local sensor) to display context-sensitive information. For this reason, it is positioned in the top left of the design space.

2. The Guide System

This section describes the GUIDE system with particular emphasis on the role of connectivity in GUIDE and the way in which the system has been designed to support wireless connectivity.

2.1 Overview

The GUIDE system has been developed to provide visitors to the city of Lancaster with context-sensitive information tailored to their particular interests and needs. The application requirements for GUIDE were obtained through an extensive requirements capture exercise [9] which involved observing activity in the city's Tourist Information Centre (or TIC) and conducting one-to-one, semi-structured, interviews with members of staff. In summary, the key application requirements for the GUIDE system were: i) the need for a flexible and tailored tourist guide, ii) the need to support dynamic information and iii) the need to support interactive services.

To use the GUIDE system, city visitors are required to carry portable GUIDE units. In terms of hardware, GUIDE units currently comprise a Fujitsu TeamPad 7600 [12] tablet PC coupled with a WaveLan PC Card [13] for network connectivity. The use of WaveLAN is an intrinsic part of the GUIDE infrastructure (described in section 2.4) and enables GUIDE units to receive beacons indicating the visitor's location and also enables parts of the GUIDE information model (described in section 2.3) to be downloaded.

The GUIDE system is web-based and each unit runs a customised web browser constructed using the HotJava HTML component. An example of the user-interface to GUIDE is shown in figure 2.

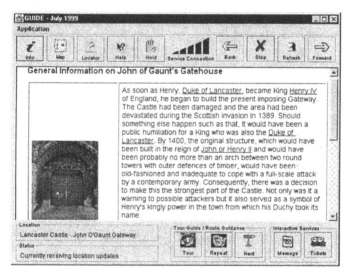

Fig. 2. The user-interface to GUIDE.

A large central area of the user interface is reserved for displaying HTML based information to the city visitor. In the screen-shot shown above, the visitor is being presented with information about the historic gateway to the city's castle and hypertext links are available should the visitor wish to find out more information on, for example, the Duke of Lancaster.

Beneath the HTML window, positioned at the bottom-left of the display, are two text message boxes, one of which is used to state the visitor's current (or last known) location whilst the other provides feedback regarding the reception of location information (described further in section 3.4). The other significant elements of the user-interface include a selection of iconised buttons for accessing the functionality supported by GUIDE (described in section 2.2) and a 'bars of connectivity' icon for providing the visitor with an awareness of their current state of connectivity (described further in section 3.1).

2.2 Functionality

The GUIDE system provides city visitors with a range of functionality. In more detail, a visitor can request the GUIDE unit to either: i) provide tailored (context-sensitive) information regarding a specific location in the city, ii) recommend a tour of the city, iii) provide access to interactive services, iv) enable browsing of the world wide web or v) send and receive textual messages.

The Provision of Context-Sensitive Information. By pressing the 'Info' button a visitor is presented with the set of options shown below in figure 3. The first two options present information based on the visitor's current location. By selecting the first option, when standing nearby the castle gateway, the page of information shown in figure 2 would be displayed.

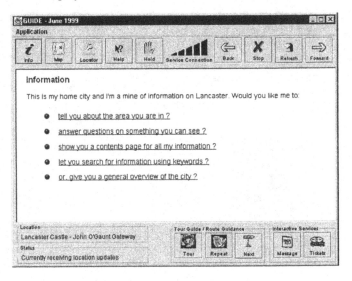

Fig. 3. The GUIDE Information Page.

The latter three options shown in figure 3 allow the visitor to request information that is not connected with the current location. An earlier version of the GUIDE system did not support these three options but instead constrained the visitor's search for information by trying to pre-empt those specific pieces of information that we believed would be of interest to a visitor at each and every location. This was achieved by providing only a limited collection of hypertext links on every page. A series of initial trials revealed that this method for enabling users to access information was unsuitable. The trials involved members of the development team escorting and observing users (comprising both experienced and inexperienced web users) whilst they used the system to tour a limited area of the city. During the trials, visitors would, on occasion, became frustrated when the system did not provide the specific hypertext link for accessing specific information. For this reason, we modified the system to include the ability for users to search for information using a keyword, to view an ordered list of all information held on the system, or to take a step back and receive an overview of the city.

On a more general point, our experience with this aspect of the GUIDE system has taught us that designers of this kind of context-aware system should be careful not to be over zealous when deciding how to constrain or scope the information provided by the system based on certain pieces of context.

Recommending a Tour of the City. When creating a tour tailored to the requirements of a visitor, the GUIDE system utilises a variety of contextual information, such as the visitor's interests, the approximate time that the tour should last, the time of day, the opening hours of the city's attractions and other factors, such as the average length of time spent at a particular attraction. A 'Guide Tour Wizard' is provided to enable visitors to quickly and easily select those attractions that they particularly wish to visit.

Note that a subset of the contextual information listed above is actually dynamic and requires updating from a remote source. The obvious example is the weather but the opening hours of the city's attractions is also liable to change. This is especially the case in Lancaster because part of the city's castle is actually used as a courtroom and therefore its opening times vary depending on the length of any scheduled trials.

Providing Access to Interactive Services. During the requirements study, it was found that visitors would often return to the TIC in order to make use of its booking services, e.g. the booking of hotel accommodation or travel. By providing remote access to these services, visitors can save time by making bookings via their GUIDE unit. In addition to providing remote access to those services provided by the TIC, the GUIDE system also enables access to other services, such as enabling visitors to query those films on show at the city's cinema and enabling visitors to book seats at the cinema remotely.

One of the future directions for GUIDE is to increase the diversity of support for interactive services and our plans for achieving this are described in section four.

Enabling Access to the World Wide Web. The GUIDE system has been designed to enable visitors to receive other remote sources of HTML based information, such as the WWW. By providing access to the web, visitors are provided with enormous potential for pursuing information that is not contained within the GUIDE information model.

Provision of a Messaging Service. To take full advantage of the network connectivity available to GUIDE units, when visitors are located within a communications cell, GUIDE supports a messaging service. This service enables groups of visitors, who may have separated in order to visit different attractions in the city, to keep in touch and also enables visitors to request information from staff at the TIC.

2.3 Information Model

The information model used by the GUIDE system represents various types of information, including: i) geographic information, ii) hypertext information, iii) active components and iv) information that can react to events, e.g. it is five p.m. and it is raining. The fact that no existing models can adequately represent all of the aforementioned information types necessitated the design of a purpose built information model (as shown in figure 4.)

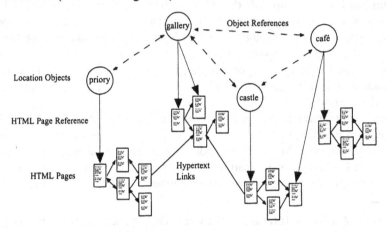

Fig. 4. The Guide Information Model.

The information model manages the requirement for representing geographic information by including special navigation point objects. These can be used in conjunction with location objects for determining the best route between a source and destination location. One example of a location object is the city's castle. This object contains state representing various attributes, such as opening times and tour costs, and also contains hypertext links to related information.

Each GUIDE unit is able to locally cache parts of the information model and is therefore able to operate even when disconnected from the network. However, during periods of disconnection the cached information model can become stale. If, for example, the opening times for the city's castle changed then the information model would become inconsistent with the server's information model and, as a result, incorrect information could be given to the visitor.

The GUIDE system has adopted an optimistic approach towards the management of potentially stale caches. If a pessimistic approach had been adopted then no functionality would have been available to visitors when out of cell coverage. The optimistic approach does, however, raise some interesting issues. For example, how can the system make the visitor aware that the information being presented to them could be out-of-date or that timely information might not be displayed because no network connectivity is available. Section three of this paper addresses these issues and describes our proposed solution for giving feedback to the user regarding the state of their connectivity.

2.4 Infrastructure

The dissemination of the information model to GUIDE units is achieved using the cell-based wireless communications infrastructure shown below in figure 5.

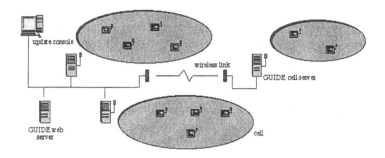

Fig. 5. The GUIDE Infrastructure.

The city contains a number of strategically positioned WaveLAN cells, each providing a shared bandwidth of 2 Mbit/s and supported by a GUIDE server. The fact that WaveLAN cells can be relatively large (up to 300 m in diameter depending on the layout of buildings) means that GUIDE servers may have to support a potentially large number of GUIDE units. This raises some important implications for the way in which information is disseminated to the GUIDE units contained in a cell.

The most significant implication concerns the mean time for a cell server to service a client's request for data. The medium access protocol used by WaveLAN is based on CSMA/CD, which means that before transmitting on the carrier a unit will listen to detect whether another transmission is currently taking place. If another transmission is heard then a random back-off will occur before another attempt to transmit is made. The implication of this is that, if a point-to-point communications method is used between a cell server and each GUIDE unit within a cell, the response times to requests would be inversely proportional to the number of GUIDE units per cell.

In order to reduce response times when the number of GUIDE units per cell is large, a broadcast based approach to information dissemination is used [14]. Each cell server thus periodically broadcasts parts of the information model relating to its cell. For example, the server for the cell containing the castle would broadcast information regarding the castle objects and other objects located close by.

3. The Implications of Disconnected Operation

Context-aware systems with a strong reliance on network connectivity, such as the Conference Assistant, are severely affected by network disconnections. However, such systems are generally intended for operation in fully connected indoor environments where disconnection is unlikely. One could argue that, in the future, fully connected environments will be commonplace in outdoor as well as indoor environments.

However, it seems unlikely that the problem of excessive power consumption, caused by fully connected operation, will disappear in the near future. For this reason, it is dangerous to simply assume that one can ignore the problems of connectivity when considering the future role of mobile context-aware systems.

The approach adopted by GUIDE has been to design a system that: 1) utilises a broadcast protocol to minimise power consumption and 2) caches information locally in order to tolerate occasional disconnection. There are, however, a number of implications that arise from adopting this approach. In particular, one needs to consider how disconnected operation might affect the visitor's trust of GUIDE given that the system relies on connectivity for the messaging service, access to interactive services, such as ticket booking, the reception of dynamic information and location information. One approach would have been to hide the issue of connectivity from the user completely. Given this approach, only when the visitor performed some action which explicitly required connectivity, such as booking a cinema ticket, would the visitor be informed that the service was currently unavailable. The problem with this approach is that the behaviour of the system would, given the anticipated switching between connected and disconnected operation, seem unpredictable and inconsistent. Predictability is a key requirement for the usability of interactive systems [15] not least because it affects the system's perceived reliability.

Clearly, if visitors perceive GUIDE as unreliable and lack trust in the system then it is unlikely to be used to its potential, if at all [16]. To help alleviate this problem, the user interface to GUIDE has been designed to encourage the user to form a suitable mental model [15] of the system, i.e. one in which the functionality of the system is not static but dependant on whether or not wireless connectivity is currently available. This is achieved by providing the user with an appropriate level of mobile-awareness [17] in order to enable them to appreciate the affect of changes in connectivity on system functionality.

The user interface effectively supports two modes of operation, one for connected operation and the other for disconnected operation. In general, modes represent hidden information and can, when poorly designed, confuse the user. However, in GUIDE we believe that we have satisfied the general principle suggested in [15] for choosing to use modes because: 1) there is sufficient reason and 2) the user is given sufficient information to tell the modes apart.

The following subsections describe the various user interface design choices we have made in order to enable the user to realise which mode they are currently in.

3.1 Use of a Metaphor to Provide Connectivity Feedback

A metaphor, that was both familiar and relevant, was required for providing visitors with feedback regarding the current state of connectivity and encouraging them to associate this with available functionality. To arrive at a suitable metaphor, we considered how connectivity feedback is provided on mobile phones. The user of a mobile phone is given feedback of their connectivity in the form of 'bars of connectivity' and when a user receives no bars of connectivity they expect limited functionality, i.e. the inability to send or receive calls. The 'bars of connectivity' metaphor has been incorporate into the user interface as illustrated in figure 6.

Fig. 6. Utilising the 'bars of connectivity' metaphor.

3.2 Disabling the 'Ticket Booking' Icon in Disconnected Mode

The user interface to GUIDE is based on the direct manipulation paradigm (although icons cannot actually be moved) and so only icons that actually allow some action to be completed should be displayed as active. For this reason, we chose to 'grey-out' the ticket booking icon when the facility is unavailable due to disconnection.

3.3 Modification of the 'Send Message' Dialogue Box

We had considered disabling the messaging icon when operating in disconnected mode, but instead chose to modify the messaging dialogue box (figure 7) to state that the message being composed would not be sent until on-line operation was resumed.

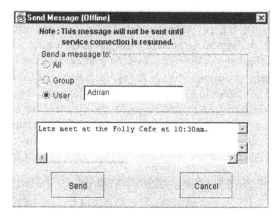

Fig. 7. Modification of the 'Send Message' dialogue box.

This approach was chosen because of the anticipated usage of the messaging component, i.e. sending informal messages to companions, and we felt that it would be most convenient for a visitor to be able to compose a message while sitting in a café even if no network connection was available therein.

3.4 Showing the Status of Location Updates

The availability of up-to-date positioning information would not always be available regardless of whether the GUIDE system received its positioning information via GPS or the coverage afforded by WaveLan cells. For example, when using GPS in a city environment the position of tall buildings can prevent the GPS system from 'seeing' a sufficient number of satellites to obtain a fix on location.

It is not necessary for the user to realise that the GUIDE system receives location information and communicates with remote services via the same wireless link. Indeed, location information could be received via DGPS, when the technology matures. In this case, a situation could arise in which location information could be received but network connectivity was unavailable or vice versa.

For this reason we have tried to encourage visitors to form a mental model in which the reception of location information and access to network based services are not inextricably linked. To this end, we chose to include a location status window in the user interface in addition to the 'bars of connectivity'.

The location status window keeps the user informed of the ongoing reception of location information by the system. When location information has not been received for a short while, the visitor is shown the time (in whole minutes) that has elapsed since the last location update was received. This information allows the visitor to backtrack to the point where location information (and in the current implementation, network connectivity) was available. Alternatively, the user could continue on their current course but in the knowledge that the system does not know (and has not known for x minutes) their location.

3.5 Using the Visitor's Assistance to Ascertain their Location

When visitors leave cell coverage, the GUIDE system can effectively 'lose' their location. Clearly, if the system erroneously interprets the visitor's location, this could have a disastrous effect on the user's trust of the system. In order to prevent this from happening, the system is designed to ask the visitor a series of questions, such as "can you see the castle?", in order to ascertain their current location. Figure 8 illustrates the way in which the GUIDE system interacts with the visitor in an attempt to gain a fix on their current location. During our initial evaluation of the system we have found the response of users to this form of questioning to be quite positive and that users are prepared to accept that the system may actually lose track of their location.

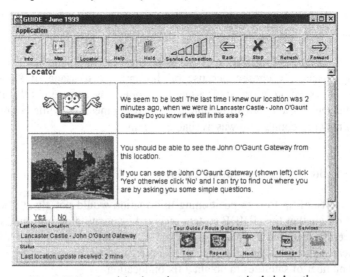

Fig. 8. Using the visitor's assistance to ascertain their location.

4. Future Directions

Our current direction for developing the GUIDE system is to extend the role of connectivity in GUIDE by supplementing the existing GUIDE infrastructure with the latest low-power, micro-cellular, wireless technologies, such as Bluetooth [18]. This will enable GUIDE to support communications within buildings. In addition, the use of micro-cellular wireless communications systems will enable us to determine users' locations with greater accuracy, without requiring bulky differential GPS equipment, and thus enhance the navigational capabilities of the system.

A further benefit of using micro-cellular wireless technologies is that the use of low-power communications devices will enable more compact end-systems (e.g. the increasingly popular PDAs, such as the palm pilot) to be used with the GUIDE system for extended periods of time.

We also plan to significantly increase the diversity of context-sensitive interactive services supported by GUIDE. Examples of such services will include: ordering a taxi or requesting the location of the nearest cash point. In both cases the system will use information about the user (taxi company preferences or bank details) and contextual information, such as the user's location and the time of day, to negotiate with the service provider on the user's behalf. Another service which we hope to provide is an awareness of others, e.g. friends, currently in the city.

Support for these new technologies and interactive services has significant implications for the role of connectivity within GUIDE and the proposed modifications will place a far greater reliance on connectivity than that of the current system. In addition, providing greater support for interactive services will require changes to underlying GUIDE protocols. In more detail, the current approach used for information dissemination and for obtaining location information relies on the network being comprised of non-overlapping cells. While such an approach has proved ideal for constructing the current GUIDE system, it is clearly unsuitable when we are aiming to provide ubiquitous access to context-sensitive services over heterogeneous networks. As a result, we will need to redesign the underlying GUIDE protocols to address these new requirements without impinging on the original GUIDE aims of providing scalable and low-power access to context-sensitive information.

In addition to modifying the protocols used in GUIDE, we will also need to provide application level components which enable context-sensitive interactions between mobile data users and local service providers, such as restaurants and taxi firms. To reduce the cost of deploying the system we are proposing that one of these components will be a generic gateway which will liaise with service providers using a range of communications techniques including synthesised speech.

5. Conclusions

This paper has considered the role of connectivity in supporting context-sensitive applications, and presented a design space that enables the positioning of context-sensitive applications depending on their reliance on network connectivity and their reliance on local storage.

The GUIDE system described in this paper occupies a central area in this design space because, although the system requires network connectivity to receive both positioning and dynamic information, the system has been designed to continue operating as a useful guide (albeit at a reduced level of functionality) even when disconnected from the network. The key design choice for enabling disconnected operation was the decision to have each GUIDE unit cache at least some portion of the information model in local memory.

However, use of this strategy alone is insufficient to solve the other problems that can occur from disconnected operation. Indeed, additional strategies were required in order to maintain the visitor's trust of the system when network communications is unavailable. In particular, the user interface was designed to encourage users to adopt a suitable mental model for using the system in both connected and disconnected modes of operation. We chose to utilise a 'bars of connectivity' metaphor in order to provide visitors with a suitable analogy for understanding at least some of the issues concerning connectivity and therefore allow the visitor's expectations of the system to be tempered by the level of connectivity available.

In addition, to cope with the situation of resolving location issues when disconnected (or when unsure of the visitor's location within a large communication cell) the visitor is asked to answer a small number of questions. Using the answers to these questions and its knowledge of the city (i.e. the locally stored information model) the GUIDE system can continue to help navigate visitors through the city.

References

1. Schilit, B., Adams, N., Want, R.: Context-Aware Computing Applications. Proc. Workshop on Mobile Computing Systems and Applications, Santa Cruz, CA, U.S. (1994)
2. Brown, P.J., Bovey, J.D., Chen, X.: Context-aware applications: from the laboratory to the market place. IEEE Personal Communications, Vol. 4, No. 5 (1997) 58-64
3. Want, R., Schilit, B., Adams, N., Gold, R., et al: The ParcTab Ubiquitous Computing Experiment, Technical Report CSL-95-1, Xerox Palo Alto Research Center (1995)
4. Dey, A.K., Salber, D., Futakawa, M., Abowd, G.D.: An Architecture To Support Context-Aware Applications. Georgia Tech, Technical Report GIT-GVU-99-23 (1999)
5. Holmquist, L.: Supporting Group Collaboration with IPAD:s - Inter-Personal Awareness Devices. Proc. Workshop on Handheld CSCW, ACM CSCW'98 Conference on Computer Supported Cooperative Work, Seattle, Washington. (1998) 37-43
6. Want, R., Hopper, A., et al. :The Active Badge Location System. Olivetti Research Laboratory, ACM Transactions on Information Systems, Vol. 10, No. 1. (1992) 91-102

7. Long, S., Kooper, R., Abowd, G.D., Atkeson, C.G.: Rapid Prototyping of Mobile Context-Aware Applications: The Cyberguide Case Study. Proc. 2nd ACM International Conference on Mobile Computing, Rye, New York, U.S., ACM Press (1996)

8. Pinkerton, M.D.: Ubiquitous Computing: Extending Access To Mobile Data, Master's Thesis, GVU Technical Report GIT-GVU-97-09 (1997)

9. Cheverst, K., Davies, N., Mitchell, K., Blair, G.S.: The Design of an Object Model for a Context-Sensitive Tourist Guide. Proc. Interactive Applications of Mobile Computing (IMC'98), Rostock, Germany (1998) 25-29

10. Davies, N., Mitchell, K., Cheverst, K., Friday, A.: 'Caches in the Air': Disseminating Tourist Information in the Guide System. Proc. 2nd IEEE Workshop on Mobile Computing Systems and Applications, New Orleans, U.S. (1999) 11-19

11. Magellan: GPS Home Page. http://www.magellangps.com/frames/frame2.htm (1999)

12. Fujitsu: TeamPad Technical Page. http://www.fjicl.com/TeamPad/teampad76.htm (1999)

13. Lucent Technologies: WaveLAN Home Page. http://www.wavelan.com/ (1999)

14. Franklin, M., Zdonik, S.: Dissemination-based Information Systems. IEEE Data Engineering Bulletin, Vol. 19, No. 3 (1996)

15. Thimbleby, H.: User Interface Design. Addison-Wesley Longman Ltd, ISBN 0-201-41618-2. (1990)

16. Sommerville, I.: Software Engineering. Third Edition, Addison-Wesley Longman Ltd, ISBN 0-201-17568-1. (1989)

17. Cheverst, K., Davies, N., Friday, A., Blair, G.: Supporting Collaboration in Mobile-aware Groupware. Proc. Workshop on Handheld CSCW: ACM CSCW'98 Conference on Computer Supported Cooperative Work, Seattle, Washington (1998) 59-64

18. The Bluetooth Consortium. http://www.bluetooth.com (1999)

Issues in Developing Context-Aware Computing

Jason Pascoe, Nick Ryan, and David Morse

Computing Laboratory, University of Kent at Canterbury,
Canterbury, Kent CT2 7NF, United Kingdom
{jp, nsr, drm}@ukc.ac.uk

Abstract. Two differing context-aware projects are described in this paper as a basis for exploring and better understanding the nature of context and context-aware applications. The investigation reveals that although indeed a useful concept, better supporting infrastructure is required before it can become a feasible mainstream technology. In particular, we propose the concept of a context information service to address this need, and define the general characteristics that such a service should exhibit.

1 Introduction

Context-awareness, the ability of a device or program to sense, react or adapt to its environment of use, is a key technology in ubiquitous, handheld and wearable computing. These new computing paradigms seek to overturn traditional desktop computing practices by either seamlessly embedding computers in the environment or task in which they will be required, or by providing a very personal computer that constantly accompanies the user and whose facilities are always at their disposal. These paradigms offer very different computing environments from each other but they are united in their aim to bring computing facilities to bear wherever and whenever the user may need them.

"Transparency of use" is often quoted as an essential quality of these devices, where they should lend themselves to the task at hand in as unobtrusive manner as possible [1]. An analogy of writing is often used, where one may write using a pen or pencil but where one's focus of attention is solely on the task of writing, the pen being transparent to that task.

Unlike pen and paper, which are typically used to perform a standard task in a standard environment (i.e. writing at a desk), the ubiquitous, handheld, and wearable computing devices will be used in a wide range of different tasks and environments. In order for these computers to integrate well with the user and the environment in which they may be used, and to offer as transparent a service as possible, knowledge of that environment and an ability to adapt to it is essential. That is, context-awareness has a key role to play in all of these new technologies that aim to place computers in much more diverse and dynamic environments (compared to the desktop).

Our research has focused on exploring context-awareness at both an application and supporting framework level. Our experiences in developing such context-aware software have led us to believe that some fundamental generic context services are required to make context-awareness a viable technology that can be easily incorporated into a variety of software. The next section of this paper describes some of our context-aware development experiences. The subsequent section presents the lessons we have learnt from these projects and is used to motivate the need for a context information service, which we discuss in the final section.

1.1 Related Work

Schilit et al pioneered the development of context-aware computing as we know it today [2]. Our generic context-aware application framework that exploits their ideas is based on Brown's concept of stick-e notes [3], a generalised electronic equivalent of Post-It notes. Other context-aware frameworks or reusable components have been devised, such as in the CyberGuide [4] and CyberDesk [5] projects that provide a modular framework for context-aware tourist guides and desktop computing environments respectively. However, they differ from stick-e notes in that they are more tightly focused on specific application domains such as tourist guides.

We have conducted a project to develop context-aware fieldwork tools, which investigates the less commonly addressed idea of authoring in context rather than retrieval in context. Other work is being done using location-aware handheld computers for ecology work [6] but it focuses on the user-interface aspects rather than the context-aware aspects that we concentrate on.

Our suggestion for the need of a context information service is substantiated by the Context Toolkit project at Georgia Tech [7]. Their similar development experiences in context-aware computing have also led them to believe in the need for generic context services. Although we share that common goal our approach to achieving it is quite different. The Context Toolkit work concentrates on developing a set of context servers that each provide different context information and that are supported by interchangeable, reusable components. Our concept of a context information service is not so focused on the provision of particular types of context. Rather, it seeks to provide a shared environment in which sensor and context components can be developed and installed, and subsequently utilised in the presentation of a common, object-oriented, contextual view of the world.

The SitComp service [8] provides context services in the form of a delivery and interpretation medium through which the applications are presented with meaningful context that is abstracted from the raw data obtained from sensors attached to a device. Our context information service concept aims to be less device/person-centric and seeks to provide a richer and more diverse sense of context by maintaining a model that presents context information as properties of the objects it describes.

All the work on context services shares a common ancestor in the form of Schilit's system architecture for context-aware and mobile computing [9], which is primarily location-based and utilises an active badge infrastructure. SPIRIT [10] expands on this work by providing a service that enables users to make use of available hardware and resources as they walk around, offering location-aware personalisation and control. The location server [11] is purely focused on providing location information and integrating different location sensing systems through a series of location mapping spaces. Although incorporating location context, our work aims to support any type of context, ranging from the user's mood to the size of a rhinoceros's footprint, and gives no special preference to any one particular type of context over another.

2 Experiences of Context-Aware Development

This section examines two of our context-aware projects. The first, the *stick-e note* framework [12], was an attempt at creating a general application framework for a particular class of context-aware applications. The second, some fieldwork tools [13], are a suite of programs designed for in-field data collection work. We conclude the section with a discussion on the lessons we have learnt from these projects.

2.1 Stick-e Notes

Brown first envisioned the concept of a stick-e note as an electronic equivalent of a Post-It note [3]. Instead of scribbling on a sticky piece of paper and then affixing it to a desk, door, etc. a user could type a message on their handheld computer and virtually attach it to a location. The computer would then redisplay the note whenever the user subsequently approached the same location. Using an electronic device rather than a paper Post-It also offered up a number of possibilities that simply aren't possible with paper notes. For example, attaching notes to contexts other than location, such as a time of day, temperature, weather condition, mood of the user, etc. Also the type of data we attached to a context need not be limited to plain text, we could consider pages of HTML, sound files, or even programs that could be executed in context.

Rather than simply developing a single electronic Post-it note application, we decided to implement the stick-e note concept as a general application framework. There are certainly many other potential applications of the general stick-e note technology. For example, a tour-guide consisting of a set of multimedia notes that present the tourist with information on the sights they visit. Our aim was to support the development of such applications by providing a general-purpose stick-e note framework that could be incorporated into applications wishing to provide such behaviour. That is, we sought to provide a processing framework that was independent of application and user interface.

The Stick-e Note Framework. Stick-e notes facilitate a form of information retrieval where the queries are automated and context-based, as opposed to the conventional manual formulation of subject-based queries by the user. We call this automated contextual retrieval process *triggering*. It is the driving force of the stick-e note framework, it is the process that defines the operation of a stick-e note program.

To support the triggering process in our project to develop a stick-e note framework we needed to incorporate three capabilities: (i) a knowledge of the user's current context (i.e. real world states, such as the user's location) in order to form a contextual query, (ii) a triggering engine that executes the contextual queries on a set of stick-e notes, and (iii) a manager entity that regulates and controls the formation and execution of queries and the dissemination of any *triggered* notes. These elements are discussed in more detail in the following three sub-sections.

Environment Module (to maintain the user's current context). The knowledge of the real world was encapsulated in an environment module so that clients (internal and external to the framework) were insulated from particular contextual and device level details. The aim was to provide a transparent and standardised interface to the 'real world' that was able to service a client's demand for the value of a particular context in a general way. For example, the client could simply ask for a location and let the environment module worry about selecting the best location-sensing device and the most appropriate data format.

In essence, clients just had to ask the environment module for a context and then this module would do the hard work of obtaining it. This approach benefits clients by insulating them from platform dependent hardware and sensor interfaces, schemes for determining best contexts, and changing device configurations. In addition, separating the context-capturing mechanism into a stand-alone module allows client context-aware applications to by-pass the stick-e note processing scheme and directly use the context data should they wish to.

Contexts were modelled in a hierarchy extending down from a completely abstract 'context' base object to generic context-type objects (e.g. location, temperature and with-person) followed by specific implementation objects (e.g. location may have point, rectangle and polygon implementations). Similarly sensor devices that provide current context data were modelled in such a hierarchy. The environment module provided an API at the level of generic context-types and hid all notion of devices. For example, a GetLocation() API call could be issued to obtain the current location, with the specific implementation and sensor devices consulted remaining hidden from the client.

Triggering Engine. When run, the triggering engine first ascertains the current context by consulting the environment module and then formulates a query based on this information. It then proceeds to execute this query on the set of notes that it has been passed (e.g. a set of notes for a guided tour of Canterbury) and produces the subset of notes that match the conditions of the contextual query (e.g. the notes describing the features of interest in the user's immediate vicinity). This process is similar to conventional search engines but there are changes in semantics that arise from the use of context as query. For example, if a stick-e note is only attached to a location context, but the query also states a temperature context, then it is likely that the desired behaviour would be to ignore the temperature context for that comparison. The triggering engine attempts to build-in as many of these implicit semantics as possible but they can also be overridden in a stick-e note itself.

Manager. The manager is responsible for maintaining the 'plumbing' between framework and applications through which one or more clients may specify their interests and receive related notes that are triggered. Clients indicate their interests by specifying the collection(s) of notes they are interested in working with (notes are grouped and stored in collections to allow for logical groupings, e.g. a set of campus tour notes). The manager then adds this collection to the pool of notes that is to be passed to the triggering engine when it is executed. Copies of any triggered notes that the triggering engine produces are then sent out to the appropriate clients.

The manager invokes the triggering engine at (configurable) time intervals and may first filter the source pool of notes based on the results of previous triggerings. One reason for performing this filtering is to prevent multiple triggering of the same note so that, for example, the initial triggering context must be cleared for a certain duration before the note is retriggered. This is useful in applications like tour guides where, after the user dismisses an information panel that has been triggered, it should not be redisplayed until the site is revisited at a later date. This may also involve detection of *border-hovering*. This is where the user is moving along the border of a contextual area, which could give the impression that they are rapidly moving in and out of that area when in fact they should be considered constantly in or constantly out of it.

2.2 Context-Aware Fieldwork Tools

Unlike the stick-e note framework, which experimented with context-awareness at a generic support level, the work on context-aware fieldwork tools took an application-oriented approach. The main aim of the work was to explore how mobile computing technology could be usefully employed to help in fieldwork environments. Equally importantly, it also gave us the opportunity to explore how context-awareness could be utilised and to evaluate its usefulness and practicality in this application domain.

Generic Data Collection Tools. We developed a suite of three programs, *StickePlates*, *StickePad*, and *StickeMap*, for the PalmPilot handheld computer. These were designed to help in the task that dominates most types of fieldwork, that is, data collection. The StickePlates program allows the user to define a data collection template, which consists of a list of fields with a name and type. After defining a set of templates the user can use the StickePad to collect their data through an electronic form interface on the PalmPilot screen. This form interface is based on one of the predefined templates. Location is provided as a unique field type in the template, and the capability to communicate with a GPS (Global Positioning System) receiver is provided. Thus, the programs were imbued with a simple location-awareness.

The StickePad utilises this location-awareness when a new note is created by automatically filling in any location field with the user's current location (derived from an attached GPS receiver). The fieldworker can therefore effortlessly, consistently, and accurately, geo-reference all of the data that she collects in the field, a process that is normally time-consuming and inaccurate using manual methods.

The StickPad's abilities are extended with context-awareness, but the StickeMap is designed specifically to exploit context-awareness. It provides a dynamic and configurable map-like interface that visualises the user's current location relative to the stored forms on the device, e.g. plotting the giraffe observations previously recorded relative to the ecologist's current location. It also serves as an alternative data access mechanism through which stored forms are effectively ordered by proximity to the current location (which often corresponds to the order of the form's current importance). This provides the fieldworkers with a very useful facility that simply isn't possible with their traditional paper-based recording methods.

The ecologists used the set of tools (and continue to do so) over two field seasons of approximately three to four months duration. The most extensive trial was in a behavioural study of giraffe in which over 6,000 notes were recorded exclusively on the handheld computer; no conventional paper-based data collection methods were used for the entire duration of the study. Using our software the ecologists were able to record more data in less time and with more reliability and consistency than was previously possible. This success, in part, is attributable to the location-awareness of the tools.

A Rhino Identification Tool. The StickPlates, StickePad and StickeMap tools are generic ones aimed not just at ecological studies but for any in-field data collection work, e.g. they are suitable for archaeologists, field engineers, etc. A more task-specific tool we have been developing is a rhino identifier to aid the ecologists. Context-awareness is at the heart of this tool as it aims to predict what rhinos are likely to be present, or were present, close to the ecologist's current context. More specifically, the current context consists of the ecologist's location, measurements of footprints found (currently manually entered but which, in future versions, may be automatically extracted via a digital camera) and time of day. This current contextual data is compared with historical contextual data of rhino sightings, home-range and footprint data, in order to produce a list of the rhinos that will most likely be discovered, or would have been, given the ecologist's current circumstances. This tool will go on trial in the next field season. If it proves successful then there are many possibilities for expanding its context-aware aspects. For example, using temperature, vegetation types, weather conditions, etc. as context, all of which could be automatically obtained through electronic thermometers, GIS/databases, and wirelessly networked weather stations, respectively.

3 Lessons Learnt

From the development of a general framework and a set of task-specific tools, we have learnt a number of lessons regarding both context-aware applications and user-interface issues for handheld computers. This paper addresses the context-aware aspects, the user-interface issues can be found elsewhere [14].

3.1 Context-Awareness is Extremely Useful

The majority of context-aware applications that we have developed thus far have been only aware of their location. However, location-awareness has proven extremely useful both as an enhancement to existing tasks, such as geo-referencing electronic forms, and also in developing completely new applications, such as the fieldworker's StickeMap. We have many other ideas for extending the use of the location-awareness still further, e.g. delivering real-time GIS information relevant to the user's current location from a base computer to their mobile handheld via a wireless link. We are also exploring the incorporation of other contexts such as direction, elevation, temperature, etc. However, we have shown that even a relatively simple context-awareness can be of great utility to the user.

3.2 On the Nature of Context

At the start of our work we had conceived of a context as being a relatively simple snapshot of a set of environmental values such as location, temperature, etc., that described a particular instance of the user's environment. But as our work has progressed it has revealed the more rich and complex nature of context.

Context and Content May Not Be So Different. In our stick-e note framework we initially made a very clear distinction between context and content. This was understandable given our concepts of Post-It notes and tourist guides in which some data was electronically attached to a particular situation. However, in developing the data collection tools for the ecologists the difference became much less distinct. When using the tools they were just as interested in the context of the note (i.e. the location in which it was recorded) as they were in the behavioural observations that they recorded. Additionally, the information they recorded, such as the current activity of a giraffe, could be considered to be as much context as it was content. To them the only distinction between the content and context of a form was that the computer automatically completed the contextual parts.

We thus changed our concept of a stick-e note to accommodate this change of perception. Instead of two separate context and content parts, there is now simply a set of fields that describe a situation.

Context Can Be Complex. Upon first consideration a context such as location may appear to be a relatively simple item of data to manipulate. However, it soon becomes apparent that there is a plethora of different location sensing systems available such as GPS [15], active badges [16], visual identifiers [17], etc. These all tend to use their own measurement systems and work in different, though sometimes overlapping, domains. For example, GPS only works outdoors and tends to use latitude and longitude measurements, whereas active badges are more often deployed indoors (due to infrastructure costs) and use a cell-based measurement system. What is more, some of these individual measurement systems have different operational attributes that can dramatically affect their correspondence with the real world, e.g. latitude and longitude is expressed in relation to a specific datum (essentially, a mathematical representation of the Earth's surface) – using the wrong datum can result in inaccuracies of as much as a kilometre. To further add to the complexity locations may be specified in a variety of ways, such as a point, a rectangle, or a polygon, each of with may have some form of accuracy or error boundary.

Providing comprehensive support for a context such as location, considering the diversity of sensors and measurement systems, is a complex task.

Context is Much More Than Location. Given the inherent mobility of handheld computers and the varying situations of ubiquitous computing, it is not surprising that the location context has been the focus of much context-aware research. Indeed, our research was initially focused on this form of context as there were a wide array of automatic detection mechanisms and obvious uses for this information. However, there are many other types of context that can be automatically detected, some of which may be more important than location, depending, of course, on the application. For example, the orientation of the user may be just as important as location in trying to determine what they are currently looking at, and in our continuing work on the fieldwork tools we are now exploring contexts as diverse as time of day, weather conditions and animal footprint measurements.

Context is an Attribute not an Entity. In our initial stick-e note framework we considered contexts as individual entities that existed in the user's environment, e.g. the location, the temperature, etc. However, context really makes no sense on its own. It inherently describes some real or virtual entity. For example, a location may be attributed to a place, a person, a car, a book, etc. A location on its own has no value unless we know what entity it is locating.

In the stick-e note model where we thought of current contexts as self-contained states existing in the environment, what we were actually doing was making implicit assumptions about what they were attributed to. For example, the current location context was implicitly attributed to the user, temperature was implicitly attributed to the local vicinity, orientation was implicitly attributed to the user, giraffe behaviour (in the fieldwork tools) was implicitly attributed to the last spotted giraffe, etc. Such implicit assumptions may work in the cases of simple applications but they are not advisable. And in more complex applications which consider the current context of more entities than simply the user and the immediate vicinity, it is essential that context be explicitly modelled as an attribute of a particular entity

Virtual Entities Can Have More Complex Context. The current context of a physical object, such as a person, can be represented by a set of otherwise unrelated fields, e.g. their location, temperature and orientation. The context of virtual entities may be represented in the same way. For example, a virtual billboard could be associated with a real location context so that the advertisement or information it presents can be displayed on a user's handheld computer when they walk by the location to which it is virtually attached. Unlike a real billboard though, the virtual billboard may be easily moved to different locations. The most interesting aspect of the virtual billboard however, and all other virtual objects, is that they need not obey the laws of physics as real objects do. The virtual billboard can therefore do otherwise impossible things like being in two or more places at the same time, being visible only to certain types of people, existing only at certain temperatures, and so on. The aforementioned attributes could be practically employed in a virtual billboard that advertises an ice-cream parlour, where the billboards could be displayed on any ice-cream lover's handheld computer when walking near the store on a hot day!

Given their unique ability to defy the laws of physics, virtual entities need to express their context in more complex terms than a simple set of fields. They require the ability to represent their context in the form of conditional expressions of context that may utilise Boolean operators.

3.3 On the Nature of Context-Aware Applications

Given our comments on our evolving understanding of context, it is perhaps not suprising that we found context-aware applications to be much more diverse in structure and more time-consuming to develop than we had first anticipated.

There are Many Classes of Context-Aware Applications. The stick-e note framework suits applications that seek to place data in context and automatically retrieve that data when the user enters that context. However, our work on the context-aware fieldwork tools illustrate other types of applications, and there are no doubt many more new and existing applications that require other forms of context-awareness beyond what is offered by stick-e notes. This will particularly be the case when imbuing existing applications with context-awareness because the developer will probably prefer to add context-awareness in very specific places, in order to add some extra 'intelligence' to the program, rather than completely rewriting the application to fit the stick-e note framework. For example, a simple calendar and to-do list program could be imbued with a context-awareness so that it knows what context the diary and to-do entries will be carried out in. The to-do list could then offer a "do now/here" view and the diary could have a more intelligent alarm system than, for example, simply beeping half an hour before a meeting even when the user is currently in a completely different city to that of the meeting.

The stick-e note framework does indeed provide useful support for a certain class of context-aware applications, but there are no doubt other general classes of context-aware applications and there are certainly applications that have their own esoteric uses of context-awareness.

Context-Aware Applications tend to be Resource Hungry. A device or program that is aware of its context must, by definition, keep watch over its environment. In its simplest form this may be performed by occasionally polling some sensors that provide the current value of a particular context. All context-aware applications need to perform this task, so if more than one context-aware application is simultaneously running on a device then there could be a competition for sensor resources and there is a danger of one of the applications locking out the others. This is especially likely for sensors that require a continuing dialogue rather than periodically broadcasting information.

For many applications obtaining the current context from a sensor is just the start of its work. For example, in the stick-e note framework the current context is obtained in order for the triggering engine to check if there are any stick-e notes that should be triggered in those circumstances. This continual triggering process, and similar processes in other context-aware applications, requires considerable processor resources and could again place the application in competition with other programs running on the device (including non-context-aware programs).

Context-Awareness has a High Development Cost. Writing a context-aware application from scratch is a hard process. To imbue a device or program with a knowledge of just a single context requires a good deal of effort. One must develop the code to communicate with some external sensing system, convert the obtained data into a desirable format, provide the necessary machinery for manipulating the data, and finally, provide an interface with which the user can work with the data. In the case of imbuing the fieldwork tools with a location-awareness, we developed the code to communicate with a GPS receiver by listening to its broadcasts of NMEA sentences (a data transmission format common to GPS receivers), provided functions to convert the latitude and longitude to other formats, e.g. UTM and OSGB (these are two co-ordinate systems that we commonly use), provided the means to calculate distances between locations, and provided a map-like visualisation of the geo-referenced forms. In other words, a large portion of the development cost was in producing the location-awareness capability.

This development effort does little to encourage the growth of the use of context-awareness in applications, especially in cases where the context-awareness is incidental to the main purpose of the application. For applications like the previously mentioned context-aware to-do list and diary, it is unlikely that the development cost could be justified for the relatively small benefits derived.

The Computing Environments are Diverse. During the relatively short time span of this work, approximately 2-3 years, we have seen many advances in the mobile computing platforms available, each offering ever more sophisticated computing capabilities. And unlike desktop computing, the world of handheld and ubiquitous devices is a very heterogeneous one, with many different computing platforms each with their own weird and wonderful operating systems.

Although this diversity makes for a quite exciting environment to work in, it does present a major drawback in developing new software: we can find ourselves spending more time rewriting the same programs for the latest and greatest platform than we can in developing the new ideas that we wanted to explore.

The Greater the Context the Greater the Application. Our work has primarily been based on handheld computers that we have equipped with sensors to detect various aspects of the immediate environment. This provides a user-centric context-awareness in which the device shares the same contextual viewpoint as the user, e.g. their location, the temperature there, etc. The more types of context we support, the better a perception of our context the device has. But perception can also be improved by incorporating the viewpoints of others, i.e. sharing contextual information with other devices to build a much more expansive contextual model of the world. Applications then have an enormous wealth of contextual information to utilise, not just about the user's context but about the context of the many other people, devices, and objects that are sharing that environment. Obviously much more sophisticated applications can be developed given such a dramatic increase in the richness of context.

4   Enabling Context-Aware Computing via a Context Information Service

This section draws together the lessons learnt in our context-aware development experiences and presents the concept of a *context information service* as a means of better facilitating the development of context-aware technology.

Through our context-aware research projects we have discovered that imbuing programs with context-awareness can greatly benefit the user. However, we have also discovered that there are many issues about the nature of context and context-aware applications that make developing such facilities less than straightforward. In the current state of affairs incorporating a context-aware capability into software could be likened to developing a program's graphical user interface by manipulating individual bits and pixels rather than using the high-level facilities provided by a common interface environment such as X-Windows or Microsoft Windows. One can easily imagine that today's user interfaces would be substantially less sophisticated without the facilities provided by these environments. It is our belief that just as generic interface services have enabled the growth and improvement of the graphical user interfaces of software, so too will generic context services support the growth and improvement of the context-aware capabilities of software. The context toolkit project at Georgia Tech [7] offers the same vision, though they focus on developing the equivalent of individual GUI widgets whereas we concentrate on developing the equivalent of the shared environment in which such widgets can be developed and made available to applications and end-users. Work in both areas in essential and complementary.

We believe that at the core of a supporting infrastructure for context-aware computing should be what we have termed a context information service (CIS) [18]. The responsibilities of this service are to gather, model, and provide contextual data, i.e. the general functionality that is required at the heart of all context-aware applications. The CIS does not attempt to impose any application semantics: its simple role is in the provision of contextual information. It is the common base on top of which more sophisticated context-aware capabilities and applications may be built.

The construction of a good CIS is an essential development to ensure the success of context-aware computing. The overall aim of a CIS is clear: to gather, model, and provide contextual information. But in order to establish more precisely what exactly a *good* CIS is we have formulated some guidelines that, based on our exploration of context-awareness and context-aware applications presented in this paper, define what we consider are the important characteristics it should exhibit:

— *Presents an object-oriented contextual model.* As we have previously described, contexts are attributes of particular entities, e.g. location may be an attribute of a person, giraffe, car keys, etc. Therefore, the CIS should model and present contextual information as a property of a real or virtual object.

— *Manages shared access to resources.* There may be a number of separate context-aware applications running simultaneously, but each will interact with the same single CIS running on the host device. This enables it to manage shared access to the host device's physical resources (such as sensors) and to present a common unified contextual model across all the applications.

— *Supports extensible and reusable components.* There is a vast array of potentially useful context types and sensors, making the development of a 'complete' CIS simply impossible. Instead it will probably be initially equipped with just a few basic context and sensor components. However, anyone should be able to develop and/or easily install new context and sensor components, e.g. akin to plug-ins for a WWW browser. Once developed for one application that extra context or sensor component is available to any other client application, or indeed to any other component that may produce a more abstract or value-added output.

— *Supports a layered service structure.* The CIS is solely concerned with the gathering, modelling, and provision of contextual information, and does not attempt to provide any application semantics. However, generic services that do, such as the stick-e note framework, are certainly useful. So the CIS is likely to form the bottom layer of a stack of services ranging from the generic to the application-specific.

— *Is globally scalable.* The CIS should be structured so that it accommodates not only an ever-growing local contextual model but also be able to incorporate and share contextual information with remote CISs. We envision a world where every device has a CIS and believe that the ability to effortlessly connect and amalgamate these CISs will yield many new exciting context-aware developments.

– *Is Platform Independent.* As much as possible the CIS should be independent of specific platforms, especially given the requirement for global scalability and its inherent need of inter-operation of heterogeneous devices.

The relative importance of these CIS characteristics of course depends on the particular client application for which it is being considered. They do, however, provide us with a good measure of the potential utility of a CIS implementation.

5 Current and Future Work

We are now in the process of developing a context information service that fulfils the guidelines that we have set out in this paper. Written in the Java programming language, it consists of four main components: (i) a *world* object that presents contextual information embedded in *artefacts* that correspond to real or virtual entities, (ii) a shared *sensor array* which can be populated with various sensors, (iii) an extensible *catalog* of context, sensor, and artefact components, and (iv) a *world archive* that facilitates the storage of contextual changes over time. We are also investigating methods of interconnecting and discovering remote CISs. Work on the ecology fieldwork tools also continues as a parallel activity, which, in the future, will utilise the context information service.

6 Conclusions

We have presented a summary of two quite different context-aware research projects, one a generic framework and the other a task-specific set of applications, and have used these as a means to better understand the nature of context and context-aware applications. A number of lessons have been learnt from those development experiences, suggesting that, although context-awareness is extremely useful, there a number of issues that must be resolved in order to make it a more viable technology for the mainstream. The concept of a context information service is proposed as a method of addressing those issues with the aim of co-ordinating the entire context gathering, modelling, and provision needs of the host device.

Acknowledgements

The "Mobile Computing in Fieldwork Environments" project [19] was funded by the Joint Information Systems Committee (JISC) Technology Applications Programme. (JTAP), grant number JTAP-3/217. We appreciate the help of all the ecologists and MSc students from Manchester Metropolitan University that gave us an insight into how electronic tools could be used in the field, and in particular Alan Birkett and Kathy Pinkney for pioneering and continuing to use our prototype tools.

References

1. Weiser, M. Some Computer Science Issues in Ubiquitous Computing. *Communications of the ACM*. 36(7), pp. 74-85.
2. Schilit, B., N. Adams, and R. Want. Context-Aware Computing Applications. *IEEE Workshop on Mobile Computing Systems and Applications*. 1994. Santa Cruz, CA, USA. pp. 85-90.
3. Brown, P.J., J.D. Bovey, and X. Chen. Context-Aware Applications: From the Laboratory to the Marketplace. IEEE Personal Communications, 1995. 4(5), pp. 58-64.
4. Long, S., et al. Rapid Prototyping of Mobile Context-Aware Applications: The Cyberguide Case Study. 2nd ACM International Conference on Mobile Computing and Networking (MobiCom '96). 1996.
5. Dey, A.K. and G.D. Abowd. CyberDesk: The Use of Perception in Context-Aware Computing. PUI 97 Perceptual User Interfaces Workshop. 1997.
6. Bailey, K. Stone Age Skills Meet the Challenge of the Techno-Age. in The Times, 8th October 1997. London. pp. 16-17 (Interface section).
7. Salber, D., A.K. Dey, and G.D. Abowd. The Context Toolkit: Aiding the Development of Context-Enabled Applications. CHI'99 (to appear). 1999. Pittsburgh, PA, USA.
8. Hull, R., P. Neaves, and J. Bedford-Roberts. Towards Situated Computing. 1st International Symposium on Wearable Computers (ISWC '97). 1997. Cambridge, Massachusetts, USA.
9. Schilit, W.N. Ph.D. Thesis. System Architecture for Context-Aware Mobile Computing. Columbia University. 1995.
10. Adly, N., P. Steggles, and A. Harter. SPIRIT: a Resource Database for Mobile Users. ACM CHI'97 Workshop on Ubiquitous Computing. 1997. Atlanta, Georgia, USA.
11. Leonhardt, U. and J. Magee. Towards a General Location Service for Mobile Environments. Third IEEE Workshop on Services in Distributed and Networked Environments. 1996. Macau. pp. 43-50.
12. Pascoe, J. The Stick-e Note Architecture: Extending the Interface Beyond the User. International Conference on Intelligent User Interfaces 1997. 1997. Orlando, Florida, USA. ACM. pp. 261-264.
13. Pascoe, J., D.R. Morse, and N.S. Ryan. Developing Personal technology for the Field. Personal Technologies, 1998. 2(1), pp. 28-36.
14. Pascoe, J., N.S. Ryan, and D.R. Morse. Human Computer Giraffe Interaction: HCI in the Field. Workshop on Human Computer Interaction with Mobile Devices. 1998. University of Glasgow, UK. GIST Technical Report G98-1.
15. Web Page: Global Positioning System Overview. Department of Geography, University of Texas at Austin. http://www.utexas.edu/depts/grg/gcraft/notes/gps/gps.html
16. Want, R., et al. The Active Badge Location System. ACM Transactions on Information Systems, 1992. 10(1), pp. 91-102.
17. Rekimoto, J. and K. Nagao. The World through the Computer: Computer Augmented Interaction with Real World Environments. UIST 95. 1995. Pittsburgh PA USA. ACM Press. pp. 29-36.
18. Pascoe, J. Adding Generic Contextual Capabilities to Wearable Computers. The Second International Symposium on Wearable Computers. 1998. Pittsburgh, PA, USA. IEEE. pp. 92-99.
19. Web Page: Mobile Computing in Fieldwork Environments Project Page. Computing Lab, University of Kent at Canterbury. http://www.cs.ukc.ac.uk/projects/mobicomp/Fieldwork/index.html

RAMSES: A Mobile Computing System for Field Archaeology

Massimo Ancona, Gabriella Dodero, Vittoria Gianuzzi

DISI - Università di Genova
Via Dodecaneso, 35 - 16146 Genova (Italy)
{ancona,dodero,gianuzzi}@disi.unige.it,
WWW home page: http://www.disi.unige.it/person/{AnconaM,DoderoG,GianuzziV}

Abstract. RAMSES (Remote Archeological Mobile Support Enhanced System) is an outdoor application of mobile computing to field archaeology, whose prototype has already been field tested in Summer 1998 at the site of Poliochni in Greece. The requirements for both hardware and software are illustrated; the system is composed by a fixed station, acting as object repository, and a few mobile units which input archaeological evidence by means of electromagnetic pen. The software components on both fixed and mobile systems and their interaction are described as well.

Topics: Handheld, wearable and environment-based appliances, Linking virtual worlds and physical worlds, Applications in arts and entertainment.

1 Introduction

When people like computer scientists think about archaeologists, the first character that strikes their mind is Indiana Jones, or, if you prefer, the figure of some old, wise gentleman with colonial hat on. Reality is quite different: working outside the civilized world is no way easy or funny. Moreover, the introduction of high technology in hostile environments (rain, cold, dust, heat etc.) today is still a challenge not simple to win.

From an engineering point of view, one of the main problems in Field Archaeology today is COMMUNICATION. If you search for tools or systems that can help archaeologists to locate new working areas or catalog thousands of objects, you can find a lot; but if you think of time spent between site excavation and publication of results (the head and tail of every archaeological research) you realize that a large amount of time is wasted for people in main digging camp to wait for return of their colleagues bringing finds from the field.

Let's see an example: we find a good place for excavations and we start to dig. When we find something interesting, we have to:

⋆ locate where the find is: its bidimensional coordinates and depth; its relative position with respect to neighboring finds;

⋆ draw a realistic sketch and take a note of color, material, possible use and dating if already known;

⋆ if the find is significant, even critical for further excavations, it could be great to have a system that allows us to communicate our discovery to other scientists at base camp, sending them its description, drawing or snapshot in real time;

⋆ in case of doubt, a comparison with other finds from the same area in previous campaigns, or from related areas, could be extremely useful.

At the end of the working day, and at the end of the campaign, all collected finds and the notes accompanying them must be analyzed and reorganized to fill the report forms and to make what has been found available to other scientists, possibly in electronic form on a site data base.

Today, such an integrated computer based system doesn't exist yet, if archaeologists have to communicate about latest finds, they are forced to leave the excavation site and go back at least to the camp (or they give up the idea of communicating, and store the finds for later show). Well, the aim of RAMSES project is the development of that system.

At present a prototype system is already working, using a network of mobile, pen-based computers which allows archaeologists to communicate in real time, from the excavation site, not only with text, but also with drawings, to other fixed hosts and to the rest of the scientific community (using a fixed host as a gateway to Internet).

The project results from a cooperation among archaeologists and computer scientists at our University, belonging to DARFICLET, the Department of Archaeology and Classical Phylology, and to DISI, the Department of Computer Science of the University of Genova. The end-user for such a system is the Italian Archaeological School in Athens, which has been responsible for more than 60 years of campaigns in the site of Poliochni, in the Greek island of Lemnos [11]. In Summer 1998, the prototype has already been field tested in the island of Lemnos, Greece, at the prehistoric site of Poliochni by the archaeological team.

The next Section describes the main requirements for a network operating in an archaeological field. Then, the functions of the two main software components, respectively running on the mobile and the fixed system, are explained. Details on how data is exchanged between the two systems is also given.

2 Wireless and Pen-Based computing for archaeological fieldwork

Laptop computers, which support a stationary working environment at different locations (such as both home and office) may already provide some of the useful features in field archaeology [9], as stated in the Introduction.

However, to allow real-time communication (networking) from the site, true mobility is needed, with **wireless communication**, such as radio connections. In fact, in contrast to what might happen in urban areas, electric power supply and telephone cable connection is seldom possible on an archaeological site: no wires can cross it, but perhaps there could be a nearby building (where archaeologists live during the campaign) where such facilities could be found. High costs and low bandwidth/reliability tradeoffs have important consequences on how wireless networking is supported. Client/server program execution, distributed file systems and data bases are not trivially made available on a wireless network. Software challenges lie both in adapting and redesign of existing pieces of software, and in design of novel applications especially addressing needs of mobile users.

Mobility is not the only requirement for a network in the archaeological site. Like most other outdoor computing environments, field archaeology is an extremely hostile computational environment. A computer should be operational in the open air, in any possible weather including heat, dust or perhaps rain: most laptops are often non-operative under such conditions. The need of being used while standing (or in some uncomfortable position) puts additional restrictions on the use of keyboard, mouse or trackball for input. Last but not least, weight of the device (which is mostly due to accumulators) should be carefully considered.

These requirements can be met by a mobile computer, which inputs from **electromagnetic or passive pens** which "write" on shock-proof liquid crystal screens. A pen immediately replaces a mouse (or other pointing devices) in menu-driven software; when a complex command or a text has to be input, some handwriting recognition software has to be used. An introduction about this technology can be found in [6].

2.1 Wireless networking outdoors

There are several kinds of "networking" environments already (or soon to be) operative in the outdoors. They may rely on high-speed cellular communication, satellite services or, as in our case, on radiofrequency. The connection to a wireless LAN and the use of a mobile device introduces the concept of AirAwareness[10], i.e. the capability of being always on-line and having the access to information anytime and anywhere. In the next future, millions of people shall connect to information sources while moving for their job by means of their personal digital assistants, as described in[5].

The major infrastructures available for data communication are Analog *Cellular systems* and *Packet Radio* systems. Both have been discarded, for our application, however, due to some their features. These include limited system capacity and low data services (about 20 Kbps from a stationary user), too low to allow transmission of drawings and snapshots of finds. Moreover, since different protocols have been adopted by different states, it could be difficult to provide a software and a target system widely usable in every excavation site, without considering the possibility of having no connection service provided at all.

Technologies like *Dual Band GSM* or *Iridium* were already foreseeable when our project started (and are available now): they have been considered out of this project's interest because of the low bandwidth they too support. Satellite coverage of areas of archaeological interest is not easy found. For these reasons we investigated the radio frequency communication devices, taking into consideration the need of being operational (almost) worldwide without obtaining special permissions for frequency use.

Among Radio Frequency systems, we selected the *Frequency Hopping Spread Spectrum* Radio technology, which offers high speed (about 2Mbps) along with reasonably secure communication data links, low power consumption and a coverage radius of about one mile without repeaters. Moreover, no license is required, and its use is accepted also in military areas, so the equipment can be easily transferred into every excavation site. The distance/speed tradeoffs for our application were all in favor of speed, and the one mile coverage was considered sufficient for most sites.

The scenario of a mobile network within an archaeological field is thus as in Figure 1. Three different entities can be identified: mobile computer units (labeled mu), mobile support stations (labeled MSS) and fixed hosts. MSS units are workstations with wireless communication interface towards mobile computers, and possibly another interface (wireless or cable) towards a WAN such as Internet. A wireless network consisting on one or more fixed workstations, and two or more mobile computers connected to a wireless LAN by radio devices, is sufficient for the needs of most archaeological excavations. The workstations are installed in some building close to the excavation site, and they are connected to Internet by telephone cables or satellite.

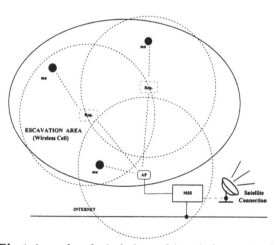

Fig.1 An archaeological site and its wireless network

Remark that in most sites a single support station is sufficient to support all MUs. It follows that we do not have the problem of locating the user unless in a very large site, which would require just a few fixed support units (see Figure 1). Even in this case, since archaeologists move by walking, MUs execute transactions while being relatively still. However, we may have a problem of elective disconnection[7], when the archaeologist is working in an inaccessible area (e.g., underground).

To this purpose, each MU has a large caching capability: it can support long periods of work without connection, thus a caching model is more suitable than a remote access model [1]. Remote access is relatively rare and only on specific user requests, where a peak of communication from the MU to the support station is needed. Typically, peak situations arise during remote data acquisition, that is in case a data acquisition device has been connected to the MU. Examples of such devices are GPS, a digital camera, or a metal detector (assuming the site includes metallic tools, coins etc. among possible finds).

The devices we are presently using are:

Palmtop computer Telxon PTC 1134 as mobile device; it runs Windows 3.x for Pen and the drawing tool has been developed using 16bit C++ and graphical libraries. The choice of such a development environment is motivated by the need to optimize tools performance on small configurations like the 16-bit one we presently have, while preserving upward compatibility for future expansions on 32-bit machines. The system is fully operational, mobile unites communicate on the network by using asynchronous message exchange (email messages) and emulated shared memory (shared directories and files).

Pentium based PCs, and DEC Alpha stations, running Windows NT and Lotus Notes operate as objects repositories (Lotus servers).

ARLAN Aironet Access Point which provides transparent wireless connectivity between the fixed station and one or more mobile computers. It incorporates industry standard IEEE 802.1d Spanning Tree protocol.

The choice of a 16-bit computer has been taken at project startup, in 1996, because of the high cost (at that time) of shockproof, weatherproof computers based on 32-bit CPUs. Even more significant is the limitation on disk capacity, which is 40MB, which obliged us to carefully select the operating system and support software. Thus, Windows for Workgroup was installed, instead of using a distributed technology like DCOM or Corba, which would not fit into such constraints. Obviously, in case further funds will be available for prototype engineering into a product, new versions of RAMSES will incorporate more advanced software support.

3 Archeo: the mobile archaeological system

Let us examine field work in more details for better understanding how mobile pen-based computers may support it. Archaeologists usually bring their paper and pencil diary in the field, where they collect daily notes. These notes are the most important, and often the only, means to record and eventually later reconstruct archaeological evidence, which is being excavated day by day. Off the field, diaries are used to extract the official archaeological reports, that is, a selected portion of their contents is copied to standard forms in order to document excavation results to the archaeological scientific community.

Several authors, like [8], consider location-awareness as an essential feature of mobile systems. RAMSES is not "location-aware", in that no GPS is connected to the mobile computer, and software is not monitoring current position. Field archaeology however requires to be aware of positioning, at various scales of resolution: these topographical information are input by the archaeologist to the system. The largest topographical unit to be considered is the _site_, an area of interest which has variable dimensions, usually very large ones as well. A site cannot be excavated at the same time in all of its surface; a selected portion of it where excavation activities are operational is called _test_. If possible, an interpretation directs a selection so that an unitary portion of the site is treated at the same time, such as a single building. It can be further subdivided into smaller units called _sectors_, whose size and shape may encompass further interpretation, e.g. a room inside a building, or may just be convenient portions of an interesting area. Inside a sector there may be several _stratigraphic units_, each of them being a convenient unit of archeological information and the basis for cataloging. A stratigraphic unit may have a volume by itself (e.g. a wall), or just be a profile or section (e.g. plain ground where several bones were found lying).

As interpretation of finds proceeds, stratigraphic units may be aggregated to form a structure called _archaeological context_, an example of which could be a small building, composed by the four walls delimiting it. Other relationships among stratigraphic units can be spatial (above, below, inside,...) sequentialization (referred to excavation time sequence: a wall has been excavated during 1996 campaign, another in 1997), and stratigraphical (referred to dating of finds: previous, subsequent, contemporary,...)

Figure 2 shows a typical section as could be reconstructed from some stratigraphic units.

The test in an excavation site is usually marked by a regular, square grid (approx. 2-3 meters each edge) identifying areas to be excavated. Each square in the grid is separately considered and in turn it is subdivided into smaller sections (approx. 30 cm. each edge), by means of strings. This subdivision allows easy identification of the exact position of finds at the current level. The current level is inspected, removed earth is sieved, and finally the fine grid is remapped at the next lower level. When current level is lowered, track is kept of the previous one by marking its orthogonal projection to vertical sides of the excavation: thus, we end up with a vertical grid too, in order to be able to identify finds proximity in 3D space.

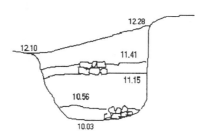

Fig.2 A section

Finds at each level are cataloged and then separately stored in boxes (one per square and level in the large grid). Information to be kept for each find are:
⋆ spatial information: its position in the tridimensional grid and its size;
⋆ additional visual details (if needed): the shape, by means of a sketch or snapshot;
⋆ classification: possible material, color traces, status and so on;
⋆ additional data (to be determined later): possible origin and period.

We then have to collect in our "digital diary" textual, visual and spatial information. The next Subsection shall detail how.

3.1   Data Entry: Drawings and Text

Textual information is locally collected on the palmtop computer by means of selectable menus, or by using special input software like the T9[12] software system, or handwriting recognizers. Until speech recognition devices shall become widely available on palmtops, textual input shall be rather difficult, and menu-based classification shall be much better achievable. If a whole text has to be entered, we developed a special software called WordTree [4] that speeds up input of text on pen-based devices.

Visual and spatial information may consist on sketch creation and retrieval, find positioning in the 3D grid, spatial relationships to other finds such as on-top-of, and association of sketch to related textual information.

We designed the special purpose software **Archeo** on top of a drawing system. Each find can be sketched on the screen of the palmtop by means of the magnetic pen; it can then be measured and related to the grid, measuring its distance from grid edges. The sketch can also be automatically adapted to measures once they have been taken (e.g. zoomed, rotated, stretched,...) for more realistic appearance. Attachment of a snapshot taken by a digital camera may be useful for the most significant finds.

The use of a graphic-based object oriented tool, allows to separately manipulate each object (find), which encapsulates all relevant attributes as defined by the archaeologist. Each object may also be spatially and thematically related to other objects, by linking them with distances and same attributes, in order to be able to recall them on the screen. In a side window, textual information can be attached to objects as annotations.

Specifically, two kinds of views are possible for each test, the map and the section. In _map mode_, objects (that is, finds) can be inserted by drawing them on the screen or by inserting some points and then interpolating a curve; they can be later merged inside a stratigraphic unit, and stratigraphic units may be merged into contexts. The correspondence of screen coordinates to surface measures is immediate; depth is also available on request. In _section mode_, inserted objects are only shown (if they belong to the selected section).

See Figure 3 for a view of Archeo interface.

Other functions are typical of drawing tools, like filling, zooming, gridding and the like; in case of zooming into some area, a global view of the whole test is kept in a side window. All acquired data can be downloaded to the central workstation and automatically inserted into the site object store (and made available, via Internet, to remote scientists). Further analysis is then possible: for example thematic 3D maps of the site are automatically updated with new finds, as soon as they are cataloged.

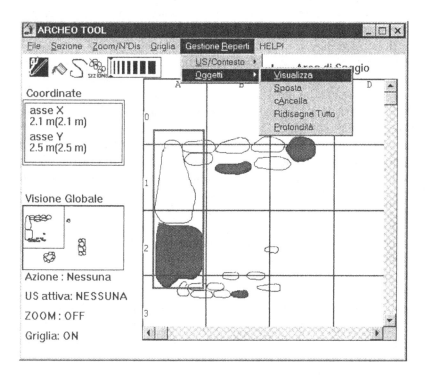

Fig.3 Drawing with Archeo

4   ADE: Archaeological Data Environment

ADE is the receiver/container application installed on fixed hosts present at base camp. All of the portable computers present in the field can connect to ADE to send or receive information. ADE purposes are: to provide physical storage for portable computer's data, to manage the radio network, to connect the base camp to remote host with WAN, acting as gateway to Internet.

The application is quite complex, and its cooperative nature has suggested the use of a powerful development tool: **Lotus Notes**. Notes allows the definition of etherogeneous documents and their storage over different machines using the proprietary method of "Replicas", which synchronizes Notes distributed database. This method is particularly efficient in low band networks such as telephone networks. Moreover, Notes automates every workflow process on documents making it easy to share information between remote posts. The last, but not least, feature of Notes is the possibility of Internet automatic document publishing (which are translated into html) and forms (so people physically far away can augment the data base by introducing their own form-based documents) using the DOMINO web server technology.

ADE consists on a collection of Notes documents glued together by a Navigator, scripts and agents. Scripts perform actions when events (like clicking a button in a form) are caused by users choices. Agents are automatically activated at given schedules (e.g. daily).

ADE documents are hypertextual documents including personal annotations by archaeologists, drawings, digital images, and a wide amount of data about referenced finds. They can be filled in by connecting at the fixed host, at base camp, or after a communication to/from a portable computer (thus receiving Archeo's data, drawings etc.).

In defining ADE documents, care has been taken to obtain total compatibility with the sheets required by Italian Ministero dei Beni Culturali, mandatory for every campaign in Italy. This causes a great improvement in the traditional archaeological fieldwork, because the so called "field diary notes", taken during actual digging work, need not be copied to official documents later on: we can now print out official documents from the field diary notes themselves.

Figure 4 shows a schema of possible communication to/from ADE.

Our system provides novel features with respect to other archaeological information systems, due to different attitudes towards data manipulation as in group activities. Notes allows to keep multiple copies (replicas), even incomplete ones, of each object repository, to be stored on different client computers. Consistency of multiple independent replicas, even when simultaneously updating the same object, is kept by Notes itself: in fact, it contains proprietary synchronization software to such purpose.

Any user, either mobile or stationary, and even connected via Internet from the University labs, may independently retrieve, update off-line and then send back to the server a selected data subset: for example, a replica may collect objects belonging to a specific test in the whole site, or to a certain period of time over all the site, or to stratigraphic units at the same level in several tests.

5 Archeo-ADE communication protocol

We have already remarked that power consumption is high when transmitting, and that power availability is limited by the weight of accumulators. Then, communication to/from the mobile system should be carefully designed.

Two kinds of information are exchanged through the wireless network: short messages (such as e-mails, or data sequences originated by remote DB queries) and long messages, represented by visual information like maps, snapshots, large drawings. They require two different mechanisms:

(1) synchronous communication in a client/server interaction fashion,

(2) asynchronous communication by means of shared files.

The system is asymmetric by nature, since handshaking cannot be activated by the fixed station when the MU is unreachable, and the MU cannot be always "listening" for incoming messages in order to save power. Hence, synchronous communication can only happen via an handshaking protocol always activated by the MU playing the role of the client with respect to the fixed station (server).

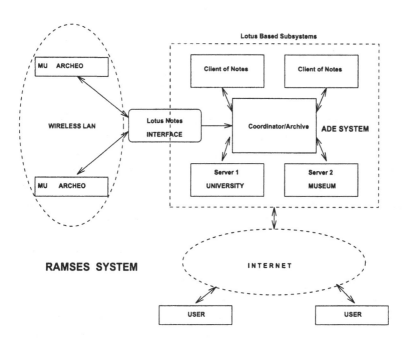

Fig.4 Possible links to/from ADE

Data exchange via shared files optimizes large data set transfer and, if files are stored on the fixed station, it may be used also when some MU is disconnected or in stand-by. The advantages are:

(a) shared files can be maintained on a queue on the fixed station when data and messages cannot be immediately sent to the MU,

(b) files are always recorded on the fixed station, thus offering a higher reliability, and coherence in case of multiple updates by many MUs can be enforced;

(c) when the fixed station is unreachable or battery is in lower state, data can be maintained on the MU local storage until the connection is established or battery are changed.

In this way we optimize both fast data exchange in real time of short messages and larger data information exchange, with minimal delays due to disconnection periods or battery discharge. All data exchange is always under user control for preventing early discharge of battery avoiding data losses.

6   Conclusions

This paper has presented how mobile computers, integrating suitable communication technology, as nowadays available inside a palmtop computer, may be used to develop field archaeology support tools. Application scenarios in field archaeology have been examined comparing present with future situations.

The most innovative aspect for field archaeology derived by our communication scenario is the possibility, for a scientist, to achieve true collaboration with colleagues, like he were on the site, thus reducing mobility costs of an excavation campaign. Similar considerations hold for several outdoor activities, where the rapid changing of the technological scenario and the need of ad-hoc solutions lead to the application of mobile technology based on wireless links supporting multimedial Data Base access.

Examples of applications can be found in the Cultural Heritage area, where the ongoing ESPRIT project TOSCA (Tourist Orientation and Support in Cultural Assisted tours) the aim of which is to provide visitors with the audio/video information needed for a cultural sight, the possibility of accessing a remote database and connecting to service centers, through mobile wireless computers. TOSCA is based on two types of services: Multimedia Personal Terminals connected, by means of mobile radio, wireless/contactless local loops, to available communication platforms, which allow a regular information updating and remote access to ISDN; and Personal Digital Assistants, the operability of which is restricted to a particular location (indoors, Museum or Gallery), which provide interactive guidance. In TOSCA some problems are very close to those we faced in RAMSES, like data base remote access, or those that we will consider in the future, like the use of speech instead of pen to insert textual information. An important feature of RAMSES which TOSCA lacks is the possibility of inserting textual and graphical information into the data base, and the special attention that has been paid in minimizing the use of both memory and battery.

The developed technology is not restricted to the Cultural Heritage area since it is applicable, with suitable modifications and extensions, to other fields such as for supporting patients and medical personnel in hospitals. Some pioneering hospitals are already experimenting mobile computing and wireless LAN technology, and applications reported in the literature include: the Good Samaritan Hospital (OH,USA), the Liverpool Women's Hospital (UK), the North Carolina Hospital, and others. The aim of these projects is to provide doctors and nurses with personal wearable handheld computers, linked via wireless networks to a server, which collects in a repository all clinical records and information on patients. Handheld computers run a specially designed application which completely replaces traditional paper-based management of clinical records.

All of them adopt the FHSS Technology for the wireless communication, since it appears to be the best for small areas, for its low power consumption, high transmission speed and lack of interference with medical equipment. Moreover, since there is no restriction for access to the radio frequency bands used by FHSS communications, this technology has been widely implemented by idividual vendors. Applications have been developed using technology provided by

Symbol Technologies, Aironet, or Netwave. For example, Good Samarital Hospital portable and handheld computers are wireless connected to the network via Aironet PC2000 Type II PC Cards and Aironet PC2000 Wireless LAN Adapter [2].

Hospital applications, even if indoor, are closer than TOSCA to our experiences, both for user interface and features, since the palmtop is heavily used as an input device. The same authors are presently undertaking a similar project.

Acknowledgements

Funds for supporting such efforts have been given by CNR, the Italian National Research Council, within the three year national project "Cultural Heritage" (1997-1999).

The authors gratefully acknowledge the programming efforts of several Computer Science students who developed the various releases of RAMSES.

Further details on this project are available at the URL:
http://www.disi.unige.it/person/DoderoG/pub_pfbc.html.

References

1. S. Ahson, I. Mahgboub, Research issues in Mobile Computing, IEEE IPCCC'98, Phoenix (AZ), Feb. 16-18, 1998, pp. 209-215.
2. Aironet at Good Samaritan Hospital,
   `http://www.aironet.com/tech/apps/goodsam/goodsam.html`.
3. Ancona, M. et al., 1998. Mobile computing for real time support in archaeological excavations, CAA97 Digest of Papers, Archaeopress, Oxford, UK.
4. M. Ancona D. Comes, WordTree - A Pen Based Software For Editing Short Notes, DISI - Technical Report, Genova - Italy 1998.
5. T. Imielinski, B. R. Badrinath, Wireless Computing, Communications of the ACM 37(10): 19-28, 1994.
6. J. Jerney, Mobile Insights: the Bright Future of Pen Computing, Pen-based Computing, The Journal of Stylus Systems (electronic version), 1994.
7. J. Kistler, M. Satyanarayanan, Disconnected operation in the coda file system, ACM Trans. on Computer Systems, 10(1), 1992.
8. Ryan, N.S., et al., 1998. Enhanced reality fieldwork: the context-aware archaeological assistant, in: CAA97 Digest of Papers, Archaeopress, Oxford, UK
9. Syslat, Aide à l'enregistrement de la documentation archeologique, Centre de Documentation Archeologique de Gard, Nimes, 1995.
10. Telxon Corporation, Beyond The Radio: Developing Complete Wireless System Solutions, `http://www.telxon.com/pp-2.htm`.
11. Tinè, S. et al. 1997. Poliochni 1991-1995. I nuovi dati, Monographies Scuola Archeologica Italiana di Atene, Roma, L'Erma di Bretschneider, Monography by the authors, 1997.
12. Tegic Communications Inc., T9 - The Ultimate Text Input Power Tool!, http://www.t9.com/palmpilot_specs.stm#features.

Token-Based Access to Digital Information

Lars Erik Holmquist, Johan Redström and Peter Ljungstrand

PLAY: Applied research on art and technology
The Viktoria Institute, Box 620, SE-405 30 Gothenburg, SWEDEN
{leh,johan,peter}@viktoria.informatics.gu.se
http://www.viktoria.informatics.gu.se/play/

Abstract. Several systems have been designed where a physical object is used to access digital information that is stored outside the object, but as yet no common vocabulary exists to describe such systems. We introduce a schema with three types of physical objects that can be linked to digital information: *Containers* are generic objects used to move information between different devices or platforms; *tokens* are used to access stored information, the nature of which is physically reflected in the token in some way; and *tools* are used to manipulate digital information. This paper gives special notice to token-based access system, and design implications for such systems are discussed. As an example of token-based access we have implemented *WebStickers*, where physical objects can be coupled with WWW pages. We present some examples of how tokens are used to access digital information in this system, and discuss future work in this area.

1   Introduction

In recent years, one of the most compelling visions of the future of computers has been that of *ubiquitous computing*, where computers would leave the desktop and move into the world that surrounds us [14]. By shifting the emphasis from the universal functionality of desktop workstations to small, dedicated computational tools, proposed ubiquitous computing environments hope to make computers as readily available and easy to use as notepads and whiteboards. In some ways, this vision is starting to make its way to reality, and with the continued miniaturisation and decreasing prices of PDAs and embedded processors, much of the technology required to make these visions a reality now exists.

However, with the increased power and complexity of portable computers, there is also the risk of simply replacing one problem with another. By moving all computing functions from one platform to another, perhaps we will not always gain as much as we would hope. Even worse, advantages taken for granted with stationary computers (large screens, high computational power, high-speed networks) are often missing on mobile devices. There is a risk that rather than simplifying the use of computers, the proliferation of a multitude of computational devices will instead make for higher complexity – thus achieving the opposite of the goal of ubiquitous computing.

An alternative approach to accessing and manipulating digital information is to use physical objects that are not in themselves computers, but nevertheless are used for representing information. Most types of information today exists in digital form, including text, images, music, films, and so on. With a suitable infrastructure, it should be feasible to have access to any book ever written, every piece of music ever recorded, any piece of art ever painted, anytime, anywhere, without the need for a physical carrier. However, this might also lead to serious problems in designing the human interface; experiences with the World Wide Web have already shown us that designing the interface to a practically limitless information space is very difficult.

But humans are inherently good at managing physical space, by ordering and sorting artifacts in their environment. Our senses give us many clues to the properties of physical objects, so that we are able to draw many useful conclusions from the way objects look and feel and how they are arranged in our environment [3]. We might take advantage of some of these capabilities when designing systems for accessing digital information, by using physical representations that are in themselves not carriers of information, but act as pointers to some online data.

In this paper, we will examine several such systems, concentrating on approaches where digital information is distributed using physical objects that represent some digital information or computational function. The process of accessing virtual data through a physical object we will term *token-based access to digital information*. The purpose of this paper is to systematise the properties of such systems, and to put them in relation to systems using other approaches, thus forming the basis for a discussion of how we can use properties in the physical world to help us better interact with distributed digital information.

2   Physical Objects as Representations of Information

There is a long history of the use of physical items to represent information, without the item actually containing the information that it represents (cf. [6, 16]). Souvenirs, photographs and keepsakes aid in the remembrance of places, past events and persons, by acting as a trigger for the user to remember certain information. The pieces used in board-games act as representations of the players through which they can perform their actions (cf. [15]). Gambling tokens used in casinos represents a value that is not inherent in the actual piece of plastic, much like the value of paper money traditionally has been guaranteed by a government's gold reserve. Cards of various kinds (calling cards, debit cards, etc.) are used to access assets – telephone call minutes, money stored in a bank account, etc. – that are not stored in the physical cards themselves.

Similarly, tokens in human-computer interaction will trigger the display of information that is digitally stored outside the token in some way. In the research community, several recent systems use physical objects without any inherent computational properties as representations of digital information in some way or another, but there is as yet a lack of vocabulary for describing and analysing such systems. To facilitate a discussion, we will first introduce three different classes of physical objects that represent digital information or computational functions: *containers*, *tools* and *tokens*.

2.1 Containers, Tools and Tokens

We will call an object a *container*, if it is a generic object that can be associated with any type of digital information. We will call it a *token*, if the digital information associated with the object is reflected in the physical properties of the token in some way, thus making the object more closely tied to the information it represents. Finally, some physical objects are to be considered as *tools*, since they are used to actively manipulate digital information, usually by representing some kind of computational function. Some accounts of related work should help clarifying these distinctions.

Containers. Several systems have been proposed in which digital information can be attached to physical objects, often to simplify the task of moving information between various computers and/or display devices. In the *pick-and-drop* approach [7], a pen was used as a container to physically "pick-and-drop" digital information between computers, analogous to how icons are "dragged-and-dropped" on a single screen. *Informative Things* [1] let ordinary floppy disks act as pointers to online information by associating them with a digital ID. A disk could thus be shared between users as usual, but would seem to have "endless" storage, since no information apart from the ID was actually stored on the disk. The authors also discuss some future scenarios where other objects might be used as "Things". *mediaBlocks* were small wooden blocks which let digital information be stored and accessed through a variety of different means [12]; for instance, after first associating a block to a digital whiteboard, the block could be used to transfer the scribbles on the whiteboard to a laser printer for printout. Finally, in the *Passage* system [8] information of various kinds could be moved between different computers by "attaching" it to small physical objects called "passengers".

Although all these systems in some sense could be said to use "tokens" to represent digital information, we prefer to call these objects *containers*. Unlike what we will term tokens, containers are generic, in that the physical properties of a container do not reflect the nature of the digital information it is associated with. Taking mediaBlocks as an example, note that by merely examining the physical form it is impossible to know if a block is associated with say a video clip, a PowerPoint presentation or a whiteboard scribble. This generic quality makes containers potentially very useful for the distribution and manipulation of a variety of digital information, but it also means that containers do not provide any additional cognitive cues for the user as to what their "contents" are. Moreover, containers are mostly used for short-term distribution and access, making them inherently transient in nature.

Tokens. In our definition, *tokens* are objects that physically resemble the information they represent in some way. Tokens are typically only transient if the token itself is short-lived. In the *metaDESK* map-display system [11], a set of objects were designed to physically resemble different buildings appearing on a digital map. By placing the models on a horizontal display, users could bring up the relevant portion of the map, and the physical form of the objects would serve as a cognitive aid for the user in finding the right part of the map to display. In the *ambientROOM* [4], objects were used to represent various types of information, and by bringing an object to an information display, an "ambient" display of that information could be accessed. For instance, by bringing a toy car close to a speaker, ambient sounds reflecting the activities in a toy project could be heard.

In the electronic tagging system described in [13], an object could be augmented with a digital ID tag allowing it to be linked to some digital information, thus letting the physical objects act as a pointer to the digital information. Some examples included a book that was associated with appropriate electronic information, such as the author's web page or a relevant page at an online bookstore, and a watch that was associated with the user's online calendar. Similarly, in the *WebStickers* system [5], users could attach barcode stickers to objects, and then associate a barcode to a web page that was somehow relevant to the object. (This system will be described in more detail later.)

Tools. Finally, some physical objects are used as representations of computational functions. We will call such objects *tools*. Some tools act as "handles" to manipulate virtual objects. In the *Bricks* system [2], a physical "brick" was attached to a graphical object on a horizontal display, and could then be used to move and rotate the on-screen object. By employing two bricks, a graphical object could be scaled and distorted. Some tools physically resemble the computational function they represent. In the metaDESK system [11], a physical representations of a magnifying glass was used to invoke functions similar to those of the *magic lenses* explored in graphical UIs [9]. By manipulating the physical magnifying glass, the user could apply the lens functions to a part of the map, thus seeing an alternative display "through" the lens represented by the magnifying glass. Other physical representations such as a "flashlight" were also used. In the electronic tagging system mentioned above (cf. [13]), a French dictionary was associated with a language translation function, so that a text could be translated simply by bringing the physical representation close to the screen where the text was displayed.

Sometimes the distinction between a tool and a token or a container will blur, since when a physical object is attached to a virtual, direct manipulation of virtual properties using the physical representation might become possible. In the metaDESK, models of buildings (tokens) were also used to scale and rotate a map, analogous to the Bricks system. In mediaBlocks, several mediaBlocks (containers) could be used in conjunction with a workbench to sequence a presentation; the completed presentation could then be associated with a new block. Such "hybrid" systems, where a physical representation has several possible uses depending on the context, are an area where we expect to see much development, but we will consider them outside the scope of this paper.

2.2 A Note on Vocabulary

The definition of *token* in the online edition of the Merriam-Webster Collegiate Dictionary includes:

1 : an outward sign or expression <his tears were tokens of his grief>
2 a : SYMBOL, EMBLEM <a white flag is a token of surrender> b : an instance of a linguistic expression

3 : a distinguishing feature : CHARACTERISTIC
4 a : SOUVENIR, KEEPSAKE b : a small part representing the whole :
INDICATION <this is only a token of what we hope to accomplish> c : something
given or shown as a guarantee (as of authority, right, or identity)
(Note: meanings 5 – *resembling money* – and 6 – *tokenism* – have been excluded)

Our intention with this choice of word is to show that a token is a "small part representing the whole", in that properties of the digital information are reflected in the token, and that the token should have some characteristic of the information it is linked to. We considered using some other term, in particular the word *phicon*, which has been used for physical counterparts to GUI icons, but decided against it. In the literature, the term phicon has been used both for what we define as tokens (e.g. the models of buildings in the metaDESK [11]) and for containers (e.g. mediaBlocks [12]), creating some confusion, which we sought to avoid with this choice of terms.

3 Token-Based Access to Digital Information

As we have seen, there are several different approaches to how we can let a physical object represent some kind of digital data or computational function. We will in the following concentrate on what we term *token-based access to digital information*, because this is an area that provides many design opportunities that calls for further exploration. We will define token-based access to digital information as:

A system where a physical object (token) is used to access some digital information that is stored outside the object, and where the physical representation in some way reflects the nature of the digital information it is associated with

A token is a representation of some digital information, but only by association and resemblance – a token is not a computer nor a display. Instead, the user will have to bring the token to some kind of external device to access the associated information.

3.1 Components

In a token-based interaction system, users will need to have access to two types of components:

- A set of physical objects which are used as representation of some digital information. These objects we will call *tokens*
- A set of access points for the digital information associated with tokens. These access points we will call *information faucets*, or faucets for short

We have chosen the term *faucet* rather than a term such as *display*, since it can be any type of device capable of presenting information, not just a graphical computer display – perhaps a speaker, a tactile device, etc. Importantly, while a token is by definition not a computer (it typically contains no computational power), neither should a faucet be considered as a computer from the user's point of view. Instead, tokens and faucets together comprise a system that provides users access to digital information – the fact that computer technology, networks, etc., might feature heavily in the implementation of such a system should not need to be of concern to the user.

3.2 Interaction in Token-Based Access Systems

Interacting with tokens can be either to access the information associated with a certain token, or to create or modify such associations. These two aspects of the human-computer interaction we will call *access* and *association*, respectively.

Access. Fundamental for any token-based system is that it allows a user to access a certain piece of information by means of presenting a token to an information faucet. By controlling the availability of tokens it is possible to control the access to information. For instance, if we allow for a number of copies of the same token to be made, several people will be able to access the information, perhaps simultaneously. Conversely, if we want to restrict access, we might only allow one instance of a token to be produced, and through some measures make it impossible to copy, thus letting the token act as the single "key" to the information in question.

We might also want to introduce some additional constraints on information access. For instance, a *combination* of tokens might be used to access the information associated with all the tokens simultaneously. A more interesting option is to use the combinations as such to form criteria for information access. For example, if two tokens represent work in a joint project, certain aspects of that work might only be accessible when both tokens are presented simultaneously, much like we might require more than one key to open a door.

Depending on the present purpose, information access might be constrained by physical *location* as well. For example, some information might only be applicable at a given location (e.g. a building) and by using tokens that only work with local faucets any distribution beyond that location can be limited. Correspondingly, public information that is meant to be widely distributed will have to use tokens that do not pose such a limitation, but instead are applicable to variety of faucets.

Association. If the association of digital information with a physical token is unconstrained and at any time allows the user to re-associate the token with any other piece of information, we are close to the properties of containers. However, when using tokens it is more interesting to investigate different ways of constraining the set of possible associations. For example, we might want to restrict the associations of a certain kind of tokens to a certain kind of information, thus avoiding some confusions between how the properties of the token are reflected in the information it represents. We might also make the associations fixed once and for all, making the connection between the token and a certain piece of information as static as possible. This would typically be the case in a public display system, say an interactive museum exhibit, where one would not want the users to be able to change the way information is associated with the physical objects on display.

Further, we might allow a user to associate more than one piece of information to a certain token. This we may call *overloading*. Overloading a token with information might have various effects. For instance, the token might represent different pieces of information at different locations or in different contexts, as is often the case with everyday objects. Alternatively, the user might be able to access several different pieces of information at the same time when applying the token to a faucet. In the latter case, the information might be displayed with a choice of which information to present.

4   A Sample System for Token-Based Access: WebStickers

As an example of token-based interaction, we have developed the WebStickers system [5]. This system is quite flexible, in that it uses the Internet for distribution of data, and thus we can use any computer with the appropriate (off-the-shelf) hardware as a faucet. The system allows users to couple identifiers in the form of barcodes to locations on the World Wide Web. Users are given a set of stickers with pre-printed unique barcodes, and can then attach the stickers to any object they want to use as a bookmark. Users then employ a barcode scanner to associate a barcode with one or more web pages, and are able to return to a page by again scanning the corresponding barcode. The idea is to allow users to take advantage of the properties of any object in their surroundings and use these properties as cognitive cues to the finding a certain web location.

The system is implemented as a database accessible via HTTP. In the database, identifiers in the form of unique character strings are coupled with URLs. An off-the-shelf barcode reader is used to scan barcode stickers, which are printed on sheets of adhesive stickers using a standard laser printer. A small client application on the user's computer monitors incoming characters from the barcode reader, matching identifiers with URLs by calling the online database, and displaying the corresponding web page in the user's browser. To create new associations, the user simply change the mode of the client program from *Goto* to *Learn*, and the currently displayed web page is associated with the scanned barcode in the server database. Using codes coupled with URLs in a database, rather than coding URLs directly into barcodes, makes it possible to create new associations or change old associations easily.

4.1   Modes of Interaction

The WebStickers system provides a basic form of access to web pages through tokens. There is currently no provision for more advanced access forms, such as those provided by combinations of tokens or based on specific locations. As for association, WebStickers currently allows totally free association between web pages and tokens, placing the responsibility of finding the correct token on the user making the association. This is reasonable considering the experimental nature of the current system, but in future versions it might be useful to introduce some restrictions. Introducing ready-made tokens for specific tasks might also be considered. (We already have one such ready-made token in the form of Post-It notes – see below.) WebStickers does allow for a form of overloading, by letting the user associate more than one web page with a single token. When such a token is accessed, the user is presented with an intermediate web page where she can choose from a list of URLs.

4.2   Types of Tokens

With WebStickers, we have been able to experiment with a variety of different tokens as representations of web-based information. Here are some examples.

Transient Tokens. For web page bookmarks that are only meant to be kept for a short time, say no more than a few weeks, we have been using books of Post-It notes with pre-printed barcodes. After associating a note with a web page users can then scribble a comment on the note that helps them remember what web page the note refers to, and attach it to their screen, their notice board, someone else's door, etc. Post-Its are explicitly designed for short-term information, making them ideal tokens to represent transient web bookmarks. After a while the glue in the note will cease functioning and the note will fall off whatever surface it is attached to, at which time the user can select to transfer the bookmark to a more permanent location, or discard it completely.

Tokens with a Direct Digital Analogy. Some WWW bookmarks have a direct counterpart in the real world. For instance, when referring to the proceedings from a conference, it is often more comfortable to use the physical book than to read from an online proceedings page. However, when a paper is to be e-mailed to someone else, when it is to be searched for specific terms, when we need to quote some sections, etc., having easy access to the electronic version is useful. We have been using the pre-existing barcodes (ISBN numbers) on conference proceedings for coupling them to their online counterpart. Since a book of proceedings is an archival object, it will mostly be stored away on a bookshelf. When working with a book, the user will take it down and bring it to her desk, and now through the WebStickers association she can have immediate access to the corresponding online documents as well.

Tokens Tied to a Certain Activity. We have experimented with using objects that are tied to a specific activity as bookmarks to related web pages. A Swedish-English dictionary has been associated with the web page of the Encyclopaedia Britannica, the thought being that when users are searching for a word this web page will come in handy if the physical dictionary is not sufficient. Similarly, a user has tied the cup used for drinking the morning coffee to the URL of the morning news (made available on the Internet by the national radio station), thus tying the activity of drinking coffee to listening to news updates.

4.3   Conclusions from the WebStickers System

By constructing a system for token-based access that allows a wide variety of tokens to be associated with a very large information space (the World Wide Web), we have been able gain experience in how virtual properties can be reflected in physical objects. We have found some very obvious correspondences, such as that between

Post-It notes and transient bookmarks, but feel that it would be useful to generalize the discussion of how to design tokens. In the following, some initial design ideas for future token-based systems will be given.

5 Fitting the Token to the Task

Since a token typically will need to have little or no inherent computational resources, many of the constraints posed on the design of ordinary computers will not have much effect. For example, a token will not need any display; it will not need to have a processor or a power supply; it will be much less sensitive to wear and tear, and so on. This leaves us with far more freedom to design and build the tokens according to other criteria.

The most important criterion will be to design the tokens in a way that clearly displays what they represent and what can be done with them, i.e. their *affordances* [3]. Matching the affordances of the token with the task it is designed to be used in, can be done in a number of different ways including the use of different materials, sizes and shapes. Since tokens are not self-contained but tied to information faucets, the interaction can also be designed to take other factors into consideration, such as the physical location or usage context.

Just like when designing graphical interfaces, care must be taken when designing tokens. For instance, often certain shapes or colours convey values or meaning specific to a culture, like the symbol of the cross does in Christian religions. Whether such cultural values should be used or avoided, will depend on the kind of information to represent and who are going to use it in what context. However, token-based interaction systems will be less loaded with predefined meaning if strongly established symbols are avoided. Below we will sketch some of the possibilities for how the properties of digital information can be reflected in the design of token-based interaction.

5.1 Materials

Tokens can be made in a variety of materials depending on what they should represent. Tokens that represent information that is only meant to last for a short while might be made of material that wears out easily. Consider for example the difference in paper quality between books and newspapers, and in the glue used on Post-It notes and postage stamps. Here, the lack of durability of the newspaper and the glue on the Post-It note are not faulty but intended, since they represent information which is only intended to be used for a short time. A book, on the other hand, is intended to be kept for some time, and a stamp should stay stuck on the envelope that it was attached to.

Similarly, tokens made in fragile materials can be used to represent information that should be handled with care. Tokens made in very heavy materials can be used to represent information that is not supposed to be transported very far from its current location. Tokens representing information that is to be used frequently by a certain user might take the form of jewellery or perhaps a belt made in some comfortable material.

5.2   Sizes and Shapes

Tokens can come in many different sizes and shapes depending on the purpose. For example: tokens that are meant to be passed between users should be graspable. Tokens that are private should afford hiding and must thus be small enough to fit into a pocket or perhaps into the palm of a closed hand. Very large tokens will be harder to move without attracting attention and thus suitable to represent information that is of public interest. If we have a large number of tokens that we need to store in the same place we might want to make them easy to stack or pile. They will then have to have a size and shape that afford this, meaning that tokens similar to cards or discs might be more suitable than tokens similar to marbles.

Further, the size and shape of the tokens can help restricting their use to avoid mistakes. Consider puzzles: besides the colour of a piece, its shape determines where in the puzzle the piece can be applied. This is especially obvious in puzzles made for small children where each of the very few pieces fit into a certain slot. In the case of token-based interaction, using shapes that only fit in certain slots can be used to determine which information faucets are applicable. If the information the token represents is of a kind that can only be accessed in certain information faucets, the shape of the token can be made in a way that only will fit into proper kind of faucets.

5.3   Usage Context

Everyday objects are often used within a special context, and when moved out of that context their "meaning" tend to change. As an example, take the many knives used in a kitchen for different purposes, e.g. cutting bread, meat, fish etc. Sometimes they are stored in drawers in the kitchen. Now imagine what happens if we instead store them in another drawer in the apartment, say, where you usually store your socks or underwear. If someone found your kitchen knifes in your bedroom drawer, he or she would definitely react differently compared to if he or she had found them in the kitchen. Thus, the very location of tools and objects can convey meaning. This should be acknowledged when using tokens for interacting with computers, by means of for example how to constrain access to (e.g. *location* and *combinations* of tokens) and associations (*overloading* tokens) with information.

Thus, we have seen how a wide variety of virtual or digital properties can be reflected in the design of the components of a token-based access system. We have in this paper only been able to sketch the outlines of these possibilities, and many practical design experiments and evaluations will be needed before any firm conclusions can be drawn or any solid design specifications can be given.

6   Conclusions and Future Work

We have attempted to show that token-based access to digital information is a valid interaction paradigm that can be used to support access to information in a distributed computing environment. Token-based access systems differ from container-based systems in that they imply a stronger coupling between physical and virtual data, i.e. the properties of a token should reflect the properties of the data it is associated with. This makes it possible to design tokens that provide users with a strong cognitive support for accessing information in distributed systems. It also opens many possibilities for building in aspects of the user interaction into the token itself, rather than having these solely confined to the virtual domain. For instance, by designing tokens with certain physical properties, say tokens that are easy or difficult to share between users, it is possible to have some desired affordances physically reflected in the token.

For future commercial applications, we can see many situations where it would be more convenient to use token-based access than a physical carrier of information. The music business is currently a good example. With forays already being made into distributing music on the Internet using the MP3 format, in the future it might be feasible that rather than buying a music carrier such as a CD or DVD, consumers will purchase a small token representing a recording. By bringing such a token to a suitable player (faucet), the user can then listen to the music associated with the token. Unlike a CD, the token would never run the risk of being scratched, and through encryption of unique IDs on each token, music companies can make sure that their music is protected. Technical realization of such a system is already possible [10].

As we have seen, several systems for token-based access to digital information have already been realized in research labs, and several systems have also been constructed where physical containers and tools are used to distribute and manipulate data. This serves to prove the technical validity of such systems, and technology for tagging and sensing objects is already good enough to construct useful applications. However, neither this paper nor most previous work has been able to more than touch on some of the most important aspects of token-based access.

In particular, matters concerning security, privacy and rights concerning information associated with tokens need to be considered. Can valuable information be safely made available on public networks without the risk for unauthorized access? Should tokens be possible to copy, and what will then happen to the information and associated access rights? Who should have the right to modify materials associated with a token, and who should be allowed to modify the associations themselves? In the experimental applications, the impact of such decisions has been limited, since the systems have been used only to a limited extent and by a limited audience of mainly expert users, but in the future these questions may come to have a serious impact. The validity of token-based access to digital information is probably more dependent on the resolution of such issues than any technological hurdles.

Before general token-based systems break into the mainstream, we will have to take these matters into consideration, and will also have to refine the way such systems are designed, improving their properties from a user perspective. In this paper we have sketched some initial possibilities for tokens-based access to digital information, but much more work needs to be done in this area. This work must be guided by experiences in disciplines such as user-interface design, industrial design and ergonomics, making for a truly cross-disciplinary challenge. We believe that with the correct approach, systems offering token-based access to digital information can prove very useful in the development of future distributed computing environments.

7 Acknowledgements

Thanks to our colleagues at the Viktoria Institute and to the HUC'99 reviewers, whose comments helped to improve this paper. This research was part of the *Intelligent Environments* project in the PROMODIS research program funded by NUTEK, the Swedish National Board for Industrial and Technical Development. Additional funding came from the *Mobile Informatics* program sponsored by SITI, the Swedish Institute for Information Technology.

References

1. Barrett, R. and Maglio, P.P (1998). Informative Things: How to attach information to the real world. In: *Proceedings of UIST '98*, ACM Press.
2. Fitzmaurice, G.W., Ishii, H and Buxton, W. (1995). Bricks: Laying the Foundations for Graspable User Interfaces. In: *Proceedings of CHI '95*, ACM Press, pp. 442-449.
3. Gibson, J. J. (1979). *The Ecological Approach to Visual Perception*. Lawrence Erlbaum Associates.
4. Ishii, H. and Ullmer, B. (1997). Tangible Bits: Towards seamless interfaces between people, bits and atoms. In: *Proceedings of CHI '97*, ACM Press.
5. Ljungstrand, P. and Holmquist, L.E. (1999). WebStickers: Using Physical Objects as WWW Bookmarks. In: *Extended Abstracts of CHI '99*, ACM Press.
6. Norman, D. A. (1993). *Thing That Make Us Smart*. Perseus Books.
7. Rekimoto, J. (1997). Pick-and-Drop: A Direct Manipulation Technique for Multiple Computer Environments. In: *Proceedings of UIST '97*, ACM Press.
8. Streitz, N.A., Geissler, J., Holmer, T. et al. (1999). I-LAND: An Interactive Landscape for Creativity and Innovation. In: *Proceedings of CHI '99*, ACM Press.
9. Stone, M., Fishkin, K. and Bier, E. (1994). The Movable Filter as a User Interface Tool. *Proceedings of CHI '94*, ACM Press, pp. 306-312.
10. Talbot, C. *Honey I Shrunk the CD*. http://www.media.mit.edu/pia/Research/CDs/
11. Ullmer, B. and Ishii, H. (1997). The metaDESK: Models and Prototypes for Tangible User Interfaces. In: *Proceedings of UIST '97*, ACM Press.
12. Ullmer, B., Ishii, H. and Glas, D. (1998). mediaBlocks: Physical Containers, Transports, and Controls for Online Media. In: *Proceedings of SIGGRAPH '98*, ACM Press.
13. Want, R., Fishkin, K.P., Gujar, A. and Harrison, B.L. (1999). Bridging Physical and Virtual Worlds with Electronic Tags. In: *Proceedings of CHI '99*, ACM Press.
14. Weiser, M. (1991). The Computer for the 21st Century. *Scientific American*, 265 (3), pp. 94-104.
15. Zhang, J. (1993). The Interaction between Perceptual and Cognitive Processes in a Distributed Problem Solving Task. In: *Working Notes of the 1993 AAAI Fall Symposium on Games: Planning and Learning*.
16. Zhang, J. and Norman, D. A. (1994). Representations in Distributed Cognitive Tasks. *Cognitive Science*, vol. 18, pp. 87-122.

InfoStick: An Interaction Device for Inter-Appliance Computing

Naohiko Kohtake[1], Jun Rekimoto[2], and Yuichiro Anzai[1]

[1] Department of Computer Science, Keio University,
3-14-1 Hiyoshi, Kohoku-ku, Yokohama 223-0061 Japan
kohtake@naohiko.com, anzai@aa.cs.keio.ac.jp
http://www.naohiko.com/
[2] Interaction Laboratory, Sony Computer Science Laboratories,
3-14-3 Higashigotanda, Shinagawa-ku, Tokyo 141-0022 Japan
rekimoto@csl.sony.co.jp
http://www.csl.sony.co.jp/person/rekimoto.html/

Abstract. Many electric appliances have recently become network reachable, and we would receive better services from them if we could use them in combination. We have therefore developed a new hand-held interaction device called "InfoStick" that serves as an "information carrier" for these appliances. For example, a user can "pick up" TV program information from a web browser and "drop" it into a VCR deck, just like moving a physical object from one place to another. Using attached visual markers, the InfoStick identifies information appliances or other physical objects and gives an appropriate choice of action to the user. This paper explains the design and implementation of the InfoStick as well as several potential applications using this device.
which looks like a laser-pointer or a small wand and allows users to operate it with only one hand. And it also describes several potential examples of using InfoStick with computer, VCR, paper, and so on.

1 Introduction

The network infrastructure has spread all over the world, and nowadays there are a variety of devices that can access the Internet. Internet access is no longer limited to personal computers or powerful workstations. And thanks to recent advances in digital and network technologies, many consumer electric devices such as VCRs, electric-organs or air-conditioners, as well as office appliances such as printers and LCD projectors are becoming "network reachable". We call these devices "Information Appliances". It is now reasonable to expect these appliances to communicate with each other in order to provide better services to users. For example, a VCR could receive a TV program information from the web browser or a printer could create a hardcopy of an image projected on a LCD projector.

However, operating these multiple devices may cause user interface problems. We might have to handle a number of remote controllers for each device, and there are few practical ways of controlling two or more appliances. When we want to "transfer" TV program information from the web browser on a computer to the VCR deck, the VCR controller does not help us. We thus need to operate information appliances in combination, that is not on their own appliance.

In addition, we also need to deal with physical (non-electric) objects such as printed paper. Even if digital and network technology becomes more advantageous, paper still has significant advantages: it is portable, writable, inexpensive, and physically visible. However, transferring data between information appliances and physical objects always requires manual operations. For instance, when we find an URL of an interesting web site on a poster, it is necessary to input the URL into a computer with a keyboard or write it down if there is no computer nearby. It would be quite useful if we could "pick up" a printed URL and "drop" it on an information appliance. In summary, we always need support for exchanging information between digital and physical objects. We call such operations "Inter-Appliance Computing".

To provide this support, we have developed a hand-held device called "Info-Stick" that serves as "an information carrier" for Inter-Appliance Computing. Using the InfoStick, a user can "pick up" TV program information from a web browser and "drop" it into a VCR deck. The InfoStick identifies information appliances or other physical objects by recognizing attached visual markers and gives an appropriate choice of actions to the user.

2 InfoStick Device

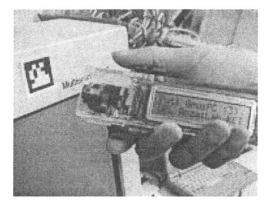

Fig. 1. External appearance of the InfoStick

The InfoStick prototype is a hand-held interaction device for exchanging information among information appliances and physical objects. Figure 1 shows the external appearance of the InfoStick. It consists of a small display to show what kind of data items can be exchanged, a video camera for object recognition, three buttons to operate data exchanges, and a micro processor for controlling all of them. The InfoStick can be connected to the Internet through a wireless network. Physically, it looks like a laser-pointer or a small wand, and can be easily pointed to target objects. Using the InfoStick is similar to drag-and-drop, a commonly used technique for interacting with GUIs.

The InfoStick automatically identifies the information appliance (e.g., a VCR) or the physical object (e.g., paper) in front of it, and shows a user a list of appropriate actions on the display. Visual markers attached to the objects are recognized by the InfoStick's camera. Among the three buttons for operating the InfoStick, the "get" button is used to "pick up" information from the target object, the "put" button is used to transfer information from the InfoStick to the target object, and the "select" button is used to select actions and information showed on the InfoStick display.

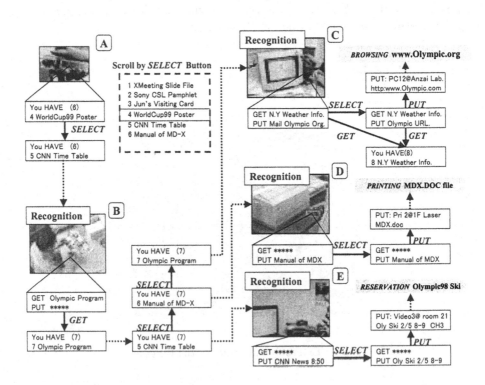

Fig. 2. Typical Information flow during the InfoStick operation

Figure 2 shows a typical information flow during the InfoStick operation. The InfoStick display shows a list of data items, and a user can scroll down the list and select one by pushing the "select" button (Figure 2 A). When a user points the InfoStick at a target object, the video camera mounted in the InfoStick detects a visual marker attached to the object (Figure 2 B). Then, the display on the InfoStick shows a list of items that can be picked up from the target object and also a list of items that can be transmitted to the target object. When the "get" button is pushed, the target object's information is stored in the InfoStick. In Figure. 2 B, a user is getting Olympic Program information.

When a user moves to another target, the InfoStick recognizes it and the available actions corresponding to the recognized object appear on the display (Figure 2 C, D, and E). And if the InfoStick has some data that can be "put" into the computer, the user can select an action by the "select" button (from the mail address to the URL in Figure 2 C). By pushing the "put" button, the user can see on the display which target and what kind of information the InfoStick has put into the computer. In this case, the target is a PC "PC12@Anzai Lab." and the "put" information is "Olympic URL", which the user can then browse. However, if the InfoStick has only one possible action corresponding to the recognized object, the displayed action does not change even if the user pushes the "select" button (Figure 2 D). So in this case, the user can do only one operation; that is, printing out "Manual of MDX file". If a user wants to select information previously put in, he can select it before detecting a visual object. Then, this information appears on the display as the possible action that he can "put" first (Figure 2 E). After that, other possible actions can be selected in turn.

During these operation sequences, the InfoStick does not directly "get"/"put" data from/to the target objects. Instead, actual data transfer occurs through the network to which all devices are connected. The InfoStick recognizes a target object according to the attached ID and issues appropriate data transfer commands to the network. In our system, we use printed 2D matrix codes (see Figure 1) as IDs. It is also possible to attach such IDs to non-electric objects.

3 InfoStick Applications

Using the prototype InfoStick, we have built several experimental applications to accomplish an interaction for Inter-Appliance Computing. We believe this technology will become a part of functions for mobile phone and each user has his own InfoStick device in the future. Some examples of these applications are given in the following sections.

3.1 Transferring Information between Computers

A basic usage of the InfoStick is to transfer digital data between several computers. At a meeting, for example, the presenter often uses a projector to support his presentation (Figure 3).

Fig. 3. At a meeting, the InfoStick creates the illusion that the presenter can "get a slide from the projector" and "put it in my computer".

The presenter can get the target presentation slide by physically pointing the InfoStick to the projector and pushing the "get" button. When he wants to take the entire slides, he can "select" the "Entire Slides" menu item and push the "get" button. After that, if he wants to create a copy of the acquired slide, he can point the InfoStick to his computer and upload the slide by pushing the "put" button. In this case, the projector itself does not have to hold the slide data. In fact, the actual slide contents are stored in servers on the network (e.g., on the presenter's computer), and the projector is used as a physical landmark for obtaining data, because it has a mental connection to the currently displayed slide. The visibility and tangibility of the user's action are important because of intuitive. A user can therefore exchange information more directly and the InfoStick creates the illusion that a user can "get a slide from the projector" and "put it in my computer".

On the other hand, if the usual file transfer method is used, a user must recognize both the target computer's name and the slide's name in order to move the slide by file transfer protocol (FTP). These operations are quite symbolic and thus invisible.

3.2 Operating Information Appliances

The second possible application of the InfoStick allows a user to operate information appliances. For example, if TV program information is stored in the InfoStick, when a user points the InfoStick to the target VCR deck, the display of the InfoStick shows the TV program names that he can reserve for recording. And after selecting the program name with the "select" button and putting it into the VCR with the "put" button, the VCR is thus programmed. (Figure 4).

Another InfoStick application is making a phone call. You normally know the person's name and phone number before calling. If you do not, you have to find them out. Without the phone number, it is impossible to call. However, with the InfoStick, a user does not have to know the number because it is stored

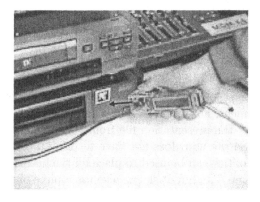

Fig. 4. The InfoStick programs a VCR to make a recording

in a server on the network. The user simply points the InfoStick at a phone and puts the person's name into the phone, which then calls the person.

3.3 Getting Information from Paper

The InfoStick can also "get" information from physical objects like paper by using visual markers. When the InfoStick recognizes the IDs, a server connected to the InfoStick displays a list of items of the recognized physical object. Then, the user can "get" the information from the target object directly by the same interaction as that with information appliances (Figure 5).

Fig. 5. A user can "pick up" a printed URL from a poster and "drop" it into a computer

3.4 Putting Information onto Paper

Another InfoStick application is to attach digital information onto paper like a tag or a document note. For example, it would be useful if we could attach presentation slide files to the corresponding document. Using the InfoStick, the user can "pick up" the slide data from the computer and attach it to the printed marker on the document. For instance, a user can simply take this document to the conference, "get" the presentation file from this marker, and "put" the file into the projector. So the user does not have to bring a computer, a projector or a floppy disk. InfoStick can be used to place all the necessary information on the presentation paper. The InfoStick can also use a piece of paper as a physical memory bank. If we want to store data for a long time, we can "put" it and write down its name as a title on a tag. Later, when a user wants to use this data, he can "get" it from the tag. This system can also be used by teachers for announcing information about exercises to students. After teachers "put" data with the title of the exercise on a tag, students use the InfoStick to "get" it from the tag on a notice board.

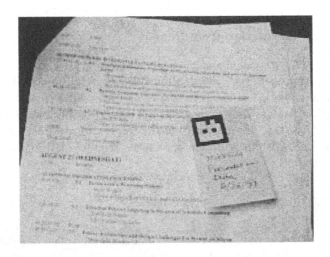

Fig. 6. A PostIt note with attached digital data

It is also possible to use a PostIt note with a printed visual marker (Figure 6). The user can attach any digital data on a PostIt note, and stick it to any objects. This usage provides a way of organizing digital data with physical documents. So even networking becomes ubiquitous, paper will still remain significant. This application of the InfoStick therefore augments electric features with advantages of paper.

3.5 Getting Information from One Object and Putting it into Many Objects

In everyday life, there are many kinds of information. A name card is a typical example of this. Generally, it gives a person's name, occupation, address, phone/facsimile number, email and URL. When we make a phone call, we intuitively select appropriate information (a phone number) from the card. When we use a facsimile, the other attribute (a facsimile number) would be used instead of a phone number. There is thus an implicit correspondence between the target device and these attributes. When the InfoStick identifies the target object, it automatically selects appropriate information by combining the attribute's ID and the target object's ID (Figure 7).

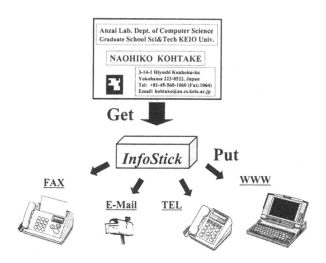

Fig. 7. Automatic selections of information according to the target object

3.6 Getting Information from a Screen

The InfoStick can recognize visual markers displayed on a screen. It is therefore possible to "pick up" the IDs from TV programs or web pages. Figure 8 illustrates this technique. When a user is watching a TV program, he finds an interesting piece of information on the TV screen. Then, he "gets" this information from the visual marker on the TV screen (above-left) and "puts" it to the nearby computer (below-left). The corresponding web page appears on the computer screen. After browsing the information from this page, he also find some information on an interesting TV program. And he "gets" it by pointing the InfoStick at the browser on the screen (below-right). Finally, he goes to the VCR deck, and "puts" it into the VCR to record the TV program (above-right).

Fig. 8. (a) Picking up a URL from a TV screen and dropping it into a computer, (b) browsing TV program information on the computer, and (c) operating a VCR by picking up the TV program information from the computer and putting it in the VCR deck

4 Implementation Details

4.1 Hardware Architecture

A prototypical InfoStick is depicted in Figure 9. We made it as compact as possible to allow the user to operate it with only one hand. The InfoStick consists of the following items: a SONY CCD-MC1 as a CCD camera to sense video images from a physical environment, three input buttons to "get"/"put"/"select", and a SUNLIKE 16×2 LCD as a display to show the particular information that the InfoStick can "get"/"put". A PARALLAX BASIC STAMP II is included in the InfoStick as a small computer for controlling the I/O signal and LCD and for exchanging data between the InfoStick and a Mitsubishi AMiTY-CN with RS-232 serial communication protocols. Parallax BASIC Stamps are small computers that run Parallax BASIC (PBASIC) programs. They have programmable I/O pins that can be used to directly interface to TTL-level devices, such as buttons, LCDs, speakers, and shift registers. And with extra components, these I/O pins can be connected to non-TTL devices, such as RS-232 networks. The Mitsubishi AMiTY-CN is located on the user's waist. It is a mobile computer for recognizing the 2D matrix code from the CCD camera's video image, by using an IBM Smart Capture Card II, and for communicating with other computers on the network. For electric appliances that are not on the network, the nearest IBM PC communicates with other PCs and controls the electric appliances through them. SONY VboxII-CI1100s connected to the IBM PCs control electric appliances.

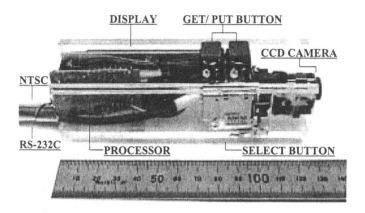

Fig. 9. Configuration of the InfoStick

4.2 Software Architecture

Figure 10 illustrates the structure of the software in the InfoStick system. A video image from the CCD camera is first sent to the Marker Reader. The Marker Reader then extracts the black-and-white pattern of the image that the InfoStick is pointing at and analyzes it. If a 2D Matrix Code is found from the image, it is converted to an ID number that will be sent to the InfoStick Controller. Then the controller receives the ID number, it searches for the target object's name and the corresponding available information that the InfoStick can "get"/"put" from the InfoStick DataBase. Marker Reader and InfoStick Controller are implemented in the InfoStick, and the other software modules are in computers connected to the network. The InfoStick DataBase contains the information received by the InfoStick and the ID Table corresponding to the ID number given by the Information Manager on the network. If the user wants to operate one of objects, he can "select" and "get"/"put" the necessary information with the input buttons. In the case of "get", the target information is added into the InfoStick DataBase. On the other hand, in the case of "put", the target physical object is operated by the Machine Controller with the necessary information obtained from the Information Manager.

All code without PBASIC is written in Java and executed on an IBM PC running Windows95. The video capturing class is of special note as it uses

JDK1.1 Java-native-interface (JNI). The Information Manager and ID table are also Java applications and communicate with other experimental applications through TCP/IP connections. All physical objects used in our applications are directly connected to the Ethernet. The InfoStick, however, uses a wireless local area network. A user therefore can take the InfoStick anywhere within wireless coverage.

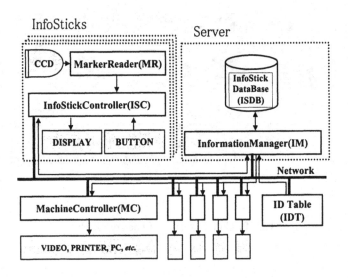

Fig. 10. Software architecture of the InfoStick system

5   Related Work

There are several hand-held devices that are designed for operating other digital and physical objects. Most of them, however, aim to operate a single target (e.g., a remote controller for a TV set), rather than to operate several target objects.

The PDA-ITV [4] uses a PDA as a commander for interactive TV. Although it uses two different displays for one task, the roles of PDA and TV are static; PDA acts as a commander only for the TV. Neither seamless manipulation is possible, nor exchanging information between the PDA and ITV is interactive. For example, it is not possible to "pick up" information from the TV screen, and then "drop" it into the PDA. The PaperLink [1] is a computer augmented pen with a video camera that is capable of recognizing text on a printed document. Although PaperLink can pick up information from paper and put it on other paper, it does not support inter object operations. For example, the user can not operate a computer object and paper information with the same PaperLink pen.

MediaBlocks [5] is a small tag used as a physical container of digital information. The user can virtually attach and carry digital data by using this tag. This system assumes every information appliance has a tag reader/writer, making it different to scale this environment. A user is unable to see the carried data until the tag is actually inserted into a tag reader/writers. Finally, the Pick-and-Drop system [2] is a direct manipulation technique that can be used to transfer data between different computers as well as on the same computer. Pick-and-Drop allows the user "pick up" an object from a display and drop it onto another display as if he were operating a physical object. Our InfoStick system is an extension of this system. Although our system also uses the Pick-and-Drop metaphor for "get" and "put" operations, the purpose of the InfoStick is to operate not only computers but all physical objects.

6 Conclusion and Future Work

We have developed the InfoStick, a new hand-held interaction device that aims to provide a uniform way of operating everyday digital/physical objects. Currently, the InfoStick recognizes the target object by using a combination of attached visual markers and a video camera. When it identifies the ID of the object, the InfoStick searches for the object's name and available information related to that name from the InfoStick DataBase on the network. The idea of deploying visual markers for object-level identification in the environment is aging. However, the use of these markers has advantages and disadvantages. This technique enables to identify an object even if it is not connected to the network, such as a printed material like a poster, a book, or a newspaper, and that visual marker can operate it with easy technology at low cost. On the other hand, a user must always know where the visual marker is. And the camera in the InfoStick needs to be pointed at it.

There are other ways of recognizing objects. They include wireless tags and infrared (IR) beacons. In the case of using a wireless tag, when a receiver approaches within about one meter of the tag, the receiver can recognize its ID number. On the other hand, the IR beacon transmits the ID number to the environment periodically. This beacon covers room-size area and is relatively robust regarding orientation of the sensors. For each method for recognizing objects, there is a different advantage and by using it appropriately, the InfoStick will become more widely used.

In addition, we are planning to provide a "docking station" of the InfoStick for easy information exchange with PCs. When a user "docks" the InfoStick, information stored in the InfoStick is transferred to the PC and the user can exchage them on the PC window. The mouse's advantages include being able to "grab", "drag" and "drop" one object from many objects on the same window. On the contrary, when the InfoStick receives a lot of information, it is difficult to select items on the LCD display. If the InfoStick icon pops up on a window when it is put into a docking station connected to a computer, we can release, delete and select objects on the window by using the mouse. (Figure 11).

258

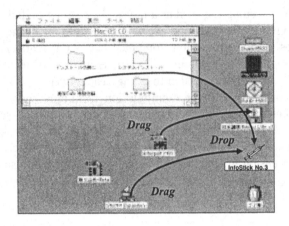

Fig. 11. Drag-and-drop to the InfoStick icon on the computer window

Acknowledgements

We wish to thank Jun Yamamoto, Nobuyuki Matsushita and Masanori Saitoh from Keio University for their contributions to this project. Several helpful discussions with members of the Sony CSL real-world UI group were also very helpful. We would also like to express our appreciation to Mario Tokoro and Toshi Doi for supporting this research.

References

1. Toshifumi Arai, Dietmar Aust, and Scott Hudson. Paperlink: A technique for hyperlink from real paper to electronic content. In*Proceedings of CHI'97*, pp.327–333, 1997.
2. Jun Rekimoto. Pick-and-Drop: A Direct Manipulation Technique for Multiple Computer Environments. In *Proceedings of UIST'97*, pp. 31–39, 1997.
3. Jun Rekimoto, and Masanori Saitoh. Augumented Surfaces: A Spatially Continuous Work Space for Hybrid Computiong Environments. In *Proceedings of CHI'99*, pp. 378–385, 1999.
4. Stott Robertson, Cathleen Wharton, Cathsrine Achworth, and Marita Franzke. Dual device user interface design: PDAs and interactive television. In *Proceedings of CHI'96*, pp. 79–86, 1996.
5. Brygg Ullmer, Hiroshi Ishii, and Dylan Glas. mediaBlocks: Physical Containers, Transports, and Control for Online Media, In *Proceedings of SIGGRAPH'98*, pp. 379–386, 1998.
6. Mark Weiser. The computer for the twenty-first-century. *Scientific American*, pp.94–104, 1991.

Using Spatial Co-location for Coordination in Ubiquitous Computing Environments

Michael Beigl

Telecooperation Office (TecO), University of Karlsruhe,
Vincenz-Prießnitz-Str. 1, D-76131 Karlsruhe, Germany
michael@teco.edu

Abstract. A problem in Ubiquitous Computing environments is the co-ordination of a multitude of different devices. This paper presents the RAUM[1]-system that provides the basis for communication between devices in a Ubiquitous Computing environment. Such communication considers the spatial order of objects in the environment similar to the way humans do. The RAUM-system uses this order to establish communication connections between objects in the environment and gives applications the possibility to react according to the spatial order. This paper proposes that in Ubicomp environments such spatial-dependent location-aware communication is superior to other communication strategies. Also three example set-ups are presented indicating that applications for Ubicomp environments benefit from the RAUM-system in various ways.

1 Introduction

Ubiquitous Computing (Ubicomp) environments can be described as places populated with a myriad of different computerized and interconnected devices. One problem in such environments is the co-ordination of and the interaction with a multitude of devices. Co-ordination of objects and applications in Ubicomp depend on conditions of the physical world, especially of surrounding objects. Such applications use for example the range of an infrared or RF transmission device to restrict the spatial range they are responsible for. Here technical restrictions are used to assign a space of interest to an Ubicomp application.

The system presented here uses spatial layout as it is perceived by a human as a strategy for structuring and restricting the space of interest for an application. Human cognition attaches importance to spatial distribution [17], using spatial order of things as a help to carry out a task. For instance, a receiver placed on a telephone indicates that calls are possible (ready for call), papers in the waste-paper-basket indicate that they could be thrown away. Another example is people talking to each other: They stand in visual and audible reach to communicate. Communication and order of objects in an environment are bound to the spatial layout, binding behavior and relation of objects in the *virtual world* to the behavior of associated objects in the

---

[1] Depending on the context the German word "Raum" could be translated as room, space, area or scope

physical world. A transfer of physical relations into the virtual world is shown in Figure 1. If two objects are close together the spatial order has a meaning that is recognized in the same way both by the human and by the system (Fig.1 circle). This leads to the following thesis:

Thesis: The communication of (computerized) objects in Ubiquitous Computing environments should, like human cognition, be spatially organized.

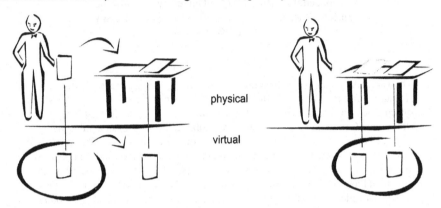

Fig. 1. Matching of physical and virtual world: If two objects (here two pieces of paper) come close in the physical world, the corresponding objects in the virtual world also come close. If they are close enough the left object recognizes the right object. They are close enough when the scope around the left object overlaps the right object.

In this paper I argue that in Ubicomp environments spatial-dependent location-aware communication is superior to other communication strategies when performing locally restricted actions. This claim is backed up and illustrated by three examples that show that applications for Ubicomp environments benefit from the proposed system.

This paper presents the RAUM system that handles communication between objects according to their spatial organisation in the environment. Therefore the RAUM concept introduces a new metaphor how communication between devices in a Ubicomp environment should be performed. The system contains the conceptual RAUM model as a theoretical base and the RAUM architecture that puts this concept in a concrete form.

In the next section an example for a spatial dependent application should clarify the problem and application area. Then the RAUM-system itself is presented. Details of the RAUM concepts and the architecture will be described next, followed by construction and implementation of the RAUM architecture, which together make up the system. The system itself will be illustrated by three example applications and related work is discussed in the end.

2 Example: ElectronicManual

The scenario "ElectronicManual" is introduced as an example to help to understand the model presented in the following sections. Purpose of the ElectonicManual application is to provide a common platform for accessing manuals of devices in the environment and for controlling these devices. The ElectronicManual scenario (Fig.2) consists of a program, the Browser, running on a handheld device and a surrounding Ubicomp environment built on top of the RAUM system. In the electronic manual example devices in the environment can communicate with each other and with the handheld device. When a manual of e.g. a video recorder located in the environment should be accessed the manual is downloaded onto the handheld device; it is then possible to read the manual and to control the video-recorder with the handheld. If multimedia content in the manual should be made available the handheld device facilitates surrounding output devices like a TV set or a HIFI in the environment to make them visible or audible. Spatial order is used in two ways in this example: First, the device that should be controlled is in a certain spatial order to the handheld device, here in front of the device. Second, the handheld device makes use of devices that are located around in a certain distance to help displaying multimedia content.

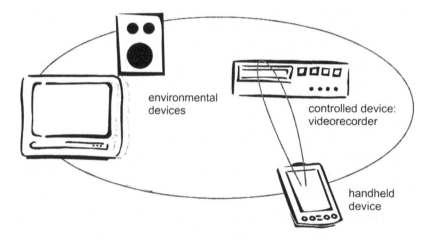

environmental devices

controlled device: videorecorder

handheld device

Fig. 2. The ElectronicManual scenario: A handheld device running the main application defines two scopes of interest. The first scope is to the device that should be controlled (here a video recorder). The second scope contains all devices in front in a certain distance. This second scope is used to ask these devices to assist the handheld device by displaying multimedia content.

3 Model

This section explains basic concepts of the RAUM-system and defines the RAUM term. Communication in RAUM is compared with other communication concepts.

3.1 Basic concepts

The way humans communicate with (computerized) objects and with each other in the physical world (source domain) is taken as a metaphor for communication between computerized objects in the virtual world (target domain). The proposed spatial structure for ordering physically existent interaction objects influences the possibility and the form of the communication. Communication is restricted to the spatial location of the object, but the object at the same time possesses the same image of the spatial environment as a user. According to the thesis the image of the distribution of objects existing in the virtual and in the physical world is equally spatially ordered. Then communication in the virtual world (i.e. between programs) occurs in the same way according to spatial structures (Figure 1). As we will see below, communication depending on the spatial layout should limit the scope of communication.

Fig. 3. Electronic applications and their paper counterparts. When a user carries out a task he recognizes the application, not the device. Using conventional interfaces these applications match to a physical object that helps to carry out the task (left: MemoPad, right: Calendar). To save space a computerized object (here a PDA) integrates several applications, but a user recognizes only the running one.

Application Objects. The term application objects (short: *objects*) stands for the combination of a physically available item (short: *item*) and a *program* serving a special purpose. This definition refers to the "obvious" function of the object to a human, the function a human recognizes as the purpose of the object at the time in question. Some items can have more than one purpose, sharing different functions over the time. In this case there is more than one object located on such an item. The set containing all objects located on one item is called an *object group*. According to the definition all objects have a physical presence when selected and a virtual presence. The virtual presence exists always in the virtual world independent of the fact whether the corresponding function is selected on the item or not.

For example a Personal Digital Assistant (PDA) handheld computer contains several programs (e.g. a memo pad and a calendar, Figure 3). In terms of the model, the item PDA hosts an object group that contains the objects "memo pad" and "calendar", because both are obvious functions when a human selects these applications on the PDA.

3.2 RAUM

The RAUM concept introduced in this paper allows modeling of objects based on a spatial order structure supporting and controlling communication. The RAUM-system defines a "location-based *R*elation of *A*pplication objects for communicating *U*bicomp event *M*essages". This relation defines the communication space containing objects that communicate among each other with the help of a spatial aware and spatial-dependent communication system.

Definition: A *RAUM* (short for RAUM scope) is defined by the relation of all *objects o*, under the restriction that the corresponding physical items lay in a *scope S*:

$$o \; \rho \; S \text{ where } o \in \{\text{all objects}\} \text{ and } S \in \text{Powerset(location description)}$$

Definition: A *scope* is a spatially defined area of the physical world that matches an according area of the virtual world.

The order of objects in the virtual world matches the order of corresponding items in the physical world. Because objects are ordered the same way in the physical and virtual world a scope defines the corresponding area in both worlds.

Scopes are defined according to a location description determining the boundaries of the scope or according to a relative range e.g. in relation to an item. Scopes are physical spaces that can be either described symbolic, geometric or hybrid; the RAUM-system follows a description method similar to [19].

Objects in RAUM communicate with each other using message events (short: *events*). Objects that take part in a RAUM receive all message events from all other objects in the same RAUM regardless of their capabilities. RAUMs are initiated by one or more objects. During initiation a scope is defined cooperatively. This scope can change over time, depending on the need of the object programs. The initiating objects describe the scope of the RAUM; objects that are in the scope of the RAUM after the definition are automatically included in the relation.

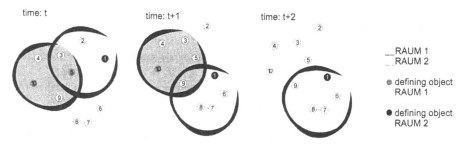

Fig. 4. Example how RAUMs are working. 3 states of a room containing 2 RAUMs: RAUM 1 with defining object 1 is moving downwards, while in RAUM 2 defining objects are giving up. As a consequence RAUM 2 vanishes

Figure 4 shows two intersecting relative RAUMs containing several objects that reflect the location of the corresponding physical items. RAUM 1 is defined by object

1; Objects 5 and 10 cooperatively define RAUM 2. Both RAUMs have objects in common. RAUM 1 is defined relative to Object 1; therefore, Object 1 is called *defining object*. As object 1 moves, RAUM 1 moves with the object (Fig.4 middle), leaving some objects behind and including others. While in Figure 4 (left) RAUM 2 is defined relative to Object 5 and Object 10, in Figure 4 (middle) Object 5 gives up his function as a defining object. Later Object 10 gives up its function as a defining object (Fig. 4 right). At the same time as Object 10 gives up its function RAUM 2 vanishes.

Every RAUM is in one of three possible states: initializing, running or dissolving. RAUMs are cooperatively created by the defining objects. The objects define the parameters of a RAUM and set the spatial definition. The definition determines indirectly which other objects take part in a RAUM. If new objects should be included as a defining object all defining objects have to agree on this.

Objects can be part of more than one RAUM. An object can even be a defining object in more than one RAUM, if the program running on the object requires this. In this case, events from one RAUM can not be seen in the other RAUM with the exception of objects located in the intersection of both RAUMs.

In the ElectronicManual example two RAUMs are defined: The first RAUM is in front of the handheld device and consists of the handheld and the device that should be controlled and whose manual should be displayed. Both devices together define this RAUM. The second RAUM is in a circle around the handheld; this second RAUM is used for dispatching multimedia content in the environment and is defined only by the handheld device.

3.3 Communication in RAUM

Communication in RAUM is *location oriented* and *spatial-dependent:* Communication partners are selected according to their spatial arrangement. In the ElectronicManual example the handheld device communicates with a radius of 2 meters in front of the device (Figure 1). This RAUM does not depend on the provided services of the objects. If a multimedia content is to be shown, an event is dropped and the appropriate device capable to handle the request picks up the event and shows the content.

On the other hand, in distributed or mobile computing systems (and also in Internet based services like the Web) communication partners are selected according to the service they provide, abstracting from the (geographical) location of the service. Here, these communication networks are referred to as *service-oriented* networks. The request for a service - e.g. a database or a printing service - as a selection criterion for the communication partner is typical for service-oriented communication. After finding this service (mostly via explicitly entering the network address as a virtual location by the user) communication is established between the service client and the service server. Physical location is not of any concern in service-oriented networks. Either location is not of interest or the assignment of virtual addresses to physical location is left to the user.

The concept of spatial-dependent communication is complementary to service-oriented communication. While spatial oriented communication abstracts from services of the communication partners, service-oriented communication abstracts from location. When creating worldwide service systems, abstracting location is a good choice as long as the service can be handled in the virtual world. In Ubicomp environments many services are performed in the physical world. Spatial-dependent communication as used in the RAUM-system supports exactly this kind of working environment: highly flexible communication directly coupled to human-computer interaction tasks. The spatial restriction of communication does not only direct communication automatically to the objects that are of interest in the local Ubicomp application, but also takes away the cognitive load from the human to imagine abstract distant devices or objects.

Communication in the RAUM-system is realized via event messages. Inside every RAUM, event messages are distributed (almost) without restriction between the objects taking part in the RAUM. The structure of events is generally freely defined. To ensure a communication basis a small number of events are predefined. Events are classified according to communication patterns. Patterns are then classified in pattern classes. Some of the patterns have to be understood by every object taking part in the RAUM-system. The common patterns cover functionality for creating, destroying, joining and dividing RAUMs. New functionality is introduced by an object through defining a pattern and ordering this pattern into the pattern class structure. In the ElectronicManual example requests for displaying multimedia content are defined as such a pattern; events built according to this pattern must be understand by devices that should take part in the ElectronicManual system. Apart from the communication pattern every event message also contains the senders location and the class of the pattern that this event belongs to.

3.4 Implications of the RAUM-system

In the following sections the major implications of the RAUM-system are described. Some principle implications concern services, network organization, communication cost, context and privacy. These implications also clearly indicate the advantages of the RAUM-system in Ubicomp environments.

Services. Services are implicitly provided in RAUM. As every object can drop an event (can be modeled as a service request) and every object can pick up events (can be modeled as a server) from the view of an object the whole RAUM reacts as one multi-purpose server. Because services in the system are bound to physical items the availability and disappearance of services can be followed by the human making applications more transparent.

Self-organizing network environment. The administrative burden of maintaining hundreds or thousands of services is taken away by the RAUM-system through restricting the number of servers via restricting the location and the use of information appliances [24] as services servers. In RAUM based systems the network and service structure is self-organizing and does not need additional environment servers or set-ups.

Reduced communication cost. To indicate the potential of the RAUM-system communication costs are compared to communication costs of service-oriented networks. The comparison is performed in a Ubicomp scenario with n objects located in a given area e.g. an office room. Let there be n_{or} objects on an average in a RAUM, and the object o should take part in n_{ro} RAUMs. Also let d be a correcting factor (because some objects are in more than one RAUM) defined as

$$d = \frac{\sum_{n} \frac{\sum \#\{\text{objects} \in \text{RAUM} \mid o_n \in \text{RAUM}\}}{\#\bigcup\{\text{objects} \in \text{RAUM} \mid o_n \in \text{RAUM}\}}}{n}. \tag{1}$$

For comparison communication costs to request a service, which is a typical communication in service-oriented systems, should be regarded; the results are similar when regarding other communication scenarios. Service based communication (e.g. Jini) normally uses a register server instance to register services and to inform other objects about services in a certain area. So in service-oriented communication first a call to such a register server is needed to request a service. Asking a register server first requires a broadcast to find the server. Next, a message is sent back to the requesting object, and then a message is sent from the requester to the actual server. Assuming all message cost as 1 the overall service call costs are:

$$\text{cost}_{\text{service}} = n_b + 2 \quad \text{for service-oriented communication.} \tag{2}$$

In the RAUM system communication costs depend on the number of objects that share a RAUM with the requesting object. The message must be sent to all these objects, therefore the cost is the cost for a multicast c to $n_{or} \cdot n_{ro} \cdot d$ objects:

$$\text{cost}_{\text{RAUM}} = n_c \quad \text{for RAUM communication.} \tag{3}$$

In the case the underlying network supports multicast and broadcast, the cost for both multi- and broadcast is 1 and there are m service request messages the overall costs for both communication methods are

$$3\,m \quad \text{for service-oriented} \qquad m \quad \text{for RAUM communication.} \tag{4}$$

indicating a clear advantage for RAUM communication.

If the underlying network does not support broadcast and multicast communication the cost increases in both cases (note: to find the register server for every service call one broadcast is needed. Due to the mobility of almost all objects in ubicomp environments objects frequently leave areas of a register server.).

$$m\,(n_{or} \times d + 2) \quad \text{(service-oriented)} \qquad m\,(n_{or}\,n_{ro}\,d) \quad \text{(RAUM).} \tag{5}$$

where x is the number of RAUMs which must be crossed by the broadcast to find the location server neglecting the costs to compute x.

We now assume a $5 \times 5\ m^2$ room with 70 RAUMs and an average of 10 objects per RAUM while every object takes part in about 3 RAUMs and a correction factor of $d=0.7$. Figure 5 shows a comparison of the cost for both communication methods. The cost for service based communication is significantly higher than the cost of RAUM communication when more than 2 Rams ($\sim 1.5\ m^2$) are needed for a broadcast to find the register server.

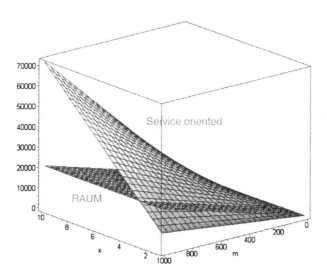

Fig. 5. Comparison of communication cost between service-oriented communication and RAUM communication. In Ubicomp environments with many objects and a high message rate RAUM communication is significantly superior to service-oriented communication

Context. Context is an important factor in Ubicomp systems. Beside location, context is needed as a decision base for many applications [26]. Context can be derived from the environment in two ways: either by equipping every object with appropriate hard- and software or through exchanging detected and preprocessed contexts among a set of objects. In a RAUM-system context is available inside the RAUM scope from all objects taking part. Every object, e.g. equipped with special sensors can transmit its findings to every other object in scope. In that way the community of objects provides a common context to every object in scope. Communication between objects is not only used for notification and command messaging but also contains sensed information. This way, the RAUM-system reduces the complexity of context detection introducing a system of shared context events.

Location based authorization. The assurance of privacy is of major concern in Ubicomp [5, 20]. Actual proposals suggest a feedback mechanism [5] so that the user knows when he is watched allowing him to move to a non-watched room, or suggest the possibility to switch off the system [15]. Both ideas are not really satisfying, because the system functionality is lost when the users do not want to be watched.

Spatial-dependent RAUM-system communication enables privacy with two concepts without loosing functionality of the system. It prohibits distribution of events e.g. movements of persons detected by sensors outside the wanted scope and allows anonymous access to sensitive data without reducing security.

Spatial limitation of communication prohibits the global access to information and prevents the set up of "Orwellian" scenarios. Communication is only allowed in specified boarders e.g. in a room. Furthermore this kind of communication allows an exact definition of the scope of events and therefore hinders supervision of persons - e.g. in a company - without reducing functionality of the system.

In spatial-dependent communication personal authorization for access can be dropped, because objects (belonging to a person) that are allowed to enter an area are allowed to use devices and data in this area. Therefore, only the location not the identity of the using object must be verified. This location based authorization metaphor is derived from daily life: Is someone authorized to enter a room, e.g. because he possesses a key for the room, he can read all documents in this room without additional identification.

4   Implementation

A couple of objects belonging to a RAUM make up a set that is modeled as a tuple space [12] with some additional operators. This tupelo space operates on the RAUM scope, or short RAUM. Tupelo spaces are a widely used basis for event communication. Examples for other systems based on tupelo spaces are Jini [30] and T Space [18]. Tupelo spaces are used to implement a RAUM communication scope. Every tupelo space contains objects that are within the scope of a RAUM relation. A RAUM is therefore implemented as a tupelo space using special operators for the setup of the RAUM and the definition of the scope. Additional operators are needed to take practical conditions of Ubicomp environments into consideration. For example, one operator set allows the determination of objects in a RAUM at a certain moment with a certain probability. Others allow asynchronous communication or the union and disunion of RAUM spaces.

4.1 Architecture

Events of an object that takes part in the RAUM are distributed to all other objects in the RAUM. If an object is a member of several rams all objects in all these rams receive events from the object. In principle, all objects in a RAUM have the same rights so dropping and accepting events is possible by all objects.

From the program's point of view object communication is handled by getting and putting event messages to the RAUM. All objects running on the same item put their event messages to the assignment level of the 3 level RAUM-system stack. At this level, events are assigned to the rams the object is member of. As a result a set of RAUM-event pairs are then passed to the RAUM-system administration level. This is the level where the RAUM-system is managed, which for example decides about creation or dissolution of a RAUM. The network layer then assigns events of rams to events to Objects, if needed by the underlying network. For example, if an IP stack of an object does not support multicast addressing, IP addresses of all RAUM-objects have to be computed at this level and events must be sent out object by.

5   Examples

Three example set-ups should illustrate the RAUM concept and application areas of location dependent communication. In the UbicompBrowser and ElectronicManual scenario surrounding computerized objects and information appliances in the environment are cooperating to enhance and simplify Human-Computer Interaction. The AmbientTelepresence system shows the integration of new kinds of computerized objects of the everyday life into application scenarios and the combination of RAUM and service-oriented communication.

5.1 UbicompBrowser

The UbicompBrowser [2] is a system that applies Ubiquitous Computing to the World-Wide Web extending the Web into our everyday environments. It extends the browser concept by replacing the standard Web user interface with a handheld access and control device and surrounding output and controllable devices. This ubiquitous user interface is determined dynamically based on the location of the handheld control. The UbicompBrowser improves Web accessibility by realizing a ubiquitous environment-based user interface, and by extending accessibility to environment-specific resources.

The UbicompBrowser setup consists of the UbicompBrowser program running on a PDA, as shown in Figure 6. This object defines a RAUM scope, which is bound to a local physical space around the PDA. When a PDA user accesses a document of a media type that can not be shown at the PDA, e.g. a movie or audio stream, the UbicompBrowser puts an event message to the RAUM asking for an object in scope to display the document. This event is taken from the RAUM by a device that matches the condition for displaying the document. Next the displaying device retrieves the document from the Web and puts out the content while synchronizing with the UbicompBrowser object via RAUM communication.

5.2 ElectronicManual

The principle of the ElectronicManual used as an example throughout the paper. The ElectronicManual [4] is build on top of the UbicompBrowser. The ElectronicManual gives users better assistance in understanding and using their devices. There are two fundamental contributions to the ElectronicManual: First the uniform access to information over devices that follows a single metaphor instead of forcing the user to rethink about the form and access method with every new device. Second the ubiquitous access to the current information, possibly enhanced with multimedia contents, learning programs and support channels. The ElectronicManual setup shows that Ubicomp environments can bring real advantages for everyday tasks. Although electronic manuals are not new, the ubiquitous access to these informations and the possibility to integrate control and information access in one user interfaces significantly improves usability.

5.3 Ambient Telepresence

The Ambient Telepresence System [3] is set up to demonstrate the connection of two or more distance rooms with the help of RAUM technology. Ambient Telepresence itself is introduced as a method to give someone the feeling that someone else is present while he is not. In contrast to other telepresence approaches, ambient telepresence is focussed on mediating background activity. Ambient telepresence is based on generation of remote presence from handling everyday objects in work environments, based on Ubiquitous Computing and context-awareness technologies. For experimentation, we have developed *MediaCups*, coffee cups in our office environment equipped with sensor, computing and communication facilities. Such a cup is an item with a corresponding program (running on a Microchip PIC microprocessor) that takes part in a RAUM. MediaCups located in dedicated office rooms (each of the office is defined as a RAUM) are interconnected with loudspeakers in the other offices. Ambient Telepresence is realized by associating cup movements to sounds: Detected cup movements of the cup are transferred as events to the remote location and made audible as associated noises. The Ambient Telepresence system interconnects two or more rams. While events in a local RAUM are detected by the RAUM-system, normal IP based communication is used for interconnecting the rams. This example setup also shows the integration of new computerized objects of the everyday life, e.g. the MediaCup.

Fig. 6. Two example set-ups of the RAUM system. The left picture shows the PDA with the UbicompBrowser, a PC based network access node and a TV set as controlled device. Right the MediaCup with an IrDA based access point as it is used in the Ambient Telepresence example.

6 Related work

Several suggestions have been made how Ubiquitous Computing environments, especially with regard to Human-Computer Interaction (HCI) problems, should be constructed or how problems that arise in this field have to be solved (e.g. [7, 21, 23, 25]). Some of these suggestions were implemented as experimental set-ups. Test-scenarios were constructed and the usefulness of these suggestions was verified. Such investigations help specifying conditions for Ubiquitous Computing systems and give guidelines for the construction of such systems.

The first Ubicomp systems ParcTab [28] and Responsive Environments [9] from XeroxParc used X-Windows based technology. ParcTab uses human computer interfaces similar to those used at desktop computers. More recent systems like Domisilica [22] from Georgia Tech also provide desktop computer bound interfaces, but additionally integrate objects of the everyday environment into the system. To interconnect both interface types, a Multi-User Dungeon (MUD) is used here as a joint communication space.

The ReactiveEnvironment [11] and the ActiveOffice [8] project at the University of Toronto are examples aiming especially at non-desktop computer interfaces. This projects deal mainly with the question of complexity of the human-machine interaction in environments enhanced with computer technology. In Active Office Buxton mentioned five Design Principles for minimising the complexity of the Ubicomp application for the user. These design principles refer to a close correlation of the *physical world* of physical items and artifacts and the *virtual (electronic) world* of programs and data. An approach to collect experience with new kind of tangible interfaces for connecting both worlds is the Tangible Bits project [16] at the MIT MediaLab.

The question of how to match both worlds is also stated as one of the major problems in other research. Some proposed Ubiquitous Computing systems match physical artifacts [7, 8, 14, 22, 29] to virtual objects. Some also have concepts for matching social interaction [8] to their virtual counterparts. All existent Ubicomp systems differ in the way, how the virtual object reflects its physical behavior. None of the above mentioned systems reflect the spatial-dependent communication concept found in the physical world. Spatial order has a role in [8] as part of the design principles. For manipulative user interfaces (e.g. [6, 13, 29]) or augmented reality systems (e.g. [10]) the meaning of spatial arrangement provides a basis for the applications functionality. Therefore, it has been implicitly implemented in these applications. Some systems [1, 10, 15, 27] use a location services to provide explicit information about the spatial layout of objects in the environment.

7 Conclusion

RAUM was introduced as a concept and a system to support co-operation and communication between objects in Ubicomp environments. RAUM communication takes the spatial order of physical objects into account. This paper indicates that in Ubicomp environments such spatial-dependent location-aware communication is superior to other communication strategies. The location-aware RAUM-model, the system, architecture and implementation are introduced in this paper. The RAUM-system supports construction and operation of Ubicomp applications in many ways. Like humans, the RAUM-system orders objects in the environment according to their spatial location making this order available to applications. Such location dependence allows users to have a transparent view of ongoing program activities. Three example set-ups show how to integrate physical devices through simply writing the service for taking part in the RAUM-system. This is even possible for very restricted devices with embedded microprocessors and small amount of storage space such as MediaCups. As a result, allowing physical set-ups to be built very fast brings the flexibility known from component-based software design to Ubiquitous Computing environments. Ubicomp environments with a large amount of computerized objects benefit also in other ways from the proposed RAUM concept. Due to the spatial restriction in RAUM privacy can be assured without crippling functionality or security, communications is carried out more efficient and management of Ubicomp environments is facilitated.

The proposed system uses exact defined boundaries for RAUM scopes (ignoring practical conditions as the uncertainty when determining a location caused by the imperfection of current technology). In contrast humans have a more blunt concept of the area they are interested in. Future experiments will show if the presented concept of exact defined scopes provides enough support for applications in Ubicomp environments or if a concept using a more blunt scope definition is significantly superior. More practical questions rise when implementing a RAUM-system. Upcoming network technologies with a very limited transmission scope (e.g. Bluetooth) facilitate the construction of spatial-depended communication, but existing network technologies must also be integrated. Criteria have to be found to optimize the setup of such mixed networks for RAUM communication.

8   References

1. Beadle, H. W. Peter, Harper, B, Maguire Jr, G. Q, Judge, J.: Location-aware Mobile Computing: Proc. IEEE/IEE International Conference on Telecommunications (ICT'97). Melbourne. April (1997)
2. Beigl, M., Schmidt, A., Lauff, M., Gellersen, H.: UbicompBrowser: 4th ERCIM Workshop on User Interfaces for All. Stockholm, Sweden. October (1998)
3. Beigl, Michael, Gellersen, Hans-Werner: Ambient Telepresence: Proceedings of the Workshop on Changing Places. London, UK (1999)
4. Beigl, Michael: ElectronicManual: 8th International Conference on Human-Computer Interaction. München, Germany (1999) to be published
5. Bellotti, V.: Design for Privacy in Multimedia Computing and Communication Environments. Technology and Privacy: In Agre, Rotenberg, : The New Landscape, MIT Press (1997)
6. Brave, S., Ishii, H. and Dahley, A.: Tangible Interfaces for Remote Collaboration and Communication: in Proceedings of CSCW '98, Seattle, Washington USA, November, ACM Press, (1998), 169-178.
7. Buxton, William A. S.: Living in Augmented Reality: Ubiquitous Media and Reactive Environments: In K. Finn, A. Sellen & S. Wilber (Eds.). Video Mediated Communication. Hillsdale, N.J.: Erlbaum, (1997) 363-384
8. Buxton, William A. S: Ubiquitous Media and the Active Office: Ubiquitous Video: Nikkei Electronics, 3.27 (no. 632), (1995) 187-195
9. Demers, Alan J.: Research Issues in Ubiquitous Computing: In Proceedings of the Thirteenth Annual ACM Symposium on Principles of Distributed Computing. Los Angeles, California, USA. August 14-17, (1994) 2-8
10. Feiner, S., MacIntyre, B., Seligmann, D.: Knowledge-Based Augmented Reality. Communications of the ACM, Vol 36, No.7, July (1993)
11. Fitzmaurice, George W. :Graspable User Interfaces: PhD Thesis. Toronto (1996)
12. Gelernter, David : Generative communication in Linda: ACM TOPLAS, Vol. 7, No. 1. January (1985)

13.Gorbet, M., Orth, M. and Ishii, H., Triangles: Tangible Interface for Manipulation and Exploration of Digital Information Topography: In Proceedings of Conference on Human Factors in Computing Systems CHI '98, ACM Press, Los Angeles: April (1998), 49-56

14.Harrison, Beverly L., P. Fishkin, Kenneth, Gujar, Anuj, Mochon, Carlos Want, Roy: Squeeze Me, Hold Me, Tilt Me! An Exploration of Manipulative User Interfaces; CHI 98, Los Angeles CA, USA, 18-23. April (1998)

15.Harter, Andy, Hopper, Andy: A Distributed Location System for the Active Office: IEEE Network, Vol. 8, No. 1, January (1994)

16.Ishii, Hiroshi, Ullmer, Brygg: Tangible Bits: Towards Seamless Interfaces between People, Bits and Atoms: CHI97 (1997)

17.Kirsh, David: The intelligent use of space: Artificial Intelligence 73(1-2).(1995) 31-68

18.Lehman, Tobin Mclaughry, Steve, Wyckoff, Peter: T Spaces: The Next Wave : Hawaii International Conference on Systems Sciences (1999)

19.Leonhardt, Ulf, Supporting Location-Awareness in Open Distributed Systems: PhD Thesis, Imperial College, University of London. May (1998)

20.Leonhardt, Ulf, Magee, Jeff: Security Considerations for a Distributed Location Service: Journal of Network and Systems Management, 6(1). March (1998) 51-70

21.MacIntyre, Blair, Feiner, Steven: Future Multimedia User Interfaces: In Multimedia Systems, Springer Verlag, (1996) 250-268

22.Mankoff, J., Somers, J., Abowd, G. D.: Bringing People and Places Together with Dual Augmentation: Collaborative Virtual Environments. Manchester. June (1998). 81-86

23.Myers, Brad, Hollan, Jim, Cruz et al Isabel: Strategic Directions in Human-Computer Interaction: ACM Computing Surveys, Vol.28, No4. December (1996)

24.Norman, Donald A: The Invisible Computer: MIT Press. (1998)

25.Salber, D., Dey, A.K., Abowd, G.D.: Ubiquitous Computing: Defining an HCI Research Agenda for an Emerging Interaction Paradigm: Tech. Report GIT-GVU-98-01. Feb. (1998)

26.Schmidt, Albrecht, Beigl, Michael, Gellersen, Hans-Werner: There is more to context than location: Proceedings of the International Workshop on Interactive Applications of Mobile Computing (IMC), Rostock, Germany November (1998)

27.Shafer, S., Krumm, J., Brumitt, B., Meyers, B., Czerwinski, M., Robbins, D.: The New EasyLiving Project at Microsoft Research: Joint DARPA/NIST Smart Spaces Workshop. Gaithersburg, Maryland. July 30-31, (1998)

28.Want, R. Schilit, B.N., Adams, N.I., Gold, R, Petersen, K., Goldberg, D., Ellis, J.R, Weiser, M.: An overview of the PARCTAB Ubiquitous Computing experiment: IEEE Personal Communications 2(6), (1995) 28-43

29.Wisneski, C., Ishii, H., Bahley, A., Gorbet, M., Braver, S., Ullmer, B., Yarin, P.: Ambient Displays: Turning Architectural Space into an Interface between People and Digital Information: Cooperative Buildings. Springer Verlag, February 25-26 (1998)

30.www.jini.org

Amplifying Reality

Jennica Falk, Johan Redström, and Staffan Björk

PLAY: Applied research on art and technology
The Viktoria Institute, Box 620, 405 30 Göteborg, SWEDEN
{jennica,johan,bjork}@viktoria.informatik.gu.se
http://www.viktoria.informatik.gu.se/play/

Abstract. Many novel applications take on the task of moving the personal computer away from the desktop with the approach to merge digital information with physical space and objects. These new applications have given rise to a plethora of notions and terms used to classify them. We introduce amplified reality as a concept complementary to that of augmented reality. To amplify reality is to enhance the publicly available properties of persons and physical objects, by means of using wearable or embedded computational resources. The differences between the two concepts are discussed and examples of implementations are given. The reason for introducing this term is to contribute to the terminology available to discuss already existing applications, but also to open up for a discussion of interesting design implications.

Keywords: amplified reality, augmented reality, ubiquitous computing, wearable computing, embedded vs. superimposed properties, private vs. public

1   Breaking away from the PC

When moving the computer away from the office desktop in order to make it fit other activities and situations, one can choose between two different approaches. Either we choose to move the computer closer to the user, making it even more personal, or we choose to move it away from the user, into the environment, making it a widely spread resource much like water or electricity.

So-called *wearable computers* take the first approach, making the computer so small and mobile that the user can carry it continuously. The aim is to create the truly personal computer, a prosthetic device closely integrated with its wearer. One important characteristic is that the wearable computer is a computational device in the user's personal and private control; the user carries the device on his or her body and is the only person to interact with it. For some illustrating examples of wearable computer systems, see [8, 11, 2]. In contrast, *ubiquitous computing*, is the approach of embedding computational resources in the environment [14]. The role of the personal computer is made less significant by placing small computers everywhere in an environment; these sense, control and display interesting information depending on some context [3]. In this approach, the user does not have to bring a computer to the task or the task to a computer, as computational resources are already present in the environment.

Currently there are a number of different approaches to merging physical space and digital information (cf. [12]), which bring together techniques from both wearable and ubiquitous computing. With ubiquitous computing, computational properties might actually be embedded into objects. However, another approach seems to have been more influential so far: wearable computers that deploy techniques to superimpose virtual properties onto physical objects, thereby giving users an *augmented reality*.

In this paper we introduce the concept of *Amplified Reality*. This concept differs from augmented reality, in that it emphasizes the importance of the shared experiences that result from *publicly available properties* of objects. Augmented reality is about how the user perceives reality, while amplified reality is about how the perceived might control how information is made available. Finally, we discuss some implications of amplified reality.

2   Augmented Reality

Augmented reality systems are systems, in which computer-rendered properties are superimposed on the real world, allowing the user to experience virtual aspects as if they were real world properties. One basic definition of the term states that augmented reality *combines virtual and real objects in real time* [1, 5].

Even though this definition does not specify how the augmented reality is presented, many "augmented realities" are only experienced through specialized equipment, such as goggles or head-mounted displays to visually enhance the user's environment [5, 10]. The use of this type of equipment allows for private information visualization, tailor-made for each specific user.

In contrast to the personal systems, some research groups are experimenting with the alternative idea of superimposing visual information that can be publicly experienced with the aid of projecting techniques [13, 15]. Such systems allow for many users to experience the same augmentation in real time, without the requirement of personal viewing equipment.

Regardless of how personal or communal the augmented experience is, the "reality" it creates is not real per se. Computer-rendered virtual properties are superimposed on real objects in such a way that the user's impression of the real world is enhanced or otherwise altered. Hence, the properties of an augmented world are associated with the observer's interpretation of the augmented reality system, rather than with the objects themselves.

3   Amplifying Reality

We will now present the concept of amplified reality as a complement to augmented reality. Part of the reason is to introduce a term that will aid in describing already existing systems, but also to point to interesting possibilities when designing mixed reality systems.

3.1 Defining amplified reality

> *To amplify reality is to enhance the publicly available properties of a physical object, by means of using embedded computational resources.*

While augmented reality is about enhancing our impressions of everyday objects in our surrounding, *amplified reality* is about enhancing the *expressions* of objects and people in the world. Since the difference may seem subtle at first, we will explain by describing the key phrases in our definition.

With *publicly available properties,* we assume that the added virtual properties are equally available to all users or everyone present. While augmented reality based on wearable technology can create large differences in how objects are presented to different users, amplified reality stresses the similarity. This is however not to say that it should be the single goal to make virtual information public in this way; sometimes a private augmented reality system will be more suitable. This can be illustrated by a simple example: suppose you want a new color on the walls of your apartment. Usually, this is achieved by painting them in the preferred color, but this result might also be achieved by wearing a pair of colored eyeglasses that make the wall appear different. In essence, the colored glass in the spectacles adds an additional layer of information on the real world, and in this way augments it. Now, re-painting the walls would correspond to amplifying reality, wearing the eyeglasses to augmented reality. If the walls are painted, anyone entering the room will be able to perceive the color; if the eyeglasses are used, only the person or persons using them will be able to see the "new" color.

An amplified object is self-contained in regards to its properties. In practice, this means that that the properties are *embedded* parts of the object. In contrast, augmented reality superimposes virtual properties on an object, which in effect does not change the actual object, but rather how we perceive or experience it. Augmented properties are not persistent outside the augmented reality. The important difference between these two approaches lie in the proprietary rights to the information. An amplified object controls the flow of information, while in an augmented reality system the perceiver is in control of the information. For instance, if an augmented reality system is used to supply its user with additional information about a person she is currently speaking to, this person has no influence over the information provided. In other words, an augmented reality systems alters the impressions of its user, without there being any corresponding properties in the *expression* of the object she is perceiving. This is quite different from ordinary life. For example, we choose what clothes to wear and thus (partly) in what way other persons will perceive us. The concept of amplified reality is designed to acknowledge this. By embedding publicly available properties, the information distributed (or the virtual properties added) will be controlled by the perceived object itself. This is perhaps most important when it comes to communication between humans, as integrity in large part has to do with what others "know" about oneself.

In an attempt to relate key attributes of amplified reality with those of augmented reality, we were able to arrange them as depicted in the figure below (see figure 1). This shows a model that groups the identified attributes of the two approaches as opposites of each other, summarizing the main differences between augmented reality and amplified reality.

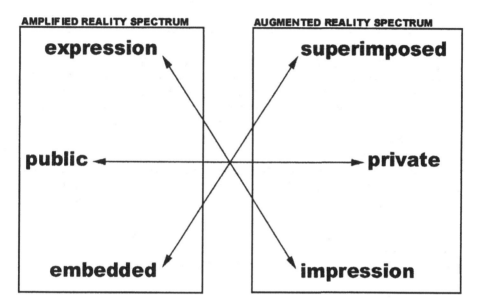

Fig. 1. Key attributes of amplified reality and augmented reality can be arranged as opposites to each other.

3.2 Examples

In order to anchor the concept of amplified reality further, we provide three examples of systems that satisfy the amplified reality definition. The first example, the Lovegety [cf. 7], is a commercial product while the following two, the Hummingbird [6] and the BubbleBadge [4], are part of our own work.

Two examples that are somewhat similar on the conceptual level can be found in the Lovegety and in the Hummingbird. Although their intended use differs, they have significant similarities that comply with the notion of amplified reality. They are palm-sized, portable electronic devices equipped with radio transceivers that continuously broadcast and listen for information. The Lovegety comes in two colors - pink for girls and white for boys. There are three user-selectable settings - "talk", "karaoke", and "get2" and when two differently colored Lovegetys on the same setting are close, an indication is given in form of a beep and a flashing light. With the

Lovegety it is possible for a user to broadcast interest in for instance karaoke, in effect providing a publicly accessible (to all who carries a Lovegety) expression about herself with the aid of technology.

The Hummingbird [6] is designed to support awareness of presence between people who frequent the same physical space. They give users constant aural and visual indications when other users carrying Hummingbirds are in the vicinity. Hence, for the user it is possible to be seen or heard by people even when out of sight, e.g. behind a closed door, or out of hearing range. Thus, the Hummingbird amplifies the user's presence.

A third example is the BubbleBadge [4], which is a wearable computer display that is worn like a brooch, hence directed towards its viewer rather than its wearer. The device is an experiment in turning a wearable computer's display inside out, effectively transforming the wearable computing concept by making digital information *public* rather than *private*. Since the device is pinned to a person, it is effectively taking advantage of its wearers mobility in serving a public audience. The BubbleBadge may be granted to show information that is private to the viewer, provided the viewer can identify herself to the device. In addition, the BubbleBadge can display public information broadcasted from locations in the environment, much like a public announcement system.

In addition, there are implementations that have a mixed approach, incorporating attributes from both amplified reality and augmented reality [13, 9, 15]. When looking at these applications we can see why they comply well with the conventional definition of augmented reality, but we can also find important and interesting attributes that do not belong in this categorization. This observation has led us to believe that it is both valuable and useful to assign a complementary term to aid us when talking about and classifying applications within these fields.

3.3 Amplifiers and Digital Sound Processing

The inspiration to the field of applications we envision in this domain, and the reason for choosing the name amplified reality, was taken from the music domain. When popular music started to develop in the early 50:s it was accompanied by an equally rapid development of musical instruments, or rather, of musical sound. Until then, electronics had not been used to alter the sound of acoustic instruments, but when microphones and amplifiers entered the stage, the sound of music was changed forever. Not only did microphones and amplifiers allow music to be played far more loudly; they also enabled musicians to change the sound qualities of their instruments. Today, digital sound processing have taken this even further, and most digital artificial reverbs, digital sound effect devices, digital instruments etc. conform to the MIDI (Musical Instruments Digital Interface) communication standard. The possibility to use MIDI to connect and control different devices, and the standard for audio contacts (making interchange of audio signals possible) imply that a MIDI set-up should qualify as a collection of appliances connected in a way characteristic to ubiquitous computing. Moreover, as far as such a set-up is used to alter the sound of an acoustic event, e.g. a person singing to an audience, it is an example of amplified reality as defined above.

4 Conclusions

We have shown two distinct strategies of how to use computers to alter or add characteristics to objects that users interact with: augmented reality and amplified reality. We introduced the term amplified reality in order to stress properties like public and embedded (compared to augmented reality's corresponding emphasis on private and superimposed) properties.

We have also shown that amplified reality can be achieved using techniques *both* from wearable computers and from ubiquitous computing. An amplified object can for instance be created by "turning a wearable computer inside out," i.e. by making the wearable computer's display available to people looking at the wearer. Further, the idea of having many amplified objects in a given area is very similar to the idea of ubiquitous computing. Usually, wearable computers and ubiquitous computing are viewed as each other's opposite, but it is not the technology as such, but the purpose of using of them that are opposite. Wearable computers focus on how to interact with information on a *private* level, while ubiquitous computing aims at enabling interaction with information on a *public* level. The concept of amplified reality breaks the linkage between hardware and software and illustrates that there can be a difference between the nature of a device and the information displayed on it. A public announcement may be displayed on a screen carried by an individual, while a private email may be shown on a communal information display (given that the owner has authorized the retrieval). How the privacy issues arising from these possibilities should be solved is a question that needs further research.

References

1. Azuma, R. (1997). A Survey of Augmented Reality. In *Presence: Teleoperators and Virtual Environments*, pp. 355-385, MIT Press.
2. Bass, L., Kasabach, C., Martin, R. et al. (1997). The Design of a Wearable Computer. In *Proceedings of CHI'97*, ACM Press.
3. Demers, A. J. (1994). Research Issues in Ubiquitous Computing. *In Proceedings of PODC'94*, ACM Press.
4. Falk, J., and Björk, S. (1997) The BubbleBadge: A Public Wearable Display. In *Extended Abstracts of CHI'99*, ACM Press.
5. Feiner, S., MacIntyre, B., and Seligman, D. (1993). Knowledge-based Augmented Reality. In *Communications of the ACM*, Vol. 36, No. 7, ACM Press.
6. Holmquist, L.E., Falk, J., and Wigström, J. (1999) Supporting Group Collaboration with Inter-Personal Awareness Devices. To appear in *Personal Technologies*, Springer-Verlag.
7. Iwatani, Y. (1998). Love: Japanese Style. In *Wired News*, 11June, 1998.
8. Mann, S. (1997). Smart Clothing: The Wearable Computer and WearCam. *Personal Technologies*, Vol. 1, No. 1, Springer-Verlag.
9. Mynatt, E., Back, M., Want, R., et al. (1998). Designing Audio Aura. In *Proceedings of CHI'98*, ACM Press.
10. Rekimoto, J., Ayatsuka, Y., and Hayashi, K. (1998). Augment-able Reality: Situated Communication through Physical and Digital Spaces. In *Proceedings of ISWC'98*.
11. Starner, T., Mann, S., Rhodes, B., Levine, J., et al. (1997). Augmented Reality Through Wearable Computing. In *Presence, Special Issue on Augmented Reality*, MIT Press.

12. Streitz, N. A., and Russel, D. M. (1998). Basics of Integrated Information and Physical Spaces: The State of the Art. In *Extended Abstracts of CHI'98*, ACM Press.
13. Ullmer, B., and Ishii, H. (1997). The metaDESK: Models and Prototypes for Tangible User Interfaces. In *Proceedings of UIST'97*, ACM Press.
14. Weiser, M. (1991). The Computer for the Twenty-First Century. *Scientific American*, pp. 94-104.
15. Wisneski, C., Orbanes, J., and Ishii, H. (1998). PingPongPlus: Augmentation and Transformation of Athletic Interpersonal Interaction. In *Extended Abstracts of CHI'98*, ACM Press.

Designing Interaction Styles for a Mobile Use Context

Steinar Kristoffersen[1] and Fredrik Ljungberg[2]

[1]Norwegian Computing Centre, Postboks 114 Blindern, N-0314 Oslo, Norway
steinar@nr.no
[2]Viktoria Institute, Box 620, SE-405 30 Gothenburg, Sweden
fredrik@viktoria.org

Abstract. Direct manipulation, which is the dominating "interaction style" for mobile computers, fails to meet the conditions of many mobile use situations. In particular, it demands too much visual attention of the user. We introduce a new, complementing interaction style (and system) for mobile computers, called MOTILE, which addresses three main requirements of interaction with mobile computers: (1) no visual attention needed; (2) structured, tactile input, and; (3) the use of audio feedback. MOTILE relies on only 4 buttons for user input and "hands free" audio for feedback.

Keywords: Mobile computers, interaction style, interface design.

1 Introduction

In the traditional office setting, the primary work tasks of users are *inside* the computer. The reason is simple: office work is to a large extent about processing documents, spreadsheets, emails, etc., and those artefacts are *inside* the computer. In a mobile use context, this is not usually the case. Maintenance workers, sales personnel, and other mobile staff do not primarily process information inside the computer. Their main tasks are *outside* the computer, e.g., meeting clients, repairing broken equipment, and so on.

Many of today's problems in the use of mobile computers derive from the fact that their interfaces are designed from the same principles as desktop computers. Desktop computers are designed on the premises of *direct manipulation*, with files and folders, drag and drop, and so on. Direct manipulation is an interaction style that demands a high degree of visual attention of the user. This may be suitable in the office (where the primary tasks are inside the computer), however it is not always the most suitable design guideline for the mobile computer. The reason is that direct manipulation paradigm is too "exclusive" for the mobile use context: it demands that the users attend to the virtual world "inside the computer" to an extent that does not agree with the conditions of the mobile use context, e.g., walking, driving, and repairing.

In this paper, we analyse the problem of direct manipulation in the context of mobile computers, derive requirements for interaction styles of mobile computers, and introduce our candidate, called MOTILE. MOTILE is an interaction style and system that seeks to complement current paradigms of interaction styles for mobile computers.

The rest of this paper is structured as follows: we first describe the mobile computer and its interface, followed by an exploration of the problem of direct manipulation in the context of mobile use. We derive a set of requirements that interaction styles of mobile computers need to meet, that served as a foundation for the design of MOTILE, which we describe next. Lastly, we review related work and conclude the paper.

2   Interacting with mobile computers

In this section, we describe the current interaction styles for mobile computers, the problems that these seem to cause, and some requirements of interaction styles in mobile use contexts.

2.1   The mobile interface

Mobile computers (or PDAs) have up to now largely been used *asynchronously*. For user input, current models rely on keyboard, pen, or both. Three main categories of operating systems for mobile computers exist. Palm Pilot computers run on the *Palm OS*, Psion computers, and new mobile phones and "hybrids" (e.g., Ericsson R380) use *EPOC*, while Palm top computers like the Cassiopeia (Casio) and Ericsson's MC 16 run on *Windows CE*. All rely to a considerable extent on the *direct manipulation* interaction style. An interaction style defines the ways in which user input and output can take place. Primary interaction styles for the PC are menu selection, form fill-in, command language, natural language, and direct manipulation [3].

Direct manipulation is the dominating interaction style for desktop computing. In a direct manipulation environment, the user operates the computer by pointing, selecting, dragging, etc., visual objects on the screen, and the results of the operations are immediately visible on the screen. The basic components of direct manipulation interfaces are windows, icons, menus and point device [2], which is the reason such systems sometimes are called "WIMP systems."

Figure 1. The three dominating mobile computer operating systems: EPOC, Windows CE, and PalmOS.

Direct manipulation demands a high visual attention of the user. Consider, for example, the OAI (Object-Action-Interface) model of direct manipulation, which is frequently discussed in the literature. The OAI model [3, p. 205] suggests three principles:

1. "Continuous representation of the objects and actions of interest with meaningful visual metaphors."
2. "Physical actions or presses of labelled buttons, instead of complex syntax."
3. "Rapid incremental reversible operations whose effect on the object of interest is visible immediately."

The consequence of these principles is an interface that is very dependent on *video*. To input information, the user needs to find the right visual object on the screen, perform the operations (clicking, dragging, etc., on the right place), and receive video feedback ("perceiving the system state", see [4]).

Let us now relate the dominating operating systems of mobile computers to the three principles of the OAI model.

- "Continuous representation of the objects and actions of interest with meaningful visual metaphors."

All three conform to this principle.

- "Physical actions or presses of labelled buttons, instead of complex syntax."

All three conform to this principle. The keyboard on most mobile computers is only used for word processing, and similar applications, not for navigating the operating system.

- "Rapid incremental reversible operations whose effect on the object of interest is visible immediately."

All three conform to this principle.

2.2 The mobile use context

The mobile use context is often heterogeneous, and for that reason it may be difficult to make general claims about it [1]. However, in many mobile situations, such as in mobile maintenance work in energy and telecommunication companies that we have studied, there is a set of common features of the use context, which in important ways differ from the traditional context of the office.

Let us compare these two use contexts, using the categories of task, hand, attention, and dynamics:

a) Task

The mobile user is often engaged with tasks "outside" the computer, e.g., implementing new equipment in the field. The office user, on the other hand, is often engaged in tasks "inside" the computers, e.g., manipulating a spreadsheet or writing a document.

b) Hands

The mobile user often uses the hands to manipulate physical objects, e.g., tools and equipment, while the office worker often easily can place the hands on a keyboard.

c) Attention

The mobile user may be involved in tasks "outside the computer" that demand a high level of visual attention, e.g., to avoid danger or monitor progress. The office user, on the other hand, can often easily direct a large degree of visual attention to the computer.

d) Dynamics

The mobile user may move during the task, as opposed to the office user who often performs the task in one single location (e.g., writing a document at the desk).

As we can see, the mobile and the stationary use context differs from each other in important ways. This suggests that interface guidelines from the office setting may not be suitable in the mobile setting, the reason being that the two use contexts simply are too different. Nevertheless, current mobile computers are equipped with interfaces and interaction styles from the office. This calls for new interaction styles that complement direct manipulation in the mobile environment. What requirements should such an interaction styles satisfy?

2.3 Requirements

When designing interaction styles for mobile computers, there seems to be at least three issues to consider. Using the terminology of Norman [4], these are:
- "Executing actions" should not demand a high degree of visual attention, among others, because, first: many users type on mobile computers with one finger on each hand, which is very difficult without looking at the keyboard;

second, localising the visual objects on the screen is very demanding visually. This calls for input methods that do not demand much video. Such methods seem likely to be very simple and structured.

- "Perceiving the systems state" should demand no or little visual attention, among others, because it may be very difficult to find a place for the mobile computer that makes the screen easily available during the entire work process. This calls for feedback and output methods that demand little or no video. Such methods may rely on audio, which is another implication.
- In most mobile situations, including rather extreme environments, users can rely on audio feedback.

These implications served as the foundation for the design of the MOTILE interaction style method described next.

3   MOTILE

MOTILE is a technique (interaction style) and a system for operating mobile computers. It is based on the three implications discussed above: no or little visual attention, structured, tactile input and the use of audio feedback. MOTILE relies on only 4 buttons for user input, and "hands free" audio feedback.

The technique comprises *binary look-up in sets of virtual keyboards*, currently with keyboards for: text input, moving the cursor, reading text and selecting links from web-pages, as well as reading and sending email. The user "encodes" input by selecting and pressing *regions* on a touch screen. *North* switches between keyboards, *East* and *West* selects the next higher or lower half of the keyboard, respectively, and *South* executes the command (e.g., types a character or takes the user to the selected web-page).

MOTILE informs the user about options and execution via a voice synthesiser. The visual channel that dominates the direct manipulation paradigm is replaced with a less obtrusive audio feedback conduit. MOTILE relies on "semantic call-back," which entails using the system as a control panel, or ultra-thin client that sends encoded instructions to dedicated servers, rather than performing actions locally. Figure 2 shows an overview of the architecture.

MOTILE consists of an ultra-thin client running on the palmtop terminal. The client communicates "orientation" (N, W, S, E) using a BreezeCom wireless LAN to the MOTILE server running on a Unix host. The simple messages are translated into selection, navigation and execution of semantic codes, which are organized in virtual keyboards. A perl script parses and returns elements of HTML from URLs. The users are continuously offered feedback on their actions via an *echoServer*, which uses a simple audio synthesiser to broadcast messages to a microwave radio. A headset is connected to the radio terminal carried by the user, thus affording non-obtrusive feedback through the audio channel. A separate server handles mail commands which it relays to *sendmail*.

The current version of MOTILE is implemented for Windows CE using Waba and Solaris servers, but any platform dependencies are external to MOTILE itself; the primary obstacle in this respect was finding drivers for Wireless LANs, and an effective voice synthesiser.

The main contribution of the current MOTILE technique is twofold:

- First, it offers an input device platform on top of which to continue experimenting with new ways of operating mobile devices, and
- Second, it demonstrates that the visual feedback channel taken for granted in the direct manipulation paradigm may indeed be challenged.

We are currently in the process of setting up a proper evaluation of the system. Thus far mainly the authors have been experimenting with the system during development only. Besides establishing that the technical configuration works well, very limited "proof-of-concept" may yet be elicited from this. We have found, however, that typing, reading and sending email, "browsing" and selecting web-pages moving the mouse cursor works, albeit slowly and requiring more concentration (mental, rather than visual) compared to the desktop-based direct manipulation counterpart. An interesting avenue for further exploration is already established, namely to attempt using a combination of "intelligent profiling" based on use patterns, to re-use frequently types combinations, and "tangible bits" [5] to reduce the stress on the user during input operations. Getting audio feedback via the synthesiser and radio, rather than visual feedback, seems to work rather well.

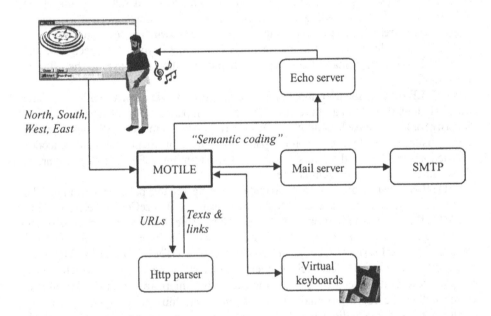

Figure 2. MOTILE.

4 Related work

There are many contributions in HCI on multi-media and multi-modal input. *Nomadic Radio*, for instance, is a wearable system for providing background awareness for mobile users [6]. It is distinguished from MOTILE, which relies on audio as a directed "foreground" feedback mechanism concerning the state of the work and available operations. In most other HCI research, audio is viewed as a means for "input." Our concern, on the other hand, is chiefly to use audio as a feedback mechanism.

The issue of interfaces on mobile computers has been debated in several recent panels. However, the perspective has mainly been one of structured output in combination with open voice input [7]. The project reported in this paper, aims to support open audio output and structured tactile input. Our concern has not been "auditory cues" [8], although we of course see them as a useful complement to the design of MOTILE. Contributions on input devices for drawing, pointing and dragging complies with the direct manipulation paradigm [9], and we have chosen not to go into these in any detail here.

One promising approach is to consider the integration or separation of input devices in terms of applications versus the mechanics of the system [10]. Rather than looking at perception as the key element, however, as Jacob et al. [10], we have looked at the social practices involved in the mobile situations that we aim to support.

5 Conclusions

We have explored the problems of applying direct manipulation in the mobile use context. We noted that the mobile *use context* in important ways differs from the office setting, which in turn has implications for the design of interfaces of mobile computers. Some important requirements that the interface of mobile computers need to meet are: *no or little visual attention, structured, tactile input and the use of audio feedback*. These requirements guided the design of MOTILE, a new and complementing interaction style (and system) for mobile computers. MOTILE offers a complementing interaction style for heterogeneous use contexts, in particular those where *tasks other than operating the mobile computer may be the most important, users' hands may be otherwise occupied, users may be involved in tasks "outside the computer" that demand a high level of visual attention, and users are highly mobile whilst performing the task.*

The direct manipulation paradigm seems *too exclusive* for the mobile use context. It rests upon the idea that users can direct very much of the attention to the computer, which, thus, circumscribes the task users want to accomplish. Accordingly, when the users are in situations where this is not the case, e.g., while driving a car or maintaining equipment in a hazardous environment, the assumptions of direct manipulation do not hold as well. Inasmuch as the mobile use context often is dynamic and involves tasks outside the computer, we argue that direct manipulation may not be suitable for mobile computers. Due to the dynamics of the mobile use context there is needed a set of interaction styles and interfaces for mobile computers from which the users can choose according to the conditions of the particular situation.

Future work involves exploring ways to enhance MOTILE, e.g., *"polar" as well as binary look-up,* by which the user can scan much faster simply by pressing the pertaining button longer or harder, *"pads" with physical scale and orientation,* rather than buttons, by which the user can jump relative to the magnitude of direction changes, and *semi-automated completion of input sequences* based on the frequency of previous user actions. We will also conduct a thorough evaluation of Motile.

6 Acknowledgements

The Mobile Informatics research program of the Swedish Information Technology Institute (SITI), and the MoBEE project with grants from the Research Council of Norway funded this research.

7 References

1 Hinckley, K., *et al.* (1998) "Two-handed virtual manipulation," *ACM Transactions on Computer-Human Interaction*, Vol. 5, No. 3, p. 260 - 302.

2 Nielsen, J. (1993) *Usability engineering,* San Diego, CA: Academic Press.

3 Shneiderman, B. (1998) *Designing the user interface. Strategies for effective human-Computer interaction,* Third edition, Reading, MA: Addison-Wesley.

4 Norman, D. (1988) *The psychology of everyday things,* USA: Basic Books.

5 Ishii, H. and B. Ullmer (1997) "Tangible bits: Towards seamless interfaces between people, bits and atoms," in *Proceedings of ACM 1997 SIGCHI Conference on Human Factors in Computing Systems,* ACM Press.

6 Sawhney, N. and C. Schmandt (1999) "Nomadic Radio: Scalable and contextual notification for wearable audio messaging," in *Proceedings of ACM 1999 SIGCHI Conference on Human Factors in Computing Systems,* ACM Press.

7 Hindus, D., C. Schmandt, and C. Horner (1993) "Capturing, structuring, and representing ubiquitous audio," *ACM Transactions of Information Systems,* Vol. 11, No. 4, p. 376 - 400.

8 Brewster, S. (1998) "Using Nonspeech Sounds to Provide Navigation Cues," *ACM Transaction on CHI,* Vol. 5, No. 3, p. 224-259.

9 MacKenzie, S., A. Sellen, and W.A. S. Buxton (1991) "A comparison of input devices in element pointing and dragging tasks;," in *Proceedings of ACM 1994 Conference on Human Factors in Computing Systems,* ACM Press.

10 Jacob, R.J.K., *et al.* (1994) "Integrality and Separability of Input Devices," ACM Transactions on *Computer-Human Interaction,* Vol. 1, No. 1, p. 3-26.

POBox: An Efficient Text Input Method for Handheld and Ubiquitous Computers

Toshiyuki Masui

Sony Computer Science Laboratories, Inc.
3-14-13 Higashi-Gotanda
Shinagawa, Tokyo 141-0022, Japan

Abstract. We introduce an efficient text input technique that can be used in various environments where conventional full-sized keyboards cannot be used. The technique, called POBox, consists of two steps for entering a word or a phrase. First, a user enters a small part of the word or some other attribute, and POBox dynamically searches a dictionary for candidate words and shows them to the user for selection. The user then selects the desired word from the candidate list, and POBox enters the word into the user's document. POBox uses the context of the user's document to help identify likely candidates. Many times POBox can predict the desired word based on the context. This allows the user to skip the first step and enter text even more efficiently. We show that the same technique can be applied to various handheld and ubiquitous computers including PDAs and cellular phones, where conventional full-sized keyboards are inadequate.

1 Introduction

Full-sized keyboards have been by far the most common and efficient text input devices. By using a keyboard, a trained user can enter hundreds of characters per minute. However, a keyboard is efficient for text input only if there is enough space to hold the keyboard, only if both the user and the keyboard are in stable positions, only if the user can use both hands freely, and only if the user is well trained. These conditions are too restrictive these days, since computers are to be used by anyone at any place. People might want to check their e-mail in a restaurant, browse the Internet in the kitchen, write an e-mail in a commuter train, write a text on a whiteboard in a classroom, write down their schedule on their handheld computers while walking, etc. In all of these cases, the user cannot use a standard keyboard, either because it is too large or because the user cannot use both hands. There is no doubt that in the future, computers will be mainly used in environments where using full-sized keyboards are inadequate. It is therefore important to develop a technique in which characters and texts can easily be entered in any of these situations.

We propose an efficient text input technique called POBox (Predictive cOmposition Based On eXample) that can be used in various environments where conventional keyboards are difficult to use. With POBox, users can efficiently enter text in any language by using menus, word prediction, and approximate pattern matching. In this paper, we first introduce various existing text input techniques which does not require a standard keyboard, and then we introduce the POBox system by showing an application of it for pen-based computers. We also introduce implementations of POBox on other handheld machines including cellular phones and wearable computers.

2 Overview of Text Input Methods

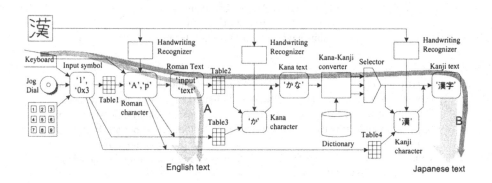

Fig. 1. Structure of various text input systems.

Figures 1 shows an overview of various existing text input systems. Line A shows how an English text is composed using a standard keyboard. Roman character codes are directly generated by the keyboard and concatenated to generate a text. Line B shows how a Japanese text is composed using a standard keyboard. Roman character strings are first converted to Kana texts which represent the pronunciation of Japanese words, and then they are converted to Kanji characters by a Kana-Kanji converter. Since multiple Kanji characters often have the same pronunciation, the user must choose the correct one by using the selector.

There are many reasons why text input on handheld computers is very slow. First, typing a key or writing a character is much slower than using a standard keyboard. Second, users have to type keys more times than when using standard keyboards, since small input devices often have smaller number of keys (e.g. cellular phones usually have only 20 keys). These keys can generate only a small number of input symbols, and combinations of the keypress must be converted to Roman characters using a mapping table (Table1.) In this way, input symbols must be converted more than once until the final text is composed. When entering Japanese text on a cellular phone, the input symbols must first be converted to Kana characters using Table3, and then Kana character string is converted to a Kanji character using the Kana-Kanji converter. A proper Kanji must then be selected using the selector. Hence, it takes a significant amount of time to follow these steps.

A variety of techniques for fast text input on handheld machines have been proposed. One approach is to make the speed of using a software keyboard faster. "QWERTY" layout is often used for the software keyboard, but QWERTY is not the best layout for a pen-based software keyboard, since frequently-used key combinations are sometimes laid out far apart and users must move the pen for a long distance to enter a text. "Fitaly" keyboard[11][3] is a layout for minimizing the pen movement on software keyboards. Since "e" and "n" often appear next to each other in many English words, they are put in an adjacent position on the Fitaly keyboard. Other layouts are also proposed to improve the input speed on software keyboards[2][4].

Another approach is to use fast handwriting recognition systems. Unistroke[1] was one of the first approaches in this direction, and similar techniques like Graffiti have become very popular on recent handheld computers including 3Com's PalmPilot. More sophisticated gesture-based techniques like T-Cube[13], Quikwriting[9], and Cirrin[5] have also been proposed.

Yet another approach is to give up entering characters one by one, and to use a word dictionary for composing a text. Textware's InstantText system[12] allows users to use an abbreviated notation of a sentence to reduce the number of input. For example, users can type "oot" to enter "one of the", or type "chrtcs" to enter "characteristics". These abbreviations are dynamically created and they do not have to be predefined. Tegic's T9 system[10] takes a different approach. T9 was originally developed for composing texts using only 9 keys on a standard telephone. On T9, instead of typing keys more than once to select an input character, more than one characters are assigned to the digit keys of a telephone so that users do not have to be concerned about the differences. Figure 2 shows a typical key assignment on a telephone keypad. When a user wants to enter "is", he pushes the "4" key first where "G", "H", and "I" are printed, and then pushes the "7" key where "P", "Q", "R", and "S" are printed. Using the combination of "4" and "7" corresponds to various two-character combinations including "hr", "gs", etc., but "is" appears most frequently in English texts, and the system guesses that "is" is the intended word in this case.

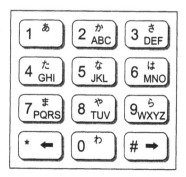

Fig. 2. Phone key assignment.

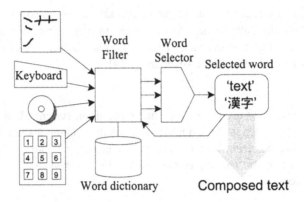

Fig. 3. POBox architecture.

3 POBox: Incremental and Predictive Text Input Method

POBox is a text input method for handheld and ubiquitous computers, with which only small number of user operations are required to compose a text. Figure 3 shows the architecture of POBox.

A text composition task with POBox consists of repetitions of the following two steps.

Filtering Step First, a user provides search keys for a word he wants to enter. Search keys can be the spelling, pronunciation, or shape of a character. As soon as he enters search keys, the system dynamically uses the keys to look for the word in the dictionary and shows candidate words to the user for selection.

Selection Step Second, the user selects a word from the candidate list and the word is placed in the composed text. Next input words are predicted from the context and are used in the next filtering step.

In most existing text input systems, users must provide all the information for the input text, either by specifying input characters or by showing the complete shape of characters by giving handwritten strokes. In POBox, users do not have to give all of them to the system; they only have to give information to the system which is enough for the search.

Users also do not have to specify all the characters or stroke elements which constitute a word; they only have to specify part of the input word and select it from the candidate list. This greatly reduces the amount of operations and time for composing a text, especially when selecting input characters is very slow or difficult.

This architecture can be applied to a variety of non-keyboard devices, including pen tablets, one-hand keyboards, and jogdial-based phones. We show how the same technique can be applied to many handheld and ubiquitous computers of different kind in the following sections.

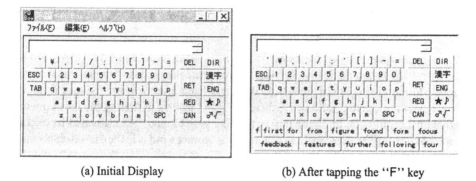

(a) Initial Display   (b) After tapping the "F" key

Fig. 4. Pen-based POBox.

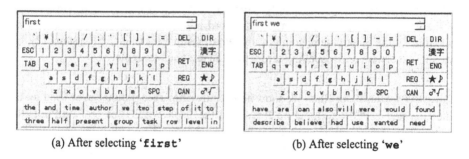

(a) After selecting '**first**'   (b) After selecting '**we**'

Fig. 5. After selecting "**first**" and "**we**".

3.1 Using POBox for Pen-based Computers

POBox was originally developed for pen-based computers[6], and it was extended to handle both software keyboards and handwriting recognition systems without changing modes[7]. We briefly review how POBox works on pen-based computers including pen-based Windows95 and 3Com's PalmPilot.

Using POBox on Windows First, we show how POBox can be used on pen-based computers. We use the previous sentence as a sample input text.

Entering English Texts Figure 4(a) shows the startup display of POBox running on Windows95. When the user pushes the "F" key, the display changes to Figure 4(b), showing the frequently used words that start with "F" in a candidate word list.

    Since the word "**first**" is a frequently used word and is found in the candidate list, the user can tap the word "**first**" so that it is put into the text area. After selecting "**first**", the display changes to Figure 5(a). In the menu at the bottom, the words that often come after "**first**" are listed in order of frequency. The next word, "**we**", often comes after "**first**", and this word is again in the predicted list of candidate words, and the user can directly select "**we**" by touching it in the menu. After selecting "**we**", the display changes to Figure 5(b).

In this way, users can repeatedly specify the search key and select a candidate word to compose a text.

Using Approximate String Matching When no word is found from the keys given by the user, POBox automatically performs approximate pattern matching in which words closest to the given pattern are listed. With this feature, even when the user does not give the correct spelling of a word, there is a good chance of finding the desired word among the candidates. In Figure 6(a), a user is trying to input "`Pithecanthropus`" without knowing the exact spelling. Even so, the correct word is in the candidate because "`Pithecanthropus`" is the word which is closest to the pattern "`piteca`" given by the user.

Also, by using the same algorithm, the user can give only part of the spelling to find the desired word. For example, if the user does not remember the spelling of "`Mediterranean`", he can specify "`mdtrn`" to see the list of words which are close to the pattern and then can find the right word in the list (Figure 6(b).) This feature is similar to the automatic creation of abbreviations in the InstantText system[12], but InstantText cannot allow spelling errors like the previous example.

Using POBox on PalmPilot We show how handwriting recognition can be used for the selection step of POBox[7]. Figure 7(a) shows the display of POBox on PalmPilot after the user taps the "ま"(ma) key on the software keyboard. The words listed are candidate words which begin with the pronunciation "ma".

When the user moves the pen after touching the tablet instead of tapping the software keyboard, the system starts handwriting recognition and interprets the strokes incrementally, and shows candidate words that begin with the strokes. Figure 7(b) shows the display after the user has drawn a line from the center of the software keyboard to the lower left corner. This is the first stroke of the Kanji character "入," and those words that begin with the character are shown as candidates. Unlike existing handwriting recognition systems that recognize characters only after all penstrokes that constitute the character have been written, incremental recognition can greatly reduce the number of penstrokes the users have to draw.

In this way, software keyboards and handwriting recognition are seamlessly integrated in POBox for pen-based computers.

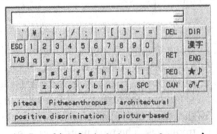 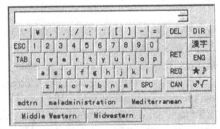

(a) Searching for '`Pithecanthropus`'   (b) Searching for '`Mediterranean`'

Fig. 6. Performing approximate pattern matching.

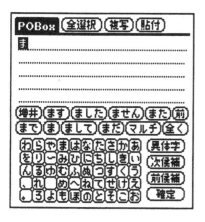

(a) Using Japanese soft keyboard   (b) Incremental handwriting recognition

Fig. 7. Using POBox on PalmPilot

3.2   Using POBox for a Cellular Phone

POBox can be used for handheld devices which do not have pen tablets. Instead of using a software keyboard or pen operations on a cellular phone, digit keys and a jog-dial can be used for the filtering step and the selection step.

Since the number of keys on a cellular phone is much smaller than the number of keys on an ordinary keyboard, it is impossible to select an input character with one keypush. We took an approach that is currently popular in commercial cellular phones; pushing the "7" key once to input "p", pushing the same key twice to input "q", etc.

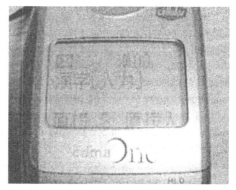

Fig. 8. CDMA cellular phone and POBox running on it.

Figure 8 shows the implementation of POBox on a CDMA cellular phone. The phone has about 20 keys on the surface and a jog-dial at the left side of the LCD display. Three or four alphabetical characters are assigned to each digit key (Figure 2) like standard push-phones in North America. Hiragana characters are also assigned to those keys in order to specify the pronunciation when used for Japanese text input.

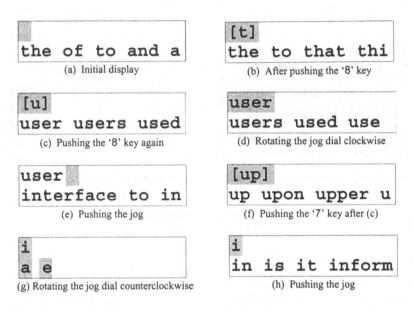

(a) Initial display

(b) After pushing the '8' key

(c) Pushing the '8' key again

(d) Rotating the jog dial clockwise

(e) Pushing the jog

(f) Pushing the '7' key after (c)

(g) Rotating the jog dial counterclockwise

(h) Pushing the jog

Fig. 9. Text input steps on CDMA phone.

Figure 9(a) shows the initial display of the phone. Frequently-used words are listed as candidates at the bottom of the display. When a user pushes one of the digit keys, the character printed on the key is shown at the cursor position and candidate words which begin with the character are shown at the bottom of the display (Figure 9(b)). When the user pushes the key again, the next character printed on the keytop is shown and corresponding candidate words are displayed (Figure 9(c)). A user can rotate the jog-dial clockwise at any time to select a candidate word. If "**user**" is the desired word, the user can rotate the jog-dial and display "**user**" at the top of the display. As the user changes the selection, more candidate words appear at the bottom of the screen for selection (Figure 9(d)). The user can then push the jog-dial to make the selection final. At this moment, next word is predicted just like pen-based POBox and next candidate words are displayed at the bottom. The user can again rotate the jog-dial to select a candidate from the list (Figure 9(e)). In Figure 9(c), if the user pushes the "7" key, "**p**" is selected as the next character for the input word (Figure 9(f)).

When a user begins rotating the jog-dial counter clockwise, the user can select input characters by the jog rotation. Input characters are sorted in frequency order; "**e**", "**a**", "**i**", etc. appear as the candidate input character as the user rotates the jog-dial. Figures 9(g) shows the display after the user rotated the dial three steps. When the user pushes the jog, the search character becomes fixed, and words which begin with the pattern are displayed as candidates (Figure 9(h)). The user can then rotate the jog-dial clockwise to select the candidate input word (e.g. "**information**".) Although using a jog-dial for

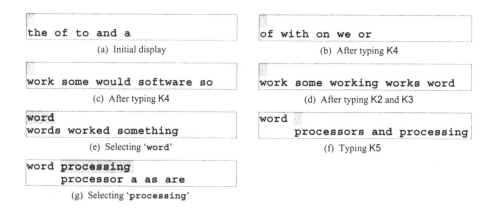

Fig. 10. Entering "**word prediction**" using one-handed POBox.

character input takes more time than using digit keys, using a jog-dial has an advantage; users do not have to touch the digit key at all and composing text only by one hand is possible.

3.3 Using POBox for One-hand Keyboards

A one-handed keyboard is sometimes more convenient for handheld or "wearable" computers. A large one-handed keyboard is sometimes more convenient for elderly people and handicapped people than using a full-sized keyboard designed for dextrous people. Some companies even claim that one-handed keyboards are the best input devices even when used on a desk.

One-handed keyboards have much less keys than full-sized keyboards, and the restrictions for text input seem to be the same as that for cellular phones. However, there are slight differences. When using a cellular phone, ordinary users cannot push more than three keys in one second. However, when using a well-designed one-handed keyboard, dextrous people can easily type more than 6 keys in one second. This means that, when using a one-handed keyboard, it is better for users to type as many keys as they can to perform an effective search of the dictionary.

With this consideration, we took an approach which is similar to the T9 system. We mapped all the alphabet keys to only four keys, each of which corresponds to each finger on one hand, excluding the thumb. All the keys which are pressed by both hands' forefinger ("f", "j", "t", "y", etc.) are mapped to one key (K2), and all the keys pressed by the middle finger are mapped to another key (K3)[1]. In this way, all the alphabetical keys are mapped to only four keys (K2–K5). So a word such as "**word**" is mapped to "K4 K4 K2 K3". On a standard ASCII keyboard, we can map the "a" key for K5, "s" for K4, "d" for K3, and "f" for K2. With this assignment, "**word**" is mapped to "**ssfd**".

Figure 10 shows how a text like "**word processing**" can be entered using this method. Figure 10(a) shows the initial display. By typing K4, K4, K2, and K3, the

---

[1] This number notation is derived from the notation used in piano scores.

display changes to (d), showing the first input word "**word**" in the candidate list. The space key is used for selecting candidates in this case, and when the user types the space key five times here, "**word**" comes to the text input area as shown in (e). When the user types K5 which corresponds to the first letter "**p**" for the next word "**processing**", the display will change to (f) and "**processing**" can be selected as the next word by typing the space key three times. From start to finish, in order to enter a text such as "**word processing**", 13 keystrokes were required in this case, which is not bad because "**word processing**" is made up of 15 characters.

This approach is similar to the approach used in the Half-QWERTY keyboard[8]. The Half-QWERTY keyboard can be considered as a "folded" keyboard where "k" and "d" are mapped to the same key position. Users can easily type "d" instead of "k" because of the symmetric nature of the human nerve system. Our method can be considered as folding the keyboard even more, until only four keys are left.

Just like T9, many different words fall into the same keystrokes in this approach. For example, "**word**", "**work**", and "**some**" are all mapped to the same keystroke "K4 K4 K2 K3". However, even when using the reduced keystrokes for the filtering part of POBox, it is not difficult to select a required word by typing the space key.

In our method, users who are able to touch-type do not have to remember new key-character mapping at all. With the key mapping on an ASCII keyboard shown above, the user only has to be careful not to move the fingers, and typing "f" instead of "r", "t", "g", etc. is not difficult.

Although this method looks similar to T9, there are significant differences. When T9 is used, users have to type n keys if they want to enter a word consisting of n characters. On the other hand, POBox does not use the length of a word as a key for searching a word, and users usually do not have to type as many as n keys before they find the desired word in the candidate list.

4   Discussions

4.1   Using POBox for Other Input Devices

We have already introduced variations of POBox using a pen tablet, a one-handed keyboard, and a jog-dial with a small number of keys on a cellular phone for the filtering step and the selection step of POBox. Virtually any input device can be used for POBox. It would also be possible to use gaze input, speech input, tilting input, etc. without big modifications.

4.2   Choosing the Best Combination

The most important design decision is to determine the interface for the filtering step and the selection step. Even for a device with very small number of input methods, this design decision is difficult. For example, in POBox for cellular phones, either a jog-dial or a keypad can be used for the filtering step and for the selection step. It is difficult to know which is better than the other. The ease of use depends on many factors including the input speed of the device, difference from existing methods, ease of understanding, etc.

4.3 Dictionary

Using an appropriate dictionary is another important point when using POBox. Since people use different phrases depending on the situations, it would be nice to be able to switch dictionaries according to the situations. For example, when replying to an e-mail, using the previous e-mail as a temporary dictionary would work well.

4.4 Other Advantages

There are more advantages of using POBox. We would like to mention other advantages of POBox not mentioned so far.

Avoidance of Spelling Errors Using POBox, all the input words are selected from the candidate list, so there is little chance of making spelling errors. This may be the reason why Japanese spell checkers are not as widely used as English spelling checkers.

Language-Independence The basic concept of POBox can be applied to any language, as long as the language has a finite set of notations. POBox can also be used for drawing symbols and diagrams if they are in a dictionary and can be searched by giving the appropriate keys for the search. Writing Kanji text with handwriting recognition is actually not very different from writing symbols.

Ease of Use POBox is an example-based input method, and users do not have to know how to write characters to compose a text as long as they know how to read characters. People who can read English are almost surely able to write English as well, but being able to read Kanji characters is completely different from being able to write them. The average Japanese person can easily read a word like "憂鬱"(melancholy), but only a portion of the population can actually write it without making a mistake. Even a pre-school child can compose text using POBox as long as he can read some of the character elements. We gave POBox on PalmPilot to a 6-year old boy without explaining what it was, and found that he was able to write a very long story without asking how to use it.

5 Conclusions

We have introduced an efficient text input technique called POBox, that can be applied to various handheld and ubiquitous computers where conventional keyboards are difficult to use. We have shown three examples of applying POBox to handheld devices, and have also shown that the same technique can be used for a wide range of handheld and ubiquitous computers.

References

1. Goldberg, D., and Richardson, C. Touch-typing with a stylus. In *Proceedings of ACM INTERCHI'93 Conference on Human Factors in Computing Systems (CHI'93)* (April 1993), Addison-Wesley, pp. 80–87.

2. Hashimoto, M., and Togasi, M. A virtual oval ieyboard and a vector input method for pen-based character input. In *CHI'95 Conference Companion* (May 1995), Addison-Wesley, pp. 254–255.

3. MacKenzie, I. S., Zhang, S. X., and Soukoreff, R. W. Text entry using soft keyboards. *Behaviour & Information Technology*. http://www.uoguelph.ca/ imackenz/BIT3.html.

4. MacKenzie, I. S., and Zhang, S. Z. The design and evaluation of a high performance soft keyboard. In *Proceedings of the ACM Conference on Human Factors in Computing Systems (CHI'99)* (May 1999), Addison-Wesley. to appear.

5. Mankoff, J., and Abowd, G. D. Cirrin: A word-level unistroke keyboard for pen input. In *Proceedings of the ACM Symposium on User Interface Software and Technology (UIST'98)* (November 1998), ACM Press, pp. 213–214. http://www.cc.gatech.edu/fce/pendragon/cirrin.html.

6. Masui, T. An efficient text input method for pen-based computers. In *Proceedings of the ACM Conference on Human Factors in Computing Systems (CHI'98)* (April 1998), Addison-Wesley, pp. 328–335. http://www.csl.sony.co.jp/person/masui/papers/CHI98/CHI98.pdf.

7. Masui, T. Integrating pen operations for composition by example. In *Proceedings of the ACM Symposium on User Interface Software and Technology (UIST'98)* (November 1998), ACM Press, pp. 211–212. http://www.csl.sony.co.jp/person/masui/papers/UIST98/UIST98.pdf.

8. Matias, E., MacKenzie, I. S., and Buxton, W. Half-qwerty: Typing with one hand using your two-handed skills. In *CHI'96 Conference Companion* (April 1996), ACM Press, pp. 51–52. http://www.dgp.toronto.edu/people/ematias/papers/chi96/.

9. Perlin, K. Quikwriting: Continuous stylus-based text entry. In *Proceedings of the ACM Symposium on User Interface Software and Technology (UIST'98)* (November 1998), ACM Press, pp. 215–216. http://mrl.nyu.edu/perlin/demos/quikwriting.html.

10. Tegic Communications. *T9*. 2001 Western Avenue, Suite 250, Seattle, WA 98121. http://www.t9.com/.

11. Textware Solutions. *The Fitaly Keyboard*. 83 Cambridge St., Burlington, MA, 01803 USA. http://www.twsolutions.com/fitaly/fitaly.htm.

12. Textware Solutions. *Instant Text version III*. 83 Cambridge St., Burlington, MA, 01803 USA. http://www.twsolutions.com/overview/overview.htm.

13. Venolia, D., and Neiberg, F. T-Cube: A fast, self-disclosing pen-based alphabet. In *Proceedings of the ACM Conference on Human Factors in Computing Systems (CHI'94)* (April 1994), Addison-Wesley, pp. 265–270.

Panel Session

Middleware for Ubiquitous Computing

Robert J. Aiken[1], Adam Abramski[2], Dr. John Bates[3], and Thomas Blackadar[4]

[1] Cisco Systems Inc., 6519 Debold Rd., Sabillasville, MD., 21780, USA,
raiken@cisco.com
[2] Sun Microsystems, 901 San Antonio RD., Palo Alto, CA., 94303, USA
adam.abramski@sun.com
[3] University of Cambridge, Laboratory for Communications Engineering,
University of Cambridge, UK
jb141@eng.cam.ac.uk
[4] FITSENSE,Wellesley, MA.,USA
tblackadar@pedinc.com

Abstract. The advent of cheap and ubiquitous computing is revolutionizing the way we work and play, as well as provide enhanced support environments for critical applications such as medicine. These computer and communications based environments will provide more capabilities and control to the applications and user and will provide them with a mobility not seen before. However, we need to first define and design some of the core middleware building blocks necessary to accomplish this evolution. This panel session will provide a short overview on the changing nature of our "electronic environment" and then the panelists will address 2 applications areas based on these new models as well as the requisite middleware to support them. The final panelist will discuss some of the underlying infrastructure to support these environments.

1   Introduction

The technological wonders of the 1980's (the PC and the local area network) and the 1990's ("dial up" access to the Internet and the Web) will soon be woven into a new tapestry that includes new modes of collaborative computing and electronic persistent presence (EPP). This new environment is based on the availability of abundant and cheap ubiquitous computing, mobile/nomadic network access, autonomous and intelligent software proxy agents, and the middleware necessary for enabling applications to utilize and manipulate the underlying infrastructure and hardware.

Local area networks that once only connected PCs and workstations are evolving to include wireless and mobile networks, body area networks (BANs), wearable computers, PDAs, as well as intelligent commercial buildings and residences. There is talk of interplanetary networks and we may soon see nano-nets. Our client-server models are evolving to include computational and informational grids, as well as teleimmersive and sensory feedback collaborative environments. All of these brave new world technologies are converging and will demand new middleware services to support them and to enable the applications to utilize these capabilities in new and innovative ways. Wearable computers will be organized into body area networks and will perform a variety of functions, such as monitoring biological signs or supporting multiple modes of communication (e.g. cell phone, video, audio) and computation. They will not only need to interact and peer with each other but also with other body area networks (BANs) as well as local area networks, building networks, wide area networks, and service level gateways. We are only now beginning the daunting task of identifying and developing the connectivity software, hardware, and protocols, as well as the enabling middleware required to support such an environment.

Imagine an icon or avatar that represents a person, process, or agent. Many types of relevant information and metadata will be associated with this icon. This information, which describes a person's or agent's status of "being on the net", will most likely be in some sort of a directory and will most likely have information indicating how that person or agent may be contacted. The status information will be under the direct control and management of the user or an agent so designated by the user. Assume that you click on my icon and if I am on the "net" via my ISDN line then the application client may spawn the audio and video connection, with perhaps other collaborative tools, sessions necessary for us to communicate. If I have just left my office and I only have mobile network access in the 32kbps to 56 kbps range then an alternative means of communication, e.g. email or audio, may be established. If I can only be contacted with a pager or cell phone the client software will dial the appropriate number that it retrieves from the directory. If my current default mode of communication indicates that I am not reachable (choice made by user) at this time then the caller can leave the appropriate type of message. Now lets go one more click further into the future. Assume that I have software and proxy agents that not only triage communication modes for me but also handle online commerce and other agent-agent transactions - even without my being on the net (I may be sleeping or on a plane). One such example is my "energy agent" which will constantly broker and negotiate, in real time, with the Utility power broker for determining the cost of a kilowatt based on my consumption requirements, time of day, and other variables. I may have many agents active all of the time (i.e. electronic persistent presence), some of them monitoring the infrastructure, others monitoring my various physical workspaces, and yet others conducting electronic commerce. These agents will be on all the time and will be communicating with other agents sans any explicit control by myself.

2 Panel Structure and Participants

The panel on middleware for ubiquitous computing will start the discussion by examining the middleware requirements necessary to support "body area networks" (BANs) as well as intelligent building area networks, which interact with their occupants. In addition, SUN's JINI will be discussed as a platform upon which one can build middleware and the necessary underlying infrastructure to support ubiquitous computing on a wide variety of heterogeneous devices.

Robert J. Aiken , Advanced Internet Initiatives Strategist, AII division, Office of the CTO, Cisco, will chair the panel and provide a very brief introduction on new environments (e.g. support mobile, nomadic, persistent, and ubiquitous computing) and the new and old middleware capabilities required to support them.

Tom Blackadar of FITSENSE will talk about bodynets, and the middleware required to make use of and manage a bodynet. For example, if sensors are used to track biological signs how will they communicate with one another and not other people's bodynets? What is the physical scope of the body network as well as what middleware is required to support new applications that can make use of this ubiquitous computing capability?

Dr. John Bates, Cambridge University, John will discuss "Active Middleware" to Support Personal Area Networking and Ubiquitous Computing". The concept is to support a number of applications, including sentient transport systems and sentient buildings (e.g. the Intelligent Hospital and the Active Home). These sentient environments support location and context-aware applications, e.g. applications follow you (patient vital signs, videoconferences etc) and the environment around you adapts to your personal preferences. He'll also mention how this technology can support augmented reality (when using "wearables"), virtual reality and a blending of the two.

Adam Abramski, SUN Systems, will speak on JINI and the middleware that is needed to enable both NEW and old applications to take advantage of this new capability and infrastructure enabled by JINI.

Towards a Better Understanding of Context and Context-Awareness

Moderators

Gregory D. Abowd and Anind K. Dey

Graphics, Visualization and Usability Center and College of Computing,
Georgia Tech, Atlanta, GA, USA 30332-0280
{abowd, anind}@cc.gatech.edu

Panelists

Peter J. Brown[1], Nigel Davies[2], Mark Smith[3], Pete Steggles[4]

[1] Computing Lab., The University of Kent at Canterbury, Canterbury, Kent, CT2 7NF, UK
P.J.Brown@ukc.ac.uk
[2] Computing Dept., Engineering Building, Lancaster University, Lancaster, LA1 4YR, UK
nigel@comp.lancs.ac.uk
[3] Hewlett Packard Laboratories, Palo Alto, CA, USA
msmith@hplmts.hpl.hp.com
[4] AT&T Laboratories Cambridge, 24a Trumpington Street, Cambridge CB2 1QA, UK
pjs@uk.research.att.com

1 Introduction

When humans talk with humans, they are able to use implicit situational information, or *context*, to increase the conversational bandwidth. Unfortunately, this ability to convey ideas does not transfer well to humans interacting with computers. In traditional interactive computing, users have an impoverished mechanism for providing input to computers. By improving the computer's access to context, we increase the richness of communication in human-computer interaction and make it possible to produce more useful computational services. The use of context is increasingly important in the fields of handheld and ubiquitous computing, where the user's context is changing rapidly. In this panel, we want to discuss some of the research challenges in understanding context and in developing context-aware applications.

We define context as any information that can be used to characterize the situation of an entity, where an entity can be a person, place, or physical or computational object. We define context-awareness or context-aware computing as the use of context to provide task-relevant information and/or services to a user. Three important context-awareness behaviours are the presentation of information and services to a user, automatic execution of a service, and tagging of context to information for later retrieval. Some of the main challenges in the area of context-aware computing are:

- the development of a taxonomy and uniform representation of context types;
- infrastructure to promote the design, implementation and evolution of context-aware applications; and
- a discovery of compelling context-aware applications that assist our everyday interactions with ubiquitous computational services.

2 Position Statements

Following are the position statements from each of the panelists.

2.1 Peter Brown (www.cs.ukc.ac.uk/research/infosys/mobicomp/Fieldwork/)

My view is that future research must focus more on the whole solution rather than on part solutions. There are two strands to this. The first is general to most research. When I was working with a company to create a hypertext product, I was told "People do not want hypertext: they want solutions. Hypertext is only likely to be PART of an solution". I often quote this maxim, as one can substitute almost any research area for hypertext. Certainly it applies to context-awareness. The second strand concerns bringing together technologies. You could get any of the following opinions from individual researchers in context-awareness:

- the key is the underlying database.
- context-awareness is a type of information retrieval.
- what we need to do is to solve the HCI issues.
- we need a solid theoretical foundation.
- if you want this to be real, you need to solve hard AI problems.
- it is a systems/software engineering problem.
- the area is waiting for the right hardware at the right price.
- context-awareness is a specialized area of distributed   systems.

All of these are at least partly true. The real key, however, is bringing the technologies together.

My theme, therefore, is that currently we researchers think too much in terms of our own pet technology. The reality is that this will only be part of context-awareness, and, if we are hoping for our research to be applied, this in turn will only be part of the solution. Certainly such success as we have had at the University of Kent at Canterbury has been the result of people with different outlooks getting together, but we, like others, still have a long way to go.

2.2 Nigel Davies (http:// *www.guide.lancs.ac.uk)*

Context sensitive systems and applications are those that respond to changes in their environment. Typically these responses are designed to improve a systems' perform- ance or to make its behaviour more relevant to the situation in which it is being used. For the purposes of this panel I propose to argue that in the near future all mobile systems will be context-sensitive: after all, why would you want a system which was not context sensitive? I will provide examples to justify this claim based on the results of our work on the Lancaster GUIDE project. This project has developed and de- ployed a context-sensitive tour guide in the city of Lancaster which combines mobile computing hardware, context-sensitive applications and wireless communications to provide visitors to the city with context sensitive, interactive applications.

A relevant publication is: Davies, N., K. Cheverst, K. Mitchell, and A. Friday. "Caches in the Air: Disseminating Information in the Guide System" Proc. 2nd IEEE Workshop on Mobile Computing Systems and Applications (WMCSA '99), New Orleans, U.S., IEEE Press, Pages 11-19.

2.3 Mark Smith

Context aware computing has the potential to allow applications in emerging service based computing architectures to provide completely new functionality. Client de- vices can use a wide variety of sensors to provide awareness of who the user is, and the location and environment in which the application is being used. Environment awareness can include such things as whether or not a user is still holding a device, if the user alone or with others, stationary or in motion, hot or cold, light or dark and so forth. Using this information, appliances and applications can be optimized and per- sonalized in ways that provide benefit to both technology providers and users. To realize this vision, I see six broad research areas in context aware computing. They cut across many of the technical areas in servers, services, transport and clients, both fixed and mobile, that make up future service centric system architectures.

1. Algorithms to render physical significance from sensor data. This is most obvi- ous in applications such as biometric based user authentication, but it can become very challenging in areas of environmental awareness. For example, an algorithm that exploits sensor data to robustly determine something seemingly simple such as if a device is still in the possession of a user can be difficult.

2. Technology for integrated sensors. Some sensors such as active pixel arrays can currently be integrated onto CMOS chips without using special processing, but what about other sensors such as motion or humidity. How can sensors be de- signed to allow multiple functionality, for example an imaging sensor that can be used for both biometrics and communication. Integrated optics is another chal- lenge both for capture and display.

3. Privacy issues. These go way beyond the security and encryption issues we have now. I would not be surprised if in the future entire conferences are given to this topic.

4. Agents that make use of sensor data. How are agents to be constructed that support dynamic persona in an application? How is the data that these agents use to be distributed? These are problems at the server and transport level.

5. Personalization of applications and appliances. One of the greatest benefits of using context aware computing is the ability to use sensor data to personalize applications and devices to conform to what the user expects. This is from the consumer's point of view the 'killer app'. These are problems at the application and client device level.

6. Capitalizing on the new spaces that context awareness enables. What customers will pay for, and what not. What partnering will be necessary across the emerging service centric computing community that is forming in order to make context aware computing real.

2.4 Pete Steggles (www.uk.research.att.com/~pjs)

What is needed in context-aware computing is a sufficient 'kit' of composable small services which really benefit from context-awareness. But with the right parts you can put together what I would call killer applications. We have just put together a system which combines follow-me desktops, camera tracking, text-to-speech, follow-me sound playing and 3D visualization to provide a recorded tour of our lab where we take a visitor round with a slide show following us, demo the technologies referred to in the show at the time, track the visitor with cameras and record the whole thing, giving the visitor a souvenir CD with a multimedia version of their tour with synchronized video. For us, when we have fully deployed our system, that will be a killer app!

Any description of the world that can be relevant to an application counts as a 'context type'. In our research we have attempted to create a very detailed model of the environment to address this. Inevitably, with so few real context-aware applications, there is doubt as to which facts will be useful and which won't. With respect to location, we have got a long way by attempting to model vague location-related facts using geometric containment and overlapping relationships. Really accurate location is 99% of the battle.

The MediaCup: Awareness Technology Embedded in an Everyday Object

Hans-W. Gellersen, Michael Beigl, and Holger Krull

Telecooperation Office (TecO), University of Karlsruhe
Vincenz-Prießnitz-Str. 1, D-76131 Karlsruhe, GERMANY.
{hwg, michael, krull}@teco.edu

Abstract. The MediaCup is an ordinary coffee cup augmented with sensing, processing and communication capabilities, to collect and communicate general context information in a given environment. In this project, coffee cups are computerized to integrate them and the information they hold—where the cup is, how it is handled, and whether it's hot or cold—as context into surrounding information ecologies.

1   Introduction

Computerization of everyday objects is a promising approach toward weaving computer usage into the fabric of our everyday lives. Many examples have been developed in which everyday objects are computerized to integrate them into specific computer supported tasks, including popular scenarios such as intelligent meal preparation with computerized kitchen gadgets, and personalized coffee consumption aided by smart coffee cups [4].

Beyond such scenarios and specific applications, we are concerned with how everyday objects can be integrated more generally into surrounding information ecologies. We propose augmentation of everyday objects with information technologies to obtain general context information, available to any application within a given environment. As an example, we have developed the MediaCup, a coffee cup augmented with sensors, processing, and communication to collect and broadcast context information obtained from ordinary use of the cup. The obtained context information—where the cup is, how it is handled, and whether it's hot or cold— has for example been used for colleague awareness.

The work we present is related to research on computerization of ordinary things, such as for instance carried out by the Things That Think consortium [4]. However a distinguishing notion is the consideration of everyday objects and of the information that can be obtained from them as general context in an information ecology. The MediaCup that we have prototyped makes a coffee cup and related information available as context, broadcast in some real or virtual environment, such as the workplace, or a multicast group on the Internet. The MediaCup work is also related to research on location- and context-awareness in smart environments, which has yielded for example active badges [5] and smart badges [1] attached to people and things to collect and communicate location information and possibly other context. In these efforts, new devices are introduced into an environment to make it smart. In contrast, in the MediaCup project context-awareness technology is built almost invisibly into already existing everyday objects, transparent to their everyday use.

2 MediaCup Implementation

The MediaCup hardware comprises sensors for temperature and acceleration, a PIC 16F84 microcontroller, an infrared diode for communication, and a standard Lithium battery (3V, 120mAh). To track movement, we have integrated the two-axis acceleration sensor ADXL202AQC of Analog Devices, which can measure both dynamic and static acceleration. The sensor uses 0,6 mA and is turned off between measurement cycles to save power. For temperature sensing we have integrated the DS1621 Dallas Semiconductor chip measuring from –55 to +125 °C, with 1μA standby current, and 400μA communication current. The microcontroller has 1792 Byte Flash RAM for programs, 68 Byte RAM, and 13 I/O ports used for control of temperature chip, accelerometer, and infrared diode. With 4 MHz, power consumption is below 2mA, and in sleep mode below 1 μA. With the Lithium battery, the MediaCup can be powered for approximately 2-3 weeks.

Sensor readings are taken every 50ms for acceleration, and every 3 seconds for temperature. The raw sensor data is processed on the MediaCup, applying heuristics to obtain cues regarding handling and situation of the coffee cup. Acceleration sensor data is mapped to three distinct cues: cup is stationary, drinking out of the cup, and fiddling around with the cup. Temperature data is mapped to the cues: filled up, cooled off, and actual temperature.

Cues are communicated every 15 seconds via a low-powered 3mm infrared sender SFH 409-s, using IrDA physical layer coding. In the MediaCup environment, transceivers already present in desktop and laptop computers can be used to receive cup IDs and cues. In addition we have built an overhead transceiver infrastructure into our office environment to connect MediaCups, and to track their location. We have used HP's HSDL 1001 IrDA Transceiver with 15 ° range, and about 1m² footprint.

Fig. 1. MediaCup prototypes.

Transceivers are connected via serial line to a computer that distributes cues in the MediaCup multicast group.

Figure 1 illustrates the evolution of MediaCup prototypes. The first version served for initial data collection but obviously was not fit for day-to-day use. With the second prototype, we embedded the MediaCup hardware in a non-obtrusive way at the bottom of a coffee cup. The third prototype now has the hardware mounted in the rubber base of the HUC99 coffee cup, allowing removal so that the cup can be dish-washed.

3   Application Experience and Future Work

We have used the MediaCup in colleague awareness applications. In a study of *Ambient Telepresence*, MediaCups and other devices in an office environment were used to track everyday activity which was then communicated to a remote workplace where it was rendered as subtle background noise, to promote a sense of remote presence in a non-obtrusive way [2]. In another colleague awareness application the MediaCup was used in conjunction with other environment based sensors to log user activity for production of a kind of comic strip of recent activity, accessible to co-workers [3].

MediaCup use in the described applications showed the utility of embedding awareness technology in everyday objects, however it also revealed shortcomings in our first prototypes. Cue recognition did not work reliably for similar cues, in particular for the cues drinking vs. playing with the cup. This is primarily due to the low frequency of accelerometer readings, a design decision to save power.

The next MediaCup implementation will be based on a PIC 16F877 or 16F876, with 14336 Byte Flash RAM to enable more sophisticated processing of sensor readings. To improve tracking of cup movement, we will integrate a 3-axis accelerometer, AMP ACH-04-08-05 of Measurement Specialities. For power management we plan to experiment with GoldCaps. Finally, we also consider integration of IrDA transmitters for two-way communication, for MediaCup uses beyond collection of sensor-based context information.

References

1. Beadle, H.W.P., Harper B., Maguire G.Q., and Judge, J. Location Aware Mobile Computing. Proceedings of IEEE International Conference on Telecommunications, Melbourne, Australia, April 1997.
2. Beigl, M., and Gellersen, H.-W. Ambient Telepresence. BHCI Workshop on Changing Places, Queen Mary and Westfield College, London, U.K., April 1999.
3. Chen, C., and Gellersen, H.-W. Cognition Based Collaboration Log for CSCW. The 2nd International Conference on Cognitive Science (ICCS), 27-30 July, Tokyo, Japan, 1999.
4. Poor, R.D., Hawley, M. and Tuteja, M. Things that Think. In: Personal Technologies, Vol. 1, No. 1.
5. Want R, Hopper A, Falcao V, Gibbons J. The Active Badge Location System. ACM Transactions on Information Systems, Vol. 10, No. 1, 1992.

Point & Click - Interaction in Smart Environments

Michael Beigl

Telecooperation Office (TecO), University of Karlsruhe, Vincenz-Prießnitz-Str. 1,
D-76131 Karlsruhe, Germany
michael@teco.edu

Abstract. A problem in smart environments is the interaction with a myriad of different devices, in particular the selection which of the devices should be controlled. Typically, different devices require different control tools. In contrast, a generic Point & Click appliance is proposed. To interact with a device in the environment this generic control appliance is pointed at devices for selection providing visual feedback to the user, obtains control information from the device, and allows control with the help of a simple user interface.

1   Introduction

An important issue in smart environments is how to interact with a wide diversity of devices, and one interesting but little explored aspect is how to select devices for interaction. Typical approaches are the use of separate controls for different devices (e.g. separate remote controls for TV and video), selection based on profiling of user action [1], and selection based on context-awareness technology [3]. As an alternative approach we propose the use of a generic Point & Click appliance. We call this appliance AIDE (Appliance for Interacting with Devices in the Environment)

Our Point & Click system consists of a control appliance, the AIDE device, for Ubicomp environments and a small extension for devices in such environments. We suggest a generic control appliance is useful in particular for interaction with devices, which possess *no own user interface*, or whose function is to be controlled although they are *in spatial distance*, but within visual proximity, and their *use is not familiar*. The following paragraph will present such a device and the belonging infrastructure.

2   AIDE: A Point & Click Appliance

"Pointing" is an important way of communication for humans, if (indirect) control over objects is to be executed: Pointing refers to things, which are of interest, both to inform about the things and to arrange control. Humans transfer this metaphor to the operation of technical devices: Although modern remote controls do not require pointing to the controlled device humans tend to direct them directly towards the device. The action of pointing is used to select an object for the following command (i.e. the device, which should be controlled). Pressing a key or the articulation of a command causes the selection to be performed. Therefore, the call of a function can be split into two phases: The pointing-phase where you select a device and the phase where a command is selected and send to the device by clicking.

2.1 Pointing-Phase

An important principle for the structure of user interfaces is feedback [2], which prescribes a response of the selected function to humans. If there are several devices located near to each other, no decision can be made which device should be controlled by simply pointing. Optical feedback has to be provided during the pointing phase before the selection itself is triggered. When pointing to a device which should be controlled the selected device has to be recognized by the human as selected. The system presented below simplifies the selection of a device by an optical feedback in form of a red laser-point. This phase of selecting a device by pointing at it and the optical feedback which device is selected are the major difference between the Point & Click appliance and universal remote control applications e.g. [4].

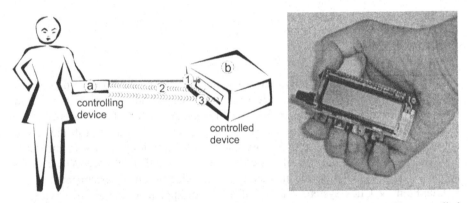

Fig. 1. The control appliance (a): A human selects a device in the environment (the controlled device (b)) with the help of a controlling device through a laser (1). After selection, commands are transmitted to the controlling device (2). A human chooses one of the displayed commands with the associated button at the Point & Select AIDE device (right figure).

2.2 Click

For pointing and selecting the device function we have developed a small control appliance (Figure 1, right), the AIDE device. AIDE has a LCD screen to display available commands that can be sent to the controlled device. The entire process of control can be described schematically as follows. First, the AIDE device (a) is directed towards the controlled device (b) and the activation key is pressed (pointing phase, 1). A laser beam gives an optical feedback, showing which device is selected. When the controlled device detects the laser beam, it transfers the control description to AIDE using infrared communication (2). This description containing all possible commands is shown on the AIDE's display. The user selects one of the displayed commands using the keys at the side of AIDE (click). The selected command is transferred to the controlled device and the action is carried out at the device (3).

3 Implementation

In order to designate the device for everyday usage it should be so small that it fits into a trouser pocket without problems. Handheld Computers as PalmPilot are still too big for the proposed usage scenario. Since no special requests regarding flexibility for communication and command display exist, we refrain from using standard markup languages and protocols as HTML/HTTP or WML/WAP. Plain text was used to describe the commands that are shown at the display. Each line of the display contains one instruction.

The AIDE system consists of two components: the AIDE control appliance and an extension for controlled devices, which can be attached to existing switching inputs (e.g. buttons). The AIDE device consists of 5 buttons, which are arranged around the LCD display, and a laser pointer, an IrDA (Infrared Data Association) communication unit and a processor. The LCD display operates in upright mode to support the handling of the AIDE device as a pointing device. The button on the right side is used as the activation key, the 4 buttons present at the left side as selection keys. The device is controlled by a PIC 16F84 microprocessor; communication is performed through an IrDA transmitter. The module used at the controlled device uses similar hardware, but without laser diode and LCD display.

4 Conclusion

We demonstrated advantage of generic control appliances as one possibility to control the diversity of devices in a smart environment. A major difference between the presented control appliance and universal remote controls is the split of interaction with devices in the environment into two phases: Point and Click, where in the pointing phase the control appliance provides a optical feedback to the user.

Further usability tests must show specific strengths of such a system. A further reduction of the dimensions of the AIDE device as well as an increase of the display resolution will widen the application possibilities.

5 References

1. Maes, Pattie: Agents that Reduce Work and Information Overload, Communications of the ACM, Vol37, No7, July (1994)
2. Norman, Donald A: The Design of Everyday Things, Doubleday (1988)
3. Schmidt, A., Beigl, M., Gellersen, H.-W.: There is more to context than location: Intl. Workshop on Interactive Applications of Mobile Computing, Rostock, Germany (1998)
4. Spinellis, D.: Palmtop Programmable Appliance Controls: Personal Technolgies, Vol 2, pp 11-17 (1990)

Wearable Information Appliances for the Emergency Services: HotHelmet

Chris Baber , David J. Haniff , & Robert Buckley

School of Electronic & Electrical Engineering
The University of Birmingham., Birmingham B15 2TT

Abstract. Much of the work into wearable computers has been concerned with the miniaturization of Personal Computers, e.g., 486 or Pentium-based. In this project, we ask whether it is possible to build a wearable device from much simpler electronic components. Specification for the device is based on the capture of user requirements, and constraints for the design are obtained from consideration of the operating environment.

1. Introduction

For wearable computers, the notion of using simple electronics in place of 'computers' raises fundamental questions concerning the nature of computers and of human-computer interaction. Norman [1] has proposed that future technologies can be considered as 'information appliances'. This links to the convergence between development of computers and development of other electrical products under the broad heading of embedded systems, e.g., see Badami and Chbat, [2]. Thus, wearable computers need not be miniaturized versions of the multifunctional Personal Computer (PC), so much as limited-function products which provide access to useful functionality when the user requires. From this argument, one can view wearable computers as embedded systems. This raises the question of how one might design 'information appliances' that can be worn by members of the emergency services.

2. Developing a Design Concept

The first stage of the design project was to demonstrate our wearable computer equipment to firefighters (see Baber et al. [3] for a description of the computer). We showed demonstrations of InterVision's ManuMax2000 with Seattle Sight head-mounted display, together with AURIX speech recognition software (from SRU, DERA, Malvern). The demonstration was enthusiastically received, with much being made of the futuristic appearance of the technology. Discussion of possible application to firefighters led to a sharp division of opinion. On the one hand, a wearable computer, with the capability to record comments and data, could be useful for Access Control Officers (ACO).[1] On the other hand, the wearable computer might be detrimental to operations on the fire-ground. Firefighters working in hazardous, often smoke-filled, conditions could have difficulty reading detailed visual displays; the displays might obscure vision, which is already limited by facemask and smoke; engaging in dialogue with the computer could distract attention from environmental hazards or other information. Currently, most communications between firefighters on the fireground is either verbal (through radio communications) or gestural. This suggests that information requirements are limited and relate to immediate needs. However, there is also concern as to whether one could monitor a firefighter's physiological status and communicate this to the ACO. There is a wide range of commercially available products which can be used to monitor basic physiological states, and work reported by Picard [4] suggests the possibility of using data collected from such measures to model the wearer's physical condition.

Manufacturers of breathing apparatus have been experimenting with the idea of using microprocessors to monitor air supply. For example, InterSpiro has produced a product which incorporate three LEDs to indicate status of the Breathing Apparatus (see figure one). The LEDs are green, yellow and red. Illumination of each, or a combination of these LEDs is used to signal specific information, e.g., a flashing red LED indicates sudden drop in pressure in the face-mask, green LED indicates 90-100% pressure in cylinder, green and yellow LEDs indicate 75-90% pressure, yellow LED indicates 50-75% pressure etc.

These developments in technology suggest that the concept could be profitably expanded to consider other measures that could be input to the processor and then displayed to the firefighter. Considering the likely user of the information, e.g., the individual firefighter vs. ACO outside the building, indicates whether information needs to be presented to the wearer or via mobile communications. Furthermore, asking what the wearer will do with the information tells us whether one needs to present digits / graphics or whether a single indicator will suffice.

Having defined a concept, the next stage has been to develop a working prototype. The design sketches show a conventional firefighter helmet fitted with a row of LEDs attached behind the visor, i.e., on the front rim of the helmet. Currently the prototype has been built using a 'Cromwell' helmet (from Helmet Integrated Systems), fitted with a row of LEDs on the inner rim of the helmet. Temperature sensing is performed using thermistors and thresholds are set using. When temperature exceeds the threshold, an LED illuminates. A countdown timer has been created using a row of 6 LEDs and a PIC microcontroller. Signals for distress and evacuation are presented using LEDs that flash in response to an external signal.

---

[1] An Access Control Officer will stand at the entrance to a building an monitor the ingress and egress of firefighters wearing Breathing Apparatus (BA crew). ACO would benefit from knowing the physical state.

Figure one: InterSpiro's Spirotroniq
breathing apparatus

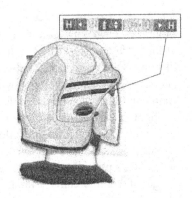

Figure two: Sketch of initial design
concept

3. Conclusions

While the equipment has yet to be trialled, it is apparent that the use of simple electronics (often employing off-the-shelf kits) has many analogies with rapid prototyping in software development. The definition of requirements has led to be construction of solutions for each requirement (which we consider an 'object') and objects are connected into a larger system. Further work will examine the co-ordination of the objects, e.g., in terms of prioritising calls between sensors and processors, and in terms of timing of events. The requirements of wearers of 'information appliances' can be met using software or hardware. This means that development of wearable technology needs to consider not only software solutions but also hardware solutions. This argument has been well-rehearsed in the embedded systems literature but could be a useful point of consideration for thinking about ubiquitous and wearable computing.

Acknowledgements
This work is supported by EPSRC grant GR / L 48508 'Human Factors of Wearable Computers'

References

1. Norman, D.A., 1998, *The Invisible Computer*, Cambridge, MA: MIT Press
2. Badami, V.V. & Chbat, N.W., 1998, Home appliances get smart, *IEEE Spectrum* (August) 36-43
3. Baber, C., Haniff, D. & Woolley, S. (1999) Contrasting paradigms for the development of wearable computers, *IBM Systems Journal 38 (4)* 1-15
4. Picard, R., 1997, *Affective Computing*, Cambridge, MA: MIT Press

Using Wearable Computer as an Audiovisual Memory Prosthesis

Jyrki Hoisko

Research&Technology, Nokia Mobile Phones, Elektroniikkatie 10,
FIN-90571 Oulu, Finland
Tel. +358 40 7080582, email: Jyrki.Hoisko@nokia.com

Abstract. This paper describes briefly the use of a futuristic audiovisual content recorder that supports retrospective episodic memory. The concept was explored by implementing a wearable prototype system, which was used to collect image and audio material over a period of several months. It was confirmed in this wearable computer context that image and audio data could help episodic memory to recall other facts related to that episode. This kind of technology could be useful in both working life as well as in free time.

1   Introduction

Progression in technology has provided mankind with ever smaller and powerful computing and recording devices. This new technology has brought new possibilities to enhance our personal lives with digital devices. With the accompanying reduction in size of imaging devices, we can assume imaging will be integrated into our digital assistants. New technologies in electronics and software make it possible to support man's most intimate mental tool, memory, in novel ways. *Memory prosthesis* supports the user in remembering personal things more efficiently. This functionality could be achieved with a carry-everywhere always-on wearable personal imaging and recording system that stores relevant information and keeps personal data warehouse of one's life by taking images and audio recordings. The relevant information can then be accessed manually by a user or automatically by a proactive device.

There are several definitions of human memory depending on the cognitive task at hand. *Episodic memory* is one's memory for personal events[1]. It has been proved that a) episodic memory is quite easy to recall and b) partial information helps to recall other facts related to that situation[2][3]. From images and audio, we ourselves can recognize cues about event like *physical location, people*, what happened *before* and *after the event, activity at hand*, and other relevant facts that work as triggers to retrieve the same moment back to our mind [4]. This way partial information may help memory to recall facts that were not even recorded by any device.

It must be noted that similar research activities do exist. Mann has conducted extensive studies with personal imaging systems [5]. Mann has also considered the use of a videographic memory prosthetic [6]. Eldridge and Lamming at Rank Xerox Research Center have studied video diaries that support human memory. They found out that a video diary works better to enhance recalling than textual representations of previous events [7]. Lamming et al. outlined the desing issues for memory prosthesis based on their experience with Pepys, Forget-me-not and ParcTabs [4][8]. Proactive agent-based Remembrance Agent by Rhodes is also closely related to the subject. His system collects textual information of user's life (emails, www-pages, persons met etc.) The system finds automatically a reference from user's memory collection to the subject at hand [9].

2 Overview of the System

At first, audiovisual material was supposed to be collected and browsed using a wearable computer (VIA II PC) attached with a digital camera and a GPS receiver. However, the system was bulky and rather uncomfortable to use. Since it was vital to collect material from everyday use, a method that is more unobtrusive had to be found. A small digital JPEG/MPEG camera by Hitachi residing in a shirt pocket provided much easier way to collect a material from places where wearable computers would have invoked too much attention. The camera allowed automatic shooting of an image every 30 seconds and had capacity for over 3000 high quality JPEGs, which were then fed to a database (e.g. once a day). Audio was recorded using binaural microphones and a portable DAT-recorder. The wearable computer was used to browse the material occasionally, however, usually collected material was put into use and browsed using desktop computer and a specifically built user interface. Both desktop and wearable computers had relational databases containing the location information, images and excerpts of audio plus additional annotations. The location information was simulated – we found that it was sufficient to enter the coarse location manually. This coarse location described only the greater scale location, like cities the user had visited.

3 Using the System

The material was collected during meetings, conferences and other events related to professional life, but also during free time activities like in parties, shopping or other casual situations. The system enabled both automatic and manual shots of images. Video wasn't used.

Queries of recorded material were made in relation to: 1) *location* in different scales, 2) a given *time-of-day*, *day-of-week*, and 3) *objects* and *activities* labelled by manual annotations, on- and off-line analysis (such as speech recognition and optical character recognition).

Since system didn't provide access to immediately recorded material, *short-term* applications were not experimented (like querying "Where did I park my car an hour ago?"). Instead, *longer-term* and *autobiographical* queries and applications were considered. Often, it was nice to browse the collected material just for fun to see what one had been doing in the past days, weeks or months. The material was browsed to see whom one had met, what interesting things there were in e.g. some conference or how the party evening had evolved. These queries were utilizing the material that was taken automatically. On other occasions the material was queried for specifically taken shots, such as manually taken shots of transparencies, papers, places or persons.

4 Utilizing Capacity

It is useful to consider theoretical recording capacities that could be utilized. The wearable computer system that was used provided over 3GB storage capacity. If we dedicate 2 GB for GSM audio (13kbit/s) and full-size digital images (~59kB each, 30 sec interval, ~15661 bits/s) and leave 1 GB for longer period thumbnails (~6.8kB each, 30 sec interval, ~1817 bit/s) we get temporal recording capacity as follows; with audio and full-size images: ~5 days, plus visual cues of 76 days. All together, this covers almost three months. The overhead caused by annotations, slack space and the database were excluded.

As storage capacities are constantly increasing, it seems like it is possible to record extensive periods of user's life. We anticipate that a hard disk of the size of a matchbox will have several gigabytes of capacity in near future. Our conclusion is that according to the available storage size, the concept of the memory prosthesis is feasible even today.

5   Conclusion

Location and time are usually sufficient query terms for retrieval, but labels and more specific query information are often needed. More infrastructure or means of analysis are needed to provide this information. It was noticed that viewing images and hearing audio of past actions could reveal and stimulate memory of ones personal history. These triggers can even help to recall things that were not recorded by any device. Pictures and audio clips can be used to support one's perception of biographical events.

The constructed prototype system proved to be beneficial and it was put to use in practice, in spite of its simplicity and primitive nature. This gave credence to the notion of the future success of more sophisticated devices of this type. The prototype clearly showed that recording capacity is not the limiting factor for these systems in near future, but rather that the means to easily retrieve material may prove a more formidable barrier. Lack of automatic annotation techniques to provide further information for retrieval is a major limitation. Furthermore social approval takes time, and social, privacy and legislative issues will doubtless emerge.

Although it seems like most of the everyday memory problems are prospective a wearable computer recording an audiovisual content could be useful for a great number of people to support their retrospective memory. This could be achieved by implementing a recorder as an intrinsic function in digital devices we would carry anyway on a daily basis. More throughout analysis on the subject can be found in [10].

6   References

[1]   Tulving, E.: How many memory systems are there? *Amer. Psychologist*, 40, (1985) p. 385-398

[2]   Wagenaar W.A.: My memory: a study of autobiographical memory over six years. *Cognitive Psychology*, Vol. 18 (1986)

[3]   Linton M.: Ways of searching and the content of memory. *Autobiographical Memory*, Cambridge University Press, New York (1986)

[4]   Lamming M. & Flynn M.: "Forget-me-not" Intimate computing in support of human memory. *Rank Xerox Research Center Technical Report EPC-1994-103* (1994)

[5]   Mann S.: Wearable computing: A first step toward personal imaging. *Computer*, vol. 30, No.2 (1997)

[6]   Mann S.: 'WearCam' (The Wearable Camera): Personal Imaging Systems for long-term use in wearable tetherless computer-mediated reality and personal Photo/Videographic Memory Prosthesis.In: *ISWC'98*. Oct 19-20 (1998)

[7]   Eldridge M., Lamming M. & Flynn M.: Does a video diary help recall? *Rank Xerox Research Centre Technical Report* EPC-1991-124 (1991)

[8]   Lamming M., Brown P., Carter K., Eldridge M., Flynn M., et. al.: The Design of Human Memory Prosthesis. *The Computer Journal* Vol.37, no.3 (1994)

[9]   Rhodes B.: The wearable remembrance agent: a system for augmented memory. *The Proceedings of ISWC'97* (1997)

[10]   Hoisko J.: Audiovisual Memory Prosthesis. Master's Thesis. University of Oulu, Dept. of Electrical Engineering, Finland. 72 p. (1999)

Today's Stories

Marilyn Panayi[1], Walter Van de Velde[2], David Roy[1], Ozan Cakmakci[2], Kristiaan De Paepe[2], Niels Ole Bernsen[1]

[1] Southern Danish University, Odense University, Faculty of Science and Engineering, Natural Interactive Systems Laboratory, Odense, Denmark.
{panayi, roy, nob@nis.sdu.dk}

[2] Starlabs, Starlab Research Excelsiorlaan 40, B-1930 Zaventem, Belgium
{ozan, wvdv, kristiaan@starlab.org}

Abstract. Research frameworks are being developed that involve very young children in the process of development of future technologies. Children, their teachers and parents from schools in Israel and Denmark are coming together with researchers, educationalists, psychologists, designers and technologists to develop a wearable technology - the KidsCam. This example of a hyper-camera will facilitate and support the development of social, communicative and emotional skills in the context of the everyday activities of children. It is envisioned that such digital technology will become embedded in educational culture and create opportunities for shared reflection on early life experiences. Issues that surround the development and deployment of new technology including those of appropriateness, need, value and ethics are an integral part of the project.

1 Introduction - Pedagogy and Interaction Technology Perspectives

The Today's Stories project is evolving a technology facilitated approach to learning for young children (4 to 8 years old) that is aimed at supporting the development of social, communicative and emotional skills of children in the context of the everyday activities. The facilitating role of technology will be complemented by the discovery of novel forms of educational interaction and the development of new media that often follows new technologies. Wearable technology will allow children to learn from reflecting on their actions and learn from other children's perspectives on their own actions. The technologies will facilitate capture and document such "reflective experiments in living". Children will build up their own but interrelated digital portfolio of their day's interesting events. A community memory of a group of children will be co-created and evolve through a didactic process of dialogue and reflection, leading to understanding. Children, teachers, parents, educationalists, developers, researchers and designers are focusing on the co-exploration of technology development in the context of a model knowledge sharing. At the Israeli site a future-oriented educational framework, *The Autonomy Oriented Education* paradigm is geared towards the development of autonomy, morality and belonging in children, Aviram [5]. In Denmark researchers are working both in local schools and focus groups to set up 'Communities of Enquiry'.

These children form groups of 'KidSearchers' ™, that are contributing to the development of this future technology. These interactive research paradigms have arisen from previous work by Roy et al [6] and Panayi and Roy [7] and are being developed within a Danish cultural context. The conditions for acceptance and success of deploying such technology in a social, cultural and ethical context are being investigated, Beach et al. [8]. It is envisioned that these interactive digital artifacts will enhance and also contribute to cross-cultural understanding and critical technology awareness.

2 KidsCam - A Deployment Scenario

The technology embodiment is currently envisioned as a **KidsCam** a 'wearable' device that audio-visually captures events in the child's daily life, and relays them to a collective memory of interrelated episodes. KidsCam is a hyper-camera, i.e. an ad-hoc network of communicating cameras that record a hyper-video document of interleaved episodes from different perspectives. The KidsCam is designed to have image and audio processing capabilities operating over a wireless local area network. The network will connect the computers to a server with two modes of operation for the KidsCam: 1) on-demand operation controlled by the children and 2) autonomous mode where the camera notices interesting events occurring and triggers the recording of cameras that share the same view.

Wearable cameras have been proposed by Starner et al [1], Healy et al in [2] and Mann in [3]. In [2] Healy describes a camera called the Startle Cam, which is triggered upon the detection of the "startle response" indicated by the wearer's skin conductivity. Techniques suggested in [2] and [6] for gathering information about the physchological states of the wearer using physiological signals, maybe of interest to Today's Stories in later stages of development. Mann proposed in a recent paper [4] the possibility of automatic generation of photo albums. These techniques maybe of interest to Today's Stories in optically determining which cameras are sharing the same visual view given that an interesting event is happening or about to happen.

Today's Stories differs from previous work by specifically targeting the ease of pedagogical implementation of new technologies in learning environments. The children will be wearing the hyper-camera during school-time. Usability issues are being explored and the interplay between functionality, novelty and intrusion are example of elements of the interaction being traced. Recognition algorithm will have two functions: 1) detection of interesting events occurring and 2) determining which children are sharing the same view given one particular interesting event. Machine vision techniques such as optical image flow are to be investigated to calculate distances between children as a feature for *"interest value"* of events. Image flow calculations can be aided by inertial data, received from accelerometers and gyroscopes as described in [9]. In [10] Davis and Bobick present a temporal template approach to represent and recognize actions such as aerobic exercises. Starlab already has a prototype of a camera that is able to gather inertial information about the camera motion, called the Metacam.

It is envisaged that temporal templates could be created, from different points of visual view. These representations of actions from each child's perspective could be used to infer specific information about interest in the visual field. Joint audio and video analysis of events may result in more robust decisions about the *'interest value'* of events. Coupling the KidsCam with biosensors is also a promising way of improving the *'interest value'* criterion. Feedback from children, during the authoring stage, could also be used to improve the recognition algorithm.

3 Artifacts for Reflection -'Composer' and 'Memory Boxes'

'The Composer' is a multi-media environment under development that will allow children to form their ongoing portfolio out of the different sequences that capture events from various perspectives. Digital events will be augmenting with voice, graphics and sound effects. A suite of annotation features will include stylized faces to express various emotions and special sound effects to highlight for example surprise or fear. A survey of state of the art multimedia editing and authoring packages and current use in educational settings is being carried out and incorporated into Roadmaps that will support the technology development [11]. A novel feature that is proposed with the 'composer' is the option for children to interact with the scene and objects at different levels of abstraction thus creating rich artifacts for reflection.

The interpretation of an event from its visual effect already influences the space that is being given to a child to express what it is that she found interesting about the event. For instance if a child gets emotionally involved in the face of a fight of two other children over a toy; and a teacher or other children see the scene depicted by images, the obvious interpretation of the scene is that it is the fight that has engaged the child. However, it may well be that the child is good friends with one of the children involved, or that it has a special emotional attachment to the toy itself.

Among the issues highlighted has been that of how to deal with the amount of information that one captures in the record. In order to explore the other end of the continuum, we are developing the **Memory Boxes**, a 'constrained record'. A Memory Box can be used to collect memories of objects, places or people (i.e. information item) which have been marked by special Memory Tags. By opening the little box in the presence of objects, places or people, a memory of them is stored into the box. Technically, a memory could be a pointer to a multi-media document that is associated with the information item - but not necessarily a representation of it. By opening the box next to a computer screen its content is visualized. By opening boxes near to each other their contents are mixed. And by shaking, a box it is emptied. With the boxes, the only 'recording' of the event will be in the collection of three pointers, 'memories' of e.g. the two children and the object. This leaves the initiative to explain what it recollects about the event and in what way it experienced it, completely with the child, and thus stimulates an alternative basis for reflection.

The 'Memory boxes' are currently being used with children to explore a number of notions of representation, relationship and interaction e.g. containment, information capture and exchange, proximity, intimacy, privacy, space and time. Digital portfolios are being created for both individual and collective using existing traditional technologies e.g. cameras, video cameras and digital toys and the new technologies as come on stream. This project provides the opportunity to explore how new technologies become embedded in educational culture, Panayi and Roy [12]. Prototypes and mockups of the Memory Boxes and the KidsCam will be available.

References

1. Starner, T., Mann, S., Rhodes, B., Levine, J., Healey, J., Kirsch, D., Picard, R. W., & Pentland, A. Augmented Reality Through Wearable Computing. Presence: Teleoperators and Virtual Environments, 6(4), (1997) pp. 386-398, MIT Press.
2. Healy, J. and Picard, R.W. StartleCam: A Cybernetic Wearable Camera. In Proceedings of the International Symposium on Wearable Computers, (1998).
3. Mann, S. A Historical Account of 'WearComp' and 'WearCam' Inventions Developed for Applications in 'Personal Imaging'. In Proceedings of the International Symposium on Wearable Computers, (1997) pp. 66-73. Los Alamitos, CA, USA: IEEE Computer Society.
4. Mann, S. Personal Imaging. ACM Mobile Networking, Vol.4 No.1 (1999) pp. 23-26.
5. Aviram A. *Personal Autonomy and The Flexible School*. International Review of Education 39(5): (1993) 419-433.
6. Roy, D. M., Panayi, M., Foulds. R., Ernshteyn. R., Harwin, W.S., Fawcus, R.: The Enhancement of interaction for People with Severe Speech and Motor Impairment through the Computer Recognition of Gesture and Manipulation. Presence: Teleoperators and Virtual Environments, 3 (3), (1993) pp.227-235, MIT Press.
7. Panayi, M., and Roy, D.: "BodyTek: Technology Enhanced Interactive Physical Theatre for People with Cognitive Impairment" in Ryohei Nakatsu, Edward J. Altman, and Claudio Pinhanez (Eds.) Proceedings of ACM 6th International Multimedia Conference, Workshop on Technologies for Interactive Movies. (1998), pp.35-39.
8. Beach, D., and et al.: Ethics of Developing and Deploying New Technologies (1999) in preparation.
9. Verplaetse, C. Inertial proprioceptive devices: Self-motion-sensing toys and tools. IBM Systems Journal Vol. 35, (1996) No. 3&4,
10. Davis, J. and Bobick, A. The Representation and Recognition of Action Using Temporal Templates. IEEE Conference on Computer Vision and Pattern Recognition (1997), CVPR'97.
11. Today's Stories Roadmaps Series - Technology Roadmap, Version 1, Internal document, www.starlabs.net. (1999).
12. Panayi, M., and Roy, D.: "Magic of Today: Tomorrow's Technology", Personal Technologies, (1999), (submitted).

On the Self Evaluation of a Wearable Assistant

Walter Van de Velde

Starlab NV/SA
Excelsiorlaan 40-42, B-1930 Zaventerm, Belgium
wvdv@starlab.net

Abstract. This note discusses preliminary ideas on evaluation the effectiveness of a wearable's role which we restric to autonomously providing advice on what may be interesting for a user to do. *Our idea is to view a piece of advice as entailing an expectation on future behavior, and to track user behavior in order to evaluate the effectiveness of the advice.* The full validation of the wearable, when taken along similar lines, requires to track how improved interests lead to new user behaviors, and we are starting to see how this could be done . The work reported in this poster presentation fits in a larger project called COMRIS[1], in which a wearable is being developed for use in a social context.

1   Introduction

The problem that we want to address in this paper is the self-evaluation of a wearable. Our concern is not the usability of the wearable, which mostly deals with interface issues and ergonomics. These are important issues, of course, and it may be impossible to detach them from any other aspect of evaluation. However, it is also the quality of the service that a wearable provides *in se* which determines its effectiveness. Before we can start to understand this effectiveness, we need thus to define what is the service that a wearable provides.

Wearables as Context-Sensitive Advisors

In this note I want to restrict myself to a particular kind of wearable, namely an output-only device that gives advice on what its user (host) may want to do. We are thinking in particular of social contexts. In the COMRIS project we develop an infrastructure to support social processes in dynamic communities, for instance at large conferences or industrial fairs. The COMRIS parrot is the most visible part of the project - but COMRIS is much more than its wearble! - and by now also its hallmark. It is a wearable device that speaks to its 'user' words of advice and hints as she walks through the fair [1].

---

[1] COMRIS (project number 26900) is partially funded by the EU in its long-term research initiative on Intelligent Information Interfaces (i3). COMRIS stands for Co-Habited Mixed Reality Information Spaces. See arti.vub.ac.be/~comris. The views expressed in this paper are not necessarily those of the COMRIS consortium.

A phrase that has regularly been used to illustrate the parrot's advice giving is the following: "A presentation on numerical learning methods, a topic you are definitely interested in, is starting in 5 minutes in room B. You may want to catch the speaker afterwards since he is a reviewer for your I3 project. Maybe you want to say hi to your friend Sandy who is near you. Don't forget to mention the present that she gave to you last time you met". This text is essentially in three parts, each of which mixes a piece of raw information, elements for personalization, and elements for contextualization.

With the word context, we refer to the spatio/temporal/social circumstances in which a wearable's user ('host') is situated [2]. The ability to perceive this context is, I believe, the key difference between wearable and other types of computing devices. With context perception it is possible for a device and for the services it provides to take initiatives based on its own perception of where the host is, what is happening around her, what she is doing, or what she is up to. Whereas traditional computing can go as far as user profiling, wearables are the obvious platform to go beyond.

The COMRIS parrot is an output-only device. This means that it requires no explicit input from its host, e.g., in the form of a command and control language. All the parrot has is context perception, which it uses as a means to find out which of the things it can do are most useful to the host. With context perception we refer to the ability of capturing, without explicit user interaction, the context in which a device is being used. In our case, since the parrot device is being worn on its human host, this context closely matches the host's context.

The COMRIS parrot is based on a StrongARM processor. In a two-layer sandwich construction we have squeezed two PCMCIA slots and all the rest that is normally found within a powerful state of the art laptop. The wallet sized pack runs LINUX, from which a LAN is wirelessly accessed and interface peripherals are addressed, in particular for speech output. The 'eyes' for context perception are no more than a bunch of active infrared to identify places and to locate other parrots, although in [2] we go much further. Apart from this, the parrot is essentially an output-only device.

2   Advice as Expectation

An output-only device has no means for the user to provide any feedback. In fact, in the spirit of a pure wearable, such feedback is likely to be always implicit. An important issue is how such a system can be evaluated or, how it can evaluate itself.

The key insight we want to build on is the following: _The parrot's advice creates an expectation on future behavior._

The COMRIS parrot is trying to bias host behavior toward those activities which it deems most likely to lead to enhancing user interests. For instance, if a user wants to know as much as possible about a certain subject area, then the parrot will aim to get its host to listen to talks on that subject, to read the relevant papers or to talk to the best people in that field (see also Sect. 3 on the notion of interest).

At a first level, then, the parrot will consider itself maximally successful if the host follows each and every advice that it is giving to it. This is, in its purest formulation, a debatable statement but it is a starting point.

Example 1. Suppose the parrot gives a nearness notification. This means for instance that a participant that a host wanted to meet (or avoid) is nearby. Such a notification thus comes in two variations: avoid or encounter. Both of these entail an expectation about future behavior. On the one hand the parrot's host is expected to avoid the neighbor entity, in the other it is expected to approach it. In other words, based on this advice, re-enforcement can be derived by tracking how long the nearness to the neighbor is maintained by the host.

Example 2. Suppose the parrot gives an advice on being in room B for an interesting talk at 2 o'clock. This corresponds to an expectation that the host will be in room B at 2 o'clock. A re-enforcement can be derived by tracking presence in room B around the time of 2 o'clock. Maximal re-enforcement can be inferred when the user is their at exactly 2 o'clock. Around this optimum a bell-shaped function reflects re-enforcement from deviating behavior.

3 Interest as Resource for Behavior

At the next level, much more difficult to deal with, the issue is how one can evaluate the overall performance of a wearable. In COMRIS the aim of the whole enterprise is to further a user's interests. For instance a user may want to know as much as possible about a certain topic, or may want to get acquainted with as many people as possible in a particular field. But these are just means to an end, the end being behavior. For the time being we represent an interest as a data structure with a measurable satisfaction function defined on it. An interest represents the pursuit of a resource for behavior, but it leaves in the middle what that behavior is. Thus, an interest is neither a goal nor a task. It is not limited in time, neither is it something reachable.

Does this mean that host behavior is 'perfect', when she always follows the parrot's advice? No, *an interest being a resource for behavior* (and thus not a goal or task), the ultimate evaluation is in the deployment of the behaviors that such resources enable, for instance better teaching, more convincing argumentation, better usage of time, and so on. This is a secondary effect of parrot advice, and more important, but also more difficult to trace and measure.

The ultimate reflection of improved interest satisfaction is thus in behavior. Consequently, it should be traceable by context perception. However, it seems obvious that for this much more fine grained context perception is required, for instance as explored in the project TEA [2]. The prospect of this is however that interests as such do not need to be measurable except through the successfulness of the behaviors which they enable.

References

1. Van de Velde, W.: Co-habited mixed realities. In *Proceedings of the IJCAI workshop on Social Interaction and Communityware,* Nagoya, Japan (1997).
2. Schmidt, A., Aidoo, K.A., Takaluoma, A., Tuomela, U., Van Laerhoven, K. and Van de Velde, W.:Advanced Interaction in Context. In *Proceedings of the Symposium on Handheld and Ubiquitous Computing.* Lecture Notes in Computer Science. Springer Verlag, Heidelberg. (1999). (this volume).

On Positioning for Augmented Reality Systems

Stelian Persa[1], and Pieter Jonker[1]

[1]Pattern Recognition Group, Delft University of Technology
Lorentzweg 1, 2628 CJ Delft, The Netherlands
{stelian,pieter}@ph.tn.tudelft.nl

Abstract. In Augmented Reality (AR), see-through Head Mounted Displays (HMDs) superimpose virtual 3D objects over the real world. They have the potential to enhance a user's perception and his interaction with the real world. However, many AR applications will not be accepted until we can accurately align virtual objects in the real world. One step to achieve better registration is to improve the tracking system. This paper surveys the requirements for and feasibility of a combination of an inertial tracking system and a vision based positioning system implemented on a parallel SIMD linear processor array.

1   Inertial tracking for Augmented Reality

Position and Orientation Tracking is used in Virtual and Augmented Reality (VR, AR). With a plethora of different graphics applications that depend on motion-tracking technology, a wide range of interesting motion-tracking solutions have been invented [1],[2]. Many applications only require motion over a small region, and these tracking approaches are usable, although there are still difficulties with interference, line-of-sight, jitter and latency. A modern six-degree of freedom sensor is the IS-600[3]. Its inertial sensor simultaneously measures 9 physical properties: angular rates, linear accelerations, and magnetic field components along all 3 axes. Micro vibrating elements are used to measure angular rates and linear accelerations. The angular rate signals are integrated in a direct manner to obtain orientation. The linear acceleration signals are double integrated to track changes in the position. However, this leads to an unacceptable rate of positional drift and must be corrected frequently by some external source. Hence the system uses an acoustic time-of-flight ranging system to prevent position and orientation drift. The accelerations are also fed into an error estimator to help cancel pitch and roll drift. The yaw drift is corrected by the acoustic range measurements simultaneously with the position drift. This leads to a:
- Max. Angular Rate: 1200°/sec [3]   - Angular Accuracy: 1.3° RMS [4]
- Translation Accuracy: 3.6 RMS(mm)[4] - Prediction: 0-50ms [3]
- Orientation Update Rate: up to 500Hz[3] - Position Update Rate: up to 150Hz [3]

The question is whether such a tracker is feasible for our Retinal Scanning Display for Augmented Reality [8]. The accuracy needed for registration of the real and virtual images on such a see-through headset involves two aspects, spatial accuracy and latency. The user of a Virtual Reality system will tolerate, and possibly adapt to errors between his perceived motion and the visual result. However, with an

Augmented Reality system the registration is within the visual field of the user and hence the visual effect may be more dramatic.

For spatial accuracy we use the fact that the central fovea of a human eye has a resolution of about 0.5 minute of arc [7] and that it is capable of differentiating alternating brightness bands of one minute of arc. For latency we can reason that at a moderate head rotation rate of 50 degrees per second the system lag must be $\leq$ 10 ms to keep angular errors below 0.5 degrees.

The IS-600 system is measured as having about 1^0 RMS static orientation accuracy and a 3^0 RMS dynamic accuracy. We must conclude that although suitable for applications in virtual reality, this accuracy is probably inadequate for AR tracking.

To illustrate this we map this error onto the 2D-image domain of our see-through headset. Considering f_x the focal length of a video camera (in pixels), L_x be the horizontal image resolution and θ_x the Field-Of-View of the camera, then the ratio of image pixel motion to the rotation angels (in pixels/degree) is:

$$\frac{L_x}{\theta_x} = \frac{L_x}{2 \arctan\left(\frac{L_x}{2 f_x}\right)} \tag{1}$$

E.g. with an image resolution of 640x480 and a focal length $f_x = 600$ pixels, the 1^0 RMS static accuracy of the tracker leads to 11 pixels misalignment between real and virtual objects on our see through headset.

2   Real-time vision for the correction of position drift

To correct positional drift in a 6-DOF inertial tracking system, some type of range measurements to known points in the environment is required. For outdoor operation, only a vision-based system is suitable, because for all the other systems the resolution is inadequate (GPS), the range is too small and/or the sensors are not suitable to operate outside (Acoustic). Hence we investigated image processing algorithms and architectures for fast feature and fiducial tracking. We foresee a vision system that searches and tracks known features in outdoor scenes, such as lines, corners and man made fiducials to calculate a pose to be used to correct the drift of the inertial tracker.

In order to obtain fast pose estimations we implemented the algorithms on a parallel architecture for real-time image processing, the IMAP-Vision board, a frame grabber and Linear Processor Array (LPA) of 256 8 bit processors in SIMD mode on a single PCI board. The board is programmed in a data parallel version of C [5].

Our line detection is a parallel Sobel edge detector followed by a parallel Hough Transform. Sobel operator and Hough transform over 1300 points takes 49 ms on the IMAP-Vision system. The error in estimation of the line segment is about one pixel for the radius and 0.7 degree for the angle. These errors can be reduced by increasing the parameter space, however, this will increase the execution time. We implemented two corners detection algorithms in a data parallel way. Our parallel implementation on the IMAP-Vision system of the Kitchen and Rosenfeld corner detector takes 7ms and about 3ms for a gradient direction corner detector. The last one needs a false corner suppression postprocessing. To regularly calibrate the AR headset on the Campus we can use man-made fiducials onto known positions. The vision system can recognise these and automatically reset position and orientation of the tracker, when sufficient correspondences are found. As fiducials we used small square red blocks (forming a dot-code) on a larger black background. Our fiducial recognition algorithm takes 25msec. and has an error of about 9mm in real world if the camera is 3m apart and the FOV of the camera is 45 degree, due to the resolution of the grabber (256^2)

Subsequent pose estimation takes from 15msec. to 2sec. on a Pentium depending on the initial guess of the pose, and with a Kalman filter we could estimate recursively the position and uncertainty of a moving feature point in each next frame. The Kalman filter also fuses the information from inertial measurement unit with the data from vision system. We estimate that on a Pentium this takes about 10msec. With a total pose update rate of 60 msec., and an accuracy of 9mm we conclude that it is feasible to make vision trackers based on parallel Image Processing Architectures, for the correction of position drift in inertial trackers for Augmented Reality applications.

3 Results and conclusions

In this paper we surveyed the requirements for and feasibility of a combination of an inertial tracking system and a vision based positioning system for augmented reality systems. At a moderate head rotation rate of 50 degrees per second, the lag of such a system must be $\leq$ 10 ms to keep angular errors below 0.5 degrees. The dynamic accuracy for rotations of 1°, yields a registration error of 11 pixels, which forms a problem for objects far away from the camera.

We developed a visual system based on a parallel image processing array. A fiducial tracker takes 25 msec and the error is about 9mm. We can conclude from this results that the IMAP-VISION board is suitable as a vision system for outdoor augmented reality applications.

This work has been conducted in the framework of the Ubiquitous Communication Project (UbiCom) from the TU Delft (http://www.ubicom.tudelft.nl/).

References

1. Christine Youngblut, Rob E. Johnson Sarah H. Nash, Ruth A. Wienclaw: Review of Virtual Environment Interface Technology, Institute for Defense Analyses
2. J. Borenstein, H.R. Everett, L. Feng. Where am I? Sensors and Methods for Mobile Robot Positioning, University of Michigan
3. InterSense IS-600 User Manual
4. F. Kuijper, A. Smits, H. Jense: Traking Systems and the Value of Inertial Technology, Proc. of SPIE Conference on The Engineering Reality of Virtual Reality, pp.386-397, 1999.
5. S. Kyo, S. Okazaki, Y. Fujita, et:A Parallelizing Method for Implementing Image Processing Tasks on SIMD Linear Processor Arrays, CAMP'97, pp.180--185, 1997
6. Azuma, R., Bishop, G. (1994). Improving static and dynamic registration in an optical see-through HMD. Proceedings SIGGRAPH '94 : 197-204.
7. Jain, A. K. (1989). Fundamentals of Digital Image Processing. Englewood Cliffs, NJ, Prentice Hall.
8. Gerardus Cornelis de Wit: A Retinal Scanning Display for Virtual Reality, PhD Thesis, Technical University Delft, 1997

Hippie: A Nomadic Information System

Reinhard Oppermann, Marcus Specht and Igor Jaceniak
GMD - German National Research Center for Information Technology
Institute for Applied Information Technology (FIT-PIC)
D-53754 Sankt Augustin
{reinhard.oppermann, marcus.specht, igor.jaceniak}@gmd.de
http://fit.gmd.de/hci/projects/hips

Abstract: Hippie is a WWW-based nomadic information system that supports users before, during, and after a visit to exhibitions. The system models the visitor's knowledge, preferences, and interests and tracks his/her position while moving in the physical space with Infrared, electronic compass and DGPS technologies. Therefore the user-modeling component of Hippie enables the system to adapt presentations, recommend tours, or alert the visitor when he/she passes hotspots in the exhibition. The underlying metaphor of connecting information space and physical space is applicable in many fields and arouses new challenges for user modeling and user adaptive systems.

1. Introduction

Hippie [1] is a WWW-based guide offering added value to current information facilities by supporting the multiplicity of activities during the preparation, the execution and the evaluation of a museum/fair visit[1]. The process orientation is made possible by the nomadic characteristic [2] of the system that allows the user to have access to his or her personal information space from all places independently from specific devices. The context takes into account the current position and direction of the user, his personal characteristics like knowledge and interests and the environmental conditions like physical arrangements and technical tools.

Table 1. Process oriented scenario

Visit-Process	Visitor Activities	System Support
Preperation (at home)	• Browsing exhibit database • Print summary information • Check pricing and opening hours • Accessing meta-information • Setting up a tour or hotspots	• Accessing the system via WWW from Home • Presenting text, graphic and animation output
Execution (in exhibition)	• Searching exhibits • Looking at exhibits • Overlaying the real artwork with explanations • Entering own annotations • Contacting people (Appointments and discussions)	• Accessing the System with mobile device via WLAN • Audio presentation (headphones), text, graphics and animations • Visitor tracking, Adaptive Maps

---

[1] The prototype Hippie was developed by GMD in the context of the project "Hyperinteraction within Physical spaces" (HIPS), an EU-supported LTR project in ESPRIT I³. The partners of the consortium are University of Siena (co-ordinating partner), University of Edinburgh, University College Dublin, ITC, SINTEF and GMD, CB&J, and Alcatel.

Evaluation (at home)	• Call to mind received information and annotations • Searching additional information	• Access to full information space and to seen objects • Address book automatically updated

Before a visit a user can browse all exhibits, prepare tours, and mark individual hotspots. The information selected and presented is adapted to the interests, the knowledge and the presentation preferences of the user [3]. During the actual visit augmented reality components for artwork interpretation and mainly audio output complement the visual modality preoccupied by the physical environment. Furthermore position tracking and location systems in the exhibition place allow for the adaptation of hippie to the current visitor position (at home or in front of a certain exhibit). The system automatically identifies the relevant objects close to the visitor and multi-modal information presentation takes into account the specific environmental constraints for information perception in the physical context.

Two main elements for the process orientation of the system, the internet-based personal information space and the learning capability of the system of the evolving knowledge and interest of the visitor, are described below in some more detail.

2. Nomadic Information Systems for Individualised Process Support

Internet connectivity provides access to the information basis from all over the world. At home the user can access the system with a desktop computer with high resolution presentations to study the site of interest, e.g., a content list and pictures of an exhibition, descriptions of individual artworks and artists as well as practical information about opening hours, ticket prices etc. Furthermore he/she can prepare an actual visit entering annotations or hotspots for important exhibits.

The visit in the exhibition is supported by a handheld/wearable computer (PDA) with wireless LAN connection. Being in the museum the user can move around and explore the environment with exhibits of particular interest for him or her. The system identifies the current position of the visitor and updates the appropriate information proposal for the visitor who can select the proposed information presentation or proceed to another interesting exhibit where information about the exhibit are welcome. The visitor access the same information space he or she is already familiar with from sessions at home including own annotations and hotspots or with a tour including exhibits of a particular importance for the visitor (see table 1).

3. Information Adaptation to User's Knowledge and Interests

The adaptive component runs a user model describing the knowledge and the interests of the user. The user model automatically evaluates the user's interaction with the system in the information space and the user's physical navigation in the museum. The adaptation to the assumed pre-knowledge is performed by avoiding redundancy and by referring to earlier presentations. When the visitor has already seen an exhibit and received a set of information presentations he or she only gets the name and a thumbnail presentation of the exhibit to ensure the user the system has selected the correct item. The adaptation to the assumed interests of the user is provided by adaptive tour and object recommendations. If a user has selected a number of objects (exhibits) the user model identifies common attributes of the selection in terms of, e.g., artist, style or genre. In case of exceeding a rule-defined threshold for a significant interest of the visitor in this kind of artworks the system initiates a "Tip" with a user specific tour containing relevant additional artworks [4].

The same rule-based mechanism is applied for the presentation of attributes of the artworks. If the user selects a set of particular interesting attributes the system recommends to present this set of attributes as a default sequence of attributes for the given class of objects or during a second stop of the visitor at an artwork the system presents appropriate attributes complementary to the attributes he or she has selected during the first stop.

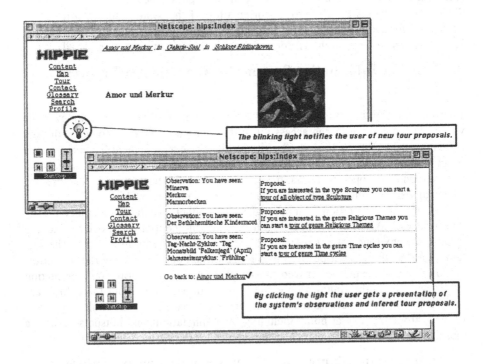

Fig 1: Notification of an adaptive tour proposal

4. Summary

Contextualised information presentation takes into account more than just the user's location [5]. A contextualised information space is defined by an information repository adapted to the location, the characteristics of the user like knowledge, interest or interaction or presentation preferences. The prototype presented in this paper supports the process of art perception at three steps, the preparation of a museum visit, the execution of the visit itself and the evaluation of the visit. The system adapts the information presentation to the evolving knowledge and interest of the visitor to enrich the benefit and the visit in terms of knowledge and enjoyment.

Formative evaluations of the system by domain and human factors experts were reflected in several redesign cycles; summative evaluations with real users are planned for this summer.

5. References

1. Oppermann, R. and M. Specht. *A nomadic Information System for Adaptive Exhibition Guidance.* in *ICHIM99, International Cultural Heritage Meeting.* 1999. Washington, D.C.:
2. Kleinrock, L., *Nomadicity: Anytime, Anywhere.* Mobile Networks and Applications, (1997). **1**(4): p. 351-357.
3. Brusilovsky, P., *Efficient Techniques of adaptive hypermedia,* in *intelligent Hypertext,* C. Nicholas and J. Mayfield, Editor. (1997), Springer: Berlin, Heidelberg, New York. p. 12-27.
4. Oppermann, R., Adaptively supported Adaptability. International Journal of Human-Computer Studies, (1994). 40: p. 544 - 472.
5. Abowd, G.D., Dey, A. K., Abowd, G., Orr, R., and Brotherton, J. *Context-awareness in wearable and ubiquitous computing.* in *1st International Symposium on Wearable Computers.* 1997. October 13-14:

A Rapidly Configurable Location-Aware Information System for an Exterior Environment

R.P. O'Rafferty, M.J. O'Grady, G.M.P. O'Hare

PRISM, Dept. of Computer Science, University College Dublin (UCD), Dublin 4, Ireland.
{Ronan.ORafferty, Michael.J.OGrady, Gregory.OHare } @ucd.ie

Abstract. This paper describes the implementation of a prototype location-aware tourist information system. Particular emphasis is paid to the layered architecture and the rapid configurability.

1   Introduction

Recent developments in Internet technology and mobile telecommunications have heralded the dawn of the "Personal Digital Assistant". One application that makes maximum use of such a device is that of an intelligent tourist guide. We have developed a prototype handheld tour-guide under the HIPS[1] (Hyper Interaction within Physical Space) project [1]. The tour-guide uses GPS to establish the users location, this facilitates presentation of contextualised information to the tourist. An essential element of this system is the ability to rapidly create tour-guides for new cities. Similar research includes that of Long *et al* [2], Davies *et al* [3] and Schilit *et al*[4]. Our research differs in that our prototype was designed with the goal of quick deployment and configuration of new tourist domains (e.g. a city, national park, or archeological site).

2   System Description

The architecture of this prototype follows a four layer model and is shown in figure 1.

Location Layer
The core component in the Location layer is the GPS receiver, namely the Garmin GPS II+ model. All GPS output complies with the NMEA 0183 standard. A position reading is sent via a serial cable to a localisation daemon running on the client. This daemon is a signed Java applet and maintains the connection to the serial port. When new position data becomes available, this data is dispatched to the server.

---

[1] We gratefully acknowledge the support of Esprit LTR through project No. 25574 and our fellow partners in the HIPS consortium.

Presentation Layer

The Presentation layer provides the user interface to the system and runs on a Toshiba Libretto 110. This interface was designed and developed by CB&J [5] for HIPS. It is not coincidental that the interface dimensions correspond to the screen size of an average PDA. The user interface is a standard web browser with RealPlayer plug-ins, through which the user receives multi-media output (HTML, JPEG, SMIL and RealAudio). User interaction and presentation delivery is controlled by JavaScript and HTML running on the client.

Server Layer

The server layer consists of a web server, RealAudio server and some Java Servlets. We use the Apache web server with the Apache JServ extension to enable execution of Java servlets. The servlets manage the connection with the client and also assemble new presentations. The server maintains a list of previously presented information and interrogates this before deciding whether a new presentation should be generated. If a new presentation is required, the multi-media database is queried and the appropriate multi-media objects are extracted. Using these objects an HTML file, and a SMIL (Synchronised Multimedia Integration Language) file are dynamically created and the client is notified that a new presentation is available.

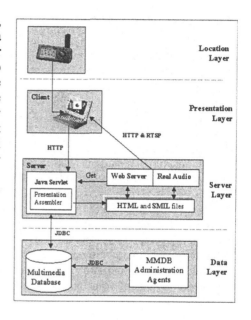

Figure 1. System Architecture

Data Layer

The data layer consists of a multi-media database namely IBM's DB2 universal database. JDBC 2.0 is utilised when performing database queries. All data maintained by the multi-media database may be classified under two headings: 1) Position-related: Lookup tables that relate an information object to a physical location. 2) Media-related: Tables relating information objects to their corresponding multi-media objects. The multi-media data types include audio, image, text, and digital video. When selecting the most appropriate information object for a users current location, their latitude and longitude position are passed to the database, and, using the *Great Circle Algorithm* the corresponding information object is identified.

Rapid Configuration

As part of the HIPS initiative, we are developing a generic location aware tour guide that is easily portable from city to city. We have developed a suite of administration agents to facilitate the database population process. These include tools to allow an administrator to easily add information objects to the database by specifying a latitude/longitude pair with a set of multi-media objects. We also provide a web-based interface to allow remote administration. For example if a new tour guide is to be developed for the campus at UCD, an administrator could collect audio, images, and video about popular tourist attractions, these could then be uploaded to the database with the corresponding global positions (established from a local map). A suitably equipped tourist could immediately utilise the system. This facility has been used for demonstration purposes both on the UCD campus and in the city of Siena.

3   Conclusion and Future Work

The work described here presents a generic location aware information system for outdoor scenarios and the need to be able to rapidly prototype tour guides for new city locations.

Our initial tests indicate that GPS, with location accuracy of less than 50 meters, is inadequate for our requirements. Consequently, we will augment our current localisation mechanism with additional technology, such as differential GPS, electronic compasses, or utilising existing cellular infrastructure to refine position (i.e. base station ID). To date our work has strived to ensure the reliability of the system, however having initially used HTTP for communication purposes, we are in the process of integrating the system with GSM. This will also facilitate the use of a thin client (e.g. a commercial PDA), as it is not practical to expect a tourist to carry such a sizeable client (i.e. Libretto). In the long term we hope to identify a subset of system functionalities that can be ported to a smart phone, utilising technologies such as the Wireless Application Protocol (WAP). Currently we are investigating system scalability issues in migrating from a campus prototype to a city wide application. We are integrating the multi-media database with a commercial GIS (i.e. MapInfo).

4   References

1.   HIPS (Hyper Interaction within Physical Space) WWW home page for the HIPS project : http://www.ing.unisi.it/lab_tel/hips/hips.html
2.   Long, S., Kooper, R., Abowd, G.D., Atkeson, C. G.: Prototyping of Mobile Context-Aware Applications: The Cyberguide Case Study. Proc. 2nd ACM International Conference on Mobile Computing (MOBICOM), Rye, New York, U.S., Pages 97-108. 1996.
3.   Davies, N., Cheverst, K., Mitchell, K., and Friday, A.: 'Caches in the Air': Disseminiating Tourist Information in the Guide System. In Proc. of 2nd IEEE Workshop on Mobile Computer Systems and Applications (WMCSA '99). New Orleans, Louisiana, 25 - 26 February 1999.
4.   Schilit, B., Adams, N., and Want, R.: Context-Aware Computing Applications. In Proc. of Workshop on Mobile Computing Systems and Applications. Pages 85-91. 1994.
5.   Broadbent, J.: HIPS User Interface Specification. HIPS Internal Report.

Mobile Computing in Machine Engineering Applications

Martin Brachtl, Lukáš Mikšíček, and Pavel Slavík

Czech Technical University, Prague, Czech Republic,
{brachtlm|miksicek|slavik}@fel.cvut.cz, http://www.cgg.cvut.cz/

Abstract. Because of limited financial resources many SMEs cannot be equipped with NC routes. A solution would be to equip a route with a low cost computer. The computer system that satisfies our requirements belongs to the class of PDA computers. The software product described in this paper is able to transform a standard NC program into form that is executable by simple control electronics attached to the route. The system is portable and it can also simulate the production process on the display of the PDA used.

1   Introduction

There are many variations of NC routes on the market that comply with current demands. Nevertheless, there is a class of users that have limited access to these types of routes. A typical user of this class can be characterized as a user working in SME with limited financial resources. This fact usually does not allow such a user to buy up to date equipment and this has fatal impact on the productivity of work and also on the financial and time expenses needed to produce a product. A suitable solution would be to equip a route with a computer system that would be able to control the route in an effective way in the same (or almost the same) manner as professional NC systems do. A possible solution could be to employ a low cost computer device that could control the route in a proper way.

2   Application of mobile computing

The requirements given above can define a class of computers that could be used for the given purpose. Another requirement for such a system could be its portability as it is necessary in many application to watch closely the production process. In such a way it would be possible to control dynamically this process as it would be possible to use various modes like a step mode when each single control step could be performed in an isolated manner.

The user should have the possibility to watch closely the course of the production process and, depending on the the current situation, be able to control the production process. The computer system chosen should allow the user to introduce flexibly new functions that could comply with specific requirements for specific products.

The computer system that satisfies all these requirements belongs to the class of PDA (palmtop, handheld) computers. The project that ran at the CTU, Prague, was targeted towards the development of the control system that would allow the user to control the route in an effective and cheap way. The final form of the software product is a system with the following characteristics:

- Transformation of a standard NC program into internal form that is executable by simple control electronics attached to the route.
- Existence of various exploitation modes (run mode, step mode, direct control mode) of a route.
- The system is portable, which allows the user to walk around the route and to watch (and also control) the course of the production process.
- Simulation of the production process on the display of the PDA used (in order to verify the control program).

The elementary control statements executable by the control electronics on the route side consists of four classes: move (line segments in 3D), turn-on and turn-off the tool, query statements (the tool position in 3D space), control the speed of the tool movement.

This means that the NC program on the PDA side (in HPGL form) had to be tranformed (also on the PDA side) into a sequence of statements that can be executable by the control electronics of the route. This conversion module was a very substantial part of the whole software system. The main problems that had to be solved were as follows:

- Transformation of primitives available in HPGL into line segments (circles, arcs etc.),
- Conversion of speeds defined in HPGL into speeds applicable for the route control,
- Maintenance of context of the environment in which the tool was working (Fig. 1, left) (the form of statements for the route had to be modified according to the given context).

As has already been mentioned it is also possible to send the control statements directly to the control electronics on the route side (Fig. 1, right). This means that this can be considered as a direct control mode as there is no program available. The user can directly control the route. This mode could be used in the future for NC programming and would give a new dimension to the NC programming in the above described environment.

3 Problems of the solution used

The software part of the solution described can be divided into two pieces: the software running on the PDA and the software controlling the electronics of the route. In both parts of the system software we can recognize some problems which were solved.

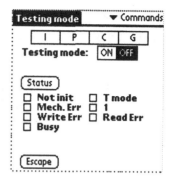

Fig. 1. PDA software screenshots

The main problem of the controlling software was to tune up the movement of the tool. The desired balance between the smoothness of the movement and the speed had to be found. Especially in the case where the move was built up from many line segments, the goal was to optimize the speed in the joining of those line segments. The optimization was based on the comparision of the first derivation of both neighboring line segments.

In the case of the second part of the software, the software running on the PDA side, a group of problems can be found. This piece of software was built on the core HPGL parser. Parsing of the source HPGL program generates the control statements for the controlling part on the route side. These control statements, and the whole communication between all the components of the system was based on the industrial I^2C bus.

4 Conclusion

The important role of the system was to make it possible to use the system in the least complicateted way. This feature is provided with the help of an "easy to use" graphical user interface (GUI). The display area of current PDAs is constrained. On the other hand, the GUI elements have to be big enough, to allow for controlling the production process with a freehand only, without the use of any pen or stylus. This problem was solved with the help of the integration of the area of press sensitive display and the set of hardware buttons of the PDA in one user interface. Because of the small amount of hardware buttons it was necessary to make the function of the buttons context sensitive.

References

1. Developing Palm OS 3.0 Applications. 3Com Corporation (1998).
   http://www.palm.com/devzone/docs.html
2. The I^2C Bus Specification. Philips Semiconductors (December 1998).
   http://www-us2.semiconductors.philips.com/i2c/

Chameleon – Reconfigurability in Hand-Held Multimedia Computers

Gerard J.M. Smit, Ties Bos, Paul J.M. Havinga, Sape J. Mullender, Jaap Smit
University of Twente, dept. Computer Science, Enschede, the Netherlands,
e-mail: smit@cs.utwente.nl

Abstract. In this paper a *reconfigurable systems-architecture* in combination with a QoS driven operating system is introduced that can deal with the inherent dynamics of future mobile systems. We claim that a radical new approach has to be taken in order to fulfill the requirements - in terms of processing power and energy consumption - of future mobile applications.

1 Introduction

In the next decade two trends will definitively play a significant role in driving technology: the development and deployment of personal mobile computing devices and the continuing advances in integrated circuit technology. The development of personal hand-held devices is quite challenging, because these devices have a very small energy budget, are small in size, but require a performance which exceeds the levels of current desktop computers. On the other hand they should have the *flexibility* to handle a variety of multimedia services and standards (like different video decompression schemes and security mechanisms) and the *adaptability* to accommodate to the nomadic environment, required level of security, and available resources. We believe that state-of-the-art system-architectures cannot provide the wealth of services required by a fully operational mobile computer given the increasing levels of energy consumption. Without significant energy reduction techniques and energy saving architectures, battery life constraints limit the capabilities of these devices. This paper discusses reconfigurability issues in low-power hand-held multimedia systems, with particular emphasis on energy reduction.

2 Energy efficiency

In the area of mobile computing it will be an enormous challenge to work with a minimal power budget. Yet, the architecture must provide the performance for functions like speech recognition, audio/video compression/decompression and data encryption. Power budgets close to current high-performance microprocessors, are unacceptable for portable, battery operated devices. We think progress has to be made in two areas in particular:

- *Reconfigurable system architectures*
  Reconfigurable architectures are flexible and adaptive, use the chip area effectively and are relatively easy to design.
- *Energy-aware operating systems*
  Mobile systems should be flexible and adaptive to the inherent unpredictability of the mobile environment, and should be able to control the multimedia streams through the reconfigurable architecture. The operating system has to be Quality of Service driven to be able to adhere to these requirements efficiently. Here QoS not only involves network performance parameters, but also energy cost and infrastructure cost. These parameters are 'vertical' controls: they have impact on all layers of the protocol stack, from applications down to the physical layer. Therefore our approach is based on an extensive use of power reduction techniques at all levels of system design.

3 Reconfigurable systems architecture

The strength of a *reconfigurable systems architecture* is its flexibility. Reconfiguration can be applied at several layers in the system and in various levels of granularity, for example: a) reconfigurable processing modules b) reconfigurable media streams, and c) system decomposition. In addition to that, a generalized QoS model that encompasses different levels of granularity of the system is essential to select an efficient configuration.

Small grain reconfigurability: Reconfigurable processing modules
Multimedia applications have a high computational complexity with a regular and spatially local computation. Communication between modules is significant. State-of-the-art application-specific coprocessors have the potential to perform multimedia tasks efficiently: both in terms of performance as well as in energy consumption. Such coprocessors are not attractive though, due to their inflexibility [1].
For a wide range of functions that use digital filtering algorithms on parallel data state-of-the-art reconfigurable devices (such as FPGAs), do not posses the required processing power. We defined a novel architecture called FP*FA*s (*Field-Programmable Function Array*). These devices have a matrix of ALUs and lookup tables [3]. A broad class of compute-intensive algorithms can be implemented on an FPFA efficiently. The instruction set of an FPFA-ALU can be thought of as the set of ordinary ALU instructions, with the exception that there are no load and store operations which operate on memories. Instead, they operate on the programmable interconnect; that is, the ALU loads its operands from neighboring ALU outputs, or from (input) values stored in lookup tables or local registers. A novel aspect in this concept is that chip design is replaced by dynamic reconfiguration and reprogramming for future applications using a highly efficient platform. In our opinion, this sheds a new light on the fundamental issues of low-power embedded systems.

Medium grain reconfigurability: Reconfigurable media streams

Much energy can be saved in multimedia systems by improving the component interaction [2]. Autonomous, reconfigurable modules such as network, video and audio devices, interconnected by a switch, offload as much work as possible from the CPU to programmable modules that are placed in the data streams. Thus, communication between components is not broadcast over a bus to main memory, but delivered exactly to where it is needed, work is carried out where the data passes through and, if memory is required at all, it is placed on the data path where it is needed. Modules are autonomously entering an energy-conservation mode and adapt themselves to the current state of resources, the environment and the requirements of the user. To support this, the operating system must become a small, distributed system.

Coarse grain reconfigurability: System decomposition

In a system many tradeoffs can be made. A careful analysis of the data flow in the system and decomposition of the system functions can reduce energy consumption considerably. For example, when we consider the transmission of an image over a wireless network, there is a trade-off between image compression, error control, communication requirements, and energy consumption. In an architecture with reconfigurable modules and data streams, functions can be dynamically migrated between functional modules such that an efficient configuration can be obtained.

4 Conclusion

Without significant energy reduction techniques and energy saving architectures, battery life constraints limit the capabilities of future mobile systems. In this paper we claim that a *flexible* and *reconfigurable* systems-architecture in combination with a QoS driven operating system is needed to deal with the inherent dynamics of future mobile systems. This reconfigurability can be found in the interaction of multimedia devices, in the media processing and in migration of functionality.

References

1. Abnous A., Rabaey J., "Ultra-Low-Power Domain-Specific Multimedia Processors," *Proceedings of the IEEE VLSI Signal Processing Workshop*, San Francisco, October 1996.
2. Smit G.J.M., et al.: "An overview of the Moby Dick project", *1st Euromicro summer school on mobile computing*, pp. 159-168, Oulu, August 1998.
3. Smit J., et al, "Low Cost & Fast Turnaround: Reconfigrable Graph-Based Execution Units", *Proceedings Belsign Workshop*, 1998.

An Evaluation of WebTwig – A Site Outliner for Handheld Web Access

Matt Jones[1], Geroge Buchanan[1] & Norliza Mohd-Nasir[1]

[1] Interaction Design Centre, School of Computing Science, Middlesex University, London
UK N11 2NQ
{m.jones, k.boone, george10, n.mohd-nasir }@mdx.ac.uk

Abstract. Interaction problems occur when small-screen devices (PDAs, Palmtops etc) are used to access Web pages designed for conventional, large-screen displays. To overcome some of these problems, we have developed a tool, WebTwig, which is designed to improve Web access on small-screen devices. We have carried out an experiment to assess the usefulness of WebTwig. Our results indicate that the tool can improve a user's performance and satisfaction.

1. Introduction

Users are beginning to use handheld computers to access Web pages. The display –area of these devices is much smaller than that found on desktop machines. Most Web pages are produced for conventional desktop viewing. In an earlier study [1], we proposed there would be serious interaction problems if handheld computers were used to access such conventional pages.

The results of our study, along with review of literature concerning information visualisation, led us to develop a new tool, WebTwig [2] that can automatically adapt conventional web sites to be more effective for handheld computers. This poster reports on an evaluation of the use of WebTwig for the task completion.

2. WebTwig

WebTwig [2] provides a tree-based outline view of an entire site. Outline views present users with a high level view of the information content which can be manipulated until the required detail is achieved. Outliners have been used in many applications from word-processing to mapping applications.

3. The study

For the study we created two handheld simulations, both simulations were able to display the same number of lines (approximately, the size found on typical Windows CE machines).

One simulation displayed the original desktop-optimised site without any adaptation for handheld displays. The other presented the WebTwig view of a site. Example screenshots of the two simulations are shown below in Figure 1, below.

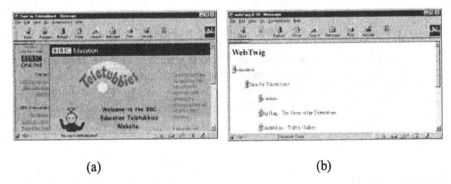

(a)   (b)

Figure 1 – example displays used in the study. (a) is the view on a small screen without any site adaptation; (b) shows an example of the site view via WebTwig – note the structured display of topics and the arrow icons which allow users to expand/ collapse topics.

Twenty-six volunteers, all with similar profiles (e.g., in terms of web literacy, experience of handheld display and so on), were used in the study. These volunteers were divided randomly into 2 groups of 13. We asked each group of user to complete 4 tasks using 4 sites (1 task per site). One group used the unadapted site view (e.g., see Figure 1(a)); the other group used the WebTwig view (e.g., Figure 1(b)).

Two of the tasks required a specific correct answer – we called these the 'direct' tasks. The other two allowed users more flexibility and choice in terms of answer – these were the 'indirect' tasks.

WebTwig builds outline views from the physical directory structuring used to organise the Web site. Two of the sites in the trial were organised with a good hierarchical structuring of Web pages (the 'structured' sites) while the other 2 had no structure ('flat' sites).

Each of the four tasks, then, involved a different combination of task type and site characteristic: direct/structured, direct/flat, indirect/structured and indirect/flat. The aim of these combinations was to ensure a fair assessment of WebTwig without biasing the results by using tasks/ sites that were could be thought of being particularly suited to the approach.

We recorded the time that each user took to complete each of the four tasks. As they completed each task, we asked them to rate the effectiveness of the simulation in helping them to reach their goals. A scale of 1 to 9 (with 1 representing very poor and 9 excellent) was used in this part of the evaluation.

4. Results

Table 2 presents an overview of the results of the study. As can be seen, overall, WebTwig users were able to complete tasks 35% quicker than the group that had to use the unadapted sites. Similarly, WebTwig was rated more highly than the un-adapted sites – WebTwig users found the WebTwig view more effective in complet-ing tasks than did the users of the unadapted sites. The better performance of WebTwig was seen in all four tasks; however, the differences in performance were less marked for the task where the task type was indirect and the site type flat.

	Average time (secs) to complete a task	Average effectiveness ranking in complet-ing a task (1-9, poor to excellent)
Group 1:Using unadapted site view	155	4
Group 2:Using WebTwig view	102	7

Table 2: Overview of study results

5. Conclusions

Our study has shown that outline views for handheld web-site use has good potential. WebTwig automatically produces such views from any site, im-proving accessibility for handheld users. We are currently improving WebTwig to provide a search mechanism so that views can be pruned and so that more than one form of outline view can be generated.

References

1. Jones, M., Marsden, G., Mohd-Nasir, N., Boone K. & Buchanan, G. (1999). Improving Web interaction on small displays. Proceedings of W8 conference, Toronto, May 1999 (Also reprinted in International Journal of Computer and Telecommunications Network-ing, 31 (1999), 1129-1137).
2. Jones, M., Marsden, G, Mohd-Nasir, N. & Buchanan, G. (1999), A site-based outliner for small screen web access. Proceedings of W8 conference, Toronto, May 1999.

Human Factors of Multi-modal Ubiquitous Computing

David J. Haniff, Chris Baber and William Edmondson*

School of Electrical and Electronic Engineering
*School of Computer Science
The University of Birmingham, Birmingham, B15 2TT

Abstract. Multi-modal interaction with Ubiquitous Computing needs to be carefully examined for its appropriate use within systems. The importance of this analysis is highlighted through the presentation of an experimental study that demonstrates that one modality could be implicit within another.

1 Introduction

A goal of Ubiquitous Computing (UC) is to make computational technology invisible; in other words, to remove the technology from an explicit role in a person's workaday activity to an implicit (supportive) role. In addition, instead of a single user interacting with one computational device the user interacts with many devices embedded into the environment to such as extent that the interaction itself becomes integrated into the real world. Weiser (1993) equates the view of ubiquitous computational technology to 'writing', in that it becomes pervasive within society and daily life.

Multi-modal interfaces attempt to provide multiple sensory channel input and output. However, the issue of appropriate modal interface representation has, to date, not been fully addressed. Whether the interface for the ubiquitous device is visual, auditory or tactile we need to assess its appropriateness for the task in order to achieve this seamless interaction. If the interface is inappropriate then the user will be distracted and the goal of invisibility will not be achieved. This paper therefore approaches the issue of multi-modal UC from a user's perspective.

2 Uni- vs. Multi-modal Interaction

Most user-interfaces are uni-modal, in that they use only one sensory channel, primarily th visual system. Multi-modal interfaces use combinations of sensory channels to provide information to the user. Gaver (1989) used sound to supplement visual tasks on a user-interface. Bolt (1980) enhanced interaction with visual objects by the use of speech and gesture. UC can use a variety of modalities in the real world to provide seamless interaction. To date, the distinction between uni- and multi- modal interfaces has tended to focus on the range of modalities which can be supported. Typically, we recognise multi-modal interfaces as having sound, vision, and (possibly) tactile properties. However, designing interfaces for UC produces a problem of defining the information which can be conveyed using different modalities and how this can be related to information from the everyday world.

The components within UC interfaces can be described as 'external representations'. Scaife and Rogers (1996) have examined visual external representations and how these relate to internal constructs. However, visual external representations commonly represent real world objects that have multi-modality associated with them implicitly. This has implications for ubiquitous multi-modal interface design. An interface with multi-modal feedback may not be necessary due to a visual representation providing the necessary information to evoke other sensory considerations. However, in order to understand how these representations work we need to examine the verbalisation of a simple real world task. We asked participants to produce instructions for building a water pump. The generation of instructions for the manipulation of these real objects allows us to analyse external representations with a task that would require multi-modal interaction (e.g. to see, touch, and pick up the objects).

3 Modal Interaction Study

The study examines instructions produced by participants to construct a water pump. The water pump consists of nine parts (see figure 1).

Figure 1: Water pump components

Method

The participants were presented with a constructed water pump and were asked to produce textual instructions to assemble the pump. In order to ascertain which parts were used in the construction the participants needed to interact with the water pump. The textual instruction phrases produced by the subjects were categorised into objects (nouns), actions (verbs), attributes (adjectives) and relationships (association between objects).

Participants

The study used ten students (aged 18 – 29) from the University of Birmingham with no prior professional experience of instruction design.

Results

The *content analysis* identified certain characteristics of the phrases produced by the subjects. Attributes describe the features of the objects used in the construction.

There were a total number of 21 attributes identified. The top five occurring attributes in the total amount of textual instructions produced are presented in graph 1.

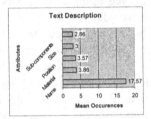

Graph1: Content analysis of instructions

Discussion

The water pump study suggests that the issue of whether or not a multi-modal interface is appropriate for a task needs to be carefully considered. The participants may have believed that the tactile features were not necessary in the production of instructions to guide others in the construction of the pump. The visual features were described but not the tactile features. This could be due to the tactile considerations being implicitly assumed by the use of visual features or due to the subjects' prioritisation of visual features over tactile due to the nature of the task. Therefore, the close examination of modal representations is required in order not to produce surplus communications to the user.

4 Conclusion

The consideration of modality perception can offer useful information for the design of multi-modal UC interactions. Multi-modal UC can offer the user interaction that models real world interactions using a variety of sensory channels. However, the study described demonstrates that the modal interaction techniques need careful consideration. In some cases different modalities may not be appropriate and introduce redundancy into the development process.

5 References

Bolt, R. (1980) "Put-That-There": Voice and Gesture at the Graphics Interface, *SIGGRAGH '80 Proceedings*,   14, No. 3 (July 1980), 262-270.

Gaver, W. (1989) The SonicFinder: An interface that uses auditory icons, *Human-Computer Interaction*, 4, 1, 67-94.

Scaife, M. and Rogers, Y. (1996) External cognition: how do graphical representations work? *Int. J. Human-Computer Studies*, 45, 185-213.

Weiser, M (1993) Hot Topics: Ubiquitous Computing, *IEEE Computer*, October.

URCP: Experimental Support for Multi-modal Interfaces

A. Donnelly & E. Barnstedt,

Department of Computer Science,
Trinity College Dublin,
Dublin, Ireland
Alexis.Donnelly@cs.tcd.ie

Abstract. We describe the design and prototyping of an experimental protocol, the Universal Remote Console Protocol (URCP), to support mobile, multi-modal, short duration interactions using a mobile console to interact with a smart building and appliances within it. Our experience thus far indicates that URCP is lightweight, easy to implement and supports flexibility in the design of user-interfaces.

1.0 Introduction & Motivation

URCP is a supporting pipeline between building applications (such as a simple appliance or a building management system), acting as a server and a mobile/wearable computing device, acting as a thin client, that supports several modes of interaction with the building user (see Fig 1). Our design is based on an idea from the Trace Research Center [2].

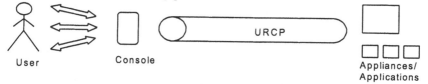

Fig. 1. URCP supports multi-modal interaction in a smart building

Typical scenarios supported by URCP include the following. Within a meeting, a speaker might run a thin client to the environmental controls (lights, projector, blinds etc) on a laptop using a conventional WIMP interface. Another speaker might prefer a small PDA connected to an earpiece and a finger keyboard concealed in a glove to suit personal presenting style. Elsewhere in the building, other information, such as the current location of a particular individual or the route to a particular room might be requested and supplied in various forms – text, graphic or audio. Similar requirements for differing modes arise in other applications of wearable computing such as aircraft maintenance. A maintenance engineer may elect to interact with a schematic database by voice while hands and eyes are busy but using a WIMP interface when seated at a workstation. Supporting the guest (language) preferences in a smart hotel bedroom is an example from a more domestic domain.

2.0 Protocol Description

URCP supports this single task/multiple mode paradigm by maintaining the abstract nature of the interaction (e.g. menu presentation and alternative selection) as far as possible along the communication path with details of user modalities left to the thin mobile client. This design is perhaps an example, in a mobile setting, of the well-known end-to-end argument in system design [1].

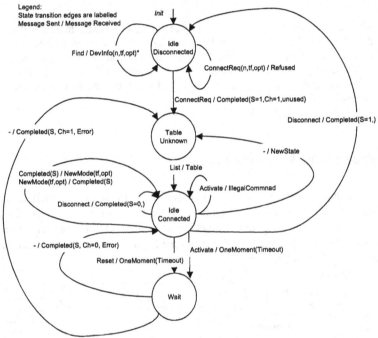

Fig. 2. Console State Transition Diagram

The console state transition diagram is shown in Fig 2. Transition arcs are labeled with "Message Sent / Message Received" with parentheses indicating the values of message content. In a typical interaction, the console requests a menu by sending a List message to which the appliance responds with a Table message containing a list of options. For each option in the Table message, its name, type (i.e. text, audio, graphic) and value are sent. The mode of interaction is set by the contents of the DevInfo and ConnReq messages during connection setup. This mode may be changed via an option explicitly offered by the appliance, or the NewMode message may be used, by either party, specifying the desired new transmission format and options. While the Principles of Universal Design, [3], are more apt for user interfaces, we have found them a useful guide in the design of URCP, if only to ensure that design options are retained at the end(s) of the pipeline.

The constraints of computing power and battery lifetime on a mobile device require simplicity and low overhead in URCP. In applications where hands and eyes are busy, a voice recognition/speech synthesis interface is required. Some mobiles may be sufficiently powerful to support this mode themselves with simple text being carried by URCP. Where this is impossible, such tasks must be off-loaded to the stationary computing infrastructure with voice traffic carried by URCP. Audio support has been included explicitly in the messages described above. This also permits implementers to take advantage of optimisations available in the lower networking layers, as envisaged in the SWAP protocol design.

As part of a feasibility study for a smart buildings initiative at TCD, we prototyped URCP on a Palm III PDA acting as console (WIMP and scan-and-select user interfaces) and several appliances (CD player, TV and building simulator) running on Win 98 with URCP above IrDA 1.0. Though very different in programming style, both implementations occupied about 1000 lines of C code. The performance of the IrDA link was disappointing, especially over longer distances. However, we determined that observed latencies were due exclusively to delays in the underlying IrDA protocol stack – URCP itself introduced very little overhead.

3.0 Evaluation & Future Work

Despite predictable deficiencies of the prototype, URCP has demonstrated promise as a simple lightweight protocol to support multi-modal interactions in a smart building environment, leaving wide scope for detailed interface design. The bi-directional nature of URCP means that a single mobile console should suffice for current and future appliances (assuming they support URCP).

One of our motivations for prototyping URCP was the absence of a full specification or any implementations of the Jini distributed architecture. The simplicity of URCP compares favourably with the more complex protocols such as RMI or IIOP associated with Jini. Experimentation based on URCP in advance of Jini may provide early insights useful in the detailed design of the evolving Jini architecture. URCP is still very much an experiment.

We hope to construct further console applications using URCP to develop our ideas and the protocol further. We envisage console applications capable of supporting several, simultaneous, interleaved interactions and experimenting further with support for changing user-interface modality during an interaction. We also intend to port URCP to a radio-based communication infrastructure such as Bluetooth, DECT, SWAP or a Wireless LAN based on IEEE 802.11.

References

[1] Saltzer J., Reed D., Clark D., "End-to-End Arguments in System Design", ACM Transactions on Computer Systems, 2 (4), Nov. 1984, pp. 277-288.

[2] Vanderheiden G., "Universal Remote Console Communication Protocol", Proceedings of the TIDE Congress – Improving the Quality of Life for the European Citizen, Helsinki, June 1998, published by IOS Press, Amsterdam, 1998, pp. 368-373

[3] Center for Universal Design, North Carolina State University, "Principles of Universal Design", Version 2.0, April 1997, Center for Universal Design, North Carolina State University, 1997 (see http://www.design.ncsu.edu/cud/pubs/udprinciples.html)

Magic Medicine Cabinet:
A Situated Portal for Consumer Healthcare

Dadong Wan

Center for Strategic Technology Research
Andersen Consulting
Northbrook, IL 60062 USA
dwan@cstar.ac.com

Abstract. In this paper, we introduce a smart appliance for consumer healthcare called "Magic Medicine Cabinet." It integrates such technologies like smart labels, face recognition, health monitoring devices, flat panel displays, and the Web to provide situated support for a broad range of health needs, including condition monitoring, medication reminders, interactions with one's own pharmacists and physicians, as well as access to personalized health information.

1. Introduction

In recent years, we have heard much about smart appliances, ranging from Internet microwaves [1] to Web refrigerators [3]. Most of these appliances, however, are little more than their traditional counterparts with Internet connection. There is little integration between the newly added functionality and what the appliance traditionally does. For instance, with Web browsing available through a microwave front panel, one can perform many functions we use our desktop computers for: home banking, electronic shopping, and even online gaming. Despite the versatility, these functions have little to do with what the microwave is being used for: speed cooking and re-heating of food.

We believe that closer integration between the traditional use of an appliance and Internet capabilities related to that use will result in smarter appliances. Our goal is to integrate the growing array of Internet resources devoted to healthcare with artifacts in the home traditionally associated with healthcare.

2. Motivation

There are two intrinsic facets to healthcare: *informational* and *physical*. Activities such as finding out the potential side effects of a given drug or scheduling an office visit with one's physician, for example, fall into the first category. On the hand, taking a pill (hopefully a right pill) or measuring one's blood pressure are physical activities. Access to the right health information is no substitute for proper physical care. Effective healthcare requires a continuous interplay of information exchange and physical care.

With the advent of the Internet and the Web, we have witnessed an explosion of healthcare information. According to a recent survey, two-thirds of Internet users use the Web to search for health information [2]. While the increasing accessibility of health information is essential to the future of healthcare, it represents only one side of the equation. To achieve the dual purpose of lower cost and higher quality of care, consumer-initiated physical care, especially at the consumer's own home, must also be encouraged and explicitly supported.

3. The Concept

The Magic Medicine Cabinet (MMC) is a smart appliance for supporting both the informational and physical aspects of consumer healthcare. Specifically, it embeds a number of technologies that, together, enable consumers to (1) perform routine physical care, such as reminding and ensuring one to take the right medication and tracking vital signs; (2) access up-to-date personalized health information; and (3) interact online with physicians, pharmacists, and other professional care providers.

In addition to bridging the gap between the physical and the informational aspects of healthcare, the MMC also embodies another important concept: it is a *situated portal*. We believe that proper healthcare is an integral part of everyday life. As a result, a supporting mechanism like MMC needs to be situated in an everyday space so that one does not have to step out of one's normal activities in order to take advantage of services rendered by such a mechanism. For example, the MMC can remind a person to take medication through both voice and the embedded display while they are brushing their teeth.

The medicine cabinet is traditionally a bathroom fixture for a reason: the bathroom is a highly frequented quarter where many daily personal care activities already take place. The MMC takes advantage of the situated nature of the medicine cabinet but extends it from a passive storage space into an interactive appliance. The implementation of the MMC incorporates the following technologies:

- *Face recognition*: it recognizes people who approach the medicine cabinet and responds with proper services.
- *RFID-based smart labels*: drug products stored in the medicine cabinet have smart labels attached to them. Hence, it can detect which product is being taken out.
- *Vital sign monitors*: one can use these monitors to track a wide range of health indicators, such as blood pressure, heart rate and cholesterol level.
- *Voice synthesis*: it allows auditory output to supplement what's shown on the cabinet display.

The MMC has a embedded Pentium-266 MHz computer and Internet connectivity. As shown in Figure 1, the MMC looks very much like a conventional medicine cabinet. One key difference is that the left panel of the cabinet has a built-in flat-panel display. The user interacts with the MMC through its touch-sensitive screen, voice output, and the cabinet display.

Fig. 1. The Magic Medicine Cabinet recognizes which medication Johnny is holding, and warns him if he is taking the wrong medication.

4. An Example Scenario

Like millions of other Americans, Johnny's life has been hampered by his chronic allergy problem. One morning, Johnny gets up and heads to the bathroom to get ready for school. He hears a voice from his medicine cabinet:

"Good morning, Johnny. I have allergy alert for you."

Johnny looks up at his medicine cabinet display, and notices the pollen count in his area is dangerously high. He also sees big red flashing letters on the cabinet display reminding him to take his allergy medication.

Johnny reaches on to the shelf of the cabinet and picks up a medicine bottle:

"Wrong...you've taken Allegra instead of Claritin!"

Johnny puts the bottle back and picks up another one:

"Great...now you have the right medicine."

Later that day, when noticing the presence of his father Dan at the bathroom, Johnny's medicine cabinet reminds him that it's time to measure his blood pressure. Dan opens the cabinet door and slips the cuff around his arm (see Figure 2). His medicine cabinet tells him that his blood pressure has gone a bit higher since the previous reading, and suggests that he might want to consult with his doctor. If he is so inclined, Dan can schedule an office visit with his family doctor right there through his medicine cabinet!

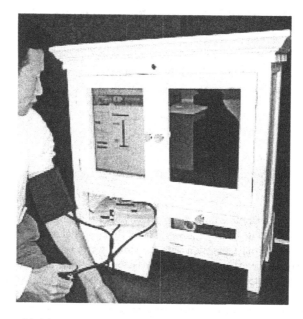

Fig. 2. Dan measures his blood pressure using the monitoring device attached to the medicine cabinet.

5. Summary

The Magic Medicine Cabinet is part of an ongoing research program in situated computing at Andersen Consulting's Center for Strategic Technology Research (CSTaR). In this program, we attempt to integrate a wide range of sensory, computing, and communications technologies to create new types of consumer experiences. One central theme of our research is to explore ways for bridging the gap between the physical world in which we live, and the virtual world on which we are becoming increasingly dependent. The MMC prototype is a good example showing how informational and physical healthcare can come together in the form of a smart appliance.

References

1. Essick, Kristi. Defrost, Cook, Send E-mail? NCR Shows Off Internet-Enabled Microwave Oven. *The Industry Standard* (September 11, 1998).
2. Hafner, Katie. Can the Internet Cure the Common Cold? *New York Times* (July 9, 1998).
3. Richtel, Matt. For the Refrigerator, A Silicon-Chip Treat. *New York Times* (February 18, 1999).
4. Williams, Thomas. There's No Place Like Home Healthcare. *Healthcare Informatics* (October, 1997).

Augmented Workspace: The World as Your Desktop

Kelly L. Dempski

Center for Strategic Technology Research (CSTaR)
Andersen Consulting
3773 Willow Road
Northbrook, IL 60062 USA

Kelly.L.Dempski@.ac.com

Abstract. We live in a three dimensional world, and much of what we do and how we interact in the physical world has a strong spatial component. Unfortunately, most of our interaction with the virtual world is two dimensional. We are exploring the extension of the 2D desktop workspace into the 3D physical world, using a stereoscopic see-through head-mounted display. We have built a prototype that enables us to overlay virtual windows on the physical world. This paper describes the Augmented Workspace, which allows a user to position windows in a 3D work area.

Keywords. Ubiquitous computing, cooperative buildings, human-computer interaction, physical space, context awareness, visualization.

1. Introduction

In our daily lives, much of what we do and how we interact has a strong spatial component. Your calendar is on a wall, or on a certain part of your desk, and sticky notes are placed on walls and whiteboards. Yet, as an increasing portion of our work is done on computers, a large majority of our interaction is confined to the small, two-dimensional workspace of the computer monitor. While windows based systems allow the user to arrange windows spatially anywhere on the monitor, these systems do not offer anywhere near the freedom of placement that is inherent in the three-dimensional physical world.

The limitations of the desktop metaphor have been known for some time [1]. The fields of Ubiquitous Computing and Wearable Computing are demonstrating the potential value in moving computing out of its traditional context of a box on a desk and out into other contexts in the physical world. . An increasing number of researchers are developing prototypes that illustrate different capabilities that become possible once one breaks out of the desktop metaphor, including a number of recent systems such as the BubbleBadge [2], and comMotion [3]. However, while these prototypes invent new and exciting applications for ubiquitous computing, they do not address how the idea of ubiquity may improve traditional computing activities such as every-day office work. Our goal in developing an Augmented Workspace is to move computing beyond the desktop but to stay within the boundaries of one's office, to see if we can enhance normal computer-oriented activities by vastly expanding the available display space.

2. The Augmented Workspace

An Augmented Workspace incorporates the technologies and concepts behind Augmented Reality [4] to create a workspace that takes greater advantage of the physical world. To use this workspace, a user wears a high-resolution stereoscopic see-through head mounted display (HMD). The HMD allows the user to interact with the real world while using head tracking to overlay computer-generated data and objects in specific spatial locations. In our prototype, "windows" are not only confined to a two-dimensional location on a screen, but can have a full three-dimensional position anywhere within the user's physical work environment. Calendars can be placed on the walls, along with sticky notes and reminders. Current work can be placed around the desk or directly in front of the user.

The result is a computing environment that takes better advantage of the physical world. Because information can be arranged throughout the entire physical environment instead of the screen, the "resolution" of the computing environment is virtually limitless. "Windows" can be projected onto nearly any surface in the user's space, or they can simply float or move around if need be.

3. A Look into the Augmented Workspace

Below are some screenshots of the prototype. They are taken from the point of view of the user, as seen through the HMD. These shots begin to show how system can be used to create an environment where the effects of the computer are truly ubiquitous.

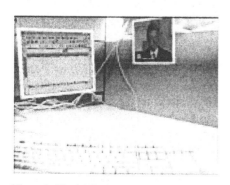

Figure 1: Work Windows

Figure 2: a Wall Calendar

In Figure 1, we see the basic windowing system. The primary work window (a word processor) is situated above the desk in front of the keyboard, while a video newsfeed is shown off to the right side.   With 3D audio, the volume from the video is lower and less obtrusive unless the user turns and focuses attention to it.

In figure 2, we see the calendar in a familiar position on the wall. Here, the calendar is placed in a position that is intuitive to this user, while still maintaining the online, dynamic properties of a computer based calendar and scheduler.

Currently, the Augmented Workspace system is built using a 400MHz PC with a 6 degree of freedom head tracker and a stereoscopic HMD. As the user's head moves, the head tracker ensures that the virtual objects stay correctly registered. Most of the rendering overhead is handled by a powerful 3D accelerator, which leaves most of the PCs computing power available for standard applications.

4. Conclusion and Future Work

Work on the Augmented Workspace is still in its early phases. We believe that the advantages of such a workspace will become very apparent as the system grows and as the equipment becomes more ergonomically comfortable. For instance, companies such as the MicroOptical Corporation [5] are introducing technologies that can place this kind of personal display in a pair of normal eyeglasses.

As work of the Augmented Workspace continues, we will begin to explore different modes of interaction with the virtual objects. Because of the 3D nature of this workspace, traditional modes of interaction may not be adequate. One alternative we will explore is using the head tracker as means to gauge which window has the user's attention. We will also use more trackers attached to hands to facilitate more natural interactions such as pointing, grabbing, and moving.

Plans are also being made to tie the Augmented Workspace in with locator and asset tracking systems. The result will be the ability to track and label people and objects in the physical world with virtual captions and labels. This extends the idea of ubiquitously located displays - the display could be virtually placed on or around the person.

5. References

1. Malone, T., How Do People Organize Their Desks? Implications for the Design of Office Information Systems. *ACM Transactions on Office Systems*, 1(1):99-112, January 1993.
2. Falk, J., Bjork, S. The BubbleBadge: A Wearable Public Display, *In Proceedings of CHI '99* (1999) 318-319.
3. Marmasse, N., comMotion: a context-aware communication system, *In Proceedings of CHI '99* (1999) 320-321.
4. Special Issue on Augmented Reality. 1993. *Communications of the ACM* 36(7)
5. The MicroOptical Corporation, http://www.microopticalcorp.com

The ChatterBox

Johan Redström, Patricija Jaksetic and Peter Ljungstrand

PLAY: Applied research on art and technology
The Viktoria Institute, Box 620, SE-405 30 Gothenburg, SWEDEN
{johan,patricia,peter}@viktoria.informatics.gu.se
http://www.viktoria.informatics.gu.se/play/

Abstract. The ChatterBox generates and presents texts based on text material produced at a certain place, for instance at an office. The idea is to create an alternative view of what is being done, that might serve as inspiration to think about existing material in new ways, as an incitement for informal discussions, as a piece of art, or just as a kind of dynamic wallpaper. In order to fulfil these aims and still not increase information overload, we aimed at making the ChatterBox an instance of calm technology designed to remain in the background of our activities. In this paper, we describe the ChatterBox concept along with some initial experiences and future research directions.

1   Introduction

The initial inspiration for the ChatterBox comes from a novel by Douglas Coupland, called Microserfs [1], in which the main character Dan at one time ponders on whether machines have a subconscious of their own or not. He starts to create a "SUBCONSCIOUS" file on his computer by writing down random words that comes across his mind. Even though the content of this file is fragmentary and largely at random, it comes to represent an alternative story or a complement to the main story of the novel.

We wanted to create a similar alternative view of what is going on at a certain place, by collecting material that is being produced, transforming it, and presenting it at public places. The idea was not to give an exact or accurate picture of the activities, but rather to create a public resource that could serve as a piece of art, as inspiration to think about the work in new ways or as a support for becoming aware of ongoing activities.

The aim was to design the ChatterBox as an instance of "calm technology" [6]. In Weiser and Brown's view, technology becomes calm when it remains in the background, or periphery, of our activities unless especially attended to, making it a readily available resource that still does not contribute to information overload. As the ChatterBox conveys information about ongoing activities, it can support some kind of awareness of these activities. However, the kind of awareness supported by the ChatterBox' fragmentary texts is more in line with abstract displays such as the Dangling String [6], Ambient Displays [8], AROMA [5] and Visual Who [2], than applications such as for instance Portholes [3] or TickerTape [4]. Further, the

ChatterBox has been designed as a resource for co-located, rather than distributed, groups of people. As the ChatterBox is not primarily intended to solve a specific task or problem, but rather to be a part of an environment, systems halfway between art and applications, e.g. [7], are important sources of inspiration.

2 The ChatterBox

The ChatterBox generates and presents texts, or short "phrases", based on text material produced by people working in an office environment. Offices seemed well suitable for this purpose, since people typically produce text at such places, and appreciate awareness of what is "going on", as well as some inspiration. The ChatterBox was designed with wallpapers, rather than ordinary information displays in mind. Thus, the presentation of the material should be aesthetically appealing and, without ceasing to be dynamic, rather slow. Instead of introducing yet another window on the desktop computer screen, the ChatterBox uses displays that are situated where people naturally move around or gather, as people should not have to attend specifically to the ChatterBox. Further, the purpose is not to make people stand and look at it for long periods of time, but to invite them to take a quick glance while passing. Displays can be placed in corridors and lunchrooms to be viewed in a relaxed manner and to provide themes for, for instance, casual discussions.

In order to make the ChatterBox fully fade to the background, no explicit actions should be required to use it. However, for privacy issues we have placed the control over what is being submitted to the system in the hands of the user. Even though automatic collection of material from local computer networks might be preferable when trying to reach beyond a traditional human-computer interface as far as possible, many privacy issues are avoided by letting users actively submit text to a dedicated email account or a directory in the computer file system. However, as the transformation of the material will be quite extensive, at least partial automatic collection of material could be acceptable in some cases.

2.1 An Early Prototype and Some Experiences

The first prototype used text documents as input and returned a continuous sequence of "phrases" made up of three to five randomly selected words from a database containing the words from the documents. Words that were not likely to convey any informative meaning, such as prepositions and conjunctions, were filtered out using an algorithm based on statistical measures of word frequencies. The generated texts were presented as scrolling text in a console window.

We have tried the prototype in two settings: at our office using a projector on a wall in the common corridor, and at a large reception party using three 100" background projection displays. Despite the lack of almost any syntactically correct sentences, it inspired informal discussions and gave its audience a few laughs. However, it was clear that the random phrases were too abstract to be informative for the purpose of supporting awareness about activities. Also, random phrases seem to require too much attention to make sense to the viewer. In future prototypes this problem will be addressed by using more advanced text processing and text generation techniques. Several other factors seemed to prevent the ChatterBox being a truly calm technology as well, most notably the displays used and the very fact that the system was novel to the viewers.

3 Future Work

Since this is research in progress, work is put on developing a second prototype that better matches the intended purposes with the ChatterBox. More advanced text processing is being applied, e.g. techniques from research in information retrieval and filtering, as well as more linguistic approaches. Automatic text tagging systems and semantic networks will enable us to use for instance finite automata for generating sentences. We will also try to transform whole sentences or even paragraphs by substituting just a few words, thereby saving more of the original context. As the ChatterBox is designed to furnish certain places, aesthetic considerations will also be important in future work and for instance the visualisation will be improved. Further, the development of electronic ink and similar non light-emitting display techniques might open up new possibilities when creating ubiquitous and calm displays.

In order to find out how well the ChatterBox performs and for whom, we will perform formative evaluations at several different locations using primarily qualitative methods. Especially, finding out how "calm" the ChatterBox can be made without losing the effect of being inspiring, entertaining and useful for conveying awareness, is an important research question in the search for calm technology.

References

1. Coupland, D. (1995). *Microserfs*. Flamingo, London, UK.
2. Donath, J. S (1995). Visual Who: Animating the affinities and activities of an electronic community. In: *Proceedings of Multimedia '95*, pp. 99-107. ACM Press.
3. Dourish, P. & Bly, S. (1992). Portholes: Supporting Awareness in a Distributed Work Group. In: *Proceedings of CHI '92*, pp. 541-547. ACM Press.
4. Fitzpatrick, G., Parsowith, S., Segall, B. & Kaplan, S. (1998). Tickertape: Awareness in a Single Line. In: *Conference Summary of CHI '98*, pp. 281-282. ACM Press.
5. Rønby Pedersen, E. & Sokoler, T. (1997). AROMA: abstract representation of presence supporting mutual awareness. In: *Proceedings of CHI'97*, pp. 51-58. ACM Press.
6. Weiser, M. & Seely Brown, J. (1996). Designing Calm Technology. In: *PowerGrid Journal 1.01*. Available at: http://www.powergrid.com/1.01/calmtech.html (1999-06-30)
7. White, T. & Small, D. (1998). An Interactive Poetic Garden. In: *Conference Summary of CHI '98*, pp. 303-304, ACM Press.
8. Wisneski, C., Ishii, H., Dahley, A., Gorbet, M., Brave, S., Ullmer, B. and Yarin, P. (1998). Ambient Displays: Turning Architectural Space into and Interface between People and Digital Information. In: *Proceedings of CoBuild '98*, pp. 22-32. Springer-Verlag.

Pollen: Virtual Networks That Use People as Carriers

Natalie Glance, Dave Snowdon

Xerox Research Centre Europe, Grenoble Laboratory,
6 chemin de Maupertuis, 38240 Meylan, France
{glance, snowdon, meunier}@xrce.xerox.com

Abstract. In this paper, we propose a novel kind of network that uses people instead of wires (or other communication media) to carry message packets between devices and between physical places. In the course of their day, people move from device to device and from location to location. We will describe how this movement of people can be harnessed to allow the communication of electronic messages, albeit in a way that is relatively unreliable and unpredictable compared with traditional networks. This new kind of network infrastructure has a number of advantages, such as low cost and scalability.

1. Introduction

The principal idea behind the Pollen network is to network devices and physical spaces using people instead of wires. Examples of devices and objects include printers, facsimile machines, video-conferencing equipment, books and other small objects. Examples of physical locations include meeting rooms, offices, and reception desks. This large variety of devices and locations is typically very expensive to network using wires. But these nodes are already connected together – by the movement of people. The Pollen network provides an infrastructure that supports the distribution and collection of information and does so without relying on traditional network technology.

Pollen also makes it possible for information to be shared and distributed where needed simply by the everyday actions of groups of people. People need not be aware of how the distribution is taking place nor of the details of their participation in the process. Information (such as hints, tips and other comments) can be associated with physical objects in the work environment and made easily available to colleagues.

This is accomplished using, for example, PDAs to perform redundant data transfer. The metaphor we use is one of plants being pollinated by insects. When an insect visits a flower to take advantage of the free supply of nectar it inevitably collects some pollen on its body. When it moves to a different flower some of this pollen rubs off. In the same way, when a user visits a device, not only can the user leave comments on the device, but the device can also transfer pieces of pollen to the user's PDA. The pieces of pollen may be either visible or invisible to the user, depending on their relevance to the user. Relevance depends on both the person's identity and the current context. Users are notified, for example, about pollen addressed specifically to them or pertaining to their current location. When the user next visits another device, the pieces of pollen stored in the PDA can then be selectively passed along. Through the cumulative actions of many people interacting with many devices in this way, messages are transferred node-by-node across the network. We are currently using Java iButtons [1] as the nodes with which the PDAs communicate but any small, rugged, device could be used or in the case of electronic devices they could be equipped with a suitable wireless or contact based interface.

An addition to this is a central organisational memory, which we also refer to as the hive. When the PDA is next docked with the user's workstation the cached pollen is uploaded to the central organisational memory. Information can also flow in the other direction. When comments become obsolete the organisational memory can transfer commands to a docked PDA instructing it to expire the comment(s) when the PDA next encounters the specified iButton(s). Although the hive is not strictly necessary for Pollen to function it allows the possibility of optimising the traffic flow since there is the possibility to learn which PDAs are most likely to visit a given node and thereby make "intelligent" routing decisions. The use of the organisational memory also allows people to obtain an overall view of the information in a Pollen network and to centrally update this information – for example to produce new manuals or Frequently Asked Question lists (FAQs) to be associated with particular devices, or to do distributed diagnosis.

Another advantage to this scheme in addition to the lack of a physical network infrastructure is that it is not restricted to an organisation. Multiple organisations (even homes) can use the same technology. We can use cryptography to ensure that the information can only be used in conjunction with a device with the appropriate keys.

2. Related Work

The work most similar to Pollen is Locust Swarm [3] which uses solar powered devices positioned in buildings to store annotations and provide location information to users via their wearable computers. Another application also from MIT, is Meme Tags [4] which allows small textual messages to be passed among users via badges worn by each user which communicate via infra-red.

We believe that Pollen has several advantages over existing network technology including: *less infrastructure* (little administration and no cabling is required), *lower cost* (iButtons are cheap and the PDAs which act as the information carriers are those that the users use as part of their everyday life) and *ease of configuration* (nodes in the Pollen network can be added or removed trivially, with almost zero administrative overhead).

There are a number of risks associated with the successful implementation of a Pollen network. The first is the storage and bandwidth limitations of the iButton and the PDAs. The second is the computational complexity, completeness and robustness of the Pollen algorithm, which as yet remains to be determined. The third is the bandwidth of the Pollen network itself, which depends on the behaviour of the pollen transmitters – that is, the PDA owners themselves. Finally, there is the need to handle inconsistent information caused by multiple copies of the same information being present on the.

3. Conclusion

We now have a prototype of the Pollen network based on Palm IIIs and iButtons [1]. We are also working on simulations of Pollen in order to better understand its behaviour – our current model is based on the concept of epidemic algorithms [2] to model the spread of messages through the network.

Another research thread involves knowledge extraction from the hive's history. Can we detect patterns in the movements of people and the use of devices, which, for example, can help us improve the working environment?

Finally, in parallel with these three research threads, we are investigating possible applications of the concept not only in the work environment, but also in the home environment, in retail and in manufacturing. Since an iButton can be placed almost anywhere (including objects which are mobile), it is possible to connect just about anything to a Pollen network with almost zero overhead, thus providing a platform for numerous new kinds of application scenarios.

Acknowledgements

The authors are indebted to Jean-Luc Meunier, for his work on a simulation of the Pollen network and Mike Glantz, Leon Rubinstein & Ian Soboroff for joining us in numerous discussions and especially for their contagious enthusiasm and support. Also many thanks are due to Nourredine Hamoudi and Nicolas Peret for their work constructing an initial prototype of the Pollen System.

References

1. iButtons, Dallas Semiconductor Corp, http://www.ibutton.com/.
2. Demers, A., Gealy, M., Greene, D., Hauser, C., Irish, W., Larson, J., Manning, S., Shenker, S., Sturgis, H., Swinehart, D., Terry, D., Woods, D., "Epidemic Algorithms for Replicated Database Maintenance" PARC report, CSL-89-1, January 1989
3. T. Starner, D. Kirsh, S. Assefa , "The Locust Swarm: An Environmentally-powered, Networkless Location and Messaging System   IEEE International Symposium on Wearable Computing, Oct. 1997.
4. Borovoy, R., Martin, F., Vemuri, S., Resnick, M., Silverman, B., Hancock, C. "Meme Tags and Community Mirrors: Moving from Conferences to Collaboration", in proceedings of CSCW'98, November 1998, Seatle, USA, pp. 159-168

VoIP in Context-Aware Communication Spaces

Theo Kanter (theo@it.kth.se), Henrik Gustafsson (hegu@it.kth.se)

Ericsson Radio Systems AB, KI/ERA/T/KA, SE-16480 Stockholm, Sweden

Abstract. Wireless and positioning technologies in combination with Internet's demonstrated capability to integrate voice and data, further leveraged by the use of software agents, allows for rapid introduction, at low cost, of a rich communication space where artifacts, people, and non-physical entities are integral parts. Given these benefits, we propose an open architecture for the integration of VoIP exemplified by a prototype of a lightweight contact center for distributed virtual networks of professionals.

1 Introduction

The Internet Protocol (IP) and processing in the end stations permits multiple applications and services to the transport medium simultaneously, where hosts have equal roles. Services may be triggered by any event, not just a (telephone) call [1] . In particular, advances in mobile computing research have shown that personal communication can greatly benefit from what has become known as context- and location-aware computing. Such applications take into account aspects such as (1) who is communicating and with whom or what, (2) the context which that person or object is in, and (3) the location or position of the person or object (since it could be an intelligent mobile object). This awareness has been shown to be highly relevant to achieving more meaningful communication. Examples of research regarding context-aware use of devices in communication are Active Badges [2] and the SmartBadge [3] . Examples of context-aware information systems are the "Forget-me-not" [4] and the Stick-e system [5] . We have come to recognize this datacom-centric approach to communication as central to the creation of new classes of personal communication services. However, the above mentioned previous work does not address the issue of incorporating multimedia communication in a datacom-centric service architecture. Recent developments that extend the scope of telephony (personal communication) to the Internet offer new possibilities in this direction. VoIP (Voice over IP) refers to the different protocols that are used to transport multimedia and the necessary signaling by means of the Internet Protocol (IP). We argue that we can only successfully deliver the new personal communication services [1] if multimedia services are delivered by the same access (IP) as opposed a traditional switched access – thus, VoIP is a key element of this new service model.

2 Communication Space

We are now able to build applications where the user is not external to a network, but a participant, immersed as it were, in a communication space of Ubiquitous Computing [6] where the application adapts to a changing context. In our model for personal communication, the services of the past will migrate and become an integral part of a communication space on the Internet and may cease to perceive them as services. This communication

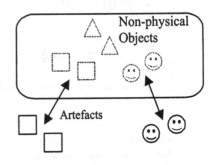

Figure 1 Communication Space

space will interact with the physical world by means context & location-aware technology. In fact the physical world can be represented and visualized, and this allows us to interact with each other and the things that we know, within this communication space. At the same time, we will interact with things in this communication space that have no existence in the physical world.

3 Prototype

In order to verify our hypothesis, we built a prototype system with location & context awareness functionality and support for mobile users that is used to improve communications both within an office environment and with others who wish to contact us in various ways. By routing communication automatically to the user's VoIP terminal (running on either stationary desktops or wearable computers connected via a wireless LAN), staff members located outside of the office but connected via remote IP-access were perceived as being 'present' just as those within the office building. The latter is important to

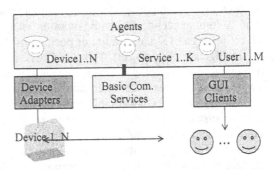

Figure 2 Architecture Overview

the maintenance of the group, despite the physical distribution. Among the scenarios that we implemented and explored were messaging and voice communication, location and presence information and a context-aware public information display in a contact-center setting. Many more scenarios are possible, and we are only at the start of research regarding such new applications. The system that has been described above has been up and running for about a year and a half in our lab network. Currently we have a number of badges, badge receivers, information displays, and users in the system. We have integrated means for remote access to our agent-enabled communication environment, such as Internet access, a web interface, remote dial-in (a modem pool), a voice gateway (for calls to and from the telephony network) and a wireless-LAN. This has contributed to the exploration of the usefulness of the applications beyond the scope of a limited office space, where one is very much aware of the presence or non-presence of users, and thus expanded its value.

4 Conclusions

Our service architecture allows for integration of VoIP in the user interface to build new applications that are open-ended in functionality and adaptability to arbitrary levels of "richness". It supports the notion of communication spaces and intelligent communication objects. In addition, we have found that the new applications that are based on an end-to-end IP-infrastructure can be installed, configured and managed entirely by end-users. There is no need to package applications and service-management support with the network access. With our architecture and prototype we have shown the ease of integrating all kinds of basic services into applications *and* we can trigger on any event, not just calls - as in telephony networks. Therefore, an architecture based on the Internet for both voice and data services modeled on distributed software agents offers a framework for the rapid introduction of new applications, and subsequent seamless integration with other services (provided they make sense to a user). While our work offers a strong argument for new applications and moving these applications to an Internet-type infrastructure, there are a number of serious obstacles (from a user's point of view) that need to be overcome. *Security* and *privacy* issues must be addressed before more than early adopters will vest their trust in these systems. These systems must be *plug and play* in order to become popular and usable. There can be no arduous installation procedures or need for central customer-administration support systems.

5 References

[1] T. Kanter, C. Frisk, and H. Gustafsson: Ellemtel - "Context-Aware Personal Communication for TeleLiving". Forthcoming publication to be published in Personal Technologies.

[2] R. Want, A. Hopper, V. Falcao, and Jonathan Gibbons - The Active Badge Location System - ACM Transactions on Information Systems, 10(1): 91-102, January 1992.

[3] G. Q. Maguire Jr., Mark T. Smith, and H. W. Peter Beadle "SmartBadges: a wearable computer and communication system" Codes/CASHE '98, 16-March 1998, Seattle, Washington, U.S.A.

[4] M. Lamming and M. Flynn, 1994. "Forget-me-not:" Intimate Computing in Support of Human Memory. In Proceedings of FRIEND21, '94 International Symposium on Next Generation Human Interface, Meguro Gajoen, Japan.

[5] Brown P J, Bovey J D and Chen X. (1997) Context-aware applications: from the laboratory to the marketplace, IEEE Personal Communications 4(5), 58-64.

[6] Mark Weiser, "The Computer for the Twenty-First Century," Scientific American, pp. 94-10, September 1991

A Platform for Environment-Aware Applications

Sven van der Meer, Stefan Arbanowski, Radu Popescu-Zeletin

[1] Technical University Berlin, Franklinstraße 28, D-10587 Berlin, Germany
e-mail: vdmeer@cs.tu-berlin.de

Abstract. Environment-aware Applications and Mobile Communications have proven significant relevance for future telecommunications and computing. This poster describes an approach to integrate heterogeneous off-the-shelf technology to fulfill the demands of environment-aware applications. The integration has been done employing a CORBA based middleware. That gave us the opportunity to define open interfaces which can be used by several environment-aware applications.

1. Introduction

The rapid progress in the melting computing and telecommunication technologies enables new application scenarios. Mobile voice and data communication, localization and positioning systems, and portable devices, have not only become available for everybody, they have even reached a degree of miniaturization that enables further integration of complex systems to hand-held devices.

Communication technology comprises available systems such as GSM-900, GSM-1800, DECT, as well as proposed systems such as wireless ATM and UMTS. Positioning and localization, scaling from global to in-house systems, is provided by miniature Global Positioning System (GPS) receivers as well as infrared tracking.

Within this context, GMD FOKUS and TU Berlin / OKS have established several projects (VISIT, Mobile Guide, PCS-Tracker, iPCSS), focusing on the integration of state-of-the-art mobile and localization and communication technology with special consideration of content handling and adaptation. The projects are based on our experience within the research institutes regarding electronic tracking, Personal Communication Support [Vdm99], filtering and dynamic conversion of communication media [Pfe97], middleware platforms [Eck97], and Mobile Agents [Arb98]. Here, we will introduce the platform of these projects which supports environment-aware applications by integrating different technologies developed during the past years.

2. A Platform for Environment-aware Applications

We have developed a platform, which offers communication, information as well as localization and controlling capabilities to business applications. To provide such a variety of services in an understandable way, the platform must have well defined *reference points* to access different services, allowing to integrate them step by step into the platform. The solution for that problem was the establishment of a Distributed Processing Environment (DPE), which has been build on top of a CORBA based middleware platform. The DPE provides well defined *interfaces* for business applications and is able to access different kinds of services, protocols, networks, or hosts through its Native Computing and Communication Environment. Therefore, it could be seen as an universal wrapping mechanism, encapsulating all underlying technologies.

The technologies we integrated in our platform are taken from recent research projects. In detail we applied to our platform:

- localization capabilities (active badge and GPS support),
- environment awareness (sensors measuring temperature, power supply status),
- communication capabilities (voice, fax, voicemail, SMS, paging, email),
- conversion capabilities (e.g. to deliver a fax to a telephone line),
- facility control capabilities (e.g. to switch on the light), and
- information storage capabilities (multimedia databases, profile databases).

2.1 Architecture

Figure 1 depicts a general overview of the layered platform architecture. That enforces strong separation of functionality and the mandatory definition of interfaces between these layers. Using these interfaces, each layer can be designed and implemented separately without facing other layers. This can be achieved through agreed services each layer offers via specified access points. On the highest layer of the architecture, several business applications could be established to fulfill certain tasks.

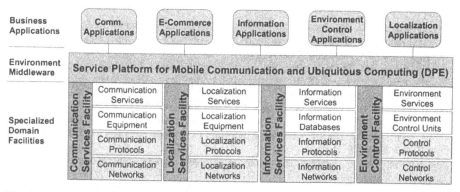

Fig. 1. Overview of the platform architecture

These applications are settled on top of our DPE which represents *the Platform for Mobile Communications & Ubiquitous Computing*. Generic interfaces have been defined for the access of the services provided by the DPE. The DPE itself uses so called "*facilities*" to react on any request.

Up to now, we have identified four facilities: communication, localization, information, and the environment. The facilities are able to interact with different architectural layers (services, equipment, protocols, network). For instances, whereas communication related application only interact with communication services, the communication facility will also interact with communication equipment to manage a communication session directly.

To access a facility, an application programmer has to use different *reference points* which are realized as CORBA objects with IDL typed interfaces. They provide generic functionality for business applications like `make_call(number)`, `find_user(user)`, or `switchON(lightID)`. Thus, the programmer has not to deal with any kind of service specific implementations.

The platform could be easily enhanced by exchanging any components with newer ones or by adding new components which are able to deal with upcoming services.

3. Summary

Our platform provides information technologies, communication technologies as well as any kind of monitoring or controlling technologies by integrating their service specific implementations in a middleware based platform. On top of this platform a variety of business applications could be established in shortest time. Up to now we have implemented a visitor information system, a unified messaging system, and a person tracking system. Currently we are focussing on Intelligent rooms, which adapt automatically temperature, light and the installed communication facilities based on personal preferences.

References

[Arb98] Arbanowski, St., Breugst, M., Busse, I., Magedanz, T.: Impact of Standard Mobile Agent Technology on Telecommunications. 5th Conference on Computer Communications, AFRICOM-CCDC'98, Tunis, October 20-22-1998

[Arb99] Arbanowski, St., v.d. Meer, S.: *Service Personalization for Unified Messaging Systems.* – Proc. of the fourth IEEE Symposium on Computers and Communications, ISCC'99, Red Sea, Egypt, July 6-8, 1999

[Eck97] Eckert, K.-P.; Festini, M.; Schoo, P.; Schürmann, G.: *TANGRAM: Development of Object-Oriented Frameworks for TINA-C Based Multimedia Telecommunication Applications.* - Proc. of the 3rd International Symposium on Autonomous Decentralized Systems: ISADS'97, Berlin, 9-11 April 1997

[Nan97] Nanneman, D.: *Unified Messaging: A Progress Report.* - in: Telecommunications Magazine, March 1997

[Pfe97b] Pfeifer, T.; Arbanowski, St.; Popescu-Zeletin, R.: *Resource Selection in Heterogeneous Communication Environments using the Tele Descriptor.* - Proc. of the 4rd COST 237 Workshop: From Multimedia services to Network services, Lisboa, Dec. 15-19, 1997, publ: Lecture Notes on Computer Science, Volume 1356, Springer: Berlin 1997

[Pfe98] Pfeifer, T., v.d. Meer, S.: *The Active Store providing Quality Enhanced Unified Messaging.* Proc. of the 5th Conference on Computer Communications, AFRICOM-CCDC'98, Tunis, October 20-22-1998

[Vdm99] v.d. Meer, S., Arbanowski, St.: An Approach for a 4th Generation Messaging System. - Proc. of the 4th International Symposium on Autonomous Decentralized Systems, ISADS'99, Tokyo, March 21-23 1999

[Zel98] Popescu-Zeletin, R., Pfeifer, T., Magedanz, T.: *Applying Location-Aware Computing for Electronic Commerce: Mobile Guide.* Proc. of the 5th Conference on Computer Communications, AFRICOM-CCDC'98, Tunis, October 20-22-1998

The Design and Implementation of the Ubidata Information Dissemination Framework

Ana Paula Afonso, Mário J. Silva, João P. Campos, Francisco S. Regateiro

Departamento de Informática
Faculdade de Ciências da Universidade de Lisboa
Phone: +351.1.7500153, Fax: +351.1.7500084
{apa, mjs, jcampos, fasr}@di.fc.ul.pt

Abstract. The dissemination model for information delivery has motivated an increasing interest, both in wired and wireless environments. In this model, the user subscribes the desired information and then passively receives new and filtered information. We propose a model for dissemination of information to mobile users, called *dynamic channel model*. It is a set of extensions to the conceptual models developed for information channels, enabling the capture of mobility-specific requirements. These are used for filtering and setting update order priorities for the information that users intend to monitor, which depends on their location and changes as they roam. This model is supported in Ubidata, an adaptable framework for information dissemination in mobile computing systems.

1. Introduction

Mobile computing environments are characterized by frequent disconnections, resource limitations, bandwidth restrictions and fast-changing locations. A requirement of any information system for such a computing environment is the efficient access to critical data regardless of location. One key constraint is that data should only be transferred between the stationary network and the mobile computer if absolutely necessary. These characteristics impose flexibility and adaptability as a key criteria in the design of mobile information systems [8].

The need for alternatives to the traditional form of data distribution (client-server model) has been identified in modern large-scale networks, and information dissemination models were proposed to support the requirements/constraints of these environments [5]. In this model, a set of publishers uses channels to disseminate information to a large set of subscribers. Recently, push-based techniques [7] has been proposed as a means of disseminating information to a large set of users in wireless and wired environments.

To address the intrinsic needs of mobile environments, we have developed Ubidata, a general and adaptable framework for mobile computing dissemination systems. This framework has been specifically designed for providing a solution to information distribution to a large set of mobile users, based on extensions to the conceptual models developed for information channels [4], and a hybrid scheme (combining push and pull) of dissemination of information [6].

2. Dynamic Channel Model

Our conceptual model, called *Dynamic Channel Model*, is inspired on the notions introduced by D. Cheriton [5]. An *information channel*, shortly *channel*, is defined as an abstraction of communication and system resources necessary to distribute information to a set of users. Our application implements the publisher/subscriber model [6]. The contents carried by a channel are grouped into logical and atomic units called *items*. An item may be a source file or a database object represented on a SQL statement in the case of a database source information. When a subscriber adds a channel to his reception list, and before starting receiving data on that channel, he must select and configure the items he is interested on.

Our work is based on a hybrid schema of data delivery [6]. We provide two different types of data delivery that may be combined to optimize application requirements: *periodic pull* and *aperiodic push*. The subscriber uses polling (periodic pull approach) to obtain data from publishers, defining individual schedules for each of the items subscribed. We use aperiodic push to broadcast information to reachable subscribers from the publisher. Publishers can associate *notifications* to the items. Push delivery is *event-driven* - a subscriber of an item with a notification receives an attention message triggered by an event such as a data modification in the item contents.

A channel item of a channel has a region to model a geographical area, represented as a composite shape. We have augmented the channel concept with this characteristic to enable the adaptation of the items' visualization behavior to the location of the subscribers. We coined the term *dynamic channels* to designate a channel with the basic adaptation properties we have just introduced. The class diagram representing our dissemination model and the detailed description of the dynamic channel model is presented in [1].

3. Ubidata

The goal of Ubidata is to provide a flexible and general framework for mobile computing information dissemination systems. Ubidata can serve as the basis for development of information systems that have in common some characteristics, such as the distribution of information sources to a potentially large set of users.

The architecture of Ubidata follows the three-tiered scheme common to information systems. The Presentation Layer, which includes the graphical interface, enables the user to view data sent by the publisher. The Application Logic Layer encloses the objects representing domain concepts that fulfil application requirements (Domain Objects) and the supporting services (Service Objects). The Storage Layer encloses databases or files that contain the information to be disseminated by the publisher and received by subscribers.

The fundamental domain objects are Transmitter and Tuner. The framework also includes a set of service objects: Positioning System Manager, Replication Manager, Web Server, Event Listener and Event Manager. The detailed description of each domain and service object is presented in [1].

Development Process

In our perspective, the elaboration and construction of information dissemination applications consists in the personalization of our dissemination model and customizing the software components of Ubidata. The development process we propose comprises the major steps of analysis, design, and implementation. We have introduced new steps to capture channel-specific information. We organized these steps in a methodology that uses UML [3]. To provide automatic support for the development process of mobile applications, Ubidata includes GIL, an open and portable tool for editing and generating dynamic channel specifications [2]. GIL is a multi-user, collaborative, editing tool. GIL is a tool that guides its users through the development of information dissemination applications, allowing them to create and characterize channel representations that automatically configure a software framework to disseminate third party contents.

4. Application

We have applied the concepts presented in Section 2 and 3 to the development of a prototype mobile information system for firefighters of the National Civil Protection Service. We developed a first version of the fire-fighters system that runs on laptops with Microsoft database and Web software (for implementation details see [1]). We intend to evaluate GIL and Ubidata usability by monitoring its use in the development of application prototypes and comparing the software metrics of these prototypes against those of identical applications built using generic software development environments. This information will be used to improve a second version of GIL and to drive further refinements to the Ubidata architecture. We are working on a second version of Ubidata to run on much smaller devices, PDAs and smart mobile phones.

References

[1] A.P. Afonso, F.S. Regateiro, and M.J. Silva, Dynamic Channels: A New Methodology for Mobile Computing Applications, Technical Report DI/FCUL TR-98-4, Department of Computer Science, University of Lisbon, April 1998.

[2] A.P. Afonso, J.P. Campos, and M.J. Silva, GIL: a Software Tool for the Construction of Information Dissemination Systems, Technical Report DI/FCUL TR-99-4, Department of Computer Science, University of Lisbon, June 1999.

[3] G. Booch, J. Rumbaugh, and I. Jacobson, *The Unified Modeling Language User Guide*, Addison Wesley, 1998.

[4] CDF documentation, http://www.w3.org/TR/NOTE-CDFsubmit.html.

[5] D. Cheriton, Dissemination-Oriented Communication Systems, Technical Report, Stanford University, 1992.

[6] M. Franklin and S. Zdonik, A Framework to Scalable Dissemination-Based Systems, *ACM OOPSLA Conference* (Invited Paper), October 1997.

[7] Push Publishing Technologies, http://www.strom.com/imc/t4a.html.

[8] M. Satyanarayanan, Fundamental Challenges in Mobile Computing, *15th ACM Symposia on Principles of Distributed Computing*, 1996.

Co-authoring in Dynamic Teams with Mobile Individuals

Cora Burger, Oliver Schramm

University of Stuttgart,
Institute of Parallel and Distributed High-Performance Systems (IPVR),
Breitwiesenstr. 20-22, D-70565 Stuttgart, Germany
E-Mail: {caburger, schramm}@informatik.uni-stuttgart.de

Abstract. Current solutions to support co-authoring of documents focus on building new systems for participants who are assumed to be connected permanently by a network. We propose an alternate approach, that copes with increasing usage of mobile/handheld devices and heterogeneous editing systems. It contains representatives for mobile participants in a fixed part of the network. By using a global standardized document format and a wide spread platform, the flexibility to constitute arbitrary teams in spontaneous manner is increased.

1 Introduction

To an increasing extent, people are working together in teams while sharing and co-authoring documents. It has been treated extensively before, how this process can be supported by computers in general and especially across spatial and temporal limits (see e. g. [4]). But besides the fact, that still some aspects are missing, new challenges come up with increasing usage of mobile devices and current development in the area of computer networks and distributed systems.

In this paper, we treat the following problems:

- mobility of users, resulting in the fact that they are not permanently connected to the rest of a team but nevertheless should not miss essential information,
- usage of different editing tools, because teams can consist of immobile and mobile participants with different facilities and/or people may favour different tools,
- dynamics, that means, for each document a new team has to be constituted and the need to cooperate can arise spontaneously.

This situation holds especially for handheld devices that are a special kind of mobile devices with a number of restrictions concerning resources. Thus, only slim versions of editors like PocketWord can be applied, whereas a wide spectrum of editors like Emacs, FrameMaker, StarOffice or MS Word is available on more powerful devices.

Current systems do not adequately cope with these conditions. They consist of special multi-user editors requiring adjustment of people. This effort as well as the installation overhead has been slightly reduced by integrating the wide spread World

Wide Web technology ([6]). A more extensive solution is given in [5], who present a suited framework to enable arbitrary configuration and tailorability including the possibility of different user interfaces for participants. But neither of these approaches takes into account mobile users with handheld devices.

2 Distributed document environment (DDE)

Figure 1 shows the architecture coping with requirements as postulated above. It can be configured and extended in a number of ways (see [7] for a detailed description). For example, we take three different users (1) with corresponding editing tools (2). A special wrapper (3) cares for connecting each of these editing tools to the rest of the world. To this end, it offers an interface (4) and uses the interface (5) of the underlying platform.

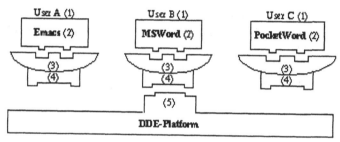

Fig. 1: DDE-Architecture

The DDE platform contains the following objects and services:
- To cope with the problem of different document formats, a global format and transformations are needed.
- Management of all objects involved. Objects are: personal participant objects representing their users even in case of connection loss, transformation objects and arbitrary kinds of document objects, e. g. books and structural elements of books.
- According to [8], enablers represent different functions that are needed in the context of supporting cooperative work (see below).
- A notification service delivering information from sources (enablers) to sinks (participant objects) by applying filtering mechanisms for privacy purposes and prevention from information flood.

For the application of co-authoring, the following types of enablers are essential:
- Share enabler to handle consistency if multiple users are modifying the same document object in the same time interval.
- Notify enabler watching modification operations according to the users interest and producing information for the notification service. Thus, other participants can be kept aware of the state of interesting document parts during the whole period from start to end of the co-authoring process.
- Version enabler for version control of document objects.
- Access control and security enabler to guarantee access according to roles and care for decryption/encryption of operations and data.

An instance of all these enablers is needed for each document object.

3 Summary and Outlook

The framework as described above enables co-authoring in a heterogeneous, dynamic and mobile environment. It allows the integration of different editing facilities and of so-called enablers realizing arbitrary consistency and awareness policies. A prototype with editor Emacs, CORBA (Common Object Request Broker Architecture) platform, transformation into SGML (Standard Generalized Markup Language) and a pessimistic consistency mechanism with total exclusion is running.

The portability of CORBA to handheld devices was studied in [3]. But the following drawback was neglected: if a user is currently disconnected, information delivered to her will be lost. To cope with this problem, the above introduced personal participant objects are informed instead. By configuring this object, a user can determine the way, she will be notified in case of being offline (e. g., a mail is created). Another solution to this problem was given in [2] by using a platform with mobile agents.

Currently, less restrictive consistency mechanisms for mobile environments (cf. [1]) are examined and implemented by taking into account special requirements of heterogeneous editing systems. It is planned to integrate further editing tools, especially those being available on handheld devices, and use XML (Extensible Markup Language) instead of SGML as global format.

References

1. Berger, M.. Generic support of autonomous work and reintegration in the context of computer supported team work (in german). Doctoral thesis, Fakultät Informatik, Technische Universität Dresden, 1999.
2. Burger, C.: Team awareness with mobile agents in mobile environments. Proc. 7th International Conference on Computer Communications and Networks (IC3N'98), IEEE Computer Society, Los Alamitos, October 1998, pp. 45-49
3. Dittrich, J., Becker , T.: Middleware for Development of CSCW Handheld Applications. Workshop Handheld CSCW, International Conference CSCW'98, Seattle, U.S.A., November 1998. See also http://www.teco.edu/hcscw/papers.html
4. Ellis, C. A. , Gibbs, S. J. , Rein, G. L.: Groupware – Some Issues and Experiences. Communications of the ACM 34:1, 38–58 (1991)
5. Koch, M., Koch, J.: Application of Frameworks in Groupware - The Iris Group Editor Environment. ACM Computing Surveys Symposium on Frameworks, 1998. See also http://www11.informatik.tu-muenchen.de/publications/
6. Salcedo, M. R., Decouchant, D.: Structured Cooperative Authoring for the World Wide Web. Computer Supported Cooperative Work: The Journal of Collaborative Computing 6: 157–174, 1997
7. Schramm, O.: Development of a distributed document environment based on CORBA. Diploma thesis No. 1708, University of Stuttgart, February 1999
8. Syri, A.: Tailoring Cooperation Support through Mediators. ECSCW'97, Proceedings 1997, pp. 157-172

A Universal, Location-Aware Hoarding Mechanism

Uwe Kubach and Kurt Rothermel

Institute of Parallel and Distributed High-Performance Systems (IPVR)
University of Stuttgart, Breitwiesenstr. 20-22, D-70565 Stuttgart, Germany
Uwe.Kubach@informatik.uni-stuttgart.de

Abstract. Hoarding is an often used technique to overcome the disadvantages of wireless wide area communication. The basic idea of hoarding is to transfer information to a mobile device before it is actually accessed on the device. The main problem is to decide which information will be needed on the devices. We propose a hoarding mechanism which exploits the fact that the information a user accesses depends on his/her geographic location.

1 Introduction

In many mobile information systems the information the users access primarily depends on their geographic position. An example for such an information system is an electronic tourist guide [1].

In an outdoor environment, as is considered in this paper, wireless wide area networks (WAN) are used for the communication between information servers and mobile devices. To overcome the drawbacks of the wireless WANs, especially the big delay and the low bandwidth, the info-station infrastructure has been proposed [2]. There, a number of high-bandwidth wireless local area networks (LAN) with a low range, so called info-stations, are placed in an area otherwise only covered by a wireless WAN. When a user arrives at an info-station, as much as possible of the information he will probably need before reaching the next info-station is transferred to his device in advance (hoarding).

A problem is how to find out, which information the user will probably need. Existing hoarding schemes have either been developed for a certain application [5] or do not consider the user's location [4]. We propose a hoarding mechanism that can be used universally and takes into account the user's location, when deciding which information should be hoarded.

2 Idea

Our idea is based on the assumption that users of mobile information systems will access quite the same information when they are located at the same position, i.e. there is some kind of geographical locality in the users' access patterns. For example, in a tourist guide application the users will probably access information about the sightseeing highlights, which are close to their current position.

For our hoarding mechanism we distinguish between two types of spatial areas belonging to every info-station: its *coverage area* and its *service area*. The coverage area is the area in which the wireless LAN belonging to the info-station is available. The service area of an info-station is the area for which the information can be hoarded at this info-station.

Basically, our hoarding mechanism works as follows: for each info-station the information system holds a table with the identifiers of the information items referenced by users during their presence in the info-station's service area. Together with every identifier a hit counter is stored, which tells how often the item has been referenced from within the service area. When a user enters the coverage area of an info-station the most frequently referenced items are transferred to his/her mobile device.

Currently, we have some possible enhancements of our mechanism in mind. Due to space limitations we cannot describe them here in detail. The enhancements include the consideration of user and application categories in order to gather the access information on a more fine-grained level. We also think about exploiting syntactic and semantic relationships between different information items. One idea is to group semantically related items in so-called semantic clusters. Further improvements will be possible by predicting the users' movement directions and by using application hints.

3 Analysis

In this section we show how our mechanism depends on the geographical locality of the users' information requests. We also compare it to the results one would get, if the hoarded items were chosen randomly.

In the model, our analysis is based on, we consider an information system that provides access to a number of information items. Only a part of these items is accessed at the service area of each info-station.

For the simulation of the users' accesses we assumed that the accesses at every info-station are distributed according to a Zipf-Distribution. Furthermore, we assumed that the reference tables at every info-station reflect the state after the info-station has been up for a longer time ("hot" tables), not the initial state.

Our experiment consisted of the simulation of 100000 information requests. We took two plots: one showing the results for our mechanism and one showing the results, we got when the hoarded items were selected randomly.

In our experiment we varied the number of different items selected at every info-station. In other words: we varied the geographical locality. The storage space available at the user's mobile device was set to 100 items. The results of this experiment are shown in Fig. 1.

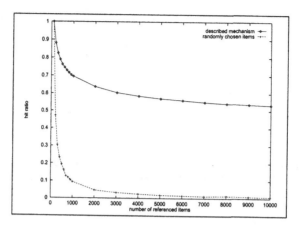

Fig. 1. Hit ratio for different numbers of items.

4 Conclusion and Future Work

In this paper we presented a hoarding mechanism which can be used universally for a large variety of information systems. We showed that with our mechanism high hit ratios are achieved as long as the geographical locality of the users' information requests is not too low.

A subject of our future work will be the test of the mechanism and the efficiency of the proposed enhancements in a real environment. Therefore, we plan to integrate our mechanism into a platform for location-aware applications currently developed at our institute [3].

References

1. N. Davies, K. Mitchell, K. Cheverst, and G. Blair. Developing a context sensitive tourist guide. In *Proceedings of the First Workshop on Human Computer Interaction with Mobile Devices*, pages 64–68, University of Glasgow, Scotland, U.K., May 1998.
2. D.J. Goodman, J. Borràs, N.B. Mandayam, and R.D. Yates. Infostations: A new system model for data and messaging services. In *Proceedings of the 47th Annual IEEE Vehicular Technology Conference (VTC '97)*, pages 969–973, Phoenix, AZ, USA, May 1997.
3. F. Hohl, U. Kubach, A. Leonhardi, K. Rothermel, and M. Schwehm. Next century challenges: Nexus – an open global infrastructure for spatial-aware applications. In *Proceedings of the Fifth Annual International Conference on Mobile Computing and Networking (MobiCom '99) (to appear)*, Seattle, WA, USA, August 1999.
4. G.H. Kuenning and G.J. Popek. Automated hoarding for mobile computers. In *Proceedings of the 16th ACM Symposium on Operating Systems Principles (SOSP '97)*, pages 264–275, St. Malo, France, October 1997.
5. T. Ye, H.-A. Jacobsen, and R. Katz. Mobile awareness in a wide area wireless network of info-stations. In *Proceedings of the Fourth International Conference on Mobile Computing and Networking (MobiCom '98)*, pages 109–120, Dallas, TX, USA, 1998.

QoS and Context Awareness for Mobile Computing

Dan Chalmers, Morris Sloman

Department of Computing, Imperial College, London SW7 2BZ, U.K.
{dc, mss}@doc.ic.ac.uk

Abstract. Systems must support context awareness for mobile applications to permit adaptation to heterogeneity of hosts and networks, and variations in the user's environment. We believe that context aware management of resources provides the most reliable basis for managing the non-deterministic behaviour of mobile systems.

1 Introduction

The integration of computing and wireless communications will facilitate mobile multimedia applications in many areas. A mobile computing device could range from notebook size to a web-enabled telephone, with considerable variation in processing power and user interface capabilities. Network connections also range from high-bandwidth LANs to low and variable bandwidth wireless. Hand-held devices often exhibit extremes of limitation and variation, and so are of particular interest.

Mobile applications have to be aware of and adapt to variations in the user's context and available resources, as discussed in [1]. Perceived quality will generally be dependant on the context [2]. In general, over-provisioning or a highly controlled infrastructure may not be practical or desirable as a means to enable QoS guarantees. We suggest that adaptive applications running in a context and resource aware environment can provide a powerful degree of autonomous context and QoS management, and so improve perceived QoS.

2 Context Aware QoS Management Architecture

Our basic framework for enabling context aware QoS management and adaptation is described in more detail in [3]. The application has QoS and context management components, which hold descriptions of the user requirements and control an adaptation engine, which interfaces to external data sources.

The context manager is provided with information from a system context manager, which handles generic context descriptions gathered from various sources. Context includes descriptions of display; user input devices; network bandwidth, delay, cost etc.; location and predicted future location; social situation and user activity.

The QoS manager negotiates with the system resource manager to reserve resources with specified characteristics. The resource manager is responsible for low-level tasks such as maintaining required throughput, while the application specifies requirements and performs large-scale adaptations affecting the presentation of data.

2.1 Context Aware QoS Management

The system context manager provides information to the resource manager on expected resource characteristics. This enables the resource manager to provide reservations against more accurate resource models. A change in resource model will cause a corresponding change in the adaptations performed by the application in order for requests to gain admission, e.g. when moving from wired to wireless networks, or areas of differing wireless network coverage. Context aware resource management also allows for intelligent selection of external resources at a system level, e.g. by mapping connections to the local mirror when moving between countries.

Resource reservation is required for QoS management of mobile applications [4,5] to make efficient use of the system's resources, while attempting to limit the application's expectations. It also provides a starting point for in-flow adaptation in the event of resource capacity deviating significantly from that expected. Reservations should be made on an end-to-end basis, where possible, in order to guarantee resources, as discussed in some depth in the QoS literature. Where end-to-end management is not supported local management based on previous characteristics is more effective than a blind best-effort system. This is especially useful in mobile systems where the network's last hop is often the limiting factor in the connection, and where wireless connections can render end-to-end guarantees meaningless.

2.2 Application Adaptation Due to Resource Variation

Applications incorporate an adaptation engine, which addresses issues of perception of quality [6]. This could be generalised to implement adaptation functions for media types and/or application classes. An adaptation engine must aim to provide an *achievable and acceptable* delivery of the data flow. By using media and/or application specific adaptation engines, the task of making the adaptations can be broken down, and an effective selection of adaptation strategy made.

An *achievable* performance region defines the capability of a resource in terms of a region of possible performance trade-off among the QoS managed parameters. An *acceptable* performance region defines the application requirements in terms of the same QoS parameters. The intersecting space then describes the "achievable and acceptable" region in the performance space, which the data flows should occupy.

A data *flow variant* defines a performance region for a specific level of compression, data resolution etc. A data flow may be provided in several variants. For instance, a map segment may be available at various scales, showing various types of feature, and covering differing areas. These changes will affect resource usage: by changing the display quality the size of the data required will change. One of those flow variants which is within the intersection of the acceptable and achievable performance regions should be selected by the adaptation engine to implement the flow, based on some goal such as maximising QoS, or minimising cost.

A change in resource availability would shift the edges of the achievable region. Changes in context might alter the boundaries of the acceptable region. If the current variant is still achievable and acceptable no change would be needed, else a different flow variant would be selected, or if none are available failure would be signalled.

2.3 Application Adaptation Due to Context Change

We also support application adaptation to context change, such as location or user activity [2]. We have experimented with the design of a web browser with an integrated location service, which enables the presentation of data relevant to location, e.g. street maps, weather forecasts etc. Where location may be predicted in advance, data can be prefetched and displayed in a timely manner. The prediction of when the location will change also provides a deadline, constraining the performance space. A device might be used in the same street by both a pedestrian and a car driver. These usage-contexts can assist the selection of types of map information to down-load: the pedestrian will not be very interested in one-way streets, while the driver is unlikely to require detailed local information, but may prefer an audio interface for safety.

3 Conclusions

The management of QoS has been combined with context management to enable improved resource and requirements management. Our framework allows the management of the uncertainty of resource characteristics inherent in mobile computing, which we believe is preferable to no management. This enables effective application adaptation and resource management for heterogeneous systems and varying user requirements, particularly where mobile devices are being used. We believe this combination of context sensitivity in applications, system management and requirements management is unusual, and can improve application usability.

We are continuing to investigate the design of adaptive applications, QoS, and context management for mobile and distributed systems, in particular for cartography.

We gratefully acknowledge financial support from the EPSRC, grant GR/L 06010.

References

1. Chalmers, D., Sloman, M,: A Survey of Quality of Service in Mobile Computing Environments *IEEE Communications Surveys*, 2(1) 1999
2. Schilit, B.N., Adams, N., Want, R.: Context-Aware Computing Applications *Proc. IEEE Workshop on Mobile Computing Systems and Applications*, Santa Cruz (1994)
3. Chalmers, D.: Quality of Service in Mobile Environments *MSc Dissertation* Dept. of Computing, Imperial College, London (1998)
4. Srivastava, M., Mishra, P.P.: On Quality of Service in Mobile Wireless Networks *Proc. NOSSDAV'97*, (1997) 147–58
5. Bolliger, J., Gross, T.: A Framework-Based Approach to the Development of Network-Aware Applications *IEEE Trans. Software Eng.* 24(5) (1998) 376–389
6. McIlhagga, M., Light, A., Wakeman, I.: Towards a Design Methodology for Adaptive Applications *Proc. MobiCom'98*, Dallas, Texas, USA (1998) 133–144

Anonymous and Confidential Communications from an IP Addressless Computer

Carlos Molina–Jiménez* and Lindsay Marshall

Department of Computing Science, The University of Newcastle upon Tyne, U.K.
{Carlos.Molina, Lindsay.Marshall}@newcastle.ac.uk

Abstract. Anonymizers based on a mediating computer interposed between the sender and the receiver of an e–mail message have been used for several years by senders of e–mail messages who do not wish to disclose their identity to the receivers. In this model, the strength of the system to protect the identity of the sender depends on the ability and willingness of the mediator to keep the secret. In this paper, we propose a novel approach for sending truly anonymous messages over the Internet which does not depend on a third party. Our idea departs from the traditional approach by sending the anonymous messages from an Internet wireless and addressless computer, such as a Personal Digital Assistant (PDA) bridged to the Internet by a Mobile Support Station (MSS).

1 Introduction

The degree of anonymity offered by anonymizers based on mediating computers is limited since there is no way the sender can hide its IP address from the mediator. Trying to send an anonymous message from an IP addressed computer is analogous to trying to make an anonymous call from a home telephone line. To make a truly anonymous call, the caller must find a public telephone box and operate it by coins. Complete anonymity is guaranteed here by the use of a non–personal terminal (the public telephone box) and by the anonymous method of payment (the coins). With this in mind, we have developed a model to send truly anonymous messages based on the functionality of the public telephone box.

2 Addressless Connection with Anonymous Payment

A well–known approach to connecting wireless computers to the Internet is the model presented in Ioannidis et. al. [1], where an MSS identifies each wireless computer by its permanent IP address. In our approach, a non–personal, temporary, random identifier (TempId) is used instead. The TempId is assigned by the MSS on a per–communication session basis. The caller pays for the call by anonymous electronic cash (e–cash) [2, 3]. Confidential communication is ensured by the use of the public key (Kpu) of the MSS and a session key (Ks) belonging to the caller.

---

* PhD student supported by The National Autonomous University of Mexico

3 The Algorithm

In our system shown in Fig. 1, Bob is the anonymous sender, Alice is the recipient of the anonymous message on her work station (WS), and Doug is the owner of the MSS and offers communication services on a pay–for–time–used basis. Claudia is a bank owner and offers support for anonymous e–cash payments to her account holders (Bob and Doug). Finally, Ebe is another PDA user. The algorithm works as follows:

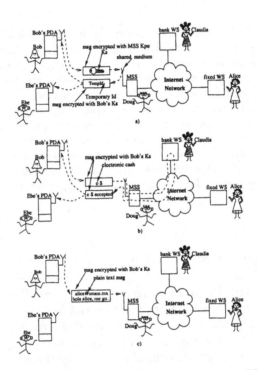

Fig. 1. Anonymous and confidential call from a PDA

1. Bob turns on his PDA and learns the Kpu of the MSS by listening to its advertisement
2. The PDA creates a Ks, encrypts it using the Kpu, and sends it to the MSS for approval, waiting t units of time for a reply
3. The MSS checks that the Ks suggested by Bob is correct and not in use. If so, it creates a TempId for Bob, encrypts it using the Ks, and sends it to the PDA as a reply. If the Ks suggested by Bob is incorrect, the MSS does not reply. If it is correct but has been assigned to an existing user, the MSS does not reply to Bob and additionally asks the user of the existing Ks to renew his Ks. After t units of silence, Bob can try again. The approved Ks is used then to encrypt and decrypt messages between the PDA and the MSS

until either the end of the session or until it has to be renewed. Messages encrypted with Bob's Ks can be overheard by Ebe but they will be ignored

4. Bob sends an anonymous e–coin to Doug to pay for the communication session. Doug consults Claudia about the authenticity of the coin before accepting or refusing it

5. If Bob wishes to anonymously e–mail Alice, he appends the message body to Alice's address, encrypts the result with Ks, and sends it to the MSS

6. The MSS decrypts the message, encrypts the enclosed message body together with Bob's TempId using Alice's Kpu, and forwards it to her

7. Alice has no means to discover the identity of the TempId holder. Yet, she can reply to Bob by addressing her response to the MSS and including Bob's TempId

8. Bob's session ends when he turns off his PDA, leaves his current MSS, or his MSS times-out his session

To stop the MSS from reading the message addressed to Alice, Bob can encrypt the message body with Alice's Kpu. Likewise, if he does not want the MSS to read Alice's reply, he can create and append a Ks to Alice's message body and ask Alice to encrypt the message body of her reply.

4 Conclusions

Aside from its obvious advantages, anonymity has several serious and negative side effects that make its deployment in the Internet a controversial issue. There are strong arguments for and against it. We believe that before saying that anonymity is good or bad, legal or illegal, we have to bring it into practice and test it rather than blindly approve or banish it.

In this work, we presented a system for sending truly anonymous and confidential messages from a PDA served by an MSS. The system imitates a public telephone box by identifying the PDA not with an IP address but with a random, temporary, non–personal identifier and by paying the MSS by anonymous e–cash for the service. An implementation model for the algorithm has been written in PROMELA code and its correctness is currently being tested using SPIN [4].

References

[1] John Ioannidis, Dan Duchamp, and Jr. Gerald Q. Maguire. IP-based protocols for mobile internetworking. In *SIGCOM'91 Conference. Communications Architecture and Protocols*, Zurich, Swizerland, September 3-6 1991. ACM.

[2] N. Asokan, Phillipe A. Janson, Michael Steiner, and Michael Waidner. The state of the art in electronic payment systems. *Computer*, 30(9), September 1997.

[3] Bruce Schneier. *Applied Cryptography*. John Wiley & Sons, Inc., second edition, 1996.

[4] Gerard J. Holzmann. *Design and Validation of Computer Protocols*. Prentice Hall, 1991.

Ad-hoc Network Routing for Centralized Information Sharing Systems

Hyojun Lim and Chongkwon Kim

Department of Computer Science, Seoul National University, Korea
{imhyo, ckim}@brutus.snu.ac.kr

Abstract. Ad-hoc wireless networking is a natural mode of communication in ubiquitous computing. In this paper, we study simple and efficient ad-hoc network routing algorithms and protocols tailored for a centralized information sharing system composed of a data repository and many remote devices. The proposed routing algorithm uses REFRESH packets that the server floods periodically to the network to set up paths from remote devices to the server. The path from the server to a device is established when the device sends a packet to the server.

1 Introduction

In a ubiquitous computing(UbiComp) environment, each person uses many computing devices to perform daily activities[3, 4]. Ad-hoc wireless networking is a natural mode of communication in ubiquitous computing[2, 3].

Many devices used in ubiquitous computing have very limited computing power. They usually use rechargeable or solar batteries and power supply is very limited also. Due to these limitations, ad-hoc routing algorithm for ubiquitous computing should be simple and energy-efficient.

In this paper, we study ad-hoc network routing algorithms and protocols tailored for specific ubiquitous computing applications. It is well known in the communications community that protocols tailored for specific applications perform better than general-purpose protocols[1]. Especially, in ubiquitous computing with devices of limited power, it would be beneficial to adopt the notion of ALF(Application Level Framing) aggressively in designing the network protocols.

The specific application that we address in this paper is centralized information sharing systems. A centralized information sharing system consists of one central information repository(server) and several handheld devices. Individuals create/collect information and input the information to handheld devices. The information is transferred to the central data repository and the information collected at the server is disseminated to individual devices. Information retrieval can occur in two modes: an automatic dissemination mode and a prompt dissemination mode where data retrieval is triggered by an explicit user request.

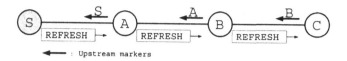

Fig. 1. Routing a packet from a device C to the server S

2 Proposed routing algorithm

Flooding is a general method to establish an initial path between two nodes in an ad-hoc network. Because the source does not know the path to the destination, it first floods a route request packet to the network. The request eventually arrives at the destination and the destination replies back to the server. This reply packet is sent to the source node along a backward path that the flooded packet has followed.

We can simplify this flooding mechanism in the specific ad-hoc network environment where the server participates in all data transmission either as the sender or as the destination. To setup routing paths from all remote devices to the server, the server periodically floods REFRESH packets to the network. The server assigns a unique ID to each REFRESH packet such that devices can detect duplicated REFRESH packets. The REFRESH packet is first delivered to devices directly reachable from the server. When a neighboring device receives a new REFRESH packet directly from the server, it marks the server's ID as its upstream marker and re-broadcasts the REFRESH packet to its neighbors. Duplicate REFRESH packets that arrive later are all ignored.

The upstream marking and re-broadcasting operations are repeated at downstream devices until the REFRESH packet is flooded to all devices. The upstream marker points the next-hop node on the path toward the server. When a remote device sends a packet to the server, the packet follows the path represented by the upstream markers.

Figure 1 shows the procedure of transmitting a packet from a device C to the server. Let us assume that after REFRESH packet flooding, devices A, B, and C have upstream markers S, A, and B, respectively. When device C sends a packet to the server, it forwards the packet to a device B as its upstream marker indicates. Device B relays the packet along its upstream device A and device A forwards the packet to the final destination S.

Let us examine the method to route a packet from a server to a remote device. In the particular application considered in this paper, the server sends information to a remote device only when the remote device sends a request packet to the server. We set up a routing path from the server to the requesting device when this request packet is forwarded to the server.

In Figure 2, suppose that a device C sends a request packet to the server. Following the upstream marker, the packet is first forwarded to a device B. When a device B receives the packet, B realizes that a device C is its direct downstream

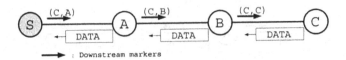

Fig. 2. Routing a packet from a server to the device C

device. B marks this fact using a downstream marker (C, C). Device B relays the packet to a device A. When a device A receives the packet, it realizes that "I can send a packet to a device C through a device B". Device A records this knowledge using a downstream marker, (C, B). This procedure repeats at the server and the server has a downstream marker, (C, A).

The server will send reply packets to the requesting device C. The reply packets can be correctly transmitted to the requesting device if we follow the successive downstream markers in intermediate devices. In Figure 2, when the server sends a packet to a device C, it examines its downstream markers. It will find a downstream marker (C, A) and forwards the packet to a device A as the downstream marker indicates. Device A relays the packet to the downstream device B and device B forwards the packet to the final destination C.

3 Discussion

A major drawback of the proposed routing scheme is that it could not support peer-to-peer communications efficiently. However, peer-to-peer communications is not entirely impossible. Suppose a device A sends packet to a device B. First, A sends the packet to the server and the server forwards the packet to B using flooding. However, flooding wastes network resources and consumes the computing and power resources of all devices. The overhead of flooding can certainly be avoided if the server has the downstream marker to B.

Depending on properties of shared information, we may be able to improve the system performance further. Suppose a device C requests particular information and the server supplies the requested information in Figure 2. The relaying nodes A and B also receives the replied information. If the information is of common interest such as user location information, then the relaying nodes intercept the flowing packets and copy their contents for later use.

References

1. Clark, D., Tannenhouse, D.: Architectural Considerations for a New Generation of Protocols. Proceedings of ACM SIGCOMM '90. 201–208
2. Starner, T., Kirsch, D., Asefa, S.: The Locust Swarm: An Environmentally-Powered, Networkless Location and Messaging System. Proceedings of First Int. Symposium on Wearable Computers(ISWC '97) (1997).
3. Weiser, M.: The Computer of the 21st Century. Scientific American. (1991) 66–75
4. Weiser, M.: Hot Topics: Ubiquitous Computing. IEEE Computer. Oct. 1993.

AuthorIndex

Lecture Notes in Computer Science

For information about Vols. 1–1616
please contact your bookseller or Springer-Verlag

Vol. 1656: S. Chatterjee, J.F. Prins, L. Carter, J. Ferrante, Z. Li, D. Sehr, P.-C. Yew (Eds.), Languages and Compilers for Parallel Computing. Proceedings, 1998. XI, 384 pages. 1999.

Vol. 1657: T. Altenkirch, W. Naraschewski, B. Reus (Eds.), Types for Proofs and Programs. Proceedings, 1999. VIII, 207 pages. 1999.

Vol. 1661: C. Freksa, D.M. Mark (Eds.), Spatial Information Theory. Proceedings, 1999. XIII, 477 pages. 1999.

Vol. 1662: V. Malyshkin (Ed.), Parallel Computing Technologies. Proceedings, 1999. XIX, 510 pages. 1999.

Vol. 1663: F. Dehne, A. Gupta. J.-R. Sack, R. Tamassia (Eds.), Algorithms and Data Structures. Proceedings, 1999. IX, 366 pages. 1999.

Vol. 1664: J.C.M. Baeten, S. Mauw (Eds.), CONCUR'99. Concurrency Theory. Proceedings, 1999. XI, 573 pages. 1999.

Vol. 1666: M. Wiener (Ed.), Advances in Cryptology – CRYPTO '99. Proceedings, 1999. XII, 639 pages. 1999.

Vol. 1667: J. Hlavička, E. Maehle, A. Pataricza (Eds.), Dependable Computing – EDCC-3. Proceedings, 1999. XVIII, 455 pages. 1999.

Vol. 1668: J.S. Vitter, C.D. Zaroliagis (Eds.), Algorithm Engineering. Proceedings, 1999. VIII, 361 pages. 1999.

Vol. 1671: D. Hochbaum, K. Jansen, J.D.P. Rolim, A. Sinclair (Eds.), Randomization, Approximation, and Combinatorial Optimization. Proceedings, 1999. IX, 289 pages. 1999.

Vol. 1672: M. Kutylowski, L. Pacholski, T. Wierzbicki (Eds.), Mathematical Foundations of Computer Science 1999. Proceedings, 1999. XII, 455 pages. 1999.

Vol. 1673: P. Lysaght, J. Irvine, R. Hartenstein (Eds.), Field Programmable Logic and Applications. Proceedings, 1999. XI, 541 pages. 1999.

Vol. 1674: D. Floreano, J.-D. Nicoud, F. Mondada (Eds.), Advances in Artificial Life. Proceedings, 1999. XVI, 737 pages. 1999. (Subseries LNAI).

Vol. 1675: J. Estublier (Ed.), System Configuration Management. Proceedings, 1999. VIII, 255 pages. 1999.

Vol. 1976: M. Mohania, A M. Tjoa (Eds.), Data Warehousing and Knowledge Discovery. Proceedings, 1999. XII, 400 pages. 1999.

Vol. 1677: T. Bench-Capon, G. Soda, A M. Tjoa (Eds.), Database and Expert Systems Applications. Proceedings, 1999. XVIII, 1105 pages. 1999.

Vol. 1678: M.H. Böhlen, C.S. Jensen, M.O. Scholl (Eds.), Spatio-Temporal Database Management. Proceedings, 1999. X, 243 pages. 1999.

Vol. 1679: C. Taylor, A. Colchester (Eds.), Medical Image Computing and Computer-Assisted Intervention – MICCAI'99. Proceedings, 1999. XXI, 1240 pages. 1999.

Vol. 1680: D. Dams, R. Gerth, S. Leue, M. Massink (Eds.), Theoretical and Practical Aspects of SPIN Model Checking. Proceedings, 1999. X, 277 pages. 1999.

Vol. 1682: M. Nielsen, P. Johansen, O.F. Olsen, J. Weickert (Eds.), Scale-Space Theories in Computer Vision. Proceedings, 1999. XII, 532 pages. 1999.

Vol. 1683: J. Flum, M. Rodríguez-Artalejo (Eds.), Co,puter Science Logic. Proceedings, 1999. XI, 580 pages. 1999.

Vol. 1684: G. Ciobanu, G. Păun (Eds.), Fundamentals of Computation Theory. Proceedings, 1999. XI, 570 pages. 1999.

Vol. 1685: P. Amestoy, P. Berger, M. Daydé, I. Duff, V. Frayssé, L. Giraud, D. Ruiz (Eds.), Euro-Par'99. Parallel Processing. Proceedings, 1999. XXXII, 1503 pages. 1999.

Vol. 1687: O. Nierstrasz, M. Lemoine (Eds.), Software Engineering – ESEC/FSE '99. Proceedings, 1999. XII, 529 pages. 1999.

Vol. 1688: P. Bouquet, L. Serafini, P. Brézillon, M. Benerecetti, F. Castellani (Eds.), Modeling and Using Context. Proceedings, 1999. XII, 528 pages. 1999. (Subseries LNAI).

Vol. 1689: F. Solina, A. Leonardis (Eds.), Computer Analysis of Images and Patterns. Proceedings, 1999. XIV, 650 pages. 1999.

Vol. 1690: Y. Bertot, G. Dowek, A. Hirschowitz, C. Paulin, L. Théry (Eds.), Theorem Proving in Higher Order Logics. Proceedings, 1999. VIII, 359 pages. 1999.

Vol. 1691: J. Eder, I. Rozman, T. Welzer (Eds.), Advances in Databases and Information Systems. Proceedings, 1999. XIII, 383 pages. 1999.

Vol. 1692: V. Matoušek, P. Mautner, J. Ocelíková, P. Sojka (Eds.), Text, Speech and Dialogue. Proceedings, 1999. XI, 396 pages. 1999. (Subseries LNAI).

Vol. 1693: P. Jayanti (Ed.), Distributed Computing. Proceedings, 1999. X, 357 pages. 1999.

Vol. 1694: A. Cortesi, G. Filé (Eds.), Static Analysis. Proceedings, 1999. VIII, 357 pages. 1999.

Vol. 1695: P. Barahona, J.J. Alferes (Eds.), Progress in Artificial Intelligence. Proceedings, 1999. XI, 385 pages. 1999. (Subseries LNAI).

Vol. 1696: S. Abiteboul, A.-M. Vercoustre (Eds.), Research and Advanced Technology for Digital Libraries. Proceedings, 1999. XII, 497 pages. 1999.

Vol. 1697: J. Dongarra, E. Luque, T. Margalef (Eds.), Recent Advances in Parallel Virtual Machine and Message Passing Interface. Proceedings, 1999. XVII, 551 pages. 1999.

Vol. 1698: M. Felici, K. Kanoun, A. Pasquini (Eds.), Computer Safety, Reliability and Security. Proceedings, 1999. XVIII, 482 pages. 1999.

Vol. 1699: S. Albayrak (Ed.), Intelligent Agents for Telecommunication Applications. Proceedings, 1999. IX, 191 pages. 1999. (Subseries LNAI).

Vol. 1701: W. Burgard, T. Christaller, A.B. Cremers (Eds.), KI-99: Advances in Artificial Intelligence. Proceedings, 1999. XI, 311 pages. 1999. (Subseries LNAI).

Vol. 1702: G. Nadathur (Ed.), Principles and Practice of Declarative Programming. Proceedings, 1999. X, 434 pages. 1999.

Vol. 1704: Jan M. Żytkow, J. Rauch (Eds.), Principles of Data Mining and Knowledge Discovery. Proceedings, 1999. XIV, 593 pages. 1999. (Subseries LNAI).

Vol. 1705: H. Ganzinger, D. McAllester, A. Voronkov (Eds.), Logic for Programming and Automated Reasoning. Proceedings, 1999. XII, 397 pages. 1999. (Subseries LNAI).

Vol. 1707: H.-W. Gellersen (Ed.), Handheld and Ubiquitous Computing. Proceedings, 1999. XII, 390 pages. 1999.